THE CAMBRIDGE COMPANION TO VICTORIAN WOMEN'S POETRY

The Victorian period has a strong tradition of poetry written by women. In this Companion, leading scholars deliver accessible and cutting-edge essays that situate Victorian women's poetry in its relation to print culture, diverse identities, and aesthetic and cultural issues. The book is inclusive in method, demonstrating, for example, the benefits of both distant and close reading approaches and featuring major figures like Elizabeth Barrett Browning and Christina Rossetti but also more than one hundred poets altogether. Thematically arranged, the chapters deliver studies on a comprehensive array of subjects that address women's poetry in its manifold forms and investigate its global context. Chapters shed light on children's poetry, domestic relations, sexualities, and stylistic artifice and conclude by looking at how women poets placed their published poems and how we can "place" Victorian women poets today.

Linda K. Hughes is Addie Levy Professor of English Literature at Texas Christian University. She is the author of *The Cambridge Introduction to Victorian Poetry* (Cambridge, 2010) and *Graham R.: Rosamund Marriott Watson, Woman of Letters* (2005), co-author of *The Victorian Serial and Victorian Publishing and Mrs. Gaskell's Work* (1999), and coeditor of the four-volume *Feminist Reader: Feminist Thought from Sappho to Satrapi* (2013).

A complete list of books in the series is at the back of this book.

T3-BHM-694

THE CAMBRIDGE
COMPANION TO
VICTORIAN WOMEN'S
POETRY

EDITED BY

LINDA K. HUGHES
Texas Christian University

CAMBRIDGE
UNIVERSITY PRESS

University Printing House, Cambridge CB2 8BS, United Kingdom

One Liberty Plaza, 20th Floor, New York, NY 10006, USA

477 Williamstown Road, Port Melbourne, VIC 3207, Australia

314–321, 3rd Floor, Plot 3, Splendor Forum, Jasola District Centre, New Delhi – 110025, India

79 Anson Road, #06–04/06, Singapore 079906

Cambridge University Press is part of the University of Cambridge.

It furthers the University's mission by disseminating knowledge in the pursuit of education, learning, and research at the highest international levels of excellence.

www.cambridge.org
Information on this title: www.cambridge.org/9781107182479
DOI: 10.1017/9781316856543

© Cambridge University Press 2019

First published 2019

Printed in the United Kingdom by TJ International Ltd. Padstow Cornwall

A catalogue record for this publication is available from the British Library.

Library of Congress Cataloging-in-Publication Data
NAMES: Hughes, Linda K., editor.
TITLE: The Cambridge companion to Victorian women's poetry / edited by Linda K. Hughes, Texas Christian University.
DESCRIPTION: Cambridge, United Kingdom ; New York, NY : Cambridge University Press, 2019. | Includes bibliographical references.
IDENTIFIERS: LCCN 2018048301| ISBN 9781107182479 (Hardback) | ISBN 9781316633571 (Paperback)
SUBJECTS: LCSH: English poetry – 19th century – History and criticism. | English poetry – Women authors – History and criticism.
CLASSIFICATION: LCC PR595.W6 C36 2019 | DDC 821/.8099287–dc23
LC record available at https://lccn.loc.gov/2018048301

ISBN 978-1-107-18247-9 Hardback
ISBN 978-1-316-63357-1 Paperback

I dedicate this book to all the scholars who have led the way in studying Victorian women poets, from the late twentieth century into the present, and to all the students with whom I have had the joy of reading and discussing Victorian women's poetry.

CONTENTS

ILLUSTRATIONS

CONTRIBUTORS

ISOBEL ARMSTRONG is Fellow of the British Academy, Senior Research Fellow of the Institute of English Studies, and Professor Emeritus of what is now the Geoffrey Tillotson Chair, Birkbeck College. Her recent books include *Victorian Glassworlds: Glass Culture and the Imagination* (2008) and *Novel Politics: Democratic Imaginations in Nineteenth-Century Fiction* (2017). She is completing a second edition of *Victorian Poetry: Poetry, Poetics and Politics* (1993) and is also a published poet.

KIRSTIE BLAIR is Chair in English and currently Head of the School of Humanities at the University of Strathclyde. She has published widely on Victorian literature, especially in the field of poetry and poetics, including *Victorian Poetry and the Culture of the Heart* (2006) and *Form and Faith in Victorian Poetry and Religion* (2012). Her current research focuses on working-class writers in Scotland and the North of England.

ALISON CHAPMAN is Professor of English at the University of Victoria. Her publications include *Networking the Nation: British and American Women's Poetry and Italy, 1840–1870* (2015) and *The Afterlife of Christina Rossetti* (2000), and she is the editor of the in-progress Database of Victorian Periodical Poetry (http://web.uvic.ca/~vicpoet/showpageimage-2/database-of-victorian-periodical-poetry/). She is completing a monograph on Victorian poetry, literary form, and Europe.

ALEXIS EASLEY is Professor of English at the University of St. Thomas. She is the author of *First-Person Anonymous: Women Writers and Victorian Print Media, 1830–1870* (2004) and *Literary Celebrity, Gender, and Victorian Authorship, 1850–1914* (2011). She also co-edited *The Routledge Handbook to Nineteenth-Century Periodicals and Newspapers* and *Researching the Nineteenth-Century Periodical Press: Case Studies* (2016, 2017), with Andrew King and John Morton.

JILL R. EHNENN is Professor of English at Appalachian State University where she teaches Victorian Studies and in the Gender, Women's and Sexuality Studies

Program. She is the author of *Women's Literary Collaboration, Queerness, and Late-Victorian Culture* (2008); articles on nineteenth-century women authors such as Dorothy Wordsworth, Elizabeth Siddal, Vernon Lee, and Lucas Malet; and multiple articles and chapters on the female co-authors who wrote as "Michael Field." Her current book project is *Michael Field's Revisionary Poetics*.

EMILY HARRINGTON is Associate Professor of English at the University of Colorado, Boulder, and author of *Second Person Singular: Late Victorian Women Poets and the Bonds of Verse* (2014).

ELIZABETH HELSINGER is John Matthews Manly Distinguished Service Professor of English, Art History, and Visual Arts Emerita at the University of Chicago. Her publications include *Ruskin and the Art of the Beholder* (1982); *The Woman Question: Britain and America, 1837–1883* (1983); *Rural Scenes and National Representation: Britain 1815–1850* (1997); *Poetry and the Pre-Raphaelite Arts: Dante Gabriel Rossetti and William Morris* (2008), and *Poetry and the Thought of Song in Nineteenth-Century Britain* (2015).

NATALIE M. HOUSTON is Associate Professor of English at the University of Massachusetts Lowell. She is currently writing a book entitled *Digital Reading: Poetry and the New Nineteenth-Century Archive*, which uses computational methods to explore the cultural function of poetry within Victorian print culture. Her research on Victorian poetry and print culture has appeared in journals such as *Victorian Studies*, *Victorian Poetry*, and the *Yale Journal of Criticism*.

SOFIA PRADO HUGGINS is a PhD student at Texas Christian University. Her research focuses on how transatlantic publishing networks enabled intersections between social reform movements. Her article "Slavery, Sex, and Social Networks: The Reception of Harriet Jacobs's *The Deeper Wrong; or, Incidents in the Life of a Slave Girl* in the British Periodical Press" appears in the April 2017 issue of *Symbiosis: A Journal of Transatlantic Literary and Cultural Relations*.

LINDA K. HUGHES is Addie Levy Professor of Literature and faculty affiliate in Women's and Gender Studies at Texas Christian University. Her books include *The Victorian Serial* (with Michael Lund, 1991); *Graham R.: Rosamund Marriott Watson, Woman of Letters* (2005); and *The Cambridge Introduction to Victorian Poetry* (2010). She is coeditor with Sharon M. Harris of *A Feminist Reader: Feminist Thought from Sappho to Satrapi* (4 vols., 2013).

LORRAINE JANZEN KOOISTRA is Professor of English and Co-director of the Centre for Digital Humanities at Ryerson University in Toronto, Canada. A specialist in Victorian illustration, her publications include *The Artist as Critic: Bitextuality in Fin-de-Siècle Illustrated Books* (1995); *Christina Rossetti and Illustration: A Publishing History* (2002); and *Poetry, Pictures, and Popular*

Publishing: The Illustrated Gift Book and Victorian Visual Culture (2011). She edits *The Yellow Nineties Online* (www.1890s.ca).

LAURIE LANGBAUER is Professor of English at the University of North Carolina at Chapel Hill. She has published in *PMLA, Novel, Victorian Studies, diacritics*, and *ELH*, among others. She wrote *Women and Romance: The Consolations of Gender in the English Novel* (1999); *Novels of Everyday Life: The Series in English Fiction, 1850–1930* (1999); and *The Juvenile Tradition: Young Writers and Prolepsis, 1750–1835* (2016). Her new project is on teen-aged nineteenth-century British artists.

CHARLES LA PORTE is Associate Professor of English at the University of Washington in Seattle. His 2011 *Victorian Poets and the Changing Bible* was awarded the Sonya Rudikoff Prize for a best first book in Victorian studies. He is presently co-editing a special issue of *Nineteenth-Century Literature* on the topic of New Religious Movements and Victorian Secularization.

MEREDITH MARTIN is Associate Professor of English at Princeton University. Her book *The Rise and Fall of Meter: English Poetry and National Culture, 1860–1930* (2012) won the MLA Prize for a First Book. She created the Princeton Prosody Archive in 2007, a curated collection containing full-text searchable works about the study of poetry and poetic language.

MONIQUE R. MORGAN is Associate Professor of English at Indiana University, where she specializes in Romantic and Victorian literature, narrative theory, and new formalist criticism. Her publications on poetry include *Narrative Means, Lyric Ends: Temporality in the Nineteenth-Century British Long Poem* (2009) and articles in *Victorian Poetry, Narrative*, and *Literature Compass*. She is currently writing a monograph on epistemology and narrative form in Victorian science fiction.

JASON R. RUDY is Associate Professor of English at the University of Maryland and the author of *Imagined Homelands: British Poetry in the Colonies* (2017) and *Electric Meters: Victorian Physiological Poetics* (2009).

MARJORIE STONE is Mc Culloch Professor of English, Dalhousie University, Canada, and volume co-editor for three of five volumes in *The Works of Elizabeth Barrett Browning* (2010), co-editor of *Elizabeth Barrett Browning: Selected Poems* (2009), and author of *Elizabeth Barrett Browning* (1995). She has also published on literary collaboration, multiculturalism, the corporate university, and other authors, including Dickens, Gaskell, Tennyson, Christina Rossetti, Frederick Douglass, and Emily Dickinson.

BEVERLY TAYLOR is Professor of English at the University of North Carolina–Chapel Hill and has published on Victorian medievalism and a range of nineteenth-century writers including Arnold, Charlotte Brontë, both Brownings, Carlyle, Elizabeth Siddal, Tennyson, and Francis Thompson. With Marjorie Stone she has co-edited a Broadview edition of Elizabeth Barrett Browning's selected poetry and co-edited three volumes in the Pickering and Chatto scholarly edition of the *Works of Elizabeth Barrett Browning*.

ANA PAREJO VADILLO is Co-director of the Birkbeck Centre for Nineteenth-Century Studies. Her books include *Women Poets and Urban Aestheticism* (2005) and *Michael Field, The Poet: Published and Unpublished Materials* (2009). She has guest edited for the journal *Victorian Literature and Culture* and *19: Interdisciplinary Studies in the Nineteenth Century*, including *The Nineteenth-Century Digital Archive* (Issue 21: 2015). She is currently writing a book on cosmopolitanism.

ACKNOWLEDGMENTS

This *Cambridge Companion* owes most to the gifted scholars whose chapters make it the exciting volume that it is. My hope from the beginning was to gather a collection of essays that exhibit the compelling interest posed by Victorian women poets, exemplify the best of scholarly methods and sensibilities, and point forward to future paths for study. This hope has been richly fulfilled by the volume authors who have distilled their groundbreaking research, presented in accessible form for a range of readers. I also thank contributors for their patience with my revision requests and many email reminders.

Warmest thanks go also to Linda Bree, who first suggested this project to me and supported it throughout its development. I likewise thank Bethany Thomas for providing a smooth transition from Linda Bree's oversight to her own; her expertise and that of the Cambridge University Press staff have been invaluable during the production phase of this *Cambridge Companion*.

Individual contributors indicate their permissions to quote or reproduce images. I express special appreciation to those institutions and individuals that provided images and reproduction permissions pro bono: the Mark Samuels Lasner Collection, University of Delaware; the Toronto Public Library; and Frances Brown's biographer Patrick Bonar.

Among my TCU colleagues, I thank Merry Roberts for assistance with preparation of the typescript, as well as the outstanding Addie Levy Research Fellows whose efforts have assisted me in recent years: Heidi Hakimi-Hood, Claire Landes, Sofia Prado Huggins, and Kaylee Henderson. I also express my gratitude to the late Linda H. Peterson, who invited me to contribute the chapter on "Poetry" to her *Cambridge Companion to Victorian Women's Writing* (2015). I have come to think of her volume and invitation as the "germ" of this present *Cambridge Companion* and welcome the opportunity to express what I and so many others, including several contributors to this book, owe to her.

CHRONOLOGY OF PUBLICATIONS AND EVENTS
Compiled by Sofia Prado Huggins

This chronology features important "firsts" and major achievements in the careers of Victorian women poets. It highlights publications and events mentioned in the chapters that follow. Birth and death dates are given at the poet's first entry.

1820	Elizabeth Barrett Barrett (later Browning, 1806–61) receives fifty privately printed copies of *The Battle of Marathon: A Poem* from her father on her fourteenth birthday. Letitia Elizabeth Landon (1802–38) places her first poem in the *Literary Gazette*, signed "L" (later "L.E.L.").
1821	Elizabeth Barrett publishes "Stanzas Excited by Reflections on the Present State of Greece" in the *New Monthly Magazine*.
1823	Mary Howitt (1799–1888) co-publishes *The Forest Minstrel and Other Poems*, with her husband William.
1824	L.E.L. publishes *The Improvisatrice*.
1825	Felicia Hemans (1793–1835) publishes *The Forest Sanctuary*.
1827	Caroline Sheridan Norton (1808–77) anonymously publishes "The Sorrows of Rosalie."
1828	Hemans publishes *Records of Woman*, her most popular volume.
1832	First Reform Act passes.
1833	Slavery Abolition Act passes.
1834	Howitt publishes *Sketches of Natural History* with her ballad "The Spider and the Fly."

1835	Elizabeth Gaskell (1810–65) and her husband William co-publish *Sketches among the Poor*, a poetry cycle, in *Blackwood's Magazine*. Eliza Cook (1818–89) publishes *Lays of a Wild Harp*. Grace Aguilar (1816–47) publishes *The Magic Wreath*.
1836	Norton legally separates from her husband and becomes a prominent campaigner for women's rights.
1837	Victoria (1819–1901) becomes queen of the United Kingdom of Great Britain and Ireland. Christian Isobel Johnstone initiates an annual anthology of working-class poetry in *Tait's Edinburgh Magazine*.
1838	Cook publishes *Melaia and Other Poems*. Irish-Australian poet Eliza Hamilton Dunlop (1796–1880) publishes "The Aboriginal Mother" in the *Australian*.
1839	Custody of Infants Act passes. *The Zenana and Other Poems* by L.E.L. is edited by Emma Roberts (1791–1840) and posthumously published after Landon's mysterious death in Africa.
1840	Frances Brown (1816–79) publishes her first poem in the *Irish Penny Journal*. Australian poet Fidelia Hill (1794–1854) publishes *Poems and Recollections of the Past*.
1842	Copyright Act extends term to forty-two years from publication or seven after author's death.
1843	Elizabeth Barrett publishes "The Cry of the Children" in *Blackwood's Magazine*. Factory Act passes, limiting women and children under eighteen to a twelve-hour working day.
1845	Elizabeth Barrett begins writing *Sonnets from the Portuguese* (published 1850) given to Robert Browning after their marriage.
1846	The Brontë sisters publish *Poems*, using the pseudonyms Currer Bell (Charlotte Brontë, 1816–55), Ellis Bell (Emily Brontë, 1818–48), and Acton Bell (Anne Brontë, 1820–49).
1847	Howitt and her husband William launch *Howitt's Journal* (1847–8).

Verses: Dedicated to Her Mother by Christina Rossetti (1830–94) is privately printed by her grandfather.

Jane Francesca Wilde (1821–96) begins contributing nationalist poetry to the *Nation* using the pseudonym "Speranza."

1848   Elizabeth Barrett Browning (EBB) publishes "The Runaway Slave at Pilgrim's Point" in the American abolitionist annual *The Liberty Bell*.

1849   Cook founds *Eliza Cook's Journal*, writing most material herself but also soliciting poetry from working-class women writers.

1850   Following Wordsworth's death in June, the *Athenaeum* proposes EBB for Poet Laureate.

Alfred Tennyson publishes *In Memoriam A. H. H.* in May and is appointed Poet Laureate in November.

The Pre-Raphaelite Brotherhood launches *The Germ*, with lyrics by Christina Rossetti as "Ellen Alleyn."

Agnes Strickland (1796–1874) publishes *Historic Scenes and Poetic Fancies*.

Jean Ingelow (1820–97) publishes *A Rhyming Chronicle of Incidents and Feelings*.

1851   EBB publishes *Casa Guidi Windows*.

Adelaide Anne Procter (1825–64) begins publishing in Dickens's *Household Words* (1840–59), sending him eight lyrics under the pseudonym Mary Berwick.

1856   EBB publishes *Aurora Leigh* (date stamped 1857).

1857   George Eliot anonymously reviews *Aurora Leigh* in the *Westminster Review*.

1858   Procter publishes *Legends and Lyrics*, first series.

1859   Isa Craig (1831–1903) wins the Burns Centenary Prize for the best poem submitted to the competition.

Dinah Maria Mulock Craik (1826–87) publishes her first collection of poetry, *Poems*. Proprietors Bradbury and Evans found the illustrated *Once a Week*, which publishes numerous poems by women.

Macmillan's Magazine, in which many of Christina Rossetti's and other women's poems first appears.

1860   *Cornhill Magazine*, edited by W. M. Thackeray, is launched; the July issue publishes EBB's "A Musical Instrument," illustrated by Frederic Leighton.

1862   EBB's *Last Poems* is posthumously published.
        Christina Rossetti publishes *Goblin Market* with illustrations and cover design by D. G. Rossetti (1828–82)

1863   Janet Hamilton (1795–1873) publishes *Poems and Essays*.

1864   First Contagious Diseases Act passes, allowing arrest and compulsory medical examination of prostitutes. The acts are a catalyst for feminist activism led by Josephine Butler (1828–1906) and helped lay the groundwork for the suffragist movement.
        Cook publishes her final book of poetry *New Echoes, and Other Poems*.

1866   Christina Rossetti publishes *The Prince's Progress and Other Poems*.
        Augusta Webster (1837–94) publishes *Dramatic Studies*.

1867   Second Reform Act passes.
        Factory poet Ellen Johnston (1835–73) publishes *Autobiography, Poems and Songs*.
        Mathilde Blind (1841–96) publishes *The Prophecy of St Oran*.

1868   George Eliot publishes her first poetry volume, *The Spanish Gypsy*.
        Hamilton receives a grant of £50 from the Royal Bounty Fund.

1870   Married Women's Property Act passes, allowing women to own the money they earn and to inherit property.
        Webster publishes *Portraits*.

1872   Christina Rossetti publishes *Sing-Song: A Nursery Rhyme-Book*.

1875   Alice Thompson (later Meynell, 1847–1922) publishes her first poetry volume, *Preludes*.
        Katherine Tynan (1859–1931) begins publishing poetry in periodicals.
        Violet Fane (Mary Montgomerie Lamb, later Singleton, later Currie, 1843–1905) publishes her verse-novel *Denzil Place*.

1876   Edith Nesbit (1858–1924) publishes her poem "A Year Ago" in *Good Words*.

1878   A. Mary F. Robinson (1857–1944), in preference to a party offered by her parents to mark her twenty-first birthday, chooses to have her first volume of poems published, *A Handful of Honeysuckle*.

1879   Webster is elected to the London School Board.

1881   Christina Rossetti's "Monna Innominata: A Sonnet of Sonnets" appears in *A Pageant and Other Poems*.
        Amy Levy (1861–89) publishes *Xantippe and Other Verse*.
        Constance Naden (1858–89) publishes *Songs and Sonnets of Springtime*.

1882   Married Women's Property Act grants women's right to own and control property after marriage.
        Ancient Ballads and Legends of Hindustan by Toru Dutt (1856–73) is published in London by John Lane, the Bodley Head Press.

1884   Third Reform Act passes.

1887   Queen Victoria's Golden Jubilee.
        May Kendall (1861–1943) publishes *Dreams to Sell*.

1889   Blind publishes *The Ascent of Man*.
        "Michael Field" (Katherine Bradley, 1846–1914, and Edith Cooper, 1862–1913) publishes *Long Ago*, a response to Sappho.
        "Graham R. Tomson" (Rosamund Marriott Watson, 1860–1911) publishes *The Bird-Bride: A Volume of Ballads and Sonnets*.
        Levy commits suicide; *A London Plane-Tree*, containing her last poems, is posthumously published.

1892   Michael Field publishes *Sight and Song*.

1895   Coventry Patmore "nominates" Alice Meynell for the poet laureateship in the *Saturday Review*.
        E. Pauline Johnson (1861–1913) publishes *The White Wampum*.

1896   Christina Rossetti's *New Poems*, edited by W. M. Rossetti, is posthumously published.

Sarojini Naidu (1879–1949) publishes "Eastern Dancers" under her maiden name Sarojini Chattopâdhyây in the August *Savoy*, edited by Arthur Symons (1865–1945).
Mary Coleridge (1861–1907) publishes *Fancy's Following*.
Meynell privately publishes *Other Poems*.

1897   Queen Victoria's Diamond Jubilee.
            National Union of Women's Suffrage Societies is founded.

1901   Queen Victoria dies on January 22.

Note: Throughout this volume, Elizabeth Barrett Browning will be referred to as EBB after a first mention of her name in full. This accords with the poet's own practice, since she signed as "EBB" both before and after her marriage. This *Companion* also adopts L.E.L., the poet's elected publishing signature, after an initial reference to Letitia (Elizabeth) Landon.

LINDA K. HUGHES

Introduction

On July 20, 1995, the world changed – or did for me, to borrow Virginia
Woolf's words – when I walked into the three-day "Rethinking Women
Poets Conference" at Birkbeck College, London. I was then working on
a biography of the 1890s poet Graham R. Tomson (later Rosamund
Marriott Watson [1860–1911]) and assumed I was doing something quirky,
at the margins of scholarship, since few scholars had heard of her.[1] Besides,
the novel then dominated studies of Victorian women's writing. At the
conference, I suddenly plunged into animated conversations among international scholars who were researching eighteenth- and nineteenth-century
women's poetry and discovering compelling work that demanded sophisticated textual, philosophical, and theoretical analysis. The conference was
swiftly followed by publication of two generously inclusive anthologies of
women's poetry, Angela Leighton and Margaret Reynolds's *Victorian
Women Poets* (1995) and Isobel Armstrong and Joseph Bristow's
Nineteenth-century Women Poets (1996).[2] Together, the conference and
the anthologies instigated new scholarship on women's poetry that continues
to this day.

Much has changed in studies of Victorian women's poetry since the mid-
1990s, however. The anthologies, often still cited (as this volume attests), are
out of print. Yet Victorian women's poetry is more available than ever to
scholars, teachers, and students thanks to digitized out-of-copyright books
by women and digital databases of nineteenth-century literary annuals and
periodicals. Attitudes toward annuals and periodicals have likewise evolved.
Once dismissed as ephemeral literary trash, they have become important sites
of research on women's poetry and women's agency as editors, writers, and
readers. Poetry dominated the letter press of illustrated annuals, which first
appeared in 1823 and flourished through the 1840s.[3] Their female editors
included poets Letitia Landon (L.E.L., 1802–38) and Mary Howitt
(1799–1888), who like other editors recruited poems from women, often
to accompany engravings. Verse written "to order" was one factor in critical

dismissals of annuals. Yet a poem like "The Romaunt of the Page" by Elizabeth Barrett Browning (EBB, 1806–61) in *Finden's Tableaux* (1839), the annual edited by EBB's good friend Mary Russell Mitford (1787–1856), also a sometime poet, became one of EBB's most popular ballads and continues to be studied by scholars of women's poetry and the nineteenth-century ballad revival. After annuals died out at mid-century, they were succeeded by an outpouring of illustrated gift books; these, too, included many women's poems.

Poets might publish a volume of poems every few years, perhaps only once in a lifetime, especially those with scant access to editors or sponsors, such as many working-class women. Annuals or seasonal gift books appeared once a year. But Victorian periodicals appeared monthly or weekly, and news-papers even daily, and they too published poems.[4] Once dismissed as uninteresting, often anonymous filler in untold magazines and newspapers, periodical poetry has reemerged as a key archive of verse by women poets ranging from Felicia Hemans (1793–1835) to Janet Hamilton (1795–1873), George Eliot (1819–80), Christina Rossetti (1830–94), and countless authors of unsigned or initialed poems.[5] Anonymity remains a challenge to scholars, as does the uneven quality of periodical poems (as in signed volumes). Still, periodicals geometrically increased the readership of Victorian women's poetry while augmenting poets' income: cheap, mass-produced print serials could sell as many as 20,000, 60,000, or more than 100,000 copies per issue. From the beginning of the Victorian era – whether dated from the first Reform Bill (1832) or Queen Victoria's ascension to the throne (1837) – women's poetry circulated regularly in periodicals through the 1880s and remained a significant presence in little magazines like the *Yellow Book* into the 1890s and the twentieth century. The millions of periodical pages now digitized further enable twenty-first-century readers to discover women's poetry and read it in its remediated print environment, although commercial databases are not universally available and represent only a portion of the original Victorian print archive. Much remains to be done, accordingly, whether by scholars working with print periodicals not yet digitized or by creating new ways to search and conceptualize digitized women's poetry.

Such massive numbers of texts, however, exert pressure on this *Cambridge Companion*'s object of study. Should "Victorian women's poetry" be approached en masse as a by-product of the Victorian publishing industry or envisioned through its high points exemplified by canonical poets such as EBB, Rossetti, and Emily Brontë (1818–48), with sidelights from distinctive poems such as "The Last Sark" by Ellen Johnston (1835–74) or "The Witch" by Mary Coleridge (1861–1907)? Classroom anthologies stage encounters with pre-selected "high points." The enormous scale of poems that Victorian women actually produced is an empirical fact that also demands attention.

This *Cambridge Companion* steers a middle course between poetry viewed on a large scale from a distance and poetry examined through historically contextualized close readings that reveal the complex techniques and voicings that make so many women's poems memorable. It thus locates "Victorian women's poetry" both in its breadth and in its depths of individual poems. Rejecting an "anthology" approach, I have invited contributions that unfold not as a chronological presentation of exemplary figures but as a series of topics that cut across a wide array of poets and allow for comparative analysis of poets and their cultural positions. Some poets, of course, are referenced more often than others, most prominently EBB and Rossetti, with frequent appearances by Hemans, Alice Meynell (1847–1922), Michael Field (Katharine Bradley, 1846–1914, and Edith Cooper, 1862–1913). More than a hundred poets are examined altogether, however, including obscure poets like Sarah Parker (1824–80) and Alice Gillington (1863–1934) or the understudied Frances Brown, (1816–79).

Since form is inseparable from any literary work, Part I (Chapters 1 through 5) addresses form and the senses – appropriately so, since printed poetry is an inherently multimedia genre that appeals simultaneously to the ear, eye, pulses, and intellect, sometimes to touch as well if readers are turning or touching pages.[6] Influenced by cultural, material, and gender studies as well as older interpretive methods, twenty-first-century scholarship has documented the cultural, physiological, and political underpinnings of form, whether in its meters, rhyming, and sonic patterns; accompanying illustrations; formats; or other cues that solicit responses from embodied readers.

Victorian women poets could choose from among a broad array of poetic genres. As Monique Morgan argues in Chapter 1 ("Genres"), women often approached genres as flexible forms that they treated experimentally. Hence, when women's practices are factored into the study of sonnets, dramatic monologues, narrative poetry and ballads, satiric and political protest poems, or epic and verse novels, genres expand beyond narrow definitions. The point is less that women's practice was often anomalous than that women could experimentally reconfigure a genre in ways intrinsic to their poetic subject and expressive aim, whether they protested artificial limits imposed on women or satirized masculine power (and ego) in terms drawn from evolutionary science.

In "Prosody" (Chapter 2), Meredith Martin extends her prior work on the cultural politics of Victorian meters to the critical reception of women poets by a largely male body of critics. Male critics repeatedly emphasized women's "naturally" poetic, song-like "melodiousness," which predisposed reviewers to approve brief lyrics more than other verse. Indeed, women poets were most often censured when they seemed to approximate prose and its capacity for argument, as with EBB's *Aurora Leigh* (1856). Such critics often ignored or underestimated learned women poets who knew Greek and experimented with classical meters, as Martin shows in discussing "The Snow Waste" (1866) by Augusta Webster (1837–94), a 371-line poem that refuses alignment of the female poet's voice with "natural" song. Referencing George Eliot's anonymous review of *Aurora Leigh* in the *Westminster Review*, Martin also reveals the difference that a learned female reviewer could make in responding to a woman poet's innovations.

In the succeeding chapter, "Haunted by Voice" (Chapter 3), Elizabeth Helsinger presents the important use that women poets could make of brief lyrics, not in conventional "melodiousness" but in Rossetti's, Meynell's, and Michael Field's artful counterpointing of voices and silence. As Helsinger observes, voice is intrinsically "ec-static," outside the self, which enables it to be heard and to create multiple voicings within a single poem, as in Rossetti's "Up-Hill." But Helsinger especially notes poets' voicings across the silences of pauses, page breaks, intervals between clinching rhymes, or the final pause of death. By foregrounding the print status, hence silence, of their lyrics, the poets examined by Helsinger offered a riposte to reductive concepts of voices confined in female bodies. These women underscored their complex artifice rather than lightsome singing.

"Floating Worlds" by Lorraine Janzen Kooistra (Chapter 4) examines appeals to eye and touch rather than ear. Kooistra approaches wood engravings that accompanied poems in books and periodicals as technologies of vision that shaped ways of seeing and knowing for women poets and their readers. After analyzing Rossetti's first book of poems, *Goblin Market* (1862) illustrated by Rossetti's brother Dante Gabriel, Kooistra turns to the mass-produced wood engravings accompanying Louisa Stewart's narrative poem "Bradmere Pool" in the periodical columns of *Once a Week* (October 22, 1859). In addition to demonstrating how an illustration constructs an interpretive frame that might alternatively contest or complement a poem's content, Kooistra models close reading of a popular illustration, which in some cases (like "Bradmere Pool") may offer more rewards than the printed poem. She also emphasizes editors' roles in selecting poems based on their picturability.

Touch receives extended attention in Jason Rudy's chapter "Embodiment and Touch" (Chapter 5); in a poem like EBB's "Runaway Slave at Pilgrim's Point," touch became an important poetic trope that intensified political protest. But Rudy especially considers the modes of embodiment in

Victorian women's poetry. As Victorian physiological studies of sensation were increasingly revealing, sensory perception depended on an interactive mind-body relationship that enabled both cognition and arousal of emotion. In *The Spanish Gypsy* (1868), for example, George Eliot represents how Fedalma's embodied act of dancing leads her outward in thought and feeling. Poetry itself could likewise lead readers out of themselves into imagined embodiments, even vicarious alterity, in vivid representations of embodied enslaved or indigenous women, as in "The Aboriginal Woman" (1838) by Eliza Hamilton Dunlop (1796–1880). In a poem like *The Ascent of Man* (1889) by Mathilde Blind (1841–96), in contrast, throbbing rhythms could evoke the throbbing pulsations of the Earth at the moment of its formation.

If the pleasures of reading poetry could lead women – and men – outward in thought and sensibility, poetry's publication in mass-distributed periodicals and newspapers alongside or in between international news, parliamentary debates, scientific discoveries, and opinion pieces meant that poems themselves did not remain bounded on a page. Rather, women's poetry spilled out into the realm of public discourse by poets' design as well as material production. Part II appropriately begins with poets' entrée to that publishing world. Alexis Easley, in "Publishing and Reception" (Chapter 6), takes a less-traveled approach to the topic by examining two poets tied closely to the laboring classes, Eliza Cook and Frances Brown, and assessing the relation between their poetry and the public personae they crafted to promote it. Easley's chapter also provides an overview of many issues recurring throughout this *Companion*. To the commentaries on reception and gendered critical reviews by Meredith Martin and Kirstie Blair, Easley adds women's agency in shaping their own receptions. Easley also, like Blair, demonstrates the importance of including working-class poets in studies of women's poetry. And she underscores the centrality of Victorian periodicals to recovering and studying women's poetry sounded earlier by Martin, Kooistra, and this Introduction as well as by Blair, Laurie Langbauer, and Beverly Taylor. Reproducing the portraits of Cooke and Brown, Easley also extends Kooistra's discussion of Victorian visuality and women's poetry. The ambiguous gendering of the portrait that Cook favored in her self-presentation, as well as the blindness of Brown, also dovetails with the attention to embodiment by Rudy and sexuality by Jill Ehnenn. As she begins her chapter, so Easley ends with intersecting differences in women's poetry and careers, and the need for all who study women's poetry to remain aware of difference as a historical fact and interpretive tool.

Chapters 7 through 10 enlarge upon women's poetry "in the world," literally so in "Transatlanticism, Transnationality, and Cosmopolitanism" by Alison Chapman (Chapter 7), who demonstrates the relevance of

Victorian women's poetry to the global turn of literary study in the twenty-first century. After noting the enabling precedent of Madame de Staël's fictional Corinne (1807), an Anglo-Italian "improvisatrice" who publicly performs her poetry, Chapman turns to three pairs of poets networked across spaces and in print: L.E.L. (London, Ghana) and Emma Roberts (1794–1840) (London, Bengal), whose work, sometimes illustrated, appeared in literary annuals and books; Toru Dutt (1856–77) (India, Hastings) and Sarojini Naidu (1879–1949) (London, India), whose hybrid identities unfolded amid cosmopolitan travel or the Indian independence movement; and EBB (London, Florence, Boston) and A. Mary F. Robinson (1857–1944) (London, Florence, Paris), whose shifting locales registered shifting marital, political, and domestic partnerships. Hybrid national affiliations of all these poets thwart customary attempts to study literature within national literary traditions.

Within Britain, too, different localities, dialects, and work experiences propelled distinctive voices and perspectives, as in the laboring women's poetry most often published in cheap periodicals at Britain's peripheries. This poetry also unsettles traditions of "national" literary culture, since women poets' allegiance to localities often superseded their British identities. In "Dialect, Region, Class, Work" (Chapter 8), Kirstie Blair examines poems that emerged from Irish, Scottish, Welsh, and English contexts. If as poets, women faced more barriers than working-class men, they were not artless singers. Prosody and diction were as important to these women poets as to their male counterparts. Choosing Scots dialect or adopting meters associated with Robert Burns could assert regional pride and politics. Whether dealing with Janet Hamilton, currently best known among working-class woman poets, or Isabella Forrest (c. 1867–1937), Blair illuminates their self-aware choices as they "code-switched" between dialect and standard English based on their complex poetics and politics.

Women poets across all classes keenly followed local, national, and international politics and participated in reform movements. Denied the vote or parliamentary representation by reason of their sex, many poets affirmed their right to speak out and adopted poetry's pithiness, memorable rhymes, rhythms, and resources of pathos to articulate their own perspectives, engage readers' sympathies, alert them to injustices, and urge activist response. In "Politics, Protest, Interventions: Beyond a Poetess Tradition" (Chapter 9), Marjorie Stone maps women poets' simultaneous involvement in multiple political movements across the decades, from child labor and the Irish famine (1840s), to the woman question, Italian Risorgimento (the movement for independence and a unified Italy), and the Crimean Wars (1850s and 1860s), to causes such as socialism, suffrage, and anti-vivisection at century's end. A complex network of international poets, reformers, and publications ensued, often involving cross-gender and cross-class activism. Aesthetically, women's political poetry frequently took experimental hybrid form, as in Caroline Norton's "A Voice from the Factories." Stone additionally details the diverse formal and political strategies of poets ranging from Cook, "Speranza" (Jane Francesca Wilde, 1821–96) or EBB and Blind to Mary Macdonald Macpherson (c. 1821–98), touching on Anglocentrism and race politics in the process.

Victorian reforms could be underwritten by religious as well as political convictions, and it seems no coincidence that both Stone and Charles LaPorte, in "Religion and Spirituality" (Chapter 10), cite "The Hebrew's Appeal" (1844) by Grace Aguilar (1816–47). LaPorte demonstrates how deeply religious conviction permeated Victorian society and its poetry and how much we miss if we ignore religion, even when religious expression, as in "The Missionary" (1846) by Charlotte Brontë (1816–55), is likely to repel twenty-first-century sensibilities. Religious convictions were far from uniform, of course, which led to competing theologies and widely variant devotional practices. His cases in point include EBB's theologically sophisticated "The Cry of the Human" (1842) and Rossetti's "Good Friday" (1864). LaPorte also looks beyond English shores to Toru Dutt – not to the poems examined by Chapman but to *Ancient Ballads and Legends of Hindustan* (1882), which drew deeply from Hindu religion yet also affirmed Dutt's Christian belief. English reception of her volume attempted to reimpose a "pure Hindu" identity on Dutt. Yet her hybrid allegiances resisted easy categorization and troubled cultural boundaries.

Part III of this book addresses two topics that Victorian commentators often considered women poets' "natural" domain: children and domesticity. If the poems women actually wrote resisted reductive formulation, so did the open secret of women's sexuality. A further challenge to domestic ideology and "natural" expression was posed by sophisticated women poets' embrace of artifice at the century's end.

"Children's Poetry" (Chapter 11) by Laurie Langbauer and Beverly Taylor attends both to the breadth of Victorian women's poetry for children and its high points. Starting with Lynn Vallone's premise that the history of children's literature is also the history of women's writing, Langbauer and Taylor document the ongoing recovery of women's poetry for children, for which Victorian periodicals are again an indispensable source.[7] After surveying poets from Jean Ingelow (1820–97) to Agnes Strickland (1796–1874), they turn to an illuminating analysis of Rossetti's *Sing-Song* (1874), noting her willingness to introduce death into a children's book, her poems' diverse aims from consoling children to teaching them to count, and the role of

Arthur Hughes's illustrations – an extension of Kooistra's discussion in Chapter 4. They end with a new generation of children's periodicals and editors such as *Atalanta*, edited from 1887 to 1896 by L. T. Meade (1844–1914). Meade's magazine reoriented children's poetry at the fin de siècle by suggesting that girls might become poets themselves and so acquire intellectual and economic agency.

Middle-class conduct books extolled marriage and motherhood as the desirable destiny of women, as did much of the age's fiction. Yet Emily Harrington reveals in "Marriage, Motherhood, and Domesticity" (Chapter 12) that women poets wrote few poems depicting happy marriages. Despite invocations of women's roles as wives and mothers in public debates over women's education, military readiness, or the franchise, marriage, motherhood, and domesticity formed only an "uneasy alliance" in the poems Harrington examines. In "The Moat House" (1886) by E. Nesbit (1858–1924), motherhood fails to coincide with marriage; even in a gift book titled *Home Thoughts and Home Scenes* (1864), mothers are most often offstage in the volume's domestic settings. Similarly, Laura and Lizzie occupy happy homes along with their children at the end of Rossetti's "Goblin Market," but no husbands are present. Altogether, Harrington's chapter offers a corrective to assumed patterns of women's poetry. The poetry may register the pressure of domestic ideology but seldom realizes domestic ideals in individual poems. And some poems actively resist them.

To fulfill the duties of marriage and motherhood, Victorian women were necessarily sexually active. In "Sexuality" (Chapter 13), Jill Ehnenn notes the challenge to Victorian female poets of representing women as sexual beings. Their formal strategies now pose challenges themselves, and Ehnenn cautions readers against projecting twenty-first-century sexual categories onto past expressions. Bringing theoretical and methodological issues into sharp relief, Ehnenn also maps diverse sexualities and their representation by Victorian women poets, from the little-known "Lines on Reading with Difficulty some of Schiller's Early Love Poems" (1883) by Fanny Kemble (1809–93) to the fallen women in poems by EBB, Rossetti, and Augusta Webster and queer sexualities that resist categorization, as in Mathilde Blind's passionately erotic nun abed in "The Mystic's Vision" (1891). Ehnenn's nuanced brief readings additionally offer methods of reading and interpreting sexuality in a wide range of verse.

Part III concludes with "Poets of Style: Poetries of Asceticism and Excess" by Ana Vadillo (Chapter 14). Keenly aware of the long history of poetic style (inherently crafted rather than natural), Vadillo focuses her discussion on two fin-de-siècle women poets who fashioned alternative styles. If Meynell was known for her lyrics' ascetic minimalism, Vadillo unexpectedly reveals links between such stylistic "purity" and literary decadence. In contrast, the poetic dramas of Michael Field, notably *The World at Auction* (1898), exhibit what Vadillo terms an aesthetic of excess, which summons artificial worlds composed from historical artifacts such as ancient coins, jewels, and garments. Michael Field's material excess deliberately counterpointed the crass vulgarity of late-century mass production of furnishings and other consumer goods. Vadillo concludes by tracing the links between these women poets' cultivation of style and Modernist poets who followed.

Two final contributions in Part IV address how we can and should read Victorian women's poetry today. In "Distant Reading and Victorian Women's Poetry" (Chapter 15), Natalie Houston models what computational analysis of a large set of texts (versus traditional "close reading") can tell us about gendered patterns in women's poetry relative to men's. Situating computational methods in relation to Annette Kolodny's feminist critical paradigm, Houston offers a "distant" reading of *A Victorian Anthology 1837–1895* (1895), edited by American critic E. C. Stedman (who gave "Victorian poetry" its name), to indicate what computational analysis can "see" that a sequence of close readings, no matter how subtle, cannot. Stedman's pattern of critical response to women's poetry parallels what Martin identifies in male critics in Chapter 2, yet Houston's analysis works with the large dataset possible only in a digital environment.

Two factors linked all the women poets examined by contributors: they were reviewed *as* women who wrote poetry, and in their daily lives and interactions within literary networks, none escaped visible embodiment as females. EBB vividly represented the effects in Book V of *Aurora Leigh*. From the heights of articulating her artistic credo, Aurora descends to her less triumphant experience as a woman at a London reception: "It always makes me sad to go abroad, / And now I'm sadder that I went to-night / Among the lights and talkers at Lord Howe's," where she wishes the host could speak to her "man to man" – which he cannot do, of course.[8]

Should Victorian women's poetry be considered apart from men's, however? To consider this, in the Afterword, Isobel Armstrong, the scholar cited more often than any other in this volume, returns to the precipitating motive behind archival breakthroughs in the 1990s – new theoretical frameworks emerging from second-wave feminism. Poststructuralist theory provided enabling heuristics to identify systemic gender differences not merely in the reception of women's poetry but also its production. Moving from this inspiring moment through Judith Butler's *Gender Trouble* (1990) and into the present, Armstrong finds reasons to resist as well as engage the study of women's poetry unto itself.[9] She emerges more skeptical about its feasibility than she once was and offers important alternative strategies.

I welcome the "gender trouble" she sets in motion at the close of this book, not as a final word but as an opening onto further study and conversations about women's poetry that this volume as a whole is designed to invite.

Notes

1. Linda K. Hughes, *Graham R.: Rosamund Marriott Watson, Woman of Letters* (Athens: Ohio University Press, 2005). N.B.: Dates of women poets are indicated on their first mention in this collection but not thereafter.
2. Angela Leighton and Margaret Reynolds (eds.) *Victorian Women Poets: An Anthology* (Oxford: Blackwell, 1995); and Isobel Armstrong and Joseph Bristow with Cath Sharrock (eds.) *Nineteenth-century Women Poets: An Oxford Anthology*(Oxford: Clarendon Press, 1996).
3. Jill Rappoport, "Annual and Gift Book," in *Encyclopedia of Victorian Literature*, 4 vols., ed. Dino Felluga, assoc. eds. Pamela Gilbert and Linda K. Hughes (Oxford: Wiley Blackwell, 2015); and *The Poetess Archive* (open-access, fully searchable website), ed. Laura Mandell.
4. Natalie M. Houston, "Newspaper Poems: Material Texts in the Public Sphere," *Victorian Studies* 50 (2008), 233–42.
5. Linda K. Hughes, "What the *Wellesley Index* Left Out: Why Poetry Matters to Periodical Studies," *Victorian Periodicals Review* 40 (2007), 91–125.
6. Marion Thain, "Victorian Lyric Pathology and Phenomenology," in *The Lyric Poem: Formations and Transformations*, ed. Marion Thain (New York: Cambridge University Press, 2013), pp. 166–70.
7. Lynne Vallone, "Women Writing for Children," in *Women and Literature in Britain 1800–1900*, ed. Joanne Shattock (Cambridge: Cambridge University Press, 2001), p. 276.
8. Elizabeth Barrett Browning, *Aurora Leigh*, ed. Margaret Reynolds (New York: W. W. Norton, 1996), 5.579–81, 811.
9. Judith Butler, *Gender Trouble: Feminism and the Subversion of Identity* (New York: Routledge, 1990).

PART I

Form and the Senses

I

MONIQUE R. MORGAN

Genres

Poetic genres are not predetermined, unchanging categories but collections of texts that are perceived to share features. When we recognize generic categories as malleable, we are more likely to welcome a wider range of texts and authors, including women writers, into the literary canon. And a more inclusive canon leads to a wider recognition of formal shapes and rhetorical effects within each genre. Studying poetry by women gives us a fuller understanding of the constraints and potentials of each genre. Of course, Victorian women writers were constrained not only by literary conventions but also by social conventions and institutional inequalities. Isobel Armstrong has explored the ways female poets both worked within and critiqued conventions of gendered experience, but she also warns, "a concentration on moments of overt protest can extract the content of a direct polemic about women's condition in a way which retrieves the protest, but not the poem."[1] In what follows, I trace women poets' protests while attending to poetic form in experiments with genre, from the sonnet to the epic. As we shall see, women poets often protest social limitations while pushing against generic constraints, finding previously untapped potential in a genre, or offsetting the limitations of one genre by incorporating the strengths of another.

Sonnet Sequences

A sonnet is made up of fourteen lines of iambic pentameter connected through an intricate rhyme scheme (though in *Modern Love* [1862], George Meredith expands his sonnets to sixteen lines). The sonnet flourished in Elizabethan England, retreated in the eighteenth century, and reemerged with new subject matter in the Romantic period with the success of Charlotte Smith's *Elegiac Sonnets* (1784). In *Sonnets from the Portuguese* (1850), Elizabeth Barrett Browning (EBB) returned the sonnet sequence to a focus on love, yet she inverted or reimagined traditional Petrarchan conceits. Whereas in sonnet sequences by Petrarch, Dante, Sidney, and Spenser, a male speaker praises a beautiful, virtuous, and unobtainable woman, EBB presents a female speaker's passionate, requited love for a man.

Sonnets from the Portuguese is based on EBB's courtship by Robert Browning; the title veiled the autobiographical elements by suggesting that the poems were translations of a preexisting work. In the opening sonnet, a personified figure claims the speaker and reveals himself to be "Not Death, but Love" (I.14).[2] Autobiographically, this evokes EBB's years as an invalid and her initial reluctance to marry before she partially recovered and accepted Robert Browning's proposal. Generically, EBB repurposes the role of death in sonnet sequences: here it is not a threat to the beloved meant to inspire the pursuit of pleasure, the legacy of offspring, or immortalization through poetry itself, but rather a temptation that the poet must overcome before pursuing love. As she struggles with her choice, she presents herself as pale and weak, and as a lesser poet than her beloved: "an out of tune / Worn viol" that may produce beautiful music in her beloved's "master-hands" (XXXII.7–8,13). This self-presentation "violates both literary and social decorum," Dorothy Mermin argues, because it "present[s] as object of desire an ill and aging woman."[3] In sonnet 23, however, the speaker boldly declares her choice of love rather than death: "I yield the grave for thy sake, and exchange / My near sweet view of Heaven, for earth with thee!" (XXIII. 13–14) The poet joyfully declares her love in EBB's most famous sonnet, which begins "How do I love thee? Let me count the ways" (XLIII.1). As Mermin explains the sequence's revolutionary aspirations, the speaker "is the reluctant object of a poet's courtship, but she is also the sonneteer ... both poet and poet's beloved" – a "doubling" that strives to "replac[e] hierarchy by equality."[4] By offering a radical alternative, EBB implicitly critiques the institutional inequalities women faced in marriage, and women's distorted representations in poetry by men.

Christina Rossetti's *Monna Innominata* (1881) overtly comments upon its relation to earlier amatory sequences and their silencing of women. Each of its fourteen Petrarchan sonnets begins with epigraphs from Dante and Petrarch. An introductory note explains that the title, which means "unknown lady," refers to Rossetti's desire to imagine a beloved woman of Renaissance sonnet sequences speaking for herself. The poems trace the speaker's intense, though ultimately unfulfilled, love for a man, and her greater love for God. Formally, the poems ostentatiously repeat words, as in the lines: "For verily love knows not 'mine' or 'thine'; / With separate 'I' and 'thou' free love has done, / For one is both and both are one in love" (4.9–11).[5] In such statements of the loss of individual identity, John Holmes reads the lovers as finding "commonality interpreted as mutual self-abnegation," while Amy Billone sees the speaker's self-assertion in the sheer frequency of the words "I" and "me."[6] In *Monna Innominata*, Rossetti models the speaker's relationship with God on romantic love; in *Later Life*, another sonnet sequence (1881), she uses Christ as a model for what human love should be.[7] Rossetti again insistently repeats words, as when she addresses God: "If making makes us Thine then Thine we are, / And if redemption we are twice Thine own" (3.9–10). The twenty-eight sonnets focus on the speaker's relationship to God through the journey of life and end with the speaker's anticipation of her own death. Rossetti's hyperbolic constraint and repetition express self-abnegation; demonstrate her mastery of the sonnet form; and create a forceful, distinctive voice.

Augusta Webster's *Mother and Daughter* (1895) depicts both the depths of a mother's love and the unidealized, ambivalent aspects of parenthood. The sonnets chart a complex pattern of memory and anticipation as the speaker considers her daughter at different ages. Webster also critiques Victorian gender ideology, perhaps most overtly in sonnet 11:

> 'Tis men who say that through all hurt and pain
>   The woman's love, wife's, mother's, still will hold,
> . . . .
> So in a thousand voices has the strain
>   Of this dear patient madness been retold,
>   That men call woman's love.   (XI.1–7)[8]

Webster emphasizes her point through the dual meaning of "strain," which conveys the music or poetry through which men expressed idealized views of women's love, and the pressure, effort, or injury such ideals force upon women. Webster frequently uses Petrarchan conceits, and though Melissa Valiska Gregory suggests that such "clichéd metaphors" derive from "a literary tradition that unreasonably insists upon total feminine purity,"[9] Webster often repurposes Petrarchan conceits for feminist ends. The speaker lists her daughter's beautiful features, but rather than compare each to a precious jewel (as in a blazon, common to sonnets), she links each to admirable qualities in her daughter's personality (II.1–14). Later, the daughter refuses to see her mother as aging: the speaker declares, "She will not have it. Loverlike to me, / She with her happy gaze finds all that's best" (XVI. 9–10). As John Holmes argues, Webster here "invert[s] the conventional trope of the sonneteer bestowing immortality on his (female) beloved through verse. Here it is the female object of the sonnet who becomes the gazer, so objectifying the speaker herself and keeping her from aging. Both mother and daughter are both subjects and objects, and their relationship is reciprocal."[10] Once again, a female sonneteer reimagines the gendered dynamics of the amatory sequence and depicts a woman in a reciprocal relationship, rather than as a silent and subservient object.

Dramatic Monologues

The great generic invention of Victorian poetry is the dramatic monologue, yet critics have always debated how best to define it. A common but tentative definition has three parts: (1) A dramatic monologue presents the speech (or writing) of one character who is clearly not the poet. (2) The poet's goal is gradually to reveal the speaker's character to the reader. (3) There is often, but not always, an implied auditor to the speech, but we have no direct access to his or her replies. Traditionally, critics have credited Robert Browning and Alfred Tennyson with simultaneously, though independently, inventing the form in the 1830s. Yet if we expand our understanding of the genre to include dramatic monologues by women, then we must not only acknowledge earlier examples by Felicia Hemans and Letitia Landon (L.E.L.) but also modify each of the three features that have defined the genre. Dramatic monologues by women sometimes blur the distinction between speaker and poet, often subordinate the revelation of character to other rhetorical purposes, and occasionally include an explicit response from another character.

Dramatic monologues have a wide spectrum of possibilities for the nearness or distance between the poet and the speaker. Some poems use characters from myth or history to establish a clear gap between author and speaker. Examples include Augusta Webster's "Circe" (1870), "Medea in Athens" (1870), and "Jeanne D'Arc" (1866), and Amy Levy's "Xantippe" (1881). Other poems feature a speaker who represents a class of women but differs from the poet's race or social status, as in Eliza Cook's "Song of the Red Indian" (1845) and EBB's "The Runaway Slave at Pilgrim's Point" (1848), and in monologues spoken by prostitutes, such as Webster's "A Castaway" (1870) and Levy's "Magdalen" (1884). Monologues with the least obvious distance between speaker and poet portray middle-class Victorian women whose experiences with courtship and marriage (or lack thereof) are more or less representative. The young speaker of Webster's "By the Looking-Glass" (1866) feels barred from love because cultural norms deem her unattractive, while the aging, unmarried speaker of Webster's "Faded" (1893) laments her lost beauty and her social insignificance. Three similarly titled poems by Adelaide Anne Procter (1825–64) each present one side of generalized courtship dialogues. In "A Woman's Question" (1858), the speaker asks her fiancé whether or not he is fully committed to their relationship. The speaker of "A Woman's Answer"

(1861) tells her beloved that she loves many things, but all for their associations with him. And in "A Woman's Last Word" (1861), the speaker ends a relationship with the man she loves.

Such poems, with contemporary female speakers describing easily generalizable experiences, offer the clearest evidence for Dorothy Mermin's claim that when writing dramatic monologues, "women seem usually to sympathize with their protagonists" and "the poet and the dramatized speaker ... blur together."[11] Glennis Byron has shown that even in monologues with a historical or mythological speaker and obvious distance between speaker and poet, women authors often sympathize with the speaker's views.[12] This emphasis on sympathy in dramatic monologues by Victorian women has led critics to reassess Robert Langbaum's foundational study, which takes the "tension between sympathy and moral judgment" in the poet's and reader's responses to the speaker as defining the dramatic monologue.[13] Rather than establishing a tension between sympathetic identification with and moral judgment of the speaker, women poets often sympathize with the moral judgments their speakers make about other people and social institutions.

As a result, women poets' "ultimate target is more the systems which produce the speakers than the speakers themselves,"[14] and this leads to their second challenge to traditional definitions of the dramatic monologue. In many monologues by women, the revelation of the speaker's character is not the primary rhetorical purpose but is instead subordinated to social critique; such poems illustrate the pernicious ways social inequality shapes women's characters. As Glennis Byron argues, "the more we move away from seeing the dramatic monologue purely in terms of character study, and the more the canon of the dramatic monologue is expanded, the more central polemic begins to appear to the form."[15]

Three dramatic monologues by Augusta Webster exemplify such polemics. The speaker of "Faded" blames society for the limited roles and value available to women. She observes that "a woman's destiny and sole hope" is to be a wife and mother (line 102), and women who miss that opportunity must spend years "withering leisurely" (line 45) because of "the merciless world / That bids us grow old meekly ... / And, being old, be nothing" (lines 51–4). Herbert Tucker finds that Webster's rhythms often allow for dual readings, either following the overall metrical pattern or deviating for rhetorical emphasis, and these alternate scansions correspond to the speaker's tension between societal expectations and individual experience.[16] In these lines, we can imagine the speaker submitting to metrical and social expectations by voicing regular iambs in "That **bids** us **grow** old **meekly**," or voicing her rebellion through a stress cluster: "That **bids us grow old meekly**." Webster expresses a similar message, with a similarly defiant possible stress cluster, in "A Castaway," in which a courtesan diagnoses that "old" is "The cruelest word that ever woman learns. / **Old – that's to be nothing**" (lines 178–80). Webster's "Castaway" also criticizes "the silly rules this silly world / Makes about women!" (lines 377–8), including ineffectual methods to educate them, and condemns the hypocrisy and destructiveness of "the virtuous worthy men / Who feed on the world's follies, vices, wants, / And do their businesses of lies and shams" (lines 92–4). In these and other critiques, "the speaker's astute social and economic analysis and her comments on the inequalities that cause and perpetuate prostitution appear, on the whole, to be thoroughly endorsed by the poet herself."[17] Webster's greatest challenge in eliciting the reader's sympathy may be "Medea in Athens"; Medea is infamous in Greek myth for murdering her children to avenge her husband Jason's abandonment of her. In Webster's poem, Medea likens her abandonment to being "put aside like some slight purchased slave" (line 224), and she blames Jason and her "dreadful marriage oaths" for her violent actions (line 208). As Melissa Valiska Gregory interprets the poem, it "contains the seeds of a wide-ranging social critique, one that implicates the ideological structures of marriage itself."[18] In these three Webster poems, however, there is no auditor for the speaker's critique, and many women's monologues portray their speakers as having limited authority and little success in expressing their grievances publicly.[19] Of course, women *authors* are able to articulate such grievances publicly, through their poetry, but they do so from behind a mask. As Isobel Armstrong argues, poems that use dramatic masks "paradoxically make possible, *because* they are distanced as drama, a far more *overt* critique ... of the cultural construction of the feminine subject."[20]

In a few experimental poems, however, an auditor is present and responds, and women poets push against the third defining feature of the dramatic monologue: its very status as a monologue. Glennis Byron has proposed the term "duologue" for these poems in which "two distinct but related monologues are juxtaposed," often to "suggest the difficulty of ever knowing the other."[21] Examples include Webster's "Sister Annunciata" (1866) and Levy's "Christopher Found" (1884) and "A Minor Poet" (1884). Most of "A Minor Poet" is spoken by a struggling author just before he commits suicide. Alone in his room, he bids farewell to other poets he admires, including "one wild singer of to-day, whose song / Is all aflame with passionate bard's blood / Lash'd into foam by pain and the world's wrong. / At least, he has a voice to cry his pain" (lines 91–4).[22] This hints at the speaker's frustration at his own inexpressiveness, a likely reason for his suicide.[23] The speaker's own cry of pain is heard only by Levy's readers; in the poem's epilogue by the speaker's friend Tom, we learn that the speaker left no written explanation for his suicide, and that Tom misunderstood his friend's suffering. The poet thus dramatizes within the poem a flawed communication, in contrast with the message the poet hopes to give more successfully, if more indirectly, to her readers. Rather than writing dramatic monologues in which there are two markedly different intentions in communication – the speaker's rhetorical purpose in talking to the auditor and the poet's purpose of revealing the speaker's character to the reader – many women poets craft monologues in which the poet and speaker share much the same message but have different levels of success in communicating it. Expanding the canon of dramatic monologues shows that the genre has a wider range of rhetorical dynamics than was previously recognized.

Protest Poems and Satiric Poetry

Pointed social critique is by no means limited to the genre of dramatic monologue. Many Victorian women poets protested by speaking on behalf of, rather than through the voice of, the oppressed, and many used direct address to accuse British readers of injustice and exhort them to reform. Identification and sympathy remain important dynamics: according to Dorothy Mermin, middle-class authors saw similarities between their own oppression as women and the more extreme oppression of the poor.[24] Sympathy and appropriation, and complex dynamics of voice, pervade many protest poems. Eliza Cook wrote "A Song for the Workers" (1853) in support of shorter hours for shop workers. It praises the virtue and self-respect of hard work but then addresses these workers by asking, "Shall ye be *unceasing* drudges?" (line 21).[25] Cook speaks to middle-class readers (and includes herself among them) when she asks, "Shall we strive to shut out Reason, / Knowledge, Liberty, and Health" from workers as a sacrifice "To the mighty King of Wealth?" (lines 45–6, 48). EBB's "The Cry of the Children" (1843) depicts the despair of children condemned to seemingly endless drudgery in mines and factories. As Caroline Levine argues, the poem depicts three types of familial connections and undercuts their claims to organize society.[26] EBB addresses her readers as "my brothers" and refers to England as "our happy Fatherland" (lines 21, 24), but she depicts working-class children as lacking comfort from their mothers and from God, who fails to act as a beneficent Father to them. At times, EBB gives voices to the child workers through imagined dialogue:

> For, all day, the wheels are droning, turning, –
>   Their wind comes in our faces, –
> Till our hearts turn, – our head with pulses burning,
>   And the walls turn in their places.   (lines 77–80)

Herbert Tucker connects this industrial subject matter to the poem's unusual meter, which he claims is not trochaic but rather stresses only one in every four syllables. "The referent of this precociously laboring, mechanically driven, metronomically merciless prosody," Tucker claims, "is the industrial experience of the child worker on whose behalf Barrett Browning presumes to speak."[27] The poem ends with the children's voices and pulses as they curse England for profiting by crushing "a child's heart" (line 154).

Adelaide Anne Procter also uses an array of voices (including her own) to decry the suffering of the poor. In "An Appeal" (1862), she speaks in her own voice, urging the English not to demand that Irish Catholics convert to Protestantism in exchange for food and shelter (a common practice in the English response to the Irish Potato Famine). "Homeless" (1862), in contrast, presents a dialogue of questions and answers to highlight the injustice that criminals, dogs, and economic goods receive better shelter and treatment than homeless children, prostitutes, and the poor do. And in "The Cradle Song of the Poor" (1858), Procter creates a fusion of dramatic monologue and protest poem. Most of the poem is a poor mother speaking to her starving infant, wishing for her child's pain to end in death, and repeating the refrain "Sleep, my darling, thou art weary; / God is good, but life is dreary" (lines 9–10).[28] The final stanza shifts to the poet's voice, as she admonishes her audience, "Such the plaint that, late and early, / Did we listen, we might hear" (lines 41–2), and urges them to be more charitable.

Some women writers engaged in public debates not through protests of current social injustices but rather through satires of recent scientific theories. Constance Naden's "Evolutional Erotics" (1887) is a series of four poems that use the structure of dramatic monologues and variations on ballad stanzas for comedic effect, social critique, and the exploration of Darwinian evolution. The speaker of "Scientific Wooing" uses language from his science classes to express his attraction to Mary Maude Trevylyan (whose name may allude to the heroines of two unhappy love poems: the title character of Alfred Tennyson's *Maud* [1855] and Mary Trevellyn in Arthur Hugh Clough's *Amours de Voyage* [1858]). Naden plays with a common trope when her speaker compares his beloved to "the palest star / That gleams so coldly from afar" (lines 52–3);[29] compare this to the title of Sir Philip Sidney's sonnet sequence *Astrophil and Stella* (1591), which means "star-lover and star." But Naden's speaker pursues his comparison with astronomical precision, longs for a spectroscope to analyze her, and speculates that "surely Love's attractive power / Directly as the mass must vary" and hence must gravitationally pull him to her massive dowry (lines 44–5). The speaker plans to woo her with science and logic, and he imagines she will relent by saying,

"*Quod erat demonstrandum!*" (line 84). This final line, "that which was to be proved," indicates the successful completion of a mathematical proof. Naden undermines the speaker's confidence, however, with her comedic choice to rhyme "demonstrandum" with "random," which introduces chance into his desired chain of causes and effects. Naden's "The New Orthodoxy" takes the form of a letter written by Amy, a student at Girton College, Cambridge, to her sweetheart, Fred. Amy inverts the usual rhetoric of faith and skepticism to voice her alarm that Fred has "been heard to say you can't / Pin your faith to Darwin" (lines 47–8), and she accuses him that regarding contemporary science, "You're a hardened sceptic!" (line 40). Her anxiety is so great that she demands an immediate answer from him and implies that their continuing engagement depends on his belief in science. Throughout "Evolutional Erotics," Naden satirizes and subverts gender stereotypes, including tropes in love poetry, expectations that science is a masculine pursuit, and stereotypes that influence scientists' understanding of sexuality.[30]

In the same year, May Kendall published *Dreams to Sell* (1887), which contains a section of poems headed "Science." The subject matter ranges from geometry to cosmology, but the majority of Kendall's "Science" poems respond to aspects of evolutionary theory. Two of the funniest, "Ballad of the Ichthyosaurus" and "Lay of the Trilobite," were previously published in *Punch* in 1885. Both feature talking fossils: the trope of prosopopoeia allows the dead to speak and allows Kendall to bridge the hundreds of millions of years between the lives of these extinct animals and the history of humankind. The Darwinian content of "Ballad of the Ichthyosaurus" is overt. The ichthyosaurus mentions Darwin by name, fixates on the relative merits of its brain and its eyes (organs that were crucial for Darwin's arguments against natural theology), and reminisces about the age of dinosaurs, when "we dined, as a rule, on each other – / What matter, the toughest survived" (lines 11–12).[31] The ichthyosaurus envies humankind's greater intelligence, but the fossil in "Lay of the Trilobite" points out human suffering, confusion, and hypocrisy; expresses satisfaction with its simpler, less conscious existence; and persuades his human listener of the merits of his less intelligent but more peaceful life. John Holmes has observed that in the accompanying illustration in *Punch*, this human auditor resembles Richard Owen, a paleontologist and prominent critic of Darwin, but the trilobite mentions Thomas Huxley, Darwin's leading defender. The poem, then, presents opposing interpretations of evolution and satirizes "all readings of evolution that see it as progressive."[32] Naden and Kendall both ridicule misapplications of science through experimental poems that combine satire, dramatic monologue, and ballad.

Ballads and Other Short Narrative Poems

Today ballads are typically defined as brief narratives focused on action and dialogue rather than feeling, told impersonally in simple language, with lines of three or four stresses. But as Letitia Henville reminds us, "most poems that were called 'ballads' by nineteenth-century poets did not contain all of these features."[33] Within this malleable genre, female poets depicted and critiqued the constraints placed on women by prescribed gender roles. In EBB's "The Romaunt of the Page" (1839), a knight and a page pause from fighting in the Crusades to talk, and the knight reveals that he agreed to marry his wife as compensation for her father's death defending the knight's father from slander. He has never seen his wife's face, and immediately after their wedding he left for Palestine. The page's sister, the page claims, was similarly married without her husband seeing her face, then disguised herself as a page and followed her husband. The knight declares he would never condone such unwomanly behavior in his wife. The page, in despair, allows herself to be slaughtered by Saracens, for the page is actually the knight's wife. The plot, though contrived, reveals that women are devalued, have limited opportunities, and are used as a means of exchange between men. Jean Ingelow's "The High Tide on the Coast of Lincolnshire" (1863) also features the tragic death of a wife. It is spoken by a rural farmer, who tells that his son's wife and her two children died when the river flooded; when the water dispersed, their bodies were left at his son's doorstep. The stanza form, intricate rhymes, and frequent repetition evoke Tennyson's "The Lady of Shalott" (1842) – another poem about a dead woman carried by a river. As Isobel Armstrong interprets it, Ingelow's poem literalizes the metaphor of overflow for poetic expression and symbolically presents the annihilation of the female subject.[34]

Not all narrative poems by women end unhappily. In two allegorical works outside the ballad tradition, Adelaide Anne Procter and Christina Rossetti imagine redemption for their female protagonists. Procter's "A Legend of Provence" (1861) tells the story of Angela, a novice in a convent whose chief duty was laying flowers by the shrine to Mary. Angela falls in love with a wounded soldier who is treated at the convent; they elope, but she realizes he is unworthy of her. She spends years as a beggar, then returns to the convent, where she sees a vision of herself as an older nun. It is Mary, who has impersonated her and performed her duties in her absence, enabling Angela to return to her life as a nun. According to the narrator, the legend's lesson is that we all can achieve "Some pure ideal of a noble life" (line 321), for "We always may be what we might have been" (line 330).

A more famous, and more ambiguous, story of redemption is Christina Rossetti's "Goblin Market" (1862). In it, a young girl exchanges a lock of her golden hair for fruit sold by goblin men. After eating, she longs for more, but denied further access to the fruit, Laura becomes sick and apathetic. Her sister, Lizzie, risks herself to acquire more fruit for Laura; after Laura licks the juice and pulp the goblins have violently smeared on Lizzie, Laura recovers. The ostensible moral is, "there is no friend like a sister / ... / To fetch one if one goes astray" (lines 562–5). Critics have generally been dissatisfied with such a simple moral for such a complex narrative and have generated an array of allegorical interpretations. Some connect the characters' acts of exchange to broader economic systems and link the profusion of exotic fruit to British imperialism. Other critics focus on the religious themes of temptation, sacrifice, and redemption. And still others emphasize sexuality. When Lizzie returns from the goblin men to save her sister, she exclaims to Laura:

> "Never mind my bruises,
> Hug me, kiss me, suck my juices
> Squeezed from goblin fruits for you,
> Goblin pulp and goblin dew."   (lines 467–70)

Here the sexual implications are too close to the surface to call them subtext, yet the passage can also be read as a version of the Eucharist. This ambiguous allegory rewards multiple readings, and, like Procter's "Legend," it implicitly critiques Victorian culture's ostracism of fallen women by suggesting that women who go astray can be redeemed.

Epics and Verse Novels

Lengthier verse narratives are usually classified as either epics or verse novels, though the boundaries are indistinct and some poets wrote hybrids of the two. Generally, the epic is distinguished from the verse novel by its more elevated style, the breadth and significance of its subject, and its more unified attitude toward its subject – what Mikhail Bakhtin has called epic's "reliance on impersonal and sacrosanct tradition, on a commonly held evaluation and point of view."[35] Herbert Tucker's *Epic* discusses nearly 350 long poems with epic pretensions published in Britain in the Romantic and Victorian periods. Of those, only fifty-eight were written by women, and only sixteen of the poems by women were published during Victoria's reign (the others having been published earlier). These sixteen long poems present an array of ambitious subjects, from the English experience of the Napoleonic wars in Sarah Stickney Ellis's *The Sons of the Soil* (1840), to Italian unification in

Mary Elizabeth Braddon's *Garibaldi* (1861), to the Biblical tale of Noah in Jean Ingelow's *A Story of Doom* (1867).

The epic poem with the broadest scope may be Mathilde Blind's *The Ascent of Man* (1889). Parts 2 and 3 offer an allegorical narrative in which a questing soul encounters Love, Sympathy, and Sorrow, ultimately suggesting that ethical striving can overcome suffering and conflict. Part 1, however, narrates the entire history of life on Earth using species and civilizations rather than individual characters and mimics the passage of time through shifting stanza forms. In 862 lines of poetry, Blind narrates the formation of the universe, the evolution of life forms, humanity's discovery of fire, the development of agriculture, the rise and fall of ancient empires, the birth of Christ, Napoleon's defeat at Waterloo, and the history of technology and art. The poem's variety of stanza forms "mimics the fecundity, profligacy, and unruliness that Darwin identifies with nature itself."[36] I argue that the *sequence* of stanza types evokes the passage of time by using forms strongly associated with specific periods in literary history: dactylic hexameter, the meter of classical epics; iambic tetrameter, which is close to the rhythms of medieval ballads; heroic couplets, popular in the eighteenth century; and elaborate stanza forms with intricate rhyme schemes and mixed line lengths, similar to Romantic poets' metrical experiments. Blind, then, reinforces the sense of rapid change through her use of stanza form.

Of much narrower scope, though of no less intensity, is Violet Fane's *Denzil Place* (1875), which offers a scandalously sympathetic depiction of adultery. Its more limited subject, focused on the two lovers and their families and its permissive attitude toward adultery, which was starkly at odds with Victorian cultural values, mark it clearly as a verse novel rather than an epic. As Stefanie Markovits has demonstrated, many Victorian long poems deal with adultery or failed marriages (in contrast to the English novel's reluctance to confront adultery directly), and they use tensions between lyric intensity and narrative progression to present tensions in contemporary ideas about love and marriage.[37] Both Fane and her heroine strive, with some success, toward reconciliation between intense but brief experiences and longer trajectories of duration and change.

EBB's *Aurora Leigh* (1856) intermixes lyric intensity with narrative duration and the epic with the verse novel. Its epic scope derives from EBB's ambition to reconcile the Real and the Ideal, which manifests in Aurora's debates with her cousin Romney about the relative merits of poetry's spiritual inspiration and philanthropy's material melioration. Romney's philanthropy is also aligned with social problem novels, while Aurora's growth into a successful poet aligns with the *Künstlerroman* (a novel of artistic development), and the heroine's courtship aligns with the marriage plot novel (specifically with *Jane Eyre*). Alison Case argues that the *Künstlerroman* and the love plot are in tension, since cultural and literary conventions require the artist-hero of the former to demonstrate narrative mastery over the story but expect the heroine of the latter to be modest and naïve about the direction of her own relationships. Case suggests that the poem's odd temporal form juxtaposes these conventions; the poem's first four books are confidently retrospective, but after the time of events catches up with Aurora's time of writing in Book 5, Aurora writes in a more immediate, diaristic manner, uncertain of the final outcome until she writes the last two books.[38] The timing of the final two books is especially strange because Aurora explicitly says she wrote them after the poem's climactic events, yet she narrates them as if she is immersed in those events and unaware of the ending. As I have argued in *Narrative Means, Lyric Ends*,[39] this temporal position that seems impossible by novelistic standards is unsurprising by the standards of lyric, which often present the poet's description as if it were simultaneous with the experience described. The generic hybridity of *Aurora Leigh* exposes and offsets the limitations of its component genres when taken individually.

In Book 5 of *Aurora Leigh*, EBB voices her own wide-ranging assessments of poetic genres through her protagonist. As Aurora reviews her poetic career, she claims:

> My ballads prospered; but the ballad's race
> Is rapid for a poet who bears weights
> Of thought and golden image. He can stand
> Like Atlas, in the sonnet, – and support
> His own heavens pregnant with dynastic stars;
> But then he must stand still, nor take a step. (5.84–9)

Here she contrasts the "rapid" narration of ballads with the lyric stasis of sonnets and moves from a quick summary of part of her career to dilate on art through an extended simile. Within this simile, her choice of pronouns genders the poet as male, which corresponds to the gender of Atlas and most early sonneteers but is an obvious mismatch to Aurora's and EBB's gender. Gender is further blurred by the "pregnant" content of the male poet's sonnet – one of many instances of maternal imagery in the poem. Another instance occurs in Aurora's admonishment to herself to

> Never flinch,
> But still, unscrupulously epic, catch
> Upon the burning lava of a song
> The full-veined, heaving, double-breasted Age. (5.213–16)

Neither EBB nor her protagonist flinches from the epic tasks they set themselves. Unhindered by scruples about generic conventions or gender ideology, they apply epic form to their contemporary moment rather than the distant past and in so doing merge novel and epic. The Victorian era as a "double-breasted Age" and the epic poem that captures that age are nourishing and generative. EBB speaks her greatest poetic ambitions through the voice of a fictional character, and her mixture of assertion and indirection, formal experimentation, and desire for social reform epitomizes the aspirations of many of the age's women poets.

Notes

1. Isobel Armstrong, *Victorian Poetry: Poetry, Poetics and Politics* (New York: Routledge, 1993), pp. 323, 319.
2. Elizabeth Barrett Browning, *The Works of Elizabeth Barrett Browning*, 5 vols., ed. Sandra Donaldson (London: Pickering & Chatto, 2010).
3. Dorothy Mermin, *Elizabeth Barrett Browning: The Origins of a New Poetry* (Chicago: University of Chicago Press, 1989), p. 131.
4. Ibid., p. 130.
5. Christina Rossetti, *The Complete Poems of Christina Rossetti*, 3 vols., ed. R. W. Crump (Baton Rouge: Louisiana State University Press, 1990).
6. John Holmes, *Dante Gabriel Rossetti and the Late Victorian Sonnet Sequence* (Burlington, VT: Ashgate, 2005), p. 52; Amy Christine Billone, *Little Songs: Women, Silence, and the Nineteenth-Century Sonnet* (Columbus: The Ohio State University Press, 2007), pp. 96–112.
7. Emily Harrington, *Second Person Singular: Late Victorian Women Poets and the Bonds of Verse* (Charlottesville: University of Virginia Press, 2014), p. 14; Holmes, *Dante Gabriel Rossetti*, p. 55.
8. Augusta Webster, *Portraits and Other Poems*, ed. Christine Sutphin (Peterborough, Ont.: Broadview Press, 2000).
9. Melissa Valiska Gregory, "Augusta Webster Writing Motherhood in the Dramatic Monologue and the Sonnet Sequence," *Victorian Poetry* 49.1 (Spring 2011), 43.
10. Holmes, *Dante Gabriel Rossetti*, p. 110.
11. Dorothy Mermin, "The Damsel, the Knight, and the Victorian Woman Poet," *Critical Inquiry* 13.1 (Autumn 1986), 75, 76.
12. Glennis Byron, *Dramatic Monologue* (New York: Routledge, 2003), p. 16.
13. Robert Langbaum, *The Poetry of Experience: The Dramatic Monologue in Modern Literary Tradition* (New York: W.W. Norton & Company, 1957), p. 85.
14. Byron, *Dramatic Monologue*, p. 59.
15. Ibid., p. 102.
16. Herbert F. Tucker, "Fretted Lines: Di-versification in Augusta Webster's Dramatic Monologues," *Victorian Poetry* 55.1 (Spring 2017), 113.
17. Byron, *Dramatic Monologue*, p. 68.
18. Gregory, "Augusta Webster," 31.

19. Helen Luu, "A Matter of Life and Death: The Auditor-Function of the Dramatic Monologue," *Victorian Poetry* 54.1 (Spring 2016), 33–5; Cynthia Scheinberg, "Recasting 'Sympathy and Judgment': Amy Levy, Women Poets, and the Victorian Dramatic Monologue," *Victorian Poetry* 35.2 (Summer 1997), 181–2.
20. Armstrong, *Victorian Poetry*, p. 373.
21. Byron, *Dramatic Monologue*, p. 97.
22. Amy Levy, *A Minor Poet and Other Verse* (London: T. Fisher Unwin, 1884).
23. Cornelia D. J. Pearsall, "The Dramatic Monologue," in *The Cambridge Companion to Victorian Poetry*, ed. Joseph Bristow (Cambridge: Cambridge University Press, 2000), p. 83.
24. Mermin, *Elizabeth Barrett Browning*, p. 96.
25. Eliza Cook, *The Poetical Works of Eliza Cook* (London: Frederick Warne and Co., 1870).
26. Caroline Levine, "Strategic Formalism: Toward a New Method in Cultural Studies," *Victorian Studies* 48.4 (Summer 2006), 640.
27. Herbert Tucker, "Tactical Formalism: A Response to Caroline Levine," *Victorian Studies* 49.1 (Autumn 2006), 88.
28. Adelaide Anne Procter, *The Poems of Adelaide A. Procter* (Boston: James R. Osgood and Co., 1873).
29. Constance Naden, *The Complete Poetical Works of Constance Naden* (London: Bickers & Son, 1894).
30. Marion Thain, "'Scientific Wooing': Constance Naden's Marriage of Science and Poetry," *Victorian Poetry* 41.1 (Spring 2003), 158; Andrea Kaston Tange, "Constance Naden and the Erotics of Evolution: Mating the Woman of Letters with the Man of Science," *Nineteenth-Century Literature* 61.2 (Sept. 2006), 204; John Holmes, *Darwin's Bards: British and American Poetry in the Age of Evolution* (Edinburgh: Edinburgh University Press, 2009), p. 193.
31. May Kendall, *Dreams to Sell* (London: Longmans, Green, and Co., 1887).
32. John Holmes, "'The Lay of the Trilobite': Rereading May Kendall," *19: Interdisciplinary Studies in the Long Nineteenth Century* 11 (2010), 4, 7.
33. Letitia Henville, "Introduction," *Victorian Poetry* 54.4 (Winter 2016), 413.
34. Armstrong, *Victorian Poetry*, pp. 355–6.
35. Mikhail Bakhtin, "Epic and Novel," in *The Dialogic Imagination*, trans. Caryl Emerson and Michael Holquist (Austin: University of Texas Press, 1981), p. 16.
36. James Diedrick, *Mathilde Blind: Late-Victorian Culture and the Woman of Letters* (Charlottesville: University of Virginia Press, 2016), p. 214.
37. Stefanie Markovits, "Adulterated Form: Violet Fane and the Victorian Verse-Novel," *ELH* 81.2 (Summer 2014), 636–40.
38. Alison Case, *Plotting Women: Gender and Narration in the Eighteenth- and Nineteenth-Century British Novel* (Charlottesville: University Press of Virginia, 1999), pp. 107–24.
39. Monique R. Morgan, *Narrative Means, Lyric Ends: Temporality in the Nineteenth-Century British Long Poem* (Columbus: Ohio State University Press, 2009).

2

MEREDITH MARTIN

Prosody

> Every woman of culture in the United States should not only own, but
> take to her heart this guide to versification, for every woman of culture is
> supposed to have the knack of rhyming, and yet, with some few excep-
> tions, a woman's poem can be told from a man's by its disregard of the
> laws of rhythm. It is a most excellent little manual, and will save many
> prayers to the Muses.[1]

Is there a reason why we should, or could, talk about prosody in gendered
terms? Seen as interchangeable, sentimental, and primarily "lyric" by the end
of the nineteenth century, poems by Victorian women have often been read
more thematically than metrically. Victorian critics rarely praised poems by
Victorian women for their prosodic innovations. It is no accident that the
most common positive descriptive term for women's versification in the
Victorian era was "melodious," since this word fulfills the expectation that
the woman poet is first and foremost a lyricist and that her access to song
(birdlike, muse-like) should be read as her natural birthright; we see this,
also, in negative assessments of women's poor versification as "laborious"
and "artificial." The idea that women should have a natural facility with
English versification follows the ideological development of an English
national meter over the course of the nineteenth century as well as the widely
circulating expectations of women's natural ability to thrive within constraint (religious and moral) and the discipline of gentle bonds.

This was not always the case. Though the proliferation of different
metrical forms and experiments by the end of the nineteenth century
may have addressed different and perhaps smaller and more specialized
reading publics, poems that used meter in new ways did not necessarily
alienate readers. Women participated in all aspects of metrical
experiment: writing in classical meters or attempting quantitative prosody, accentual meter, syllabics (counting the number of syllables in a line
irrespective of number of accents), and the accentual-syllabic tradition of
English prosody (metrical feet based on the Greek). But rather than
writing women into prosodic history, the critics of the Victorian era

tended to treat women's verses as beholden to the ideals of a certain kind of English poetic lyric.

Compare the reception of Felicia Hemans to that of Alice Meynell. Hemans was seen as a national poet with "high-toned and musical versification, in accordance with the sentiment and subject";[2] although W. M. Rossetti praised her "aptitude and delicacy in versification" in the collection he edited, he dismissed her poetry as both feminine and female, having "the monotone of mere sex."[3] As George Bethune writes in *The British Female Poets*, Hemans was "the most generally admired of all English female poets" (188). She possessed many of the requisite skills: a private education in the classics and "genius" that could inspire in the reader "a passion for the ethereal, the tender, the imaginative, the heroic" (191).[4] But her verse suffered (said the "cant of criticism") for its quantity (she wrote too much of it) and its sameness.

Meynell's posthumously published poems "The Laws of Verse," and "The English Meters" are stand-ins for the English nation (even if the names of the metrical feet she celebrates are Greek):

> Dear laws, come to my breast!
>   Take all my frame, and make your close arms meet
> Around me; and so ruled, so warmed, so pressed,
>   I breathe, aware; I feel my wild heart beat.
>
> Dear laws, be wings to me!
>   The feather merely floats. O be it heard
> Through weight of life – the skylark's gravity –
>   That I am not a feather, but a bird.[5]

Meynell addresses the laws of English meter as "dears," playing on the maternity for which she was known and claiming the meters as not only hers but also all women's. Yopie Prins reads this "passionate attachment to form itself" as a "formalization rather than a personalization of passion."[6] And, indeed, whereas the "dear laws" seem like little children, we see that she uses them to assert, at the end of the poem, that she not only watches over them but also uses them to elevate herself to the position of the bird/bard who can understand and display them. Meynell thus claims mastery for the song-bird; the laws could pull her down ("the weight of life"), as could the gravity of tradition (if the skylark is a stand-in for Romanticism), and yet she announces, "O be it heard" that she is a different kind of bird, and she does not want us to take her lightly.

In the companion poem "The English Meters," Meynell authoritatively asserts that classical feet are the representative measure of English poetry.

"English meters" exist and have characteristics that align them with the nation, with all that is right and good about English:

> The rooted liberty of flowers in the breeze
>   Is theirs, by national luck impulsive, terse,
> Tethered, uncaptured, rules obeyed 'at ease'
>   Time-strengthened laws of verse.
>
> Or they are like our seasons that admit
>   Inflexion, not infraction: Autumn hoar,
> Winter more tender than our thoughts of it,
>   But a year's steadfast four.
>
> Redundant syllables of Summer rain,
>   And displaced accents of authentic Spring;
> Spondaic clouds above a gusty plain
>   With dactyls on the wing.
>
> Not Common Law, but Equity, is theirs –
>   Our metres; play and agile foot askance,
> And distance, beckoning, blithely rhyming pairs,
>   Unknown to classic France;
>
> Unknown to Italy. Ay, count, collate,
>   Latins! With eye foreseeing on the time
> And numbered fingers, and approaching fate
>   On the appropriate rhyme.
>
> Nay, nobly our grave measures are decreed:
>   Heroic, Alexandrine with the stay,
> Deliberate; or else like him whose speed
>   Did outrun Peter, urgent in the break of day.[7]

Though the English meters are natural in this poem, their modification – indeed, codification – might be seen as unnatural or external. Alice Meynell herself celebrated periodicity. Her well-known essay "The Rhythm of Life" begins: "if life is not always poetical, it is at least metrical"; and the essay ends by citing the "law that commands all things – a sun's revolutions and the rhythmic pangs of maternity," gesturing to a career-long project of spiritualizing literature – especially poetry – and feminizing poetic form.[8] Evacuating the kind of effusive passion for which Hemans and other poetesses were known, Meynell's poems were seen by Harriett Monroe in 1916 as "severe," "austere," and missing "mystical rapture or ritualistic color."[9] That mystical rapture was clear in her essays but was also a crucial part of her prosody. Meynell corresponded with Coventry Patmore, the foremost prosodic critic of her day, and developed a metrics of the repetitive pauses and silences that mapped onto the widely held view that short, personal, devotional poems were where women's poetry most excelled. But contrasting the two women, we can see that by the early twentieth century, the "monotone of sex" that William Rossetti found in Hemans's poems was transformed into a natural affinity for national meters. Meynell was a product, then, of a century in which women poets were increasingly praised for their ability to write short, powerful, lyric poems so that the terms "poetess" and "lyric" became practically synonymous.

Indeed, the most virulent critiques of poems by Victorian women stretching prosodic norms applied to poems that ventured threateningly too close to prose. The case of half-rhymes in *Aurora Leigh* by Elizabeth Barrett Browning (EBB) is the most famous example of this transgression. George Saintsbury wrote, "Her ear for rhyme was probably the worst on record in the case of a person having any poetic power whatever."[10] But EBB's rhyming innovations and prose-like blank verse may have been less offensive to critics if the argument of *Aurora Leigh* had not been that a true female artist must strain against traditional poetic and gender norms. Critiques of George Eliot's *Spanish Gypsy* were no less scathing, and it was the "argument" that she

> put in too consecutive a shape for poetry – a certain inconsequence, inconsideration, absence of logical method, being characteristic of the forms of poetic argument. Poetry does not reason, it illuminates. It does not persuade, it flashes conviction; it reaches its conclusions by a road that logic doesn't know; it is a revelation not a syllogism. George Eliot has much subtlety of intellectual perception, but when she attempts to realize a high transcendental mood of feeling, she is apt to fail.[11]

For both EBB and Eliot, the revelations and illuminations of poetry were gendered; by using reason, argument, narrative, and logic, they were working against the expectation that their poems – and their gender – needed to operate as flashes of feeling. Rather than appealing only to an emotional register, the forms of *Aurora Leigh* and *The Spanish Gypsy* appealed to both sentiment and intellect. In this way, the very act of composing long narrative poems in blank verse with female heroines worked against the formal logic of Alfred Tennyson's *The Princess* (1847, revised 1850), in which the women are expected to sing songs as the men recover from the hard work of narrative. Just as poems by women were criticized in the Victorian era for attempting to use logic or to address issues and emotions that were seen as beyond the expectations of their gender, so, too, were women poets often praised when they wrote short poems that adhered to the expected "kindred points of heaven and home"; on the surface, it would seem that women poets wrote patriotic and religious verse with characteristic formal and thematic restraint and patriotic and political verse with rhythms praised for inspiring just the right kind of affect.

Victorian women's prosody has continued, into the twentieth and twenty-first centuries, to be read through a lens that considers it as either restrained or effusive, but with a critical difference: rather than reading Victorian women's prosody as limited by the separate spheres, contemporary critics read double poems and political critique in the expected rhythms and meters – and themes – of Victorian women's poetry.[12] By reading poems by Victorian women for hybrid discourses or as primarily lyric, much contemporary criticism unwittingly upholds the expectations promoted by the male-dominated field of Victorian prosodic criticism, but it also begins to show us how women poets used their poetic forms to transform conventions and to push the boundaries of what was expected of them.[13] Women poets wrote in a variety of verse genres, manipulating and expanding the possibilities of each genre's themes and meters; indeed, because poetic meters were so often read expressively by Victorian critics, it comes as no surprise that women poets used meters to manipulate the emotional tenor of their poems, but they also manipulated the emotional tenor of their poems to call attention to the performance of meter.

Necessary Drudgery: Women's Versification and Education

Many of the ways we read Victorian women's prosody now were presaged by mid- and late-nineteenth-century considerations of women's verses. The first collections of women's poetry at mid-century set the tone for EBB, Eliot, and the poets of the Victorian era: Bethune's *The British Female Poets: with Biographical and Critical Notices* (1848), Rufus Wilmot Griswold's *The Female Poets of America* (1853), and Frederic Rowton's *The Female Poets of Great Britain* (1854). These three anthologies all contained biographical and critical "notices" where women might have gathered information about how women's poetry was being read (or not being read) for its formal qualities. Bethune describes Hemans, for instance, as follows: "Though high poetical talent cannot be ascribed to her, her versification is easy and graceful, winning for her many admirers ... The selections we subjoin will exhibit the literary and moral traits of this amiable and industrious woman, in a good light."[14] Young poets like Eliza Cook are described as charming and "whole-souled"; "It may be hoped ... that she will take more pains in the finishing of her verses, than she has hitherto done, and avoid a repetition of ideas, a fault to which she is somewhat prone." EBB also possesses a "disdain of carefulness." Bethune continues,

Her lines are often rude, her rhymes forced, from impatience rather than affectation; and for the same reason, she falls into the kindred fault of verbose-ness, which is always obscure ... Her Greek studies should have taught her more sculptor-like finish and dignity; but the glowing, generous impulses of her woman's heart are too much for the discipline of the classics.[15]

Griswold simply describes nearly every instance of versification as "melodious."[16] The influence of an English father's books on the young poetess is evident in the critical notice of the third anthologist, Frederic Rowton, who died the same year his anthology was published. In his head-note to the poems of Miss Elizabeth Carter, he writes:

Her father appears to have taken the greatest possible pains with her education; and, although at first slow and inapt at study, she eventually became remark-ably distinguished for her extensive and varied acquirements. She was well acquainted with Greek, Latin, Hebrew, French, Italian, Spanish, and German languages; and, in later life, attained considerable knowledge of Portuguese and Arabic. Miss Carter acquired great celebrity by her translation of Epictetus, and was intimately acquainted with Dr. Johnson and the other chief literary characters of the day.[17]

Though Carter's *Ode to Wisdom* appeared in Richardson's *Clarissa* (1747–8), the connection between a woman's facility with versification and her access to education is a theme that continues throughout the late nine-teenth century. Women's verses should be natural and genuine, with varia-tion matching variation in feeling, but this may be attainable only for women who can access a classical education and who (unlike EBB) take the right lessons from it.

Otherwise, the majority of poems by women resemble Babbage's early computer, "a machine for calculating logarithms; poetry of this sort might, one would think, be made to order by a like device. Read these lines aloud, and you may almost hear the turning of a handle."[18] E. L. Bryans's 1871 essay "Characteristics of Women's Poetry" implicitly upholds the natural rhythms praised by Griswold and Bethune, and he critiques "over-carefulness of versi-fication." For him, repetition and lack of variety in women's verses are due to lack of training: "To undergo this training, much restraint, one might almost say, education, must be submitted to. Metre, rhyme, rhythm, must all be mastered, and to submit to the necessary drudgery is more than some people are prepared for."[19] Bryans's critique of *Aurora Leigh* is precisely that EBB treats subjects better left to men (he describes her verses as "poetry in spasms and eloquence in shrieks") but, expectedly, he continues, "In devotional poetry or poetry of a religious tone, women have been specially successful – indeed, one might say, more successful than men; for a woman's mind is more

adapted for the comprehension of the poetic side of religion, and more inclined
to the contemplation of religious subjects than a man's."[20] Devotional poems,
often written in common measure, could display the proper sort of controlled
and measured emotion.

Too Exclusively Identified with Song

Alfred Miles, George Saintsbury, and Robert Bridges, in their late-nineteenth-
and early-twentieth-century assessments of women's poetry, solidify these
earlier characterizations. Robert Bridges describes Mary Coleridge's poems
as "irrepressible songs of fancy," a perfect blend of "the Greek attainment
and the religious ideal."[21] In Volume 7 of Miles's *The Poets and Poetry of
the Century* (devoted only to women writers), we have Arthur Symons's
effusive praise for Christina Rossetti: "no surge of personal feeling disturbs
the calm assurance of the rhythm, the solemn reiterance of the tolling
burden of rhyme. Indeed, the more deeply or delicately felt the emotion,
the more impressive or exquisite, very often, is the art."[22] George
Saintsbury gives what is by far the most intense and praise-filled reading
of Christina Rossetti's *Goblin Market* in the third volume of *The History of
English Prosody*. The regulative patterns he finds in the long poem are akin
to regulation of the poem's overall moral, and yet he denies her the understanding necessary to pull it off knowingly:

> I daresay Miss Rossetti had never heard the words "equivalence" or "substitu-
> tion" in their prosodic meaning, and though it is extremely unlikely that she
> ever consciously realized Shakespeare's use of shortened and lengthened norms
> in, say, *Hamlet*; if she had set herself to give a demonstration of these things, as
> they appear in their very artfullest and yet most seeming-simple shape, she
> could hardly have succeeded better.[23]

Rossetti's religious poems and her virtuosic *Goblin Market* were praised for
their skill with versification. And the meters she upheld in *Goblin Market*
were quintessentially English:

> Like so many other metres, this has for regulative pattern, with the cautions so
> often given, the rock-and-oak-born octosyllabic couplet – oak of English
> rhythm and rock of Romance metre. It appears, now and then, in sober
> completeness, as here:

> > Beside the brook, along the glen,
> > She heard the tramp of goblin men.

Though the poem contains a variety of meters (he enumerates them all),
Saintsbury names the "Skeltonic" its primary measure – a sometimes two- or

three-stress, four-to-six syllable line supposedly invented by fifteenth-century poet John Skelton. He concludes his several-page section on Rossetti's prosody by stating, "On the whole, late nineteenth-century poetry has hardly, on the formal side, a more characteristic and more gifted exponent than Christina Rossetti. Read her, and read all of her."[24]

Saintsbury and Symons both name Rossetti the foremost female prosodist of her day. Rather than disregard her prosodic training, contemporary critic Anne Jamison has properly situated Rossetti among the prosodic discourses that may have precipitated the meters of *Goblin Market*. For instance, Jamison explores the ways Skeltonics were seen favorably by Isaac D'Israeli but suspiciously by Edwin Guest, whose *A History of English Rhythms* was published in 1832.[25] Were Skeltonics playful or were they genealogically tied to Anglo-Saxon rhythms? How would understanding Christina Rossetti's manipulation of a meter with an unstable provenance have changed her reception? We can see from Saintsbury's and Symons's readings the clean line they see from Rossetti to Meynell: Rosetti's verses are calm, delicate, and reticent and yet her meters display an intricate understanding of the national metrical history Saintsbury believed in.

Though Christina Rossetti's "natural" (as opposed to overly learned) versification expertly teaches us about English meter, Augusta Webster uses her "expertness" with meters to protest against the characterization of women poets as natural, lyrical agents of the nation. Mackenzie Bell's introduction to Augusta Webster in Alfred Miles's volume is striking for showing Webster's experiments in a positive light:

> Although Augusta Webster's poetry, whether rhymed or unrhymed, cannot be said to show any great musical impulse, her knowledge of metrical laws, and her expertness in the use of meters is striking. This is very observable in "The Snow Waste." It opens and concludes with a short passage in blank verse, but the body of the poem is written in eight-line stanzas. In each of these stanzas only one rhyme is employed, and the repetition of the same rhymes, which produces a sense of gloomy monotony, is managed with extraordinary skill.[26]

He also, expectedly, praises her knowledge of Greek ("Naturally both plays bear witness to the influence of her classical studies, and, indeed, could only have been written by a scholar"), her translations, and her versions of Italian short poems.[27] Just as many poems by women were praised as merely melodious, so, too, did acknowledgment of a woman's mastery of Greek (sometimes Latin) begin to sound like a trope in introductions to women's poetry. The praise of the poetess's classical education signaled not only that the female poet required something outside of her realm of regular experience to succeed but also that the classics were, as Yopie Prins has shown, accessible to and manipulated by women poets in ways we have just begun to understand.[28] EBB, Eliot, Webster, and other famous poetesses of the Victorian age chafed against the characterization that they were mere songbirds. Compare the blank verse opening of "The Snow Waste" to the eight-line stanza that follows it:

> I saw one sitting mid a waste of snow
> Where never sun looked down nor silvering moon
> But far around the silent skies were grey,
> With chill far stars bespeckled here and there,
> And a great stillness brooded over all.   (lines 1–5)

The narrator's scene-setting opening describes the character's tone:

> He uttered speech
> That was as though his voice spoke of itself
> And swayed by no part of the life in him,
> In an uncadenced chant on one slow chord
> Dull undulating surely to and fro.   (lines 14–18)

This "uncadenced chant" with only one rhyme for each eight-line stanza is difficult to maintain. Webster's poem essentially tries to take meter out of the equation but cannot quite:

> Ye dead who comrade me amid this snow,
> Where through long aeons I drag me to and fro,
> I speak again to ye the things I know
> But, knowing, cannot feel, that haply so
> I may relight in me life's former glow
> And thaw the ice-bound tears in me to flow,
> If I might into sentient memory grow
> And waken in me energy of woe.   (lines 19–27)

The poem purposefully resists the kind of metrical address that would move us to a passion of the ethereal or heroic; indeed, it is not even addressed to the reader but to "ye dead who comrade me amid this snow" to attempt to "relight" in him some feeling or passion. The stanza avoids metrical modulation just as the character's tone is supposedly monotonous. And, indeed, his own memories are

> like a book whose fair-writ phrases lie
> All shapely moulded to word-harmony
> But void of meaning in their melody,
> Vague echoes that awaken no reply.   (lines 30–4)[29]

Webster's own shapely molded words, here, studiously avoid the faint praise of "melodious" that described and minimized so many of her predecessors. Herbert Tucker rightly calls Webster "an exquisite innovator in the resources of blank verse."[30] Meter's monotony, in Webster's poems and elsewhere in the Victorian period, could be used to distance the reader from identifying rhythmic modulations with emotional expression – from identifying too closely with the poet's own feelings – and to redirect attention to the meta-poetic commentary available in the poem's rhythm.

The Mere Pleasure of Bondage

In 1916, Alice Meynell published *The Art of Scansion,* an edition of a letter that EBB wrote in 1827 to her then neighbor Uvedale Price (1747–1829) in response to his *An Essay on the Modern Pronunciation of Greek and Latin.* Meynell introduces the letter by delighting in the eagerness with which EBB argued her positions – by Meynell's moment, the question of English meter seemed (to Saintsbury, to Meynell) to be settled once and for all. But it was far from settled, and writers like both EBB and Eliot and others like them found themselves participating in arguments and quibbles over meter that prolifer-ated nearly every time a writer attempted to scan a line. "It is remarkable," Meynell wonders, "that she never uses the word 'stress' in writing of English prosody. It seems to me to be the only safe word: 'accent' being alien and ambiguous, and 'quantity' a valuable but nearly lawless part of our metre – present in every poet's intention in his line, but perhaps unnamed."[31] EBB's early participation in the prosody wars signals a poet keenly aware of the stakes of prosodic choices. Displaying her knowledge of Price's earlier work as well as passages from French literary historian Jean-Françoise Marmontel, EBB defends the metrical feet she believes are getting short shrift, like the choriamb: "I like so much all you say about choriambi, that I am the more sorry you should shut the door of English poetry in their face."[32] The choriambus is a four-syllable word (or, as EBB would call it, "tetrasylla-ble") with a trochee followed by an iamb, and she is particularly aware that she is trying to convince Price that, imperfect as it is, "the foot is considerably *mutatus ab illo* [changed from what it once was] in the process of its natur-alization into our language."[33] Her canny examples of compound choriambs "Overfatigue – overdelight – conquerer like sex" show, nevertheless, how she was trying to win recognition for the metrical foot that would be useful to her, later, as she composed verses criticized for being too much like prose.

In a letter to Anna Jameson in 1857 about *Aurora Leigh,* EBB writes, "I am entirely astonished at the amount of reception I have met with – I who expected to be put in the stocks and pelted with the eggs of the last twenty years' 'singing birds' as a disorderly woman and freethinking poet!"[34] The *Blackwood's* reviewer W. E. Aytoun was particularly upset that the poem did not idealize its language, did not ascend to pure or lofty heights:

> In this poem she has willfully alternated passages of sorry prose with bursts of splendid poetry; and her prose is all the worse because she has been compelled to dislocate its joints in order to make it read like blank verse ... The tendency to experiment, which is simply a token of a morbid craving for originality, has been the bane of many poets ... Mrs. Browning, beyond all modern poets, has no need of resorting to fantasias for the sake of attracting an audience. For whenever she deserts her theories, and touches a natural chord, we acknowledge her as a mistress of song.[35]

The ars poetica at the beginning of the fifth book of *Aurora Leigh* thematizes the limits of being a "mistress of song" and, indeed, dismantles many of the assumptions about the limits of women's artistic abilities. She moves through the ballad, the sonnet, and the descriptive poem, the pastoral, before naming her project an "epic":

> Never flinch,
> But still, unscrupulously epic, catch
> Upon the burning lava of a song
> The full-veined, heaving, double-breasted Age:
> That, when the next shall come, the men of that
> May touch the impress with reverent hand, and say
> 'Behold, – behold the paps we all have sucked!
> This bosom seems to beat still, or at least
> It sets ours beating: this is living art,
> Which thus presents and thus records true life.'
>
> What form is best for poems? (V. 213–23)

Much of the ars poetica reclaims for women the kinds of poems that exceed the limited expectations of women's verses and justify her blank verse overflowing, lava-like, the bounds of poetic tradition:

> We, staggering 'neath our burden as mere men,
> Being called to stand up straight as demi-gods,
> Support the intolerable strain and stress
> Of the universal, and send clearly up
> With voices broken by the human sob,
> Our poems to find rhymes among the stars! (V. 384–8)

The themes and form of *Aurora Leigh* generated a vast number of reviews, nearly all of which commented on "its form infelicitous."[36] Eliot's 1857 review was an exception. She singled out "the most striking characteristic" of the poem to be the way the form of the poem was infused with the far-reaching and genuine nature of a true and complicated mind:

> [I]ts melody, fancy, and imagination – what we may call its poetic *body* – is everywhere informed by a *soul*, namely, by genuine thought and feeling. There is no petty striving after special effects, no heaping up of images for their own sake, no trivial play of fancy run quite astray from the control of deeper insensibility; there is simply a full mind pouring itself out in song as its natural and easiest medium. The mind has its far-stretching thoughts, its abundant treasure of well-digested learning, its acute observation of life, its yearning sympathy with multiform human sorrow, its store of personal domestic love and joy; and these are given out in a delightful alternation of pathos, reflection, satire playful or pungent, and picturesque description, which carries us with swifter pulses than usual through four hundred pages, and makes us sorry to find ourselves at the end ... It has the calm, even flow of a broad river, not the spray and rainbows of a mountain torrent.[37]

Eliot renames her excerpts as if they were smaller poems, starting with "Mother's Love," the passage that shows how mothers pass on language to their children:

> a simple, merry, tender knack
> Of tying sashes, fitting baby shoes,
> And stringing pretty words that make no sense,
> And kissing full sense into empty words ...
> children learn by such.   (I. 49–54)

Here is the natural side of a woman's "knack," contrasted with the "Portrait" of Aurora Leigh's aunt, who

> had lived
> A sort of cage-bird life, born in a cage,
> Accounting that to leap from perch to perch
> Was act and joy enough for any bird.   (I. 304–7)

The contrast of mother's love and the grown woman's cage is striking; Eliot shows, here, what EBB and other women poets are up against – both the bias that she should be natural and that she should remain happy in her prescribed poetic cage. She then quotes the section of the poem, which she titles "Seriousness of Art," in which Romney prepares Aurora Leigh for the ways that male critics will receive her book "not as mere work, but as mere's woman's work," echoing several lines earlier in which he dismisses "mere women" and tells Aurora of her ambitions, "We shall not get a poet, in my mind" (II. 225):

Expressing the comparative respect
Which means the absolute scorn. 'Oh, excellent!
'What grace! What facile turns! What fluent sweeps!
'What delicate discernment . . . almost thought!
'The book does honour to the sex, we hold.
'Among our female authors we make room
'For this fair writer, and congratulate
'The country that produces in these times
'Such women, competent to . . spell.'   (II.235–42)

Aurora Leigh halts Romney's rant with "Stop there" to finish the two syllables that would make up this line's ten. Her blank verse makes room for the chatter of the critics, and the ellipses as Romney hesitates to find the most insulting description of mere women's talents could be read, too, as a signal to the reader that there is a metrical incompetence to the eight-syllable line. Eliot could have taken these reviews from any of the introductions I cite earlier. The fact that Eliot renames this section the "Seriousness of Art" shows how seriously she takes her role as a woman artist and how disappointed she is in criticism that diminishes women's potential ("discernment . . . almost thought" "competent to . . spell"). In fact, she italicizes the last four lines of Aurora Leigh's response to Romney. She would rather dance on tightropes

> than shift the types
> *For tolerable verse, intolerable*
> *To men who act and suffer. Better far,*
> *Pursue a frivolous trade by serious means,*
> *Than a sublime art frivolously.*   (II. 255–9)[38]

EBB and Eliot were tired of the way women's verses were characterized as frivolous, as sentimental. Eliot was a scholar of blank verse, in particular, and in her essay "Versification," she writes: "Time, accent, melodic utterance, have to be so inwrought with the emphasis, the tones, the gradations of rapidity which belong to the passionate or intellectual intention of the verse, that the versification shall be to the meaning as the mythical wings to the strong quadruped."[39] EBB's intellectual intention was clear to Eliot as it is clear to us now.

Though Eliot's essay "Versification" was not published in her lifetime, her reviews, letters, and notebooks show that she was working through several theories of versification in English to develop her own theories about poetic form. "All valid rules," she writes, "all rules not voluntarily assumed for the mere pleasure of bondage – must have a psychological or physical basis."[40]

In the same notebook, she copied passages from Joseph Haselwood's *Ancient Critical Essays upon English Poets and Poësy* (1815), James Sylvester's *The Laws of Verse; or, Principles of Versification* (1870), and Edwin Guest's *A History of English Rhythms* (1838), the volume that Jamison cites as informing Christina Rossetti's *Goblin Market*. Rather than write her own prosodic treatise, however, Eliot worked out some of her reading in two shorter notebook essays and in her verse experiments.

Like *Aurora Leigh*, the *Spanish Gypsy* received its share of negative reviews, especially its use of dialogue. John Skelton (the Victorian critic, not the fifteenth-century poet) writes: "It seems to me that the diagnosis of the clever experimentalist has here failed significantly." He continues, "To my ear ... it is entirely wanting in any true rhythmic sweetness or music. The soft melodious pulse of life beats in the verse of Keats and Coleridge; George Eliot's is hard, sharp, and galvanic."[41] But perhaps holding Eliot's poems to the "melodious pulse of life beats" limits our reading of her poetry. James Ashcroft Noble (author of *The Sonnet in England, & Other Essays*), in his introduction for Miles's volume, both summarizes and faults critics of Eliot's poetry for being too narrow in their views of verse genres. When we fault Eliot for writing poems that lack "pulse beating in the verse," we are betraying a narrow understanding of poetry by limiting it only to the identification of song – the very identification that so many women poets found restrictive:

> Mr. Oscar Browning, George Eliot's most recent biographer, denies to her not only "the passionate fire, without which," he says, "no poet can excel," but also "the gift of melodious language." "Verse to her," says Mr. R.H. Hutton, "is a fetter, not a stimulus." "A large rhythm," writes Mr. Edward Dowden, "sustains the verse, similar in nature to the movement of a calmly musical period of prose; but at best the music of the lines is a measurable music; under the verse there lies no living heart of music with curious pulsation, and rhythm which is a miracle of the blood ... She could not sing." These three criticisms are fairly representative: George Eliot was not a poet; she was not a singer; verse was a fetter to her; – the second and third statements being justifications for the first. The verdict sounds very formidable, but it may lose some of its formidableness if we see in it only an illustration of a habit which has recently been growing among the critics of demanding in all poetry the presence of certain characteristics which necessarily belong only to poetry of the lyrical kind, – an effusion, an abandonment, a sense as of a pulse beating in the verse. Poetry has, in fact, been too exclusively identified with song, whereas many conceptions which are purely poetical, and which clothe themselves in verse as naturally and inevitably as other conceptions clothe themselves in prose, are not of a nature to ally themselves with song or to allow of being sung.[42]

Indeed, the infection of "certain characteristics which necessarily belong only to poetry of the lyrical kind" dogged women poets throughout the Victorian era – that is, the expectation that their verse should be only song, or merely melodious. By the end of the century, this gendered critique was spilling into critical discourse for *all* poetry. Whereas "effusion" or "abandonment" may have been seen as the lyrical, songlike realm of women poets, by the turn of the century critics were mis-identifying all poetry *as* lyric. Contemporary critics must look past this deeply engrained habit of lyric reading, past the lack of a prosodic handbook authored by a woman, and past the mostly male-authored reviews and critiques of women's poetry to see how women participated in and responded to prosodic discourse in their poems and in their unpublished writing. Not just thematically, as in EBB's *Aurora Leigh*, but also formally, as in Webster's "The Snow Waste," women used meter to display their education, their expertise, and their ability to be read by audiences who expected more than mere songbirds. Though reviews of women's poetry tried to delineate the boundaries of poetry versus prose and emotional versus intellectual subjects, meter moved from an appropriate vehicle of the passions, in the early nineteenth century, to an intellectual subject in its own right. Victorian women poets capitalized on the allegorical meanings of meter as labor, discipline, and restraint, and they also used their mastery of meter to display their education and to access new topics. Though many readings of Victorian women poets still collapse a vast array of poetic meters into the catchall generic category of the lyric, the more we uncover women's writing about prosody – in unpublished writing, in periodicals – the more accurately we can add to the historical record of women's versification beyond the merely melodious.

Notes

1. *Philadelphia Press* advertisement for Thomas Hood's *The Rhymester,* printed in the back of Ella Rodman Church's *The Home Needle* (New York: D. Appleton and Company, 1882).
2. *The Poetical Works of Mrs. Felicia Hemans* (London: Grig & Willmot, 1845), p. xiv.
3. *The Poetical Works of Felicia Hemans, Edited with a Critical Memoir by William Michael Rossetti* (London: Ward, Lock, and Co, 1873), pp. xxvi–xxvii.
4. George Bethune, ed., *The British Female Poets with Biographical and Critical Notices* (Philadelphia: Lindsay & Blackiston, 1848), pp. 188, 191.
5. Alice Meynell, *The Complete Poems of Alice Meynell* (London: Burns, Oates & Co, 1923), p. 130.
6. Yopie Prins, "Patmore's Law, Meynell's Rhythm," in *The Fin-de-Siècle Poem: English Literary Culture in the 1890s,* ed. Joseph Bristow (Athens: Ohio University Press, 2005), pp. 276–7.

7. Meynell, *Complete Poems*, p. 133.
8. Alice Meynell, *The Rhythm of Life* (London: John Lane, 1896), pp. 1, 6.
9. Harriet Monroe, "Alice Meynell," *Poetry* 4 (1914), 70–1.
10. George Saintsbury, *A History of English Prosody from the Twelfth Century to the Present Day*, vol. 3 (London: Macmillan and Co, 1910), p. 241.
11. Shirley [John Skelton], "Poetry and George Eliot," *Fraser's Magazine* 78 (October 1868), 474.
12. Isobel Armstrong, *Victorian Poetry: Poetry, Poetics, and Politics* (London: Routledge, 1993).
13. Fabienne Moine, *Women Poets in the Victorian Era: Cultural Practices and Nature Poetry* (Surrey: Ashgate, 2015); Lee O'Brien, *The Romance of the Lyric in Nineteenth-Century Women's Poetry: Experiments in Form* (Newark: University of Delaware Press, 2013); Sarah Parker, *The Lesbian Muse and Poetic Identity, 1889–1930* (London: Pickering & Chatto, 2013).
14. Bethune, *British Female Poets*, p. 125.
15. Ibid., p. 452.
16. Rufus Wilmot Griswold, *The Female Poets of America* (Philadelphia: H.C. Baird, 1853), pp. 227, 311.
17. Frederic Rowton, ed., *The Female Poets of Great Britain* (Philadelphia: H. C. Baird, 1854), p. 178.
18. [E. L. Bryans], "Characteristics of Women's Poetry," *Dark Blue* 2 (December 1871), 484.
19. Ibid., pp. 488–9
20. Ibid., p. 491.
21. Robert Bridges, "The Poems of Mary Coleridge," *Cornhill Magazine* n.s. 23 (November 1907), 595.
22. Arthur Symons, "Christina G. Rossetti," in *The Poets and Poetry of the Century*, Vol. 7: *Joanna Baillie to Mathilde Blind*, ed. Alfred H. Miles (London: Hutchinson & Co., 1907), p. 431.
23. Saintsbury, *History of English Prosody*, p. 354.
24. Ibid., p. 359.
25. Anne Jamison, *Poetics en Passant: Redefining the Relationship between Victorian and Modern Poetry* (New York: Palgrave Macmillan, 2009).
26. Mackenzie Bell, "Augusta Webster," in *Poets and Poetry of the Century*, pp. 501–2.
27. Ibid., pp. 505–6.
28. Yopie Prins, *Ladies' Greek: Victorian Translations of Tragedy* (Princeton: Princeton University Press, 2017); and *Victorian Sappho* (Princeton: Princeton University Press, 1999).
29. Augusta Webster, *Dramatic Studies* (London: Macmillan and Co, 1866), pp. 113–32.
30. Herbert Tucker, "Fretted Lines: Di-versification in Augusta Webster's Dramatic Monologues," *Victorian Poetry* 55 (2017), 106.
31. Alice Meynell, ed., *The Art of Scansion* (London: privately printed by Clement Shorter, 1916), pp. viii–ix.
32. Ibid., p. 4.
33. Ibid., p. 5

34. Qtd. in Elizabeth Barrett Browning. *Aurora Leigh*, ed. Margaret Reynolds (New York: W.W. Norton & Co, 1996), p. 342.
35. W. E. Aytoun, in *Aurora Leigh*, ed. Reynolds, pp. 417, 420.
36. *Aurora Leigh*, ed. Reynolds, p. 404.
37. [George Eliot], "Contemporary Literature," *Westminster Review* 67 (January 1857), 307.
38. Ibid., p. 309 (Eliot's emphasis).
39. George Eliot, "Versification," *George Eliot: A Writer's Notebook 1854–1870*, ed. Joseph Wiesenfarth (Charlottesville: University Press of Virginia, 1981), p. 286.
40. Ibid., p. 288.
41. [Skelton], "Poetry and George Eliot," 474, 476.
42. James Ashcroft Noble, "George Eliot (Mary Ann Cross)," in *Poets and Poetry of the Century*, pp. 296–7.

3

ELIZABETH HELSINGER

Haunted by Voice

Voice may still be poetry's preferred medium, the figure through which we understand even printed verse, shaped for speaking by prosody and rhetorical figures of sound.[1] But voice was problematic for Victorian women poets, as scholars have been reminding us for some time. Angela Leighton, Margaret Reynolds, and Daniel Karlin have traced the intertwined tragic histories of Sappho, Corinne, and the singer of Letitia Landon's (L.E.L.'s) "L'Improvisatrice" and their silencing effects on later women poets, from Christina Rossetti, Alice Meynell, and Michael Field through Agnes Mary Robinson, Mary Coleridge, Charlotte Mew, and Mathilde Blind.[2] Philomela's song has its origins in a rape. The pain inflicted by that truly careless poet, the god Pan, on the nymph Syrinx (in Elizabeth Barrett Browning's [EBB's] "A Musical Instrument") evokes the memory of all those (usually male) poets who, like Pan, rudely wrest a woman's body to serve as an instrument for their songs. EBB approached the forms and figures of vocal expression in her poems with well-advised caution, wary of the all-too-convenient myth of the artlessly expressive female singer and its potentially blighting consequences for the serious woman writer. She devoted much of her long poem *Aurora Leigh* to showing the years of study and apprenticeship to the craft of verse writing that her fictional woman poet undertook. Women had much to gain by emphasizing the textuality of their poetry.[3] They were not included in the company of bardic singer-poets among whom the young W. B. Yeats wished to be counted. Like William Blake, William Wordsworth, S. T. Coleridge, Alfred Tennyson, D. G. Rossetti, A. C. Swinburne, and William Morris, Yeats chanted his poetry aloud, claiming the aural power of a prophetic medium.[4] Women poets did not. As Yopie Prins, Emily Harrington, and Marion Thain have argued, they embraced a poetry of silence and intimacy: a poetry of the page.[5] Yet this does not mean the question of voice in their work can be easily dismissed.

"Voice is not so much poetry's 'origin,'" writes David Nowell Smith, "as that towards which it continually reaches – not an object to be grasped but a plurality of voicings it opens to us, and to which we as readers are attuned each time anew."[6] Such voicings exist as an array of possibilities offered to a reader – possibilities opened up by the play of sense with and against the possible sounds and shapes of words put into the forms of verse: into lines and stanzas, rhymes and rhythms and meters. "To speak of voice," Nowell Smith suggests, "is, in this sense, to attend to its configurations, to the patterns of its self-configuring [in verse], but it is also to reconstruct voice as necessarily ec-static, necessarily medial: voice only becomes 'voice' as outside itself, other to itself."[7] This is literally accurate: what we hear as voice we hear only after it has left the body: "voice is *of* the body only insofar as it is *from* the body. Voice appears precisely when it leaves the body and hovers in the air," as Lawrence Kramer notes.[8] The inscription on page or tape or disk is also dis-embodied, waiting to be voiced by mechanical or human means before it can be heard. Smith's observations on the "medial" character of voice in poetry are helpful for thinking about Victorian women's poetry in the second part of the century. Unlike Robert Browning, whose poetry repeatedly draws attention to the embodied character of its speakers' words, women poets often preferred the smoother textures of verse that did not try to sound like talk. They continued to invoke the singing voice as a figure for poetry, but they also came to think of voice as something other than personal or natural: as dis-embodied, other to the poet, and plural, as something they might actively solicit and shape in a medium of silence.

Silence is an active force shaping later Victorian women poets' voice-in-verse. All four of the poets whom I will discuss experimented with verse dialogue, but all also discovered silence or absence to be a necessary shaping medium. In "To Silence," for example, Alice Meynell writes of the "moulding" of "melody-shapes" by silence, its "fine intrusions," "afterthoughts," and "wandering . . . grace, within the poet's line."[9] The "silence-bounded singing" of her poetry (line 2) is at once the silence of the printed page, the active pauses of a prosody, and the (usually) silent pressure on the present by its own future (and reciprocally, on that future by the present) that are recurrent subjects in her poems. The place of silence in all three senses – as textuality, prosody, and poetic subject – was something Christina Rossetti had earlier explored in the dialogue forms of her ballads and religious verse. For Rossetti, a silence-shaped practice of poetry at its best anticipates the possibility of song – a singing not to be found this side of the grave, that silent land where the dead pass the blank time between death and a distant resurrection, when all saints will sing together in paradise. For Katharine Bradley and Edith Cooper, writing together as Michael Field, the spaces and silences of the page supported the hidden converse between two lovers (visible in their jointly written journal and their letters to each other) that produced their voice-in-verse. Writing verse dialogue seems to have been a necessary practice for them, composed for the verse dramas that they wrote in great quantities throughout their joint poetic career. But silence also served as the provocation that focused each of their first three lyric volumes: the silence of Sappho, whose fragmented textual remains are all that survive of that first singer; the silence of the paintings that were the subject of *Sight and Song* (1893), with which I will be concerned here; and the silence of the "songs" in Persian and Elizabethan poetry. (Michael Field's third volume of short verse was in part inspired by the ekphrastic challenge of song. *Underneath the Bough*, 1893, gestures both to Edward Fitzgerald's 1859 translation of the Persian poet Omar Khayyam and to the songs found in Elizabethan song books and plays that were reprinted, without music, by A. H. Bullen in multiple volumes, beginning in 1887.) In the work of all four poets, voice is recognized as unnatural artifact when the poet attempts to construct a conversation with an other across an intervening silence, a silence of prosody, page, time, grave, or medium. The resulting poems are at once constrained and enormously ambitious: outward reaching, engaged with other texts and media, and seeking vocal realization on the lips (and the pulses) of others. Voice is ec-static, outside its material embodiments – and perhaps fundamentally plural.

In the ballads that Christina Rossetti composed in the 1850s and 1860s, she adopted that form's characteristic use of dialogue as an economic mode of narration, replacing exposition and commentary with the immediacy of impersonated conversation.[10] Much is left unexplained in this mode of narration; what is passed over in silence is left for the reader to supply. "Noble Sisters" and "Maude Clare" rework "The Cruel Sister" and "Lord Thomas and Fair Elinor," two ballads Rossetti would have known from Walter Scott's *Minstrelsy of the Scottish Border* (1802–3) and Bishop Thomas Percy's *Reliques of English Poetry* (1765), respectively – collections much loved by the young Rossetti and her siblings. Rossetti's versions pay particular attention to the fraught relations between women that the two ballads put on display, narrating the scenes between them in charged dialogue. The silence of the unsaid supports the sharp exchanges between sisters or between a spurned mistress and a wedded wife. Rossetti casts a number of her religious poems into a similarly dialogic form. "Up-Hill" (1858), for example, takes the form of a catechism where the nature of life and death is taught under the figure of the journey:

> Does the road wind up-hill all the way?
>   Yes, to the very end.
> Will the day's journey take the whole long day?
>   From morn to night, my friend.[11]

Question and answer are portrayed as a cooperative endeavor that depends on a deliberately cryptic silence as to the real subject of discussion. Division of labor becomes a way not only of seeking but also of performing belief. It is Rossetti's preferred mode. Unlike the seventeenth-century prayer poems of George Herbert or Henry Vaughan (in which God rarely replies to the poem's intimate address), Rossetti's prayer poems are frequently duets, where human and divine participants exchange the roles of petitioner and petitioned from poem to poem. The silence and privacy that devotional poetry elsewhere assumes have their origin, however, in texts that represent voice or sound. To take only the opening lines of a random series of poems, we find "Vanity of vanities, the Preacher saith" ("One Certainty"), "Flowers preach to us if we will hear" ("'Consider the Lilies of the Field'"), "By day she woos me, soft, exceeding fair" ("The World"), "Passing away, saith the World, passing away" (Part 3 of "Old and New Year Ditties"), and "Sound the deep waters: / – Who shall sound that deep? – " ("Sleep at Sea"). Others' words, often direct quotations from the Bible, become the prelude to poems that unfold as conversation.

When overt dialogue is missing, Rossetti characteristically uses repetition and rhyme to create effects of dialogue by formal textual means: to solicit into responsiveness the absent lover of "Echo," for example.[12] Crucial to such effects is the separation between repeating and rhyming lines. Rossetti rhymes across silence, the pauses and blank spaces of the printed text, forcing our attention to the page as poetry's silent medium. As we learn to read her, we find that the silence of the beat or syllable that is not uttered and the pauses between lines or stanzas take on thematic importance that derives from their formal function. In "Song: Oh roses for the flush of youth," for example, the pause between stanzas allows years to pass.[13] Silence separates and enables the rhyming repetitions of youth (in the first stanza of "Song") with age (in the second), of anticipation with regret.

The greatest challenge to such temporally and spatially distanced rhyming, as one might guess, is the silence of the grave – and that, of course, is the silence to which Rossetti's poems repeatedly turn. Here again, ballad dialogues provided one example. Rossetti's "The Poor Ghost" – where the ghost of a dead husband pleads with his weeping wife to stop disturbing him in his grave – recalls a similar conversation between the living Margaret and her ghostly lover in the well-known ballad of "Clerk Saunders" and its variant, "Sweet William's Ghost."[14] (Elizabeth Siddal, Rossetti's sister-in-law, illustrated it with a beautiful watercolor that Rossetti may have seen.) It should recall as well Rossetti's own early poem, "Song: When I am dead, my dearest."[15] Both Rossetti poems value the silent land – the place of the grave, where dis-embodied lovers no longer even want to converse with the living while they wait for a final resurrection, when their re-embodied voices will join the communion of saints singing together. That possible, imagined singing, harmonizing many voices (perhaps like the unison chanting introduced into Rossetti's high-Anglican Church), becomes both a formal and a metaphysical goal for Rossetti's religious poetry in her last decades, perhaps best realized in the circling repetitions and pauses of the roundel. Adopting the roundel (a form she took from Swinburne) in place of the dialogues of her earlier verse, she sought to attune her poetry to the finer sounds she hoped to hear on the other side of the long silence of the grave: "Tune me, O Lord" is the recurring refrain of one such roundel.[16] Silence, for Rossetti, is at once necessary and desired, a medium without which there can be no conversing in verse and no possibility of that which surpasses conversation, when many voices will sound together. Silence becomes the place of anticipation – of listening (as Harrington has argued) but also of an active and collaborative rehearsal of multitudinous voicings working in harmony. Voice, for Rossetti, is indeed as Nowell Smith describes it: "that towards which [the poem] continually reaches – not an object to be grasped but a plurality of voicings it opens to us, and to which we as readers are attuned each time anew."

Not the end of time (the silent land, the grave, the place of waiting) but time itself is the silent presence inviting conversation in Meynell's poetry. She returns again and again to the possibility that young hopes and old regrets might "converse," repeat, or rhyme in a poem: as if each could guess or read the other's shaping influence across intervening years of silence. This thought is explored in formal dialogues like "The Poets" and "The Poet to His Own Childhood," but more commonly in poems where the poet imagines how her words might be heard or read by the same poet in her past or future. This strategy multiplies potential voice by self-division, with time as the silent force shaping their relation and summoning them into a conversation made possible by the lyric poem. That curious poem "A Letter from a Girl to her own Old Age" is only the most obvious example. "Listen," "A Letter" commands,

> and when thy hand this paper presses,
> O time-worn woman, think of her who blesses
> What thy thin fingers touch, with her caresses.[17]

Rapid shifts between the young woman and her older self are contained in a single sentence, each line uniting but dividing around its caesura the "time-worn woman" from "her who blesses," "thy thin fingers" from "her caresses." The older woman is enjoined first to "Listen" and then to "Hush," but we cannot hear a voice that is mediated by the silent years that separate the young woman from the old. Harrington has drawn particular attention to the way "Meynell allies maternal creation with poetic creation," using its "rhythms of intimacy . . . the dynamic of closeness and distance, of union and painful separation."[18] In this poem the copresence of youth and age creates a paradoxically reversible relationship. The future self in "A Letter" is both "O mother, for the weight of years that break thee!" (line 4) and "O daughter, for slow time must yet awake thee" (line 5) – a doubled role that belongs no less to the younger self as she might be addressed by the older woman she has engendered.

Time that estranges creates a strangely doubled bond that continues to fascinate Meynell as she probes its complexity. "O Poet of the time to be" begins "The Spring to the Summer: The Poet Sings to her Poet," "My conqueror, I began for thee."[19] But the conquered is also aware of her power:

> I have set thy paths, I guide
> Thy blossoms on the wild hillside.
>> And I, thy bygone poet, share
>> The flowers that throng thy feet where'er
> I led thy feet before I died.　　　　　　(lines 16–20)

She began the poem, as well as the life, and set its metrical rhythms, choice of subject, and emotional tone. This is exactly what the poet of "The Poet to His Childhood" will complain of: "How dared you use me so? For you bring my ripe years low / To your child's whim and a destiny your child-soul could not know."[20] The prosodically embodied power to "set ... paths" and lead "feet" is resisted. With the regardless courage of youth, as the older poet sees it, the younger poet chooses to follow poetry's high and narrow paths without thought of others, confidently embracing "my thought and labouring to be / Unconsoled by sympathy" (lines 7–8). The older poet must live with the consequences of that choice, both prosodic and emotional, but insists (in the rhythms she must follow):

> I rebel *not*, child gone by, but obey you wonderingly,
> For you knew not, young rash speaker, all you spoke, and now will I,
>> With the life, and all the loneliness revealed that you thought fit,
>> Sing the Amen, knowing it.　　　　　　(lines 41–4)

But that "Amen" is hedged: the displaced beat on an italicized *not*, like the foreshortened, closing line are both an assent and a sounding of difference, the prosodic embodiment of a conversation between two voices that are *not* the same, however much one may engender the other. The shift is enabled by time; it is the measuring of time by the insertion of silence, and it produces a different reading and a different voicing. "We speak in unknown tongues, the years / Interpret everything aright," as the "Builders of Ruins" put it in the poem of that title.[21] "Our purpose is distinct and dear, / Though from our open eyes 'tis hidden. / Thou, Time to come, shalt make it clear" (lines 41–3). But only because time is also an "undoing" (line 44): "O years that certainly will bless / Our flowers with fruits, our seeds with flowers, / With ruin all our perfectness" (lines 48–50). The work of silent time and time's silences will produce a reading that is at once an interpretation, a clarification, and the undoing of what the original builders, like the poet in her youth, intended. Meynell's delicate tact prevents the collapse of plural possible voicings into one. The two voicings with their different rhythmic emphases are copresent but not identical in the simultaneity of the lyric poem, as Meynell explores the inevitable imbrication of the future in its own past and vice versa. Her tact is particularly evident in the process that her poems so often stage, the acts of reading toward which, as she understands, all poems must reach to realize their voices.

Meynell ventured only once onto the terrain that Michael Field were to take as their own in their early volumes: that particular quest for voicing in the face of silence that we call ekphrasis. Meynell is less concerned with the music specified in her poem's subtitle "A Rondeau by Couperin" than with an image suggested by that piece's enigmatic name, which she takes as the title of her own meditation on ekphrasis, "Soeur Monique."[22] Meynell's poem is what John Hollander terms a "notional ekphrasis": a poem that does not describe an actual work of art but rather "conjure[s] up an image," a fictional work – Meynell's "quiet form of silent nun" (line 1).[23] Her poem belongs to a modern tradition of reflective ekphrasis that includes poems by her beloved Keats and the more proximate Dante Gabriel Rossetti; it reflects upon the challenges of its own task and the limitations of its possible achievements. "Soeur Monique" begins (as many ekphrastic poems do) by addressing unanswerable questions to the silent figure she has conjured from Couperin's title, and it proceeds to a meditation on what Hollander describes as "the contingent and even fragile quality of the relation of any description to its object."[24]

Meynell's hesitations are of a piece with her tact in the treatment of future versions of herself; as Harrington points out, she "invents a relationship" with her nun only to pull back from what she acknowledges to be projections of her own feelings, choosing to leave the figure of the nun as she found her, an unknowable other.[25] Yet she is an other to whom Meynell nonetheless turns as to a guardian angel, a creature of her imagination yet separate from the poet, who has power to "remember me" and "pray for me": to be an active and even a vocal reader of Meynell's poem, sent across the silent distances of time or eternity (lines 96, 100). "Soeur Monique" becomes another self-generated extension of the self, not only daughter and mother but also sister (and Sister) to Meynell, removed from the poet by time and death but present to her in the poem as "you, / In the fields of heaven" (the poem's last words). As in so many of Meynell's poems, a constructed relationship with another self distanced by time (or beyond time altogether) and addressed in the intimate tones of familial conversation holds out the promise of listening to, or reading, the printed voice of the poet herself from a perspective outside herself. These conversations are Meynell's way of exploring the more abstract questions of the nature of poetic voice that most engage her. Like Keats, she ponders a "silent form" that "dost tease us out of thought," an unseen, perhaps unheard presence that both is and is not the poet's waking dream.[26] Through that silent form she discovers a poetic voice that is necessarily ec-static and dis-embodied; guardian angel-sister, mother, and daughter to the poet in the present of her poem. Meynell, one might say, creates a printed voice outside herself that she and other readers might vocalize – and, in this way, might hear.

Unlike Rossetti or Meynell, Katharine Bradley and Edith Cooper were not by temperament silent, as the exuberant verbal energy of their twenty-seven verse dramas and the conversations represented in their multivolume journal attest. In their shorter poems, however, Michael Field embraced a formal shaping that strives to erase the conversations that produced it. The achievements of their lyric volumes were made possible by interlacing (their term) lines and thoughts or half-thoughts from two poets and then rigorously cutting and revising to produce a single textual artifact: "the work is a perfect mosaic: we cross and interlace like a company of dancing summer flies."[27] The poets emphatically claimed their work as poems for the page. They were not overly impressed with the young Yeats's projects for reviving the arts of chanting poetry aloud. (One or both poets heard Yeats chant poetry on several occasions in 1901.[28]) Their own lyric poetry looked to a modernism that seemed to leave voice behind.

The title of their second volume of short poems, *Sight and Song,* might seem a mistake, then. Perhaps the volume might better be described as a visible translation of one silent art form (painting) into another, a "sculpting" of language into visible, almost tactile shapes, as Marion Thain has suggested.[29] Michael Field's ekphrastic poems are a limit case for the late-nineteenth-century lyric's efforts, particularly marked among women poets, to fully embrace textuality even to the materiality of the page, expelling the aural. What is left of voice is in Michael Field partly an excess to which Thain also points, an energy or restlessness that is verbal but also bodily (and sexual).[30] That restless energy is most evident in their correspondence, in their journal, and in their verse dramatizations of characters speaking under the stress of high passions. Yet voice also haunts *Sight and Song*. These ekphrastic poems are organized throughout by vocal gestures, particularly by vocatives of direct address, by interjections and exclamations, and by periodic shifts from simple indicative to interrogative or imperative mood. These residual signs of voice or instructions for voicing are indispensable to the relations between sight and song explored in this volume.

Those relations are not simple: in fact, "song" describes not only the poem but the picture, just as "sight" does. As Michael Field's Preface makes clear, song is a figure for the poetry that "translates into verse" painting's lines and colors, but it is also a figure for what, the poets insist, "the lines and colours ... sing in themselves."[31] Each picture, then, already "objectively incarnates" silent song.[32] Sight similarly applies to works in both media. It is that which appears to the poets' eyes as they study, describe, and then read and discuss each other's descriptions of each picture in their journal, careful not to privilege foreground over background, one figure over another, and trying to let the arrangements of the work's own composition prevail, at least at first, over their instinctive re-ordering of a work according to necessarily idiosyncratic interests. But sight is also the resulting poem, a text whose organization we grasp, at least in part, from the visible shapes it makes on the page. (This is a dimension of the poem to which they, like D. G. Rossetti, paid a great deal of attention, working with small presses and their artist friends and insisting on the importance of every visible aspect of their small book, not least its typography.[33]) And sight is further those acts of looking represented *in* the picture, usually the gaze of one figure in particular. These figures give meaning and emotional tone to the land- and figure-scapes of the painted canvas, making the painting's colors and lines "sing in themselves." Our attention is drawn to these figures, invoked as presences endowed with memories and imaginations that are not our own, by the vocal gestures of the poem.

We begin to see how this works in the opening poem. "*L'Indifférent*: Watteau, The Louvre" serves as a warning against overly zealous ekphrastic questioning but also as a demonstration of how both painting and poem can be at once sight and song. Watteau's picture shows a young page, arms outstretched to either side for balance as he draws his pointed feet into single line, one behind the other, centering his body in the picture space as if caught mid-motion in a pirouette. The poem, like the picture, catches him forever in his youth, poised "on a toe / As light as Mercury's" – as, visually, is the first stanza of the poem, its uneven lines outstretched equally to either side, turning forever around an invisible point.[34] As sight, the printed poem underlines the book's claim to try "to see things from their own centre."[35]

But the poem's indicative descriptive sentences are twice interrupted by imperative address, the change of verbal mood underlined by the urgency of italicization in the first stanza's third line "*Sweet herald, give thy message!*" and again in the third and fourth lines of the second stanza, "*Gay youngster, underneath the oak, / Come, laugh and love!*" (lines 3, 13–14). He does not, of course, reply; rather, his dance *is* his reply: "No, / he dances on," "In vain we woo . . . / No soul, no kiss, /No glance nor joy!" (lines 3–4, 15–17). The comma and line break after "No" in line three underline the firm negative enacted by the still-dancing, silent figure. "To merely dance where he is found / Is fate to him / And he was born for that," the first stanza surmises; "He is a boy, / Who dances and must die," the second stanza more ominously concludes (lines 8–10, 19–20). If the picture's lines and colors "sing" – or dance – if they suggest sound or movement, they do so because the poem's verbal gestures, interrupting its scrupulous descriptive statements, effectively impute consciousness to the painted boy, whose centering as a visible image (in paint or print) perforce limits his ability to answer questions or leave off his pirouetting dance.

Watteau is second only to Botticelli as the painter whose works Michael Field most often take as ekphrastic challenge – probably because two of Watteau's pictures (like all three of the Botticellis) offer a figure of Venus as the potential center of consciousness. The poets' preferred subject takes up visible residence and becomes their inner standing point (in D. G. Rossetti's terms) and the organizing focus for their poems.[36] Thain has drawn attention to the way they use the pale, troubled Venuses of *Spring* and *The Birth of Venus* to impute to painted images, caught in a single still moment, an imagination of a future into which only poetry can enter – a future when love will disappoint and dancing boys or girls will die.[37] In both Watteau's *A Fête Champêtre* and *L'Embarquement pour Cythère*, Venus is still more obviously a pale figure apart, for she is a statue largely unnoticed by the amorous figures that make up the scenes. The poems for these paintings have more work to do to make these stone Venuses the focal points of our attention and the organizing forces of the poem. Once again, however, shifts of verbal mood gradually focus our attention on figures whose imputed thoughts apparently control the tonalities of color and feeling. In the autumnal landscape of the *Fête Champêtre*, Venus's chilling presence is prepared slowly, by verbal interjections ("*Beware!*", "Ah, youth!" "Cupid knows not why").[38] These interjections, breaking away from the indicative of description, direct us first to figures engaged (according to the poem) in resistant or expansive conversation on the subject of love, but eventually to the one human figure who stands "Withdrawn and tart, / . . . in reverie apart," "ironical," and looks at the statue whose back is turned to us and to him (lines 31–2, 41). Conditionals and subjunctives proliferate as we follow his glance toward a cold, impassive Venus ("As though her bosom were exempt / From any care," lines 54–5), preparing us for the final projection from past to unseen future that can be the poem's alone: "Soon shall all hearts forget / The vows they swore / And the leaves strew the glade's untrodden floor" (lines 87–9).

The poem for *L'Embarquement pour Cythère* similarly directs us to the statue of Venus that "none sees" – except, of course, the poet: "her marble mien, / Secret, imperial, blank."[39] This longest of ekphrastic accounts concludes – and concludes the volume – with an envoi, italicized and set apart from the preceding stanzas, where the poem's long clauses give way to a series of short ones that gradually lengthen (with the approach of twilight and autumn) to include the stone Venus, whose thoughts the envoi seems to voice as she contemplates a future beyond that of the painting's (or the book's) moment, one that only the poem can guess:

> *Now they are gone: a change is in the light,*
> *The iridescent ranges wane,*
> *The waters spread: ere fall of night*
> *The red-prowed shallop will have passed from sight*
> *And the stone Venus by herself remain*
> *Ironical above that wide, embrowning plain.*　　(lines 141–6)

In Michael Field's ekphrastic translations of painting into poetry, vocal gestures engage the silent picture in a form of conversation, thereby letting it answer the questions of ekphrasis in the only way it can. The picture's silence becomes less a barrier than a means to achieve what they call in their Preface the "clearer, less passive, more intimate" relationship between poetry and painting to which they aspire, as they seek to translate one kind of visible pattern into another in a way that will also translate mute "singing" into visible and voiceable song.[40]

I want to close these meditations on voice in women's poetry by reminding us of Vernon Lee's short prose fiction "A Wicked Voice." The story, one of those collected as *Hauntings* (1890), can stand as a parable of what happens to those who refuse voice. This is a story of the revenge of the excluded aural. Vernon Lee confidently rewrote the familiar story of the raped female singer. In place of the violence visited on mythical women to make them instruments of passionate vocal production, she offered a tale of the haunting of a male musician by a musical voice equally the product of a violent act, the voice of an eighteenth-century castrato whose fabled singing was said to produce in female listeners the desire for a death as real as it was metaphorical (their ecstasies were both sexual and mortal). The young Swedish composer, visiting Venice and ambitious to write a great Wagnerian multimedia work, despises the castrato's outmoded vocal sound. Lee describes the mysterious voice five times, giving textual presence to a sound she and her readers would probably never hear (by the late nineteenth century, the trained castrato singer had all but disappeared, even in Italy). The first three times Lee describes that voice the singer is hidden. It is the swelling sound alone that takes on uncanny agency:

> [A] thread of sound slender as a moonbeam, scarce audible, but exquisite, which expanded slowly, insensibly, taking volume and body, taking flesh almost and fire ... The note grew stronger and stronger, and warmer and more passionate, until it burst through that strange and charming veil, and emerged beaming, to break itself in the luminous facets of a wonderful shake, long, superb, triumphant.[41]

The sustained and swelling note, rendered in the long and sinuous sentences of Lee's Paterian prose, seems to push beyond the powers of any ordinary singer (castratos harnessed the lung capacity and breath control of an adult to the eerily soprano range of the boy), climaxing in that triumphal, orgasmic burst of ornamentation just when the listening narrator (and Lee's reader) can bear no more.[42] At last the narrator sees the possessor of the voice he hates but cannot escape. The singer's actual body disgusts him – yet once again sound works its mesmerizing enchantment. This time the fevered narrator watches a woman die in an ecstasy of listening. The young composer recovers from his fever but henceforth finds himself unable to compose except for that hated voice. He is possessed by a silent, ghostly sound that is emphatically not his own.

Lee's parable seems at first reading a satisfying riposte to the presumptions of male musicians (and poets) who would make instruments of women's bodies to produce their own songs. Perhaps it is also a poignant commentary on the poetry of her female contemporaries, who like Lee's fictive young composer banished the embodied voice (turning by preference to silent arts) only to become voice's chosen medium. But this is also their accomplishment. Victorian women poets, I have been arguing, had indeed learned by mid-century to underline the status of their work as writing and to embrace a poetry of dis-embodied conversation, brevity, and silence. Yet as in Lee's story, their poetry conjures voice as a spectral presence, now to haunt the modern reader. Voice, in their poems, is sound that cannot be imprisoned in the singularities of the gendered body. Their conscious, intentionally crafted verse sings silently, producing the illusion or imitation of voice by textual means. Plural and dialogic, voice in their poetry becomes other to the poets: ec-static, medial, and shaped by the silences of time, space, painting, death, and the page. It demands to be realized through the listening, reading, and voicing of others.

Notes

My thanks to Marion Thain and Linda Hughes for helpful questions in response to an earlier version of this essay, presented at the NAVSA-BAVS-AVSA conference in Florence in May 2017; and to Herbert Tucker for his paper on Robert Browning's embodied verse, part of the same panel.

1. David Nowell Smith, *On Voice in Poetry: The Work of Animation* (Basingstoke, Hampshire: Palgrave Macmillan, 2015), pp. 28, 3.
2. Angela Leighton, *Victorian Women Poets: Writing Against the Heart* (Charlottesville: University of Virgina Press, 1992); Margaret Reynolds, "'I lived for art, I lived for love': The Woman Poet Sings Sappho's Last Song," in Angela Leighton, ed., *Victorian Women Poets: A Critical Reader* (Oxford: Blackwell, 1996): 277–306; Daniel Karlin, *The Figure of the Singer* (Oxford: Oxford University Press, 2013), esp. pp. 41–58.
3. Karlin, *The Figure of the Singer,* esp. pp. 117–39.
4. Ronald Schuchard, *The Last Minstrels: Yeats and the Revival of the Bardic Arts* (Oxford: Oxford University Press, 2008), pp. 1–31.
5. Yopie Prins, "A Metaphorical Field: Katherine Bradley and Edith Cooper," *Victorian Poetry* 33.1 (spring 1995), 129–48, esp. 135; Emily Harrington, *Second Person Singular: Late Victorian Women Poets and the Bonds of Verse* (Charlottesville: University of Virginia Press, 2014); and Marion Thain, *The Lyric Poem and Aestheticism: Forms of Modernity* (Edinburgh: Edinburgh University Press, 2016), esp. pp. 39–46, 153–9.
6. Nowell Smith, *On Voice in Poetry,* p. 104.
7. Ibid., p. 137.
8. Lawrence Kramer, "Song as Paraphrase," *New Literary History* 46 (2015), 579.
9. Alice Meynell, "To Silence," in *The Poems of Alice Meynell* (London: Oxford University Press, 1940), p. 176, lines 3, 6, 8, 9–10.
10. Elizabeth Helsinger, "Conversing in Verse," *ELH* 84.4 (Winter 2017), 979–1003; and *Poetry and the Thought of Song in Nineteenth-Century Britain* (Charlottesville: University of Virginia Press, 2015), pp. 117–48.
11. Christina Rossetti, "Up-hill," in *The Complete Poems of Christina Rossetti,* 3 vols., ed. R. W. Crump (Baton Rouge: Louisiana State University Press, 1979), 1.65–6, lines 1–4.
12. Harrington, *Second Person Singular,* p. 15; Rossetti, "Echo," *Complete Poems,* 1.46.
13. Rossetti, "Song: Oh roses for the flush of youth," *Complete Poems,* 1.40.
14. Rossetti, "The Poor Ghost," ibid., 1.120–1.
15. Rossetti, "Song: When I am dead, my dearest," ibid., 1.58.
16. Rossetti, "Tune me, O Lord, into one harmony," *Complete Poems,* 2.255.
17. Meynell, "A Letter from a Girl to Her Own Old Age," *Poems,* pp. 17–19, lines 1–3.
18. Harrington, *Second Person Singular,* p. 139.

19. Meynell, "The Spring to the Summer: The Poet Sings to her Poet," *Poems*, p. 8, lines 1–2.
20. Meynell, "The Poet to His Childhood," *Poems*, pp. 48–50, lines 9–10.
21. Meynell, "Builders of Ruins," *Poems*, pp. 23–5, lines 9–10.
22. Meynell, "'Soeur Monique': A Rondeau by Couperin," *Poems*, pp. 28–31.
23. John Hollander, "The Poetics of Ekphrasis," *Word and Image* 4.1 (1988), 209.
24. Ibid., p. 210.
25. Harrington, *Second Person Singular*, p. 126.
26. John Keats, "Ode on a Grecian Urn," in *Poetical Works of John Keats*, ed. H. Buxton Forman (London: Oxford University Press, 1922), p. 234, line 44.
27. Bradley, writing to Havelock Ellis in May 1886; quoted in Mary Sturgeon, *Michael Field* (London: George G. Harrap, 1922), p. 47.
28. *Works and Days*, entries for January 1, June 5, June 10, 1901 (BL Add.MS 4679).
29. Thain, *The Lyric Poem and Aestheticism*, p. 157.
30. Ibid., pp. 44–5.
31. Michael Field, *Sight and Song* (London: Elkin Matthews and John Lane, 1892), p. v.
32. Ibid.
33. Nicholas Frankel, "The Concrete Poetics of Michael Field's *Sight and Song*," in *Michael Field and Their World*, ed. M. D. Stetz and C. A. Wilson (High Wycombe: The Rivendale Press, 2007), pp. 211–21.
34. Field, "*L'Indifferent*: Antoine Watteau," *Sight and Song*, pp. 1–2, lines 1–2.
35. Field, *Sight and Song*, p. vi.
36. Dante Gabriel Rossetti, *The Stealthy School of Criticism* (London: Ellis & Green, 1871), p. 15.
37. Thain, *"Michael Field": Poetry, Aestheticism and the Fin de Siècle* (Cambridge: Cambridge University Press, 2007), pp. 66–89.
38. Field, "*A Fête Champêtre*: Antoine Watteau," *Sight and Song*, pp. 59–64, lines 13, 26, 30.
39. Field, "*L'Embarquement pour Cythère*: Antoine Watteau," *Sight and Song*, pp. 117–25, lines 45, 49.
40. Field, *Sight and Song*, p. vi.
41. Vernon Lee, *Hauntings: Fantastic Stories* (Doylestown, PA: Wildside Press, n.d.), p. 141.
42. Martha Feldman, *The Castrato: Reflections on Natures and Kinds* (Berkeley: University of California Press, 2015), and Bonnie Gordon, "It's Not About the Cut: The Castrato's Instrumentalized Song," *New Literary History* 46 (2015), 647–67.

4

LORRAINE JANZEN KOOISTRA

Floating Worlds
Wood Engraving and Women's Poetry

Poetry is a visual way of expressing ideas, emotions, and experiences. Its iconicity on the printed page forms in short lines of type floating in white space; its poetic language evokes images in the visual imagination. In Victorian illustrated books and periodicals, poems were paired with eye-catching black-and-white art, making poetry uniquely visual. The new relationship between picture and word was enabled by the reproduction technology of wood engraving, which occasioned what Jean-Louis Comolli has called a "frenzy of the visible" in the second half of the nineteenth century.[1] This chapter examines the ways in which wood engraving shaped ways of seeing, knowing, and feeling for women poets and their readers. To frame the chapter's themes, I begin with an extended close reading of the title page to Christina Rossetti's first commercially published book, *Goblin Market and Other Poems* (1862), and end by returning to its frontispiece. One of the Victorian period's finest poets, Rossetti brought a Pre-Raphaelite interest in the interaction of image and text to her highly visual poetics. Bound in a striking cover designed by her brother, Dante Gabriel Rossetti, and prefaced by two of his wood-engraved illustrations, Christina Rossetti's *Goblin Market and Other Poems* serves as an object lesson in the critical convergence of Victorian women's poetry, visuality, and optical discourses.

Framing and Viewing

The title page for *Goblin Market and Other Poems* presents as a series of frames and borders, marking off white space as well as decorated, lettered, and pictorial sections (Figure 1). Its balance of whites and blacks – negative and positive spaces translated into ground and figure – fundamentally expresses the medium of wood engraving, a point to which I shall return. First, however, I want to address the title page's component parts. The design's features allude to cover and contents, outside and inside; symbolically, these are the material and metaphysical elements that make

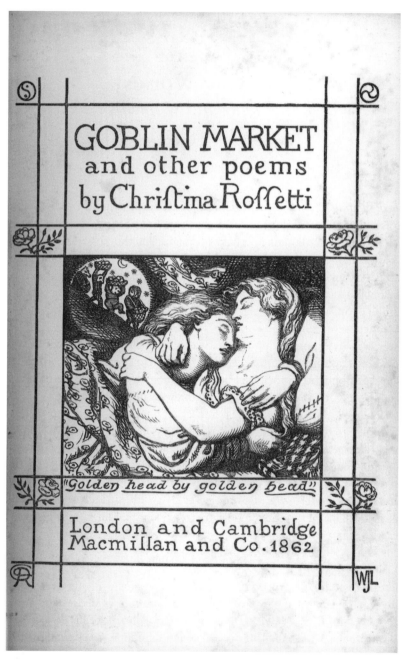

Figure 1 "Golden head by golden head." Wood engraving by W. J. Linton after Dante Gabriel Rossetti for Christina Rossetti, *Goblin Market and Other Poems* (1862): title page. Courtesy of Mark Samuels Lasner Collection, University of Delaware Library.

up Rossetti's poetics. The vertical and horizontal lines stamped in gilt on the blue covers become, on the title page, a double series of black lines framing the white space around the letterpress and inset vignette.

The central frame made by the double rules creates four squares, each containing a laurel branch and a rose. These devices are not merely ornamental. They function both as complex tributes to Rossetti herself – the laurel is a traditional symbol for the poet, while the rose signifies her surname – and as visual references to the book's poetic contents, where natural forms symbolize deeper meanings. In "Song," for instance, Rossetti uses the rose and the laurel to represent, respectively, hope for and recognition of poetic achievement. "Oh roses for the flush of youth, / And laurel for the perfect prime," the lyric speaker sings, ultimately settling for "the withered leaves I chose / Before in the old time."[2] The emblematic devices of the title page work, like Rossetti's poetry itself, to turn material images into transcendent symbols, overlaying collective experience and past traditions with the personal insights of the present. The inset vignette similarly functions as ornament and symbol, illustrating a specific line from the title poem, "Golden head by golden head," while also illuminating thematic concerns in Rossetti's collection as a whole. Tinged, like the vignette, with an inexplicable sense of sorrow and loss, these themes involve the complex ways in which the seen and the unseen shape women's experiences. In this way, the framing, ornamentation, and picturing of the title page provide a series of visual lenses through which to view the poems that follow.

A window into the collection, the vignette establishes a viewing point for witnessing a theatrically staged tableau, complete with curtains and an almost camera-like close-up of Lizzie and Laura, the sisters featured in "Goblin Market." Here we can see how theatrical spectacle, optical instruments, and illustration mutually inflected one another in Victorian visual discourses. If the title-page vignette is presented as a proscenium stage with the fourth wall removed for voyeuristic pleasure, contemporary theater was "described as a 'giant peepshow' (and the stage presented as a 'picture')."[3] Peepshows were popular street entertainments for children and adults alike, offering scopic views of familiar and fantastic scenes within darkened boxes, where moving shadows created a sense of life. The title-page vignette references the Victorian peepshow with both its staging and its figuring of an atopic visual scope, one that is "out of place" in the field of vision. The circular aperture of the upper left corner offers a disorienting glimpse into the outdoor, nighttime world of lively goblins in contrast to the inside, domestic space of sleeping sisters. Like the peepshow itself, the vignette oscillates "between two types of 'distortion' created by the absence of spatial markers on the one hand and overdetermined distinctness on the other."[4]

"A Peep at the Goblins," Rossetti's first title for "Goblin Market," evokes the scopic view of this Victorian optical instrument.[5] The peepshow portal in the vignette draws our attention to the ways in which disorienting perspectives inform the sisters' encounters with the shape-shifting goblins and their deceptive wares. For Victorian women poets, seeing and being seen were complex social negotiations as well as contested cognitive processes. Rossetti's "Goblin Market" is invested in the problematics of looking and the possibilities of vision for women in a "market" controlled by masculine purveyors.

Writing about Victorian visuality and optics, Isobel Armstrong observes that what is at stake in the peepshow "is the definition of Anamorphosis, figure and ground."[6] As an object of vision, the vignette plays with our understanding of represented space. Does the scopic aperture open a window into an outside world, giving us access to a sight that the subjects of the picture, the sleeping sisters, do not have? If this opening is a window, how does it mediate between inside and outside? Are the goblins able to peek into this intimate domestic space? Or perhaps the aperture is not a window at all. Perhaps it functions as a dream bubble, representing the night visions of one of the sleepers. The vignette challenges perspectival perception and stable spatial relations, just as Rossetti's "Goblin Market" unsettles black-and-white interpretations of women's lives. While the drama of the poem turns on the consequences that follow Laura's transgressive looking, its resolution depends on Lizzie's willingness "for the first time in her life … to listen and look."[7] Lizzie's decision to engage with the world results in Laura's cure. Anchored by the poetic passage inscribed below the vignette, "Golden head by golden head," the title-page image visualizes the sisters' sameness – "Like two pigeons in one nest" – rather than their difference in life choices or experiences. In this way, the image also looks proleptically forward to the coda, where the sisters are pictured living together happily, telling stories about their past to their children.[8]

In addition to framing, scopic views, and figure/ground relations, the title page for Rossetti's *Goblin Market and Other Poems* highlights two other aspects of women's poetry, visuality, and illustration that I explore in this chapter: the trope of the sister arts and the technology of wood engraving. The scene pictures sisters so intimately connected that it is difficult to see where one begins and the other leaves off, let alone distinguish Lizzie from Laura. In this way, the vignette offers a visual emblem for the "sister arts" of poetry and pictures. A tradition extending back to classical times, the Horatian "*ut pictura poesis*" (as a picture, so also a poem) concept of the sister arts dominated Victorian interart discourse.[9] Core to the Pre-Raphaelite movement of poets and artists in which Christina Rossetti was involved was a visual-verbal aesthetic concerned with the interaction of image and word. Pre-Raphaelite painters often took scenes from literature for their subjects, and many of them became leading black-and-white illustrators for books and magazines. Throughout the nineteenth century, illustrated periodicals popularized the visual trope of the sister arts by depicting two female figures, one with a pen and one with a brush, on their covers and contents pages. The sister arts are personified in this way from the moment the first pictorial weekly, the *Illustrated London News,* appeared in the 1840s, to the fin-de-siècle emergence of *Atalanta,* a monthly magazine for girls. For Victorian readers, then, the relationship of poem and picture on the printed page was visualized as feminine and sororal, and thought of as mutually supportive, aesthetically enhancing, and intimately interactive.

The close relationship of the sister arts in Victorian books and periodicals was made possible by the technology of wood engraving, which enabled a new approach to illustration and an interactive visual/verbal reading practice. As the dominant form of picture reproduction, wood engraving introduced the integration of image and text in mass print culture. Previous image reproduction technologies required a different printer from that used for the letterpress, resulting in the separation of picture and word. For example, the illustrated annuals popular between the 1820s and 1850s relied on steel-plate engraving, which meant that separately printed pictorial plates had to be inserted between pages of letterpress. The books and periodicals of the second half of the century, on the other hand, featured wood-engraved illustrations on the same page as the text because wood engraving, like moveable type, is a form of relief printing. To enable printing on the same press, blocks of boxwood were prepared to be type high: that is, of identical height to the typeface. Woodblocks could thus share what printers call a "bed" with lines of type, allowing them to be printed together.

From this perspective, *Goblin Market*'s title-page vignette of the sisters in bed symbolizes the intimate relationship between wood engraving and letterpress, and their radical sameness despite distinct differences. Like typography, wood engraving mediates between creator and reader. Dante Gabriel Rossetti drew the title-page design, including the caption, in reverse on the woodblock, and W. J. Linton engraved it for reproduction. Notably, there is a direct correlation between the size of the printed image and the size of the woodblock. Since boxwood is a small tree, blocks were seldom larger than five-inch squares; the borders of *Goblin Market*'s title page measure approximately 3¾ inches in width and 5¼ inches in height. Above and below the pictorial vignette, the wood-engraved, ornamental frame creates space for the insertion of the paratextual information of title, author, publisher, and date. Combining manual and mechanical methods and assembled out of fragments by many hands, the title page expresses the modular modernity of Victorian print culture. Paper provides the ground on which alphanumeric and iconographic figures convey meaning in the common medium of black ink. However unconsciously, readers must decipher this printed page by interpreting the relationship between positive and negative spaces, black lines stamped on a white ground.

While wood engraving has long been recognized as the dominant technology of reproduction in the Victorian period, its influence on ways of seeing, knowing, and representing the world has been less considered, particularly with respect to women's poetry. However, as my analysis of the title page for Rossetti's *Goblin Market and Other Poems* suggests, the linear language of wood engraving informed visual discourse by its demarcation of space through a variety of framing devices, its establishment (and questioning) of figure/ground relations, and its creation of scopic views and seeing positions. Wood engraving enabled the sister arts of poem and picture to share the printed page and develop the multimodal hybridity characteristic of Victorian books and periodicals. In the remainder of this chapter, I examine some vital connections between women's poetry and illustration by exploring wood engraving as a technology of vision under the following headings: floating worlds, cuts and openings, and ornaments and fragments.

Floating Worlds

Victorian art critic John Ruskin succinctly defined wood engraving as the "Art of Scratch" and simplified its methodology: "In wood engraving, you leave ridges, rub the tops of them with ink, and stamp them on your paper."[10] Likening the practice to cutting furrows in the earth, Ruskin called attention to the affective register of engraving: "The central syllable of the word has become a sorrowful one, meaning the most permanent of furrows [the grave]."[11] The Japanese word for wood-block prints, *ukiyo-e*, translates as "floating worlds" but also chimes with the word for the sadness of life.[12] In both Eastern and Western traditions, then, the medium of wood engraving creates "floating worlds" formed by ridges above chasms, expressing the transience of life and its inevitable end, even as it strives to achieve permanence through multiplicity and dissemination. In his *Treatise on Wood Engraving* (1839), William Chatto noted that "at least one hundred thousand good impressions can be obtained from a wood-cut, if properly engraved and carefully printed."[13] By the second half of the century, the possibilities for producing multiple images seemed virtually infinite, as electrotypes were cast from the wood engraving to preserve the original block as a matrix for future molds.[14] Taking his stand against industrial modernity, Ruskin objected to wood engraving's technological capacity, claiming that "*Permanence* ... is the object, not multiplicability."[15] In Victorian Britain's ever-accelerating "frenzy of the visible," however, not even Ruskin could stem the mass dissemination of what Walter Benjamin famously named "the work of art in the age of mechanical reproduction."[16]

Print culture in the second half of the nineteenth century was dominated by date-stamped, illustrated serials, produced to be momentarily consumed and discarded, and focused on the everyday life of readers. Many poems pictured in periodicals depicted worlds of fantasy and legend in ways similar to *Goblin Market*'s title page; others explored aspects of modern experience. Whether they were nostalgic evocations of past worlds and imagined societies or mirrors of contemporary life, however, illustrated poems presented magazine readers with floating worlds in a sea of transience. Marked off by white space and irregular wood-engraved lines in sharp contrast to the standardized lines of type set up in regular columns, these islands of aesthetics and affect were highly visible in Victorian print culture. Notably, editors frequently selected poetry by women writers for visualization, making their work more culturally visible than ever before. The pictorial treatment given to women's poetry in these magazines – narratives and ballads, lyrics of love and loss, poems of nature and religion – speaks to a cultural investment in their power to connect with a wide range of readers in an increasingly urbanized, modern world.

The era of illustrated weekly entertainment was launched in 1859 with *Once a Week*, under the editorship of Samuel Lucas. As Linda K. Hughes has shown, Lucas "not only made illustrated poems a central feature of *Once a Week* but in the process also invented a range of effects generated by paired poems and images in a magazine context."[17] Louisa Stewart's "Bradmere Pool," a romantic ballad extending over the opening three pages of an early issue of *Once a Week*, exemplifies the importance of pictured poetry to the magazine and its middle-class readership (Figures 2 and 3).[18] As the leading item in a twenty-two-page number, "Bradmere Pool" aims to capture reader interest with a thrilling poetic narrative and pictures by one of the period's best-known illustrators, Hablot K. Browne. As "Phiz," Browne illustrated the novels of Charles Dickens for over twenty years, from *The Posthumous Papers of the Pickwick Club* (1836–37) to *A Tale of Two Cities*, which was coming out serially the same year that "Bradmere Pool" appeared in *Once a Week*. Lucas's allocation of page space and pictures for this poem indicates a significant investment. Browne's three vignettes on the opening page are artfully connected by tree roots and branches, which would require finicky work in the printing office when the blocks were set up with the letterpress

Figure 2 Wood engraving by Swain after Hablot K. Browne for Louisa Stewart, "Bradmere Pool," *Once a Week* 1.17 (22 October 1859), p. 329. Courtesy of Mark Samuels Lasner Collection, University of Delaware Library.

Of the wild bee's placid murmur, of the breeze and
  of the wave,—
Gies of mothers for their offspring, and of wives for
  those still dearer,
And of children calling fathers from the crystal of
  their grave.

And the crazed yet harmless Amy wander'd hither
  every morning,
Through the driving snows of winter and the summer
  green and cool,—
Talk'd in fancy to her William till the holy angels
  call'd her :
And this short but tragic legend is the tale of Bradmere Pool.   LOUISA STEWART.

THE COOK OR THE DOCTOR?

IT is always with a shock of surprise and pain
that we read, in the Registrar's Reports, and in
the accounts of Coroners' Inquests, of death from
starvation. Everybody says the same thing on
every occasion of the kind ;—that there must have
been great fault somewhere, because the law of
the land provides subsistence for every person in
it. Let it be granted that deaths from destitution of the necessaries of life are gratuitous :
this is but a small part of the mortality from
hunger. The number of persons who die annually
from being underfed is very great. The victims
themselves are often unaware of the fact : and so
are their neighbours generally. Whatever disease
last lays its grasp upon them,—invited by their
low condition of body,—is called the cause of their
death ; but if the truth were fully understood,
we should see in the register, instead of columns
of entries of low fevers, tubercular diseases, and
fatal affections of the viscera, one comprehensive
term,—deficient nutriment.

If this kind and degree of mortality were owing
to national poverty, or to social arrangements
which condemn large classes to destitution, this
would not be the place for any remarks on the
subject. It would be a political topic of extreme
gravity, which ought to occupy the full attention
of Queen, Lords, Commons, and the political
press : but it is far otherwise. There never was
a time when work and means of subsistence were
so generally diffused in the United Kingdom, as
in the middle of the nineteenth century. There
is every reason to believe that there is food enough
in the country to keep up the health and strength
of every person in it : and it is only the deficiency
of our knowledge and skill in regard to food which
causes a large number of men, women, and children
to be underfed in the midst of abundance.

It is a rare thing to find the head of a household in any rank of life well informed as to the
right kind and degree of nourishment for any one
person. Hence there is such a thing as a family
being underfed in the midst of wealth. This
happens where the quantity which goes down the
throat is considered to be the same thing as so
much nutriment. The same mistake is to be
expected in the labourer's home ; and it is found
there, with the aggravation that the food which is
eaten, whether more or less nourishing at best, is
in great part spoiled by bad cookery. If it was
thoroughly well known throughout the country
how much nourishment every body ought to have,
what articles of food yield that nourishment best,
and how they may be best prepared, there need
be no underfeeding, from the palace to the
labourer's cottage. It is only within a short time
that this has been fully understood. The knowledge is now being applied to improve the diet and
the health of our soldiers : and we must hope that
the benefit will extend to all other classes.

The main principle of the matter is simply this.
A large proportion of the food we eat is mere
water and material which does not nourish.
What *is* nourishment? What is the precise meaning of it ?

There are two kinds of nourishment in good
and sufficient food ; but they are not quite of
equal necessity ; they are of very different pro-
portions ; and the smaller amount (by weight), is
the most indispensable. This smaller element is
absolutely necessary to life, as it goes to repair that
waste of the substance of the body which never
stops. When this waste is not supplied by food
containing this element, the parts perish very
soon. A person starved to death on a desert
island lives only a few days. I am acquainted
with one who lived thirty days under these circumstances : but he was the only survivor of his
party ; he was barely breathing when assistance
came; and his case is considered almost unparalleled.

He and his comrades had been set ashore in a
mutiny. He made the Freemasons' sign to the
leading mutineer, and the man returned in thirty
days, landed with a kettle of hot brandy-and-
water in his hand, and found my friend sense-
less under a bush, with the bodies of his comrades
lying about him. His appearance was extraordinary ever afterwards, as if every fibre in his
face was vibrating without ceasing ; but he recovered to be a world's wonder, for having lived
thirty days through the waste of his frame, without its having been repaired more or less. Four
days of absolute fasting is, I believe, usually con-

Figure 3 Wood engraving by Swain after Hablot K. Browne for Louisa Stewart, "Bradmere Pool," *Once a Week* 1.17 (22 October 1859), p. 331. Courtesy of Mark Samuels Lasner Collection, University of Delaware Library.

(Figure 2). Notably, this time, attention, and expense were lavished on the work of a relatively unknown poet. Louisa Stewart may have been the author who, after her marriage in 1861, became the popular writer of children's literature and novels, Mary Louisa Molesworth (née Stewart).[19] However, the uncertainty about her identity today highlights my point that visuality took precedence over authorial status in *Once a Week*. Lucas made his selection of "Bradmere Pool" as the leading illustrated item for a weekly number based on the poem's readerly appeal and picturable subject matter, rather than the reputation of the poet.

The relative costs for poem and pictures highlight that the magazine's biggest investment was in the drawings and their reproduction. While Lucas would likely have given Stewart the standard two guinea payment for her lengthy poem, he would have paid the well-known Browne two to three guineas for each drawing, or between eight and twelve guineas for all four.[20] Added to this would be a payment to Swain for engraving the woodblocks and preparing the electrotypes for printing. Why did Lucas invest so much money in a poet with no public profile? The answer seems to lie in the cultural value of pictured poetry to Victorian readers, rather than in the name recognition or canonicity of the author. Illustrated periodical poems challenge us to shift our attention from author-centric approaches to more material and reader-based approaches that consider the function of poetry in the modern world of Victorian print. Such an approach brings to light many women poets who, like Louisa Stewart, were read by mass audiences in their own day but are relatively unknown today.

The first page of "Bradmere Pool" presents the reader with floating worlds of wood, literally referencing the medium out of which the figural ridges were formed (Figure 2). Shaped out of twisted twigs, the initial letter "W" connects to the tree trunks, branches, and roots that function as framing devices for three inset temporal scenes. Each vignette operates as a Wordsworthian "spot of time," creating an image that draws the viewer into a remembered or imagined past, evoked in the interaction of poetic language and visualized scene.[21] The natural imagery and organic frames link to a lost pastoral world, while the theatrical tableaus – the proposal of the rich William to the peasant Amy, the tender scene showing the lord-turned-miner embracing his wife and babe before leaving for work, and the idyllic view of the graceful mother and child running through the woods to meet him at the end of the day – enable the reader to view the plot proleptically and affectively, prior to reading the narrative. In this visual context, the verses on the first page act as a verbal teaser: the opening stanzas introduce a number of rhetorical questions about how to stage the story, without naming either its main characters or its location. Not until after the first page turn (when the poem appears in double columns of unadorned type) does the narrator signal that the tale will be a dark one, advising readers to "Choose the night to hear a legend on the brink of Bradmere Pool."[22] One can picture the middle-class family sitting around the hearth on a late October evening, opening their new issue of *Once a Week* to read the tale as autumn darkness descends.

In contrast to the transient worlds of love and beauty floating on the first page, the two columns of type on the second – framed on all sides by double rules and white space, and centrally divided by a vertical line – express a mechanized modern world stamped by standardization. In this sense, the poem's second layout is also iconic and expressive, reminding readers that the flooded mine and dead miners might result as much from industrial capitalism as natural phenomena. The human cost is articulated on the third page of the weekly number. Stewart's poem is punctuated by a final wood-engraved vignette, with "the crazed yet harmless Amy" wandering in the woods talking to her dead husband, who drowned in the mine whose flooding created Bradmere Pool (Figure 3). This picture recalls to the mind's eye, but re-visions, the third scene of the opening page, where Amy and her son are depicted running joyfully in a light-filled glade (Figure 2). Instead of an innocent idyll, now the pictured scene shows a disheveled Amy and her frightened child in a dark and brooding wood. In contrast to the first page, where three floating images are linked by organic framing devices, the single image on the final page is boxed in by two columns of letterpress subdivided into four spatial units (Figure 3). The constraining effect of the lines of type framing the image is emphasized by the wood engraver's echoing use of horizontal lines to create the dark tones of the picture.

In wood engraving, the only way to create tonal variations is to carve out the negative space in gradations of width and depth, leaving the ridges that take the ink farther apart (for lighter effects) or closer together (for darker effects). The open feeling of the first-page vignette of mother and child is created by excavating most of the background, leaving fine lines to give shape to the figures and landscape (Figure 2). In the final scene, only small amounts of negative space have been excavated, illuminating human limbs and foliage to emphasize the overall darkness of this shadowed scene (Figure 3). In this way, the blackness of the image heightens the sorrow implicit in the medium. As Ruskin observed: "Now the eye is not in the least offended by quantity of white, but is, or ought to be, greatly saddened and offended by quantity of black."[23] Tinged with sadness, regret, and loss, Victorian women's illustrated poetry floats in the sorrow of wood engraving and its ongoing dialectic of transience and permanence.

Cuts and Openings

Victorians used the colloquial term "cuts" to refer to wood-engraved illustrations, which are often described as being "let in" to the letterpress. The language of the cut and the opening is central to wood engraving's influence on visual discourse. As we have seen, the woodblock was a modular unit that could be set up with lines of type: the final "cut" for "Bradmere Pool" was "let into" the letterpress in this sense, as if the image were a guest on the textual page (Figure 3). The setup of the first page of "Bradmere Pool," however, suggests a different relationship between the sister arts, one in which the pictorial matter acts as host, "letting in" a few brief stanzas (Figure 2). Here, rather than lines of type framing an inset picture, wood-engraved imagery frames the typographic text: the visual literally provides the optical entry into the poem. This setup happens frequently in Victorian illustrated periodicals, which, as we have seen, were experimental and inventive in their diverse approaches to integrating image and text.

Many examples of this inventiveness are evident in *Good Words*, a popular monthly with a religious outlook appealing to middle-class households with high-quality literature and pictures suitable for family reading. A competitor that long outlasted *Once a Week*, *Good Words* had a circulation between 80,000 and 130,000 in the 1860s.[24] Publisher Alexander Strahan and editor Norman Macleod ensured that more than half the magazine's poems were illustrated in its early years, so pictured poetry was clearly a selling feature for readers.[25] Notably, *Good Words* published a great deal of women's poetry, including both poets who continue to be studied today (such as Dinah Craik, Dora Greenwell, and Jean Ingelow) and less well-known authors. The editor's primary concern was to identify poems appropriate for *Good Words*, select those that could be pictured, and then commission artists based on the type of illustration required.[26] After receiving a block in the size wanted by the editor, the artist would draw his design in reverse on the flat surface and then send it on to the engravers for cutting. Most of the engraving for *Good Words* was carried out by the Dalziel Brothers.

In 1869, Macleod selected Thomas Sulman, an artist known for his expertise in ornamental borders and vignettes, to illustrate a lyric by hymn writer Anna Letitia Waring.[27] Waring's "Passing Pleasures" offers a good example of a page setup that required readers to view verses through the optics of a symbolic frame.[28] In such pairings of picture and poem, *Good Words* inculcated readers in the religious emblem tradition of reading for spiritual meaning by attending to the interrelations of the sister arts. To understand how this dialogic form entered periodical culture and engaged with readers, it is important to understand the centrality of the visual in the poem's mode of production. In "Passing Pleasures," poem and picture appear as a multimodal unit.

The Dalziel Brothers' Proofs Book for 1869–70, made up at the time of printing, shows that the wood engraving was produced as a frame for the poem out of four separate woodblocks, which would have been bolted together at printing time; fine horizontal lines in the proof indicate where the joins were made (Figure 4).[29] The engraving depicts a beautiful world of fragile living things created out of black lines, textures, and white spaces. Within a series of printed rules, wide strips of botanical and zoological designs border a twig-framed white space. The white of the page serves variously as the physical ground out of which plants grow and insects thrive; the sky in which birds fly; the color and texture that give shape and pattern to flowers, eggs, and butterflies; the highlights on the knobby twigs forming the frame; and the medium on which the lines of verse for Waring's poem can be set. Cognitively, the viewer's brain processes all this information by recognizing the co-dependent forces and tensions in the linear art of wood engraving and the oscillating distinctions between figure and ground in this fleeting world.

On the printed page of *Good Words,* the letterpress is literally "let in" to the wood-engraved receptacle created to hold it (Figure 5). Waring's stanzas are centered within the ornamental border, whose artful assemblage of living things born to flourish and die creates the edges of meaning for "Passing Pleasures." Read through the irregular black-and-white lines of the design, the meaning of the verses becomes illuminated. Readers are instructed to read the material world, in all the delights of its ephemeral beauty, lights, and shadows, as material symbols testifying to a promised future when they will "See greater things than this." The trope of weak and diminished sight, in "gentle training / To bear the perfect light," plays on both biblical teaching and Victorian emblematic discourses, which required readers to move between pictures and words in an ongoing hermeneutic process. In this sense, the ornamental border of "Passing Pleasures" is both decorative and readable. Forming an optical opening into the verses, the cut visualizes the meaning of poetic lines in its own linear language.

Ornament and Fragment

How did the black-inked ridges floating above the excavated furrows of wood-engraved illustrations affect Victorian aesthetics and poetics? In 1865, Gerard Manley Hopkins, then an undergraduate at Oxford, wrote

Figure 4 India ink proof of wood engraving by Dalziels after T. Sulman for "Passing Pleasures,"
Dalziel Proofs Book Volume 26 (1869-70). © The Trustees of the British Museum.

Floating Worlds

Good Words, June 1, 1869.]   PASSING PLEASURES.   401

PASSING PLEASURES.

THESE blessed passing pleasures !
   We need not let them waste,
We need not leave their treasures
   Behind us in our haste.
We need not doubt their fitness
   Where earth's deep shadows fall ;
God giving, He is witness
   That we shall want them all.

Amid the old sad story
   Of human shame and sin,
If He gives gleams of glory
   We ought to let them in.
And oh, when brought before us
   Where heart and soul can see,
How mighty to restore us
   Love's little signs may be !

A bird, a tree, a flower,
   A creature just as frail,
Will take us in His power
   To Him within the veil ;
Will come, if He has bidden,
   Amidst the darkening fight,
And leave us safely hidden
   Behind a shield of light.

Perhaps His angels see us
   Disquieted in vain ;
Perhaps His watch would free us
   From some ensnaring pain ;
But only He can measure
   Who sees our nature through
The good that in His pleasure
   A passing joy may do.

If but for one bright minute
   Through gathering clouds it break,
There is a token in it
   That He would have us take.
And His least sign obeying,
   No wealth our hearts shall miss,
Even when we hear Him saying,
   " See greater things than this !"

For He the dull ear gaining,
   Meeting the dim weak sight,
Our faith is gently training
   To bear the perfect light.
And while His mercies guide us,
   We in one sure belief
May trust the joy beside us
   Even as we trust the grief.
            A. L. WARING.

X—28

Figure 5   Wood engraving by Dalziels after T. Sulman for A. L. Waring, "Passing Pleasures,"
Good Words 10 (June 1869), p. 401. Courtesy of Toronto Public Library.

73

an essay entitled "On the Origin of Beauty: A Platonic Dialogue." Hopkins sets his dialogue in a college garden, where a professor, explaining his theory of beauty to a student and an artist, takes the frontispiece for Christina Rossetti's *Goblin Market* as his example. Claiming that beauty results from the contrast between continuity and discontinuity, he argues that the three unconnected dots forming a triangular pattern on Laura's dress "are prettier ... than actual triangles would be" because they require the perceiving eye to complete their forms.[30] The frontispiece illustration, "Buy from us with a golden curl," is a masterpiece of design, but Hopkins bypasses its figurative, narrative, and compositional properties to focus on the aesthetics of ornament: the design within the design (Figure 6). In so doing, he registers how much the picture's material means of expression, wood engraving, influenced ways of seeing and appreciating beauty in the nineteenth century.

Using a variety of tools and cutting methods, wood engravers create irregular and discontinuous ridges to take the ink. To form the repeating triangular pattern of three dots on Laura's dress, the engraver had to laboriously gouge out the surrounding negative space to shape tiny black circles. In carving this pattern, the engraver also had to attend to the drapery of the dress on which the design appears. More black lines, some cut in parallel grooves, others cross hatched, and still others outlining the curvaceous shape of Laura's kneeling legs under the fabric, create tint and shadow within a black-and-white register (Figure 6). In instancing the ornamental pattern of a dress in a printed image as an example of beauty, Hopkins's essay testifies to the power of wood engraving as a technology of vision in Victorian visual discourse. Wood engraving creates beauty out of fragments, floating worlds out of multiple tiny cuts. While the engraver – eyes fixed on a small block of wood for hours at a time, hands making miniscule furrows to create lines as fine as hair – would see each square inch as an assortment of abstract linear patterns, the viewer of the printed image cognitively assembles the discontinuous and irregular lines to perceive a whole. Essential to meaning making in all acts of perception and interpretation, the act of closure took on heightened importance in wood-engraved illustrations in Victorian books and periodicals.

Exemplifying this aesthetic of ornament and fragment, one title, *Beauties of Poetry and Gems of Art* (1864), might apply to the gift-book genre as a whole. The popular gift books of the second half of the nineteenth century combined poetry and wood-engraved illustrations in ornate bindings. Designed to be domestic ornaments on the drawing-room tables of middle-class homes and marketed as gifts for the Christmas season, these illustrated collections and anthologies of poems were targeted at women readers and often featured women poets. *Goblin Market and Other Poems*, for example,

Figure 6 "Buy from us with a golden curl." Wood engraving by Morris, Marshall, Faulkner, and Co., after Dante Gabriel Rossetti for Christina Rossetti, *Goblin Market and Other Poems* (1862): frontispiece. Courtesy of Mark Samuels Lasner Collection, University of Delaware Library.

was intended for Christmas sale, but owing to delays in preparing the cuts, the collection did not appear until spring.[31] Other illustrated collections by women – for example, Eliza Cook's *Poems: Selected and Edited by the Author* (1861), Adelaide Procter's *Legends and Lyrics* (1866), and Jean Ingelow's *Poems* (1867) – were published as gift books lavishly illustrated with wood engravings. Even more popular than collections of individual women authors were edited anthologies. Some of these, such as *Home Thoughts and Home Scenes* (1865), published women poets exclusively, celebrating their insights into the everyday experiences depicted in the accompanying images. Others, such as the perennially popular *Poets of the Nineteenth Century* (1858) and *English Sacred Poetry* (1862), included both male and female authors. As editor R. A. Willmott explained, "Our Poetry owes many beauties to womanly genius, and in the following pages some specimens of it will be found."[32] The language of "beauties" and "specimens" highlights the illustrated gift book's aesthetic of ornament and fragment. Pairing the sister arts of poetry and picture through the technology of wood engraving, ornamental gift books shored up cultural fragments of beauty in a modern, industrial world of passing pleasures.

Out of the fragmented lines and cuts on the wood-engraver's block a new set of engagements with the visual took shape in the nineteenth century. Schooled in wood engraving's visual discourse, a generation of women poets was ready to engage in the sister arts when illustrated periodicals and gift books heightened poetry's visibility at mid-century. New women poets at the fin de siècle continued the tradition. In "Poet's World," published in *Atalanta* in 1895, Scottish poet Margaret Armour writes about a poetic vision that works like an engraver, "pierc[ing] [the] way through sadness, / Deep to the everlasting heart / Of purity and gladness."[33] From outside to inside, dark to light: addressing the senses of sight and touch, wood engraving shaped an affective visual aesthetic for women poets.

Coda: Seeing/Feeling

According to Armstrong, the "doubleness of women's poetry comes from its ostensible adoption of an affective mode, often simple, often pious, often conventional," whose surface expression is investigated, questioned, or undermined by a "more difficult poem ... beneath it."[34] While Armstrong convincingly demonstrates that music informs women's expressive poetics, I have argued that wood engraving also contributed to the doubleness of women's poetry. Addressing the senses of sight and touch by digging meaning out of negative space, wood engraving shaped an affective aesthetic of surface and secret, floating worlds of the everyday.

In using Christina Rossetti's *Goblin Market and Other Poems* as an object lesson for understanding wood engraving as a technology of vision, I have treated it as a touchstone in the literal sense of something that can be seen with the eyes and felt with the hands rather than, as Matthew Arnold would have it, an evaluative measure for assessing poetry's greatest hits.[35] If the aesthetic of ornament and fragment and the affective undercurrent of sorrow characterize Victorian women's illustrated poems, our best route to reading them today is in their contemporary context of wood engraving. Assembling fragments and views out of cuts and openings, and intimately relating the sister arts of pictures and poetry in mass print culture, wood engraving framed ways of seeing, knowing, and feeling for readers and writers in the second half of the nineteenth century.

Notes

1. Jean-Louis Comolli, *Cinema Against Spectacle: Technique and Ideology Revisited* (Amsterdam: Amsterdam University Press, 2015), p. 284. *Open Access Books*, accessed August 2, 2017.
2. Christina G. Rossetti, "Song," *The Complete Poems of Christina Rossetti*, 3 vols., ed. R. W. Crump (Baton Rouge: Louisiana State University Press, 1979), 1.40.
3. Raymond Johnson, "'Tricks, Traps, and Transformations': Illusion in Victorian Spectacular Theatre," *Early Popular Visual Culture* 5.2 (2007), 151.
4. Isobel Armstrong, *Victorian Glassworlds: Glass Culture and the Imagination 1830–1880* (Oxford: Oxford University Press, 2008), p. 257.
5. R. W. Crump, note to "Goblin Market," in Rossetti, *Complete Poems*, 1.234.
6. Armstrong, *Victorian Glassworlds*, p. 257.
7. Rossetti, "Goblin Market," *Complete Poems*, 1.19, lines 327–8.
8. Ibid., 1.16, lines 184–5.
9. Lindsay Smith, *Pre-Raphaelitism: Poetry and Painting* (Tavistock, Devon: Northcote House, 2013), p. 61.
10. John Ruskin, *Ariadne Florentine: Six Lectures on Wood and Metal Engraving* (New York: Longmans, 1904), pp. 25, 59.
11. Ibid., p. 9.
12. *"Ukiyo-e": The Art of Asia*, Minneapolis Institute of Arts, http://archive.artsmia.org/art-of-asia/explore/explore-collection-ukiyo-e.cfm, accessed July 18, 2017.
13. William Chatto and John Jackson, *A Treatise on Wood Engraving, Historical and Practical* (London: Charles Knight, 1839), p. 733.
14. Simon Cooke, *Illustrated Periodicals of the 1860s: Contexts and Collaborations* (London: British Library and Oak Knoll Press, 2010), p. 173.
15. Ruskin, *Ariadne Florentine*, p. 25.
16. Walter Benjamin, "The Work of Art in the Age of Mechanical Reproduction," in *The Nineteenth-Century Visual Culture Reader*, ed. Vanessa R. Schwartz and Jeannene M. Przyblyski (New York: Routledge, 2004), pp. 63–70.
17. Linda K. Hughes, "Inventing Poetry and Pictorialism in *Once a Week*: A Magazine of Visual Effects," *Victorian Poetry* 48.1 (2010), 67.
18. Louisa Stewart, "Bradmere Pool," illustrated by Hablot K. Browne, *Once a Week* 1.17 (October 22, 1859): 329–31.
19. "Mary Louisa Molesworth," in *Orlando: Women's Writings in the British Isles from the Beginnings to the Present*, ed. Susan Brown, Patricia Clements, and Isobel Grundy (2006–2017), web, accessed July 13, 2017.
20. William E. Buckler, "*Once a Week* under Samuel Lucas, 1859–65," *PMLA* 67.7 (1952), 937.
21. William Wordsworth, "The Prelude," in *English Romantic Writers*, ed. David Perkins (Fort Worth: Harcourt Brace, 1995), pp. 307, 288.

22. Stewart, "Bradmere Pool," 330.

23. Ruskin, *Ariadne Florentine*, p. 60.

24. Amy Lloyd, "*Good Words* (1860–1911)," *Dictionary of Nineteenth-Century Journalism*, ed. Laurel Brake and Marysa Demoers, ProQuest (2005–2017), web, accessed July 14, 2017.

25. Caley Ehnes, "Religion, Readership, and the Periodical Press: The Place of Poetry in *Good Words*," *Victorian Periodicals Review* 45.4 (2012), 470.

26. Cooke, *Illustrated Periodicals*, p. 85.

27. Simon Houfe, "Sulman, T.," *Dictionary of British Book Illustrators and Caricaturists 1800–1914* (Woodbridge, Suffolk: Antique Collectors Club, 1981), p. 473.

28. A. L. Waring, "Passing Pleasures," illustrated by T. Sulman, *Good Words* 10 (June 1869), 401.

29. "India-Proofs of Wood-Engravings by the Brothers Dalziel," 1869 and 1870, vol. 26, collection of Proofs Books, Dalziel Collection, British Museum, Prints and Drawings Department.

30. Gerard Manley Hopkins, *Oxford Essays and Notebooks, 1863–1868*, ed. Lesley Higgins (Oxford: Oxford University Press, 2006), p. 155.

31. Lorraine Janzen Kooistra, *Christina Rossetti and Illustration: A Publishing History* (Athens: Ohio University Press, 2002), pp. 10–11, 62–4.

32. R. A. Willmott, ed., *The Poets of the Nineteenth Century*, illustrated with one hundred engravings (London: George Routledge, 1858), p. vi.

33. Margaret Armour, "The Poet's World," illustrated by Edith S. Moore, *Atalanta* 8 (May 1895), 484.

34. Isobel Armstrong, *Victorian Poetry: Poetry, Poetics, Politics* (London: Routledge, 1993), p. 324.

35. Matthew Arnold, "The Study of Poetry," *Essays in Criticism*, 2nd series (London: Macmillan, 1888, p. 17). Internet Archive, accessed July 20, 2017. https://archive.org/details/essaysincriticisooarnorich/page/n31

5

JASON R. RUDY

Embodiment and Touch

From Arthur Henry Hallam's 1831 assessment of Alfred Tennyson as a "poet of sensation" to Robert Buchanan's 1871 critique of Dante Gabriel Rossetti and the "fleshly school," nineteenth-century critics positioned poetry in necessary relation to the human body. Developments in the fields of natural biology, medicine, and physiology suggested that thoughts and feelings were rooted in the material body, having their origins in pulsing blood and nerve-cell transmission. To speak of embodiment in relation to Victorian women's poetry, then, is also to consider emotion and cognition. Given the commonplace Victorian association of women with unregulated feeling – tears, heartbeats, gushing sentiment – women's poetry played an oversized role in nineteenth-century debates concerning the moral, philosophical, and potentially insalubrious affects of poetry in relation to the human body. As Emma Mason writes, "it was women's assumed receptivity to sensation that rendered them ideally suited to the vocation of poet."[1] The same assumed receptivity to sensation raised pointed concerns for those women exposed to poetry's seemingly unregulated affects.

"What *is* poetry," asked John Stuart Mill in 1833, "but the thoughts and words in which emotion spontaneously embodies itself?"[2] In poems such as Tennyson's "Mariana," Mill argued, words and images combine in the reader's mind to "summon up ... a state of feeling."[3] For Mill, such states of feeling are both physiological and intellectual. "The noblest end of poetry as an *intellectual* pursuit," he writes in an 1835 review of Tennyson's poetry, is to act "upon the desires and characters of mankind *through their emotions*, to raise them towards the perfection of their nature."[4] Embodiment, feeling, and emotion all signal that for Mill the experience of reading poetry is conspicuously physiological, a version of the poetics of sensibility popularized by late-eighteenth-century poets like Mary Robinson and Charlotte Smith. Both male and female poets participated in this style of writing, but for women "the language of emotion, affect, and feeling," as Isobel Armstrong notes, was "powerfully overdetermined."[5]

79

Conservative critics objected stridently to such privileging of feeling. In 1834, Henry Taylor, an outspoken anti-Romantic, mocked poets for whom a "feeling came more easily ... than a reflection."[6] Taylor epitomizes a prominent Tory aesthetic that emerged in direct response to Hallam and Mill. John Keble, professor of poetry at Oxford, similarly encouraged poetic restraint in a lecture from 1832: "the glorious art of Poetry [is] a kind of medicine divinely bestowed upon man: which gives healing relief to secret mental emotion, yet without detriment to modest reserve: and, while giving scope to enthusiasm, yet rules it with order and due control."[7] Keble's "order" and "control" here link poetry to both the Tractarian doctrine of reserve, which focused on modesty and self-restraint, and a conservative Tory politics. The idea was becoming familiar across conservative media: "everything is poetry," wrote John Wilson in a *Blackwood's* essay of the same year, "which is not mere sensation."[8]

British women poets by contrast embraced the language and tropes of physiology. In Felicia Hemans's "Properzia Rossi," from *Records of Woman* (1828), for example, the sculptor Rossi carves out a sculpture of Ariadne to embody the tragedy of her own failed romance:

> The bright work grows
> Beneath my hand, unfolding, as a rose,
> Leaf after leaf, to beauty; line by line,
> I fix my thought, heart, soul, to burn, to shine,
> Thro' the pale marble's veins. It grows – and now
> I give my own life's history to thy brow,
> Forsaken Ariadne! thou shalt wear
> My form, my lineaments; but oh! more fair,
> Touch'd into lovelier being by the glow
> Which in me dwells, as by the summer-light
> All things are glorified.[9]

The artist's touch transmits to the sculpture her own "glow," turning rock into a lifelike form. Readers who take Mill's essay to heart may imagine in "Properzia Rossi" a similar process of transmission from poem to reader, whereby those exposed to Hemans's lines resonate with an affective "unfolding"; her poem "summon[s] up ... a state of feeling," turning adamantine readers into burning, affective subjects. The poem's heroic couplets suggest that both sculptor and reader retain some degree of control over that feeling; with such a strict form, feeling cannot go too far astray. We might think of the poem as a controlled space for feeling strongly, a place for readers temporarily to indulge in emotion.

The language of embodiment is everywhere in Elizabeth Barrett Browning's (EBB's) *Aurora Leigh* (1856), and we find it with especial urgency at the moment Aurora as a young woman first discovers poetry:

> But the sun was high
> When first I felt my pulses set themselves
> For concord; when the rhythmic turbulence
> Of blood and brain swept outward upon words,
> As wind upon the alders, blanching them
> By turning up their under-natures till
> They trembled in dilation.[10]

Aurora's poetic awakening is distinctly a physiological experience. As with Properzia Rossi's sculpting, the imagery here moves from interior to exterior, in this case from "blood and brain" to the words of poems. The poet's intense feeling takes "outward" form in language that reveals an "under-nature," like the wind that turns over a tree's leaves to reveal their tender, white undersides. EBB's imagery remains attentive to the poet's own body; the alder leaves that "trembled in dilation" point readers back to Aurora herself, she whose "soul, / At poetry's divine first finger-touch, / Let go conventions and sprang up surprised" (p. 31). To discover poetry, EBB suggests, is to achieve a more intimate relationship with one's own body. Even more: poetic inspiration seems contingent on the feeling body. Notice how in rhythmic terms Aurora subordinates personal pronouns to bodily sensation; the iambs of her line emphasize *felt* and *pulses* over *I* and *my*, suggesting the significance of physiological experience to one's sense of self.

Embodiment often also leads from the individual outward, from the self to other selves. In George Eliot's verse drama *The Spanish Gypsy* (1868), the protagonist Fedalma dances in a public square while a crowd looks on, enthralled:

> she, sole swayed by impulse passionate,
> Feeling all life was music and all eyes
> The warming quickening light that music makes,
> . . . .
> Moved in slow curves voluminous, gradual,
> Feeling and action flowing into one.[11]

Fedalma moves to her own passionate impulse, unself-consciously, and the watching crowd eventually finds itself swayed by the performance:

> Swifter now she moves,
> Filling the measure with a double beat
> And widening circle; now she seems to glow

With more declaréd presence, glorified.
Circling, she lightly bends and lifts on high
The multitudinous-sounding tambourine,
And makes it ring and boom, then lifts it higher
Stretching her left arm beauteous; now the crowd
Exultant shouts, forgetting poverty
In the rich moment of possessing her.[12]

Fedalma's dance bridges her own internal passion with the apparently universal nature of the world around her. Her body glows, visible to all, and her tambourine playing sends out resonant waves, eliciting cries of pleasure from all those present. Eliot in effect imagines through this scene what was implicit in both Hemans and EBB, the movement out of physiological experience from the individual poem to a broader audience or readership. Just as those watching Fedalma respond to her dancing and playing, so too readers of Hemans and EBB were meant to feel physiologically the emotions their poems embodied.

Politically Embodied

Projecting embodied feeling outward toward readers was understood to affect social and political change, or at least to have the chance of doing so. Women poets embraced the political opportunities opened up by their work, and they took full advantage of them. In particular, poets used embodiment and touch to encourage sympathetic identification with those different from their mostly middle-class and white readers.

Among the most well-known examples of such poems is EBB's "The Runaway Slave at Pilgrim's Point" (1848), published in a Boston antislavery journal, *The Liberty Bell*. An escaped slave narrates the dramatic monologue, detailing her traumatic life on a plantation and her eventual escape. Written in the present moment as she rushes to evade her pursuers, the poem recounts the slave's murder of her own child – the product of her master's sexual assault – and her eventual capture and likely death. Throughout the poem, EBB draws attention to the slave's body: "I am black, I am black!" is her refrain.

The runaway slave narrates the death of her lover in especially physical terms:

We were black, we were black,
  We had no claim to love and bliss,
What marvel if each went to wrack?
  They wrung my cold hands out of his,

> They dragged him – where? I crawled to touch
> His blood's mark in the dust ... not much,
> Ye pilgrim-souls, though plain as *this!*[13]

The stanza details several kinds of touching: first the lovers' hands holding one another, then the hands that pull the lover away, and finally the slave's hand as she touches her lover's blood. That trail of blood leaves a kind of writing on the ground, a "mark in the dust." EBB here plays with our sense of the poem's corporeality. The lover's ephemeral trace, his blood on the ground, is as "plain as *this*": as plain, we might imagine, as the mark at Pilgrim's Point from which the slave tells her tale. Or perhaps as plain as the slave herself, a black woman we are meant to imagine dramatically declaiming the poem. Or, equally likely, as plain as the text of the poem, written on the page before us. A productive ambiguity emerges from the unclear deictic, *this*, which encourages the conflation of location, speaker, and printed text, all through the image of blood.

Whatever one ultimately makes of the simile, this textual move invites readers to identify more viscerally with the speaking slave. Picturing the nightmare scene of a lover's death, the horror of watching him dragged away, and the trail of his blood on the ground, readers almost certainly wind up in a position of stronger sympathy with the speaker, sympathy made more instinctive by the stanza's constant language of touch and embodiment. EBB seems to embrace an idea of sympathy similar to that expressed in Adam Smith's *Theory of Moral Sentiments* (1759). "By the imagination," Smith writes, "we place ourselves in [the] situation" of a man suffering "upon the rack"; "we enter as it were into his body, and become in some measure the same person with him."[14] So too readers may well imagine "becom[ing] in some measure" EBB's runaway slave as she watches her lover dragged away to his death. What would it feel like, we are meant to ask ourselves, both physiologically and emotionally, to occupy the position of this suffering woman?

Whether one might genuinely inhabit such imaginative sympathetic spaces, however, has been the subject of philosophical debate. Audre Jaffe suggests that one's sympathy at such literary moments reflects not identification with a suffering other but instead our own individual "self-definition and self-identification"; in Jaffe's view, we come to a firmer sense of who we are through our *distance* from another's suffering.[15] EBB's mostly white and middle-class readers from this perspective would have enjoyed their obvious detachment from the hardships and perils of the runaway slave. Or perhaps they would have intuited the capriciousness of their own bourgeois identities, the malleability of their feelings, discovering as Andrew Miller suggests, "our thoughts are not our own," that "they are instead called forth by other people."[16] Sympathetic identification from this perspective unsettles not just our relation to others but also our relation to ourselves, opening fissures in our sense of who we are. Whether the reader's experiences of EBB's poem lead to sympathetic identification with the runaway slave (following Smith's model), complete distance from the slave (Jaffe), or a modified sense of self (Miller), the poem yokes us to the speaking woman's body; our encounter with the runaway slave begins as an embodied experience.

As EBB's poem progresses and we learn that the runaway slave has murdered her own child, readers find themselves in an increasingly difficult position, sympathizing on the one hand and withdrawing in revulsion on the other. Linda K. Hughes writes that "categories of guilt, sanity, and justice" in the poem "are hopelessly complicated."[17] The poem as a whole refuses an easy conclusion regarding guilt, even as EBB's language of embodiment tugs us closer to the slave woman's experience. Robert Langbaum long ago identified such tension between sympathy and judgment as foundational to the dramatic monologue as a literary form.[18] I wish here to highlight the degree to which both sympathy for EBB's runaway slave and judgment of her actions emerge from a kind of embodied identification.

The scene of infanticide unfolds with a physiological punch as visceral as the death of the slave's lover: the infant child "moaned and trembled from foot to head, / He shivered from head to foot; / Till after a time, he lay instead / Too suddenly still and mute."[19] Brutal in its cold abruptness, the dramatic monologue places readers in the horrific position of a mother murdering her own child. Ultimately, that imagined embodiment pushes readers to conceive the suffering that could have compelled a woman to such an extreme act. EBB here takes a great risk; the scene of infanticide threatens to push readers too far, breaking the bonds of sympathy they might have felt for the slave woman. But the poet clearly aims to leave her readers in a position of significant discomfort, accomplished by placing us as much as possible in the body of the slave woman herself.

A different form of sympathy emerges from Eliza Hamilton Dunlop's "The Aboriginal Mother" (1838), a poem written in response to the murder of twenty-eight Indigenous Australian men, women, and children at Myell Creek, New South Wales. Eleven stockmen had massacred the community, part of an ongoing conflict over land use in the Liverpool Plains region that resulted in widespread slaughtering of Indigenous peoples by European colonialists.[20] Dunlop was an Irish immigrant, having first arrived in the colony just prior to the horrific event. Published in the *Australian*, a Sydney newspaper, her poem unfolds dramatically as a surviving mother addresses her infant baby. Like EBB's "Runaway Slave," Dunlop's poem takes

84

dramatic form, so a reader imaginatively inhabits the speaking position of the Indigenous mother. To speak the words of the poem, then, is to imagine oneself as the embodied Indigenous woman, hiding as she holds and addresses her baby. She begs the child to "hush" so the "pale faced men / Will [not] hear thy piercing wail"; she then details the murder of her "first-born treasure" who was beheaded in the massacre as she looked on.[21] In the context of 1830s Sydney, Dunlop's poem was deeply unsettling in both humanitarian and political registers. In effect, "The Aboriginal Mother" positioned British colonial readers in sympathetic relation to a people whose displacement and murder had been methodically excused and some-times celebrated. The poem was set to music and performed, with politically mixed reviews, on Australian stages.

Dunlop was just one of many British and colonial women poets encoura-ging readers to imagine forms of embodied alterity. These "political poe-tesses," as Tricia Lootens calls them, show the extent to which "even the whitest of Victorian 'private spheres'" – the belief that women belonged in the drawing room and not the public square – "could hardly be quarantined from conscious histories of enslavement and of race relations."[22] Victorian women poets, in other words, engaged actively in political discourse, espe-cially with respect to human rights issues. We find another fine example of sympathy resulting from imaginative identification in Felicia Hemans's "Indian Woman's Death Song" (1828), likely one of Dunlop's inspirations for "The Aboriginal Mother." Heading downriver in a canoe toward a cataract and certain death, Hemans's Indian woman "press[es] her child, / In its bright slumber, to her beating heart" and sings a broken-hearted lament.[23] Physiological touching may seem incidental here, but it deftly suggests the mother's love for her daughter and encourages readers – understood primarily as white, middle-class, and female – to envision them-selves in the position of the Indian mother. Touch, that is, stands out as a point of connection between radically distinct subjects.

Other forms of alterity abound in Victorian women's poetry. EBB offers us a working-class woman in *Aurora Leigh*'s Marian Erle. Augusta Webster's *Portraits* (1870) features dramatic monologues in the voices of classical figures such as Medea and Circe: women generally framed as monstrous but reclaimed as sympathetic in Webster's telling. In "A Castaway," Webster takes on the voice of a Victorian kept woman who looks back on her life of trials and asks "Choice! what choice / Of living well or ill? could I have that?"[24] Amy Levy's dramatic monologue "Xantippe" climaxes in an upsurge of feeling as the speaker, wife of Socrates, revolts against the mis-ogyny of her husband: "with both angry hands I flung / The [wine]skin upon the marble, where it lay / Spouting red rills and fountains on the white."[25]

Levy's overflowing wine offers a vivid physiological metaphor for Xantippe's emotional gushing. In each of these poems, strong feeling invites readers to sympathize with women outside the mainstream of acceptable Victorian culture, to "become in some measure the same person," in Smith's terms.

That these women's voices take dramatic form, in what Carrie Preston calls "genres of first-person presentation," facilitates their political ends.[26] In the *Athenaeum*'s words, here writing about Webster's *Portraits*, "In most of [Webster's poems] there is moral significance, and, being moulded in dramatic form, they teach without preaching, and produce deeper effect than so-called didactic poetry."[27] These are voices, in other words, distinct from the women who created them, allowing them to avoid the perception of moralizing. Instead, readers experience "deeper effect," in large part through acts of sympathetic, embodied identification. As a result, we find ourselves compelled to political thinking – about slavery, women's rights, colonialism – on more intimate terms, leaving us perhaps more open to having our opinions swayed.

Embodied Rhythm

"If life is not always poetical, it is at least metrical," wrote Alice Meynell in the title essay of her 1892 volume *The Rhythm of Life*.[28] Embodiment takes its most profound poetic form in rhythmic pulses, the structural foundation not just of poetry but also, as Meynell argues, all of life too. Periodicity and recurrence, like those found in lunar and tidal patterns, shape the human experience of the world just as internal heartbeats, breathing, and women's reproductive cycles govern our embodied lives. Kirstie Blair's study *Victorian Poetry and the Culture of the Heart* shows the intertwining of metaphorical and literal in nineteenth-century poetry of the heart, "the inevitable presence of the physical heart in poetic usage and . . . the way in which that presence is embodied in form and meter."[29] Across the century, Victorian metrical and rhythmic experimentation engaged with notions of embodiment and physicality, playing with the idea that a poem's rhythm might literally feel like a bodily pulse, alternately quickening and slackening, sometimes irregular but mostly steady.

Inspired by the rise of the evolutionary and biological sciences, the fin de siècle in particular was a time of heightened awareness of the connection between poetic rhythm and bodily sensation. Just as the American Oliver Wendell Holmes suggested that "the form of verse is conditioned by . . . those muscular movements which insure the oxygenation of the blood," Meynell writes of "the metrical rule of the interior heart."[30] Throughout the nineteenth century, schoolchildren in both Britain and the United States knew this to be true, as poetic memorization and recitation were compulsory elements of their education. This was a time, as Catherine Robson has shown, "when poetry was experienced in and through the body": literally, with children standing before their peers, feeling in their heartbeats and breathing the rhythmic patterns of the poems they memorized and recited.[31] Victorian readers who grew up reciting poetry in the classroom would have necessarily had a visceral, bodily connection to poetry as a genre.

Embodied rhythm is foundational to Mathilde Blind's evolutionary epic *The Ascent of Man* (1889), a critique of Darwinian evolution based on complex metrics. Blind was a German-born emigrée raised in London, and her *Ascent of Man* tackles Darwin's theories head on, arguing that humankind develops upward, ascending always toward a more ideal state (Darwin suggested instead that evolution results in changes that may or may not be progressive). As I have argued elsewhere, Blind's epic shifts among a range of metrical forms that alternately suggest disorder and calm.[32] For example, the poem's opening dactylic hexameter throbs with a deeply felt physiological energy meant to mimic the scene it describes:

> Struck out of dim fluctuant forces and shock of electrical vapour,
> Repelled and attracted the atoms flashed mingling in union primeval
> And over the face of the waters far heaving in limitless twilight
> Auroral pulsations thrilled faintly, and, striking the blank heaving surface,
> The measureless speed of their motion now leaped into light on the waters.[33]

Any reader of these lines will feel the driving "pulsations" of the dactyls, a rendering into poetic form of the scene Blind imagines. The hexameter form itself offers another layer of suggestiveness, pointing back to the *Iliad* and the *Odyssey,* poems written in a Greek version of dactylic hexameter. To feel the pulses of Blind's *Ascent*, then, is possibly to feel a pulse readers have known for millennia: an embodied connection stretching back to the origins of literary tradition.

EBB had imagined a similar process of poetic transmission across time. Aurora famously insists that to be great, poetry must address "this live, throbbing age," such that future readers will

> touch the impress with reverent hand, and say,
> 'Behold, – behold the paps we all have sucked!
> This bosom seems to beat still, or at least
> It sets ours beating: this is living art,
> Which thus presents and thus records true life.'[34]

Aurora's extended metaphor refers to drying lava, which the poet will "impress" as it hardens into a set form. Whether that form is understood as metrical, conceptual, or both, the poet's physical body is the impetus behind its shaping. The resulting art, the form created by the poet's impressing, will be "living art" because its origins stem from a living artist. Significantly, and as many scholars have noted, the poet Aurora envisions is female, and her imagery, from erupting volcanos to "the paps we all have sucked," sets poetic inspiration firmly in relation to women's bodies.

Performances of women's poetry, sometimes by the poets themselves, intensified the embodied language and rhythm of these poems. Pauline Johnson, daughter of a Mohawk father and an English mother, offers an extreme example. Johnson was famous at the turn of the century in both North America and Britain for reciting her dramatic monologues in First Nations costume. Kate Flint writes that "onstage, Johnson did not so much blur [the] borders" between Native and Canadian, "as flamboyantly call attention to them in order to make increasingly political, as well as theatrical, capital from assumptions surrounding her ethnicity."[35] The poem "Ojistoh," for example, tells the story of a Mohawk woman kidnapped by a Huron warrior: "I am Ojistoh, I am she," the poem opens, and we might imagine Johnson herself declaiming the lines before her spellbound audiences.[36]

The kidnapped Ojistoh ultimately seduces her captor into complacency – "I like thee well, and wish to clasp thee close," she tells him – and then she abruptly kills him:

> My hand crept up the buckskin of his belt;
> His knife hilt in my burning palm I felt;
> One hand caressed his cheek, the other drew
> The weapon softly – "I love you, love you,"
> I whispered, "love you as my life."
> And – buried in his back his scalping knife.[37]

Gendered embodiment here strikes back with a vengeance. Readers and auditors familiar with the sentimental tradition of women's touch may well recoil as Ojistoh's hands work doubly: one caressing the Huron's cheek, the other reaching for his knife. Though Johnson herself was raised in a position of relative privilege and was never involved in the violence of the North American frontier, her identity as part Mohawk allowed audiences to conflate her identity with those she performed: a frightening possibility given the violence of a poem like "Ojistoh." The driving rhythms of the poem, which Johnson performed with zeal, further encouraged that connection:

> I lashed
> That horse to foam, as on and on I dashed.
> Plunging thro' creek and river, bush and trail,
> On, on I galloped like a northern gale.[38]

Embodied Ideals

The physiological sensationalism attached to women's writing raised concerns about the overall health and well-being of readers, particularly young women. Writing for *Popular Science* in 1888, Mary Bissell lamented the "undue stimulation" of women's "emotional nature." In particular, "the literature which little girls are permitted to read may be held responsible for much emotional stimulation of an unhealthy character."[39] An 1874 essay on "The Pathology of the Passions" warns that "as a vibrating chord determines vibration in a neighboring chord, so a passion produces in those who are the witnesses of it a passion or a tendency to a passion of the same kind ... All passions, whether good or bad, are contagious."[40]

Attention to sensory experience seemed dangerous among Victorian moralists in part for its distance from reasoned thought. The contagious "pathology" of passion manifested when individuals felt strongly without thinking deeply. Such would be one possible interpretation of the lesson Christina Rossetti had in mind for "Goblin Market" (1862). Rarely has a poet captured embodied experience as intensely as Rossetti, who depicts a woman's deep pleasure in "plump unpecked cherries, / Melons and raspberries, / Bloom-down-cheeked peaches, / Swart-headed mulberries," and much more.[41] In keeping with Mary Bissell's association of sensation and danger, the young woman who enjoys this savory fruit soon after falls victim to an unexplainable decline: "Her hair grew thin and grey; / She dwindled."[42] Readers who salivate at the poem's opening lines, beware!

But one would be mistaken to imagine the privileging of embodiment as necessarily anti-intellectual by nature. EBB is explicit that Aurora's poetic impulse, for example, is equally sensation and philosophy:

> While Art
> Sets action on the top of suffering:
> The artist's part is both to be and do,
> Transfixing with a special, central power
> The flat experience of the common man,
> And turning outward, with a sudden wrench,
> Half agony, half ecstasy, the thing
> He feels the inmost, – never felt the less
> Because he sings it.[43]

The artist's private sensation radiates outward to transform the common man's "flat experience" into something more, raising the mundane into the extraordinary. In passages such as this, EBB seems almost to anticipate Isobel Armstrong's call "to rethink the power of affect, feeling and emotion in a *cognitive* space," to see thought and feeling as intertwined rather than opposed.[44] On just this convergence, Yopie Prins writes that "throughout *Aurora Leigh*, Aurora struggles to unify mind and body in poetry." The result is a progressive chain of influence radiating out from the poet:

> To embody the spirit of the age, the poetess must transform the rhythmic figure of the body into the rhythm of the poem, the rhythmic figure of the poem into the rhythm of history, and the rhythmic figure of history into the rhythm of nature: the heart beating in the verse of the poetess could then be understood, at least in its ideal form, as a law of the universe.[45]

In fact, *Aurora Leigh* was interpreted as equally intellectual and affective from the time of its first publication. Writing anonymously for the *Westminster Review* in 1857, George Eliot argued that the poem was like no other work of the day in its "[embrace of] so wide a range of thought and emotion." This combination, writes Eliot, fully absorbs the reader into the text:

> This mind has its far-stretching thoughts, its abundant treasure of well-digested learning, its acute observation of life, its yearning sympathy with multi-form human sorrow, its store of personal domestic love and joy; and these are given out in a delightful alternation of pathos, reflection, satire playful or pungent, and picturesque description, which carries us with swifter pulses than usual through four hundred pages, and makes us sorry to find ourselves at the end.[46]

The negotiation that Eliot perceives between "far-stretching thoughts" and "swifter pulses" plays out in the verse-novel's conclusion, in the wedding of Aurora's artistic inspiration with her cousin Romney's social ideals. These two individuals, butting heads from the start, eventually fall in love and discover in their affection for one another a way of linking "sensuous form / And form insensuous."[47] For poetry to succeed, in other words, it must negotiate between the embodied world of its readers and the ideal world – philosophical, spiritual – to which readers were meant to aspire.

Eliot's own poem "Stradivarius" (1873), about the eighteenth-century genius instrument maker, succinctly expresses the need for the real to help make manifest the ideal:

> 'Tis God gives skill,
> But not without men's hands: He could not make
> Antonio Stradivari's violins
> Without Antonio.[48]

Stradivarius's hands – working physically in the material world – create the instruments that allow for musical transcendence. "Inspiration," writes Charles LaPorte with respect to Eliot, "must find its completion in real praxis or craft."[49] That praxis or craft then turns full circle, returning listeners to the inspiration that set Stradivarius to building violins in the first place. The point, as we saw with EBB, is that the ideal cannot exist in isolation from the real. Whether we understand that ideal in philosophical or spiritual terms, to access it one must first pass through the physical world and the physical bodies we inhabit in it.

This balancing between real and ideal reflects a careful negotiation characteristic of Victorian women's poetry. Conscious of the criticism likely to be lodged at any extreme, be that extreme political, cultural, affective, or otherwise, nineteenth-century British women poets showed both skill and savvy in navigating those potential hazards. They provoked, for the most part without overstepping, pushing readers to the edge of comfort but rarely beyond. This chapter has shown the degree to which such provocation was enabled by the metaphors and formal mechanisms associated with embodiment and touch. Political and emotional possibilities opened at just those points of imagined connection between a poem and its reader, between a poet and her audience.

Notes

1. Emma Mason, *Women Poets of the Nineteenth Century* (Horndon, UK: Northcote, 2006), p. 2.
2. John Stuart Mill, "The Two Kinds of Poetry," *Monthly Repository* 7 (August 1833), 715.
3. John Stuart Mill, "Tennyson's Poems," *London and Westminster Review* 2 (July 1835), 405.
4. Ibid., p. 419. Italics mine.
5. Isobel Armstrong, "The Gush of the Feminine: How Can We Read Women's Poetry of the Romantic Period?" in *Romantic Women Writers: Voices and Countervoices*, ed. Paula Feldman and Theresa Kelley (Hanover, NH: University Press of New England, 1995), p. 24.
6. Sir Henry Taylor, *Philip van Artevelde; a Dramatic Romance* (London: Edward Moxon, 1834), I:xii.
7. John Keble, *Lectures on Poetry, 1832–1841*, trans. Edward Kershaw Francis (Oxford: Clarendon Press, 1912), I:22.
8. [John Wilson], "Tennyson's Poems," *Blackwood's Edinburgh Magazine* 27 (June 1830), 721.
9. Felicia Hemans, *Records of Woman: with Other Poems* (Edinburgh and London: Blackwood, 1828), p. 49.
10. Elizabeth Barrett Browning, *Aurora Leigh* (London: Chapman and Hall, 1860 [1856]), pp. 32–3.
11. George Eliot, *The Spanish Gypsy* (Boston: Ticknor and Fields, 1868), pp. 49–50.
12. Ibid., p. 53.
13. Elizabeth Barrett Browning, *Poetical Works* (New York: Thomas Y. Crowell, 1886), p. 318.
14. Adam Smith, *The Theory of Moral Sentiments* (Indianapolis: Liberty Fund, 1984), p. 9.

15. Audrey Jaffe, *Scenes of Sympathy: Identity and Representation in Victorian Fiction* (Ithaca: Cornell University Press, 2000), p. 7.
16. Andrew Miller, *The Burdens of Perfection: On Ethics and Reading in Nineteenth-Century Literature* (Ithaca: Cornell University Press, 2008), p. 105. See too Rae Greiner, *Sympathetic Realism in Nineteenth-Century British Fiction* (Baltimore, MD: Johns Hopkins University Press, 2012).
17. Linda K. Hughes, *The Cambridge Introduction to Victorian Poetry* (New York: Cambridge University Press, 2010), p. 20.
18. See Robert Langbaum, *The Poetry of Experience: The Dramatic Monologue in Modern Literary Tradition* (New York: Norton, 1963 [1957]), pp. 75–108.
19. Elizabeth Barrett Browning, *Poetical Works*, p. 319.
20. For a more thorough historical account of the event, see Thomas Keneally, *Australians: Origins to Eureka* (Crows Nest, NSW: Allen and Unwin, 2009), pp. 401–5.
21. Eliza Hamilton Dunlop, "Songs of an Exile (No. 4): The Aboriginal Mother," *Australian*, December 13, 1838, 4.
22. Tricia Lootens, *The Political Poetess: Victorian Femininity, Race, and the Legacy of Separate Spheres* (Princeton: Princeton University Press, 2017), p. 40.
23. Hemans, *Records of Woman*, p. 105.
24. Augusta Webster, "A Castaway," in *Portraits* (London: Macmillan, 1893 [1870]), p. 46.
25. Amy Levy, "Xantippe," in *A Minor Poet and Other Verse* (London: T. Fisher Unwin, 1884), p. 27.
26. Carrie J. Preston, *Modernism's Mythic Pose: Gender, Genre, Solo Performance* (New York: Oxford University Press, 2011), p. 56.
27. "New Poems," *Athenaeum*, June 11, 1870, 770.
28. Alice Meynell, *The Rhythm of Life and Other Essays* (London: John Lane, 1905 [1892]), p. 1.
29. Kirstie Blair, *Victorian Poetry and the Culture of the Heart* (Oxford: Oxford University Press, 2006), p. 3.
30. Oliver Wendell Holmes, "The Physiology of Versification," in *Pages from an Old Volume of Life* (Boston: Houghton, Mifflin, 1899), p. 316; Meynell, *The Rhythm of Life*, p. 5.
31. Catherine Robson, *Heart Beats: Everyday Life and the Memorized Poem* (Princeton: Princeton University Press, 2012), p. 14.
32. Jason R. Rudy, *Electric Meters: Victorian Physiological Poetics* (Athens: Ohio University Press, 2009), pp. 156–62.
33. Mathilde Blind, *The Poetical Works*, ed. Arthur Symons (London: T. Fisher Unwin, 1900), p. 158.
34. Elizabeth Barrett Browning, *Poetical Works*, pp. 188–9.
35. Kate Flint, *The Transatlantic Indian, 1776–1930* (Princeton: Princeton University Press, 2009), p. 277.
36. E. Pauline Johnson, *Flint and Feather: The Complete Poems*, 7th ed. (Toronto: Musson Book Co., 1921), p. 3.
37. Ibid., p. 5.
38. Ibid.
39. Mary T. Bissell, "Emotions *Versus* Health in Women," *Popular Science* 32 (1888), 504, 505.

40. Fernand Papillon, "The Pathology of the Passions," *Popular Science* 4 (1874), 661.
41. Christina Rossetti, *Goblin Market and Other Poems* (London: MacMillan, 1862), p. 1.
42. Ibid., p. 15.
43. Elizabeth Barrett Browning, *Poetical Works*, p. 194.
44. Isobel Armstrong, *The Radical Aesthetic* (Oxford: Blackwell, 2000), p. 87.
45. Yopie Prins, "Patmore's Law, Meynell's Rhythm," *The Fin-de-Siècle Poem: English Literary Culture and the 1890s*, ed. Joseph Bristow (Athens: Ohio University Press, 2005), p. 271.
46. [George Eliot], "Belles Lettres," *Westminster Review* 67 (January 1857), 306, 307.
47. Elizabeth Barrett Browning, *Poetical Works*, p. 177.
48. George Eliot, *Poems* (New York: White, Stokes, and Allen, 1885), p. 143.
49. Charles LaPorte, *Victorian Poets and the Changing Bible* (Charlottesville: University of Virginia Press, 2011), p. 192.

PART II

Women's Poetry in the World

6

ALEXIS EASLEY

Publishing and Reception

Victorian women poets worked in a print culture largely controlled by male editors, publishers, and reviewers. Yet their experience in the literary market-place was not determined solely by their gender identity but rather by the intersection of gender and other markers of difference – for example, race, class, age, ethnicity, religion, and sexuality. As Kimberlé Williams Crenshaw points out, to understand "how the social world is constructed" we must examine "multiple grounds of identity."[1] A working-class woman poet living in Glasgow during the 1860s, for example, had a very different experience in the literary marketplace than a middle-class woman poet living in London during the same time period. A recognition of such heterogeneity undermines master narratives about a unified notion of "Victorian women's writing," let alone a unitary definition of the "Victorian woman poet."

Women's complex identities not only played an important role in deter-mining their level of access to the publishing industry but also influenced the critical reception of their work. The "poetess" was often held to a lower critical standard than her male counterparts due to assumptions about women's limited capacity for producing high art. Markers of difference in auto/biographical narratives often led critics to focus more on women's life stories than on their literary achievements. As Susan Brown puts it, the "biocritical method formed part of a trend that plagued women writers throughout the century and beyond."[2] Nevertheless, women were able to use difference as a form of self-marketing – as a way to define themselves as unique voices within broader literary communities. Emphasizing difference and iconoclasm also allowed them to reach niche markets associated with the marginalized groups to which they belonged – for example, Irish, Jewish, or working-class social networks.

The emergence of "poetess" as a catchword for a diverse array of identities in Victorian culture was inseparable from the proliferation of new publishing outlets for women. With the reduction in taxes on print, the number of newspapers and periodicals increased markedly, expanding into mass-market publications and a variety of niche-market periodicals aimed at specific communities of readers. Sometimes these communities overlapped: readers might peruse a mainstream paper such as the *Times* but also the more specialized *Jewish World* or *Suffragette*. Similarly, writers might emphasize particular aspects of their unique identities when seeking outlets for their poetry. In the 1840s, a woman poet might publish her work in a local paper such as the *Halifax Guardian*, a women's annual such as the *Keepsake*, and a magazine of popular progress like *Tait's Edinburgh Magazine*.

Within an expanding and increasingly differentiated market, poetry assumed a variety of important functions – inculcating domestic values, arguing for political change, commenting on the news, or simply inspiring moments of meditation and laughter on a Saturday afternoon. The demand for periodical poetry created new publishing opportunities for women. Some used the periodical press as a launching pad for book publication, while others wrote strictly for periodicals and newspapers. Many poems were published with authorial signature, but the convention of anonymity enabled women to publish without exposing their identities to public view. This meant that they could choose to reveal or suppress markers of difference, if editorial policy allowed.

In some instances, women had little control over how their poems or names would be presented to the public. Editors often cut and pasted material from one periodical to another, sometimes without acknowledging the original author or source publication. A lack of copyright protection for poetry made it difficult for women to assume control of their periodical verse as intellectual property – or to gain remuneration for their reprinted work.[3] However, as Ellen Gruber Garvey observes, publishing houses "noted an author's popularity in newspaper exchanges as a sign that the writer's reputation was substantial enough to carry a collection of the pieces into a book."[4] Consequently, some poets actively encouraged the reprinting and wide circulation of their newspaper verse to develop celebrity identities and to build an audience for volume editions of their work.

In this chapter, I focus on two women poets whose complex identities shaped their experience of the literary marketplace and their reception within Victorian print culture. The careers of Eliza Cook (1812–89) and Frances Brown (1816–79) together illustrate the ways in which the identity of the "working-class woman poet" during the early Victorian period was complicated by notions of geography, sexuality, physical disability, and class status. Born just four years apart, Brown and Cook could be said to be of the same generation. Both poets took advantage of the same developments in popular print culture that provided unprecedented access to women writers in the literary marketplace. However, both writers faced a distinct set of challenges and opportunities based on markers of difference that worked in tandem with gender ideology in shaping their poetic careers.

Eliza Cook

Eliza Cook was born in Southwark, London, the daughter of a brass crafts-man, which placed her family in a fairly prosperous class of artisan workers. Largely self-taught, she published her first book, *Lays of a Wild Harp* (1835), when she was just twenty-three. During the next few years, she published poems anonymously in periodicals, including the *Metropolitan Magazine* and *New Monthly Magazine*. Equally important to her early career was the *Weekly Dispatch*, a cheap newspaper, that from 1836 published her poems in its "Facts and Scraps" column.

Miscellaneous "facts and scraps" columns were a feature of many popular weekly papers published in the 1830s and 1840s. These columns published original and reprinted snippets – anecdotes, humor, kitchen wisdom, and most importantly poetry. This verse was largely domestic, sentimental, and patriotic, all of which fell within the purview of the "poetess" as it had been defined in criticism of earlier women writers such as Caroline Norton and Felicia Hemans.[5] Because papers like the *Dispatch* had large circulations and were aimed at a broad audience of artisans and lower middle-class readers, they provided an important publishing venue for working-class writers like Cook, who used periodical publication to construct a public identity and to generate an audience for volume editions of their work.

Like many novice contributors to the *Weekly Dispatch*, Cook at first published her work anonymously, signing her poems "C" or "E. C." The suppression of her name obscured her sex and enabled her to avoid the negative stereotypes associated with feminine writing during the 1830s and 1840s.[6] Yet Cook needed to establish a name for herself if she wanted to make a living as a writer. Once her poetry became popular, she began signing poems with her full name. The poems she published in the *Weekly Dispatch* with signature tell us much about the celebrity identity she wished to con-struct. Her first signed work, "The Thames," begins,

> Let the Rhine be blue and bright
> In its path of liquid light,
> Where the red grapes fling a beam
> Of glory on the stream;
> Let the gorgeous beauty there
> Mingle all that's rich and fair;
> Yet to me it ne'er could be
> Like that river great and free,
>   The Thames! the mighty Thames![7]

Cook introduces herself to readers by evoking a familiar symbol of metropolitan English life – the River Thames. As it flows through London, it bears no "azure wave" but nevertheless represents a kind of natural freedom within the city. As the stanzas unfold, the river becomes a symbol of childhood joy in nature, which alludes to definitions of the poet set out by William Wordsworth and other Romantic writers. Yet for Cook, it was the urban riverside, not an idyllic rural environment, that informed her childhood development: "Though no pearly foam may lave, / Or leaping cascades pour / Their rainbows on its shore; / Yet I ever loved to dwell / Where I heard its gushing swell" (lines 11–15). The personal becomes then political as the river transforms into a symbol of national strength: "Can ye find in all the world / A braver flag unfurled / Than that which floats above / The stream I sing and love?" (lines 19–22). In this way, Cook defines herself not only as a latter-day Romantic bard but also as a metropolitan, national poetess.

Less than a month after "The Thames" appeared, Cook published another poem in the *Weekly Dispatch* celebrating the natural environment. However, in this poem, "A Song for Merry Harvest," she foregrounds the physical labor of working-class people in an idealized rural setting. The poem is written in first person, which suggests that the poet-speaker identifies with the working-class people she describes:

> Bring forth the harp, and let us sweep its fullest, loudest string;
> The bee below, the bird above, are teaching us to sing
> A song for the merry harvest; and the one who will not bear
> His grateful part, partakes a boon he ill deserves to share.
> The grasshopper is pouring forth his quick and trembling notes;
> The laughter of the gleaner's child, the heart's own music, floats:
> Up! up! I say, a roundelay from every voice that lives
> Should welcome merry harvest, and bless the Hand that gives.[8]

Written as a song meant to accompany labor in the fields, the poem's form reflects its working-class subject matter. But the poem also reinforces the sort of values – hard work and religious faith – that could also be applied within the urban context familiar to readers of the *Weekly Dispatch*. At the same time that Cook was attempting to instill a common set of values among readers, she was also fashioning her own identity as a female working-class poet who spoke of and for the people. For the next few years, her poetry dominated the "Facts and Scraps" column of the *Weekly Dispatch*, and sometime in the mid-1840s she became its editor, a position that allowed her to promote the work of fellow women writers such as Caroline Orne, Maria Abdy, and Charlotte Brontë. This editorial position came with a stable salary of £200 per year, an income that provided her with a sense of financial security as she built her poetic career.

By the mid-1840s, Cook was a major celebrity whose poetry had been published in two popular volumes, *Melaia and Other Poems* (1838) and *Poems, Second Series* (1845). The sale of these volumes was enhanced by the frequent republication of her poems in periodicals and newspapers both in Great Britain and abroad. Her verse was also advertised as a chief attraction of the *Weekly Dispatch*. In 1847, it distributed a portrait of Cook to its 60,000 subscribers, advertising this "free gift" in various periodicals (Figure 7). Soon her name became ubiquitous, not only in British homes but also in billboard advertisements throughout the city. As the *Sheffield and Rotherdam Independent* put it in 1847, "Waiting an hour to cross one of the blocked-up thoroughfares of the metropolis, and nothing to look at besides huge bills, which stop his path, with DISPATCH and ELIZA COOK upon them, a man must be 'unlettered' indeed that could then remain ignorant of those names."[9] The effect of such advertisements was to link the *Weekly Dispatch* to Cook's reputation and public image as a national celebrity poet. By depicting a woman as its figurehead, the *Dispatch* was implicitly extending an invitation to women readers and writers to take part in its mixed-gender enterprise.

As can be seen in the portrait distributed by the *Weekly Dispatch*, a "masculine" style of dress was part of Cook's public image. Her iconoclastic appearance and ambiguous sexuality drew some negative criticism, but, overall, her carefully crafted public image functioned as a self-branding strategy that set her apart from the burgeoning mass of more conventional women poets. If, as Susan Brown suggests, the Victorian poetess was often aestheticized as an object of beauty, then Cook seems to have self-consciously presented herself as an exception to the rule.[10] Her poem "Song of the Ugly Maiden" seems to poke fun at her status as a single, homely woman, and her various love poems to actress Charlotte Cushman did not attempt to mask her same-sex desire. This sense of sexual difference carried over into her major editorial project, *Eliza Cook's Journal* (1849–54).[11] Like many other popular progress magazines founded in the 1840s, *Eliza Cook's Journal* was affordably priced at 1½ d., was directed to an artisan and lower-middle-class family audience, and was part of a broader middle-class movement to promote social progress and sympathy between divergent class positions. Containing an engaging mixture of poetry, short articles, and other miscellaneous content, the magazine was immediately successful, achieving a circulation of 50,000 to 60,000. *Eliza Cook's Journal* provided the kind of "useful knowledge" associated with magazines of popular progress, yet it also regularly incorporated articles and editorials

Figure 7 Eliza Cook by Henry Adlard, after Wilhelm Trautschold, stipple engraving, 1847. Reproduced with Permission of the National Portrait Gallery.

addressing women's issues.[12] Even though Cook was the main poet featured in the journal, it published a number of poems by other women writers, including Elizabeth Carey and Elizabeth Roberts, whose verse appeared in the journal's first volume.

Given the prominence of women poets in *Eliza Cook's Journal*, it is surprising to come upon Anna Maria Sargeant's rather critical portrayal of the writing life in "The Poetess," a short story published in the journal in 1850.[13] The protagonist, Isabel Egerton, is an esteemed yet unhappy poet who is envious of her married sister Effy's happy domesticity. Eventually Effy brings about a match between Isabel and her husband's friend Thornton, and soon the "fair Poetess was led forth, clad in bridal ornaments, to pledge her faith to one who, to own the truth, had long held her heart captive" (p. 150). On their honeymoon abroad, she is a "gifted bride, whose rare mental endowments, and true appreciation for the sublime and beautiful in nature, gave every scene a double charm" (p. 150). Her poetic training is thus shown to be compatible with her wifely duties, yet it is unclear in the end whether she continues to write or has given it up completely.

The story concludes by simply noting that Isabel fulfills the role of ideal helpmeet, the "high destiny for which she was created" (p. 150). This conclusion echoes the story's opening epigraph, an excerpt from Hemans's "Properzia Rossi" (1828): "Thou shalt have Fame! O mockery! give the reed / From storms a shelter – give the dropping vine / Something round which its tendrils may entwine / Give the parched flower a raindrop – and the meed / Of Love's kind words to woman" (p. 147). Extracted from a dramatic monologue, this epigraph is quoted out of context to suggest that Hemans herself values love over fame. The epigraph and the story together paint a portrait of the female poetess as an upper-class, self-indulgent dilettante who is better off dedicating herself to domestic concerns. This portrayal stands in stark contrast to Eliza Cook herself, who was well known as an iconoclastic independent woman – a poet who had rightfully dedicated her life to verse and had made a living as the editor of a popular journal with her name on its masthead. The contrast between Sargeant's fictional Isabel and Cook's carefully constructed editorial persona draws attention to the heterogeneity of the poetess identity. Cook is no pining, middle-class dilettante but a working-class woman of letters and a single, independent woman. Differences of class, marital status, and sexuality, embedded within specific periodical contexts, shaped the ways women's poetic identities were received and understood.

Despite Cook's editorial control over her public persona, she could not completely control representations of her life and work in the popular press.

Punch, for example, poked fun at her seasonal verse in its *Almanack* for 1846. The poem, titled "Song of November (after Eliza Cook)," begins,

> That gridiron by the mantel-piece
> Its look gives every nerve a thrill;
> That thing of home begrimed with grease,
> Whereon our sprats we learn'd to grill.
> November – month to childhood dear,
> Old month of Civic feasts and sights,
> To see that gridiron so near,
> Fills my sad heart with home delights.

The anonymous poet makes fun of Cook's sentimental approach to humble domestic objects and childhood memories by effusing over the idea of cooking sprats (small sea fish). Feeling nostalgic, the writer searches out "sprats in which childhood might confide"; however, after buying some and throwing them on the gridiron, he realizes that they are "spoiled."[14] The elevation of the mundane thus falls flat – and by implication so does Cook's poetry. Nevertheless, the satire draws attention to Cook's growing celebrity and her brand of sentimental poetry, which was becoming a ubiquitous feature of everyday life in periodicals, newspapers, and volumes. The punning on Cook's last name of course also alluded to women's traditional roles as keepers of the hearth and working-class women's roles as cooks in middle-class homes. Cook, too, made playful reference to her last name in *Eliza Cook's Journal*, where she described her editorial role as "simply [preparing] a plain feast, where the viands will be all of my own choosing, and some of my own dressing."[15] She thus simultaneously depicted herself in a conventional role as household "cook" and in a more iconoclastic vein as Eliza Cook, the powerful editor of a popular magazine.

Cook's image as a spokesperson for domestic values was always in tension with the edginess of her nonnormative sexuality and persona. With time, however, the transgressive aspects of her popular persona fell away, leaving only the conventional aspects of her brand in public memory. This was partly because Cook went into retreat in 1854 due to poor health, a physical challenge that made it difficult for her to enjoy the same level of access to the literary marketplace or control over her public persona that she had enjoyed in earlier years. Even though portraits of her appeared in periodicals from time to time and her books of poetry were frequently republished, she was not as visible as she had once been – or as active in constructing her own public identity. While her working-class status and homely, masculine appearance had been important aspects of her identity that had helped develop her unique brand in the literary marketplace, by the fin de siècle these markers of difference were interpreted as the stuff of comedy. *Punch* antici-pated the later vilification of her verse and physical appearance at the hands of the New Critics. In 1930, for example, her poems were selected for inclusion in *The Stuffed Owl: An Anthology of Bad Verse*, which character-ized her as a "rather soft and silly spinster lady" whose work "appealed very strongly to the middle classes."[16] Such a characterization ensured that her work would receive little serious attention for the rest of the century.

Frances Brown

Frances Brown and Eliza Cook were contemporaries, and their life stories and poetic careers overlapped in significant ways. Yet their differences informed their experiences in the literary marketplace. Like Cook, Brown was working class, but her impoverished upbringing as the daughter of a postmaster in a remote Ulster village, Stranorlar, placed her on a lower rung of the social ladder than Cook with fewer resources at her disposal. She lost her sight to smallpox when she was eighteen months old and learned about the world by listening to her siblings' lessons and having family members read aloud to her. Once she began writing, her sister Rebecca (and later a paid secretary, Eliza Hickman) served as her ama-nuensis. Like Cook, Brown was able to use markers of difference to sell her work to diverse audiences and achieve success in the literary world. However, because her financial standing was more precarious than Cook's and her work options were limited due to her physical disability, she struggled to make ends meet throughout her life. She eventually turned away from poetry to capitalize on the demand for prose in the expanding magazine and book markets.

In 1840, Brown published her first poem in an unnamed provincial paper and a handful of other verses in the *Irish Penny Journal* (1840–41). Like many women writers making a debut in the literary world, she developed her love of poetry in part from reading provincial newspapers.[17] So it made sense for her to choose cheap weekly papers as her first publication outlets. Significantly, the *Irish Penny Journal* was published in Dublin, the literary hub of Ireland at the time, but it was not just proximity that made it an ideal vehicle for her poetry. As the editorial introduction notes, the journal was "devoted to subjects connected with the history, literature, antiquities, and general condition of Ireland."[18] As Francesca Benatti calculates, "Overall, in its fifty-two issues the *IPJ* included forty-four articles on Irish topography, forty-two poems, twenty-three translations from the Irish language and forty-six short stories on Irish subjects."[19] Although it aimed to address "all classes of the community," it especially targeted those of "humble means."[20] The journal's remit clearly complemented Brown's identity as a rural Irish working-class poet.

Like Cook, Brown initially published her work using only her initials. Her first contribution to the journal, "The Pilgrim at the Well" (February 27, 1841), depicts a blind girl at an Irish holy well who naïvely clings to the belief that the magic waters will "banish the blight of her life away."[21] The poem concludes,

> Oh! is there not many a weary heart,
> That hath seen the greenness of life depart,
> Yet trusted in vain in a powerless spell,
> Like her who knelt by the Holy Well! (lines 41–4)

For those who knew the identity of "F. B.," the poem was a poignant reflection on loss, the blind poet's hopeless wish for the "promise of light" (line 6). For other readers, the poem most likely would have recalled a famous painting, *The Blind Girl at the Holy Well*, by Irish painter F. W. Burton, which had debuted at the Royal Hibernian Academy the previous year and had been widely circulated as an engraving created by the Irish Art-Union.

The *Irish Penny Journal* alludes to the painting in a June 19, 1841, article, "Saint Senan's Well," which praises Burton as "our own great national painter" and draws attention to the painting's "interest and picturesqueness" as a depiction of pagan Irish ritual. Echoing Brown's poem, which had been published just four months earlier, it notes that holy well shrines "supply the most touching evidences of the strength of that [Irish] devotional instinct, however blind and misapplied, that humble faith in the existence and omnipotence of a Divine Intelligence."[22] In the essay, as in Brown's poem, blindness is a metaphor for foolish belief, but the practice of visiting holy wells is ennobled by its poignancy and cultural value, as well as its celebration of spiritual devotion. Thus, Brown's poem, like most periodical poetry, speaks to its publishing context – a periodical concerned with reconstructing Irish national identity. At the same time, it resonates with representations outside the text, in this case a popular painting that would have been familiar to readers of the *Irish Penny Journal*.

Brown's identity as an Irish poet is reinforced in her second poem published in the *Irish Penny Journal*, "Songs of Our Land." This often reprinted piece echoes Cook's "The Thames" in its use of the river as a metaphor for national strength:

> Songs of our land, ye are with us for ever,
> The power and the splendor of thrones pass away;

But yours is the might of some far flowing river,
    Through Summer's bright roses or Autumn's decay.
Ye treasure each voice of the swift passing ages,
    And truth, which time writeth on leaves or on sand;
Ye bring us the bright thoughts of poets and sages,
    And keep them among us, old songs of our land.[23]

In this stanza, she presents herself as a contributor to an Irish poetic tradition that outlasts monarchical power. This message was well suited to the *Irish Penny Weekly*, which often published woodcut illustrations of ruined Irish castles and crumbling antiquarian landmarks. Implicitly, both "The Pilgrim at the Well" and "Songs of Our Land" define "F. B." as an Irish national poet. Only later would her status as a disabled working-class woman writer become an integral part of her celebrity image.

Having achieved some success in an Irish penny paper, Brown next placed her work in a high-profile metropolitan journal, the *Athenaeum*. Such a move was necessary for relocating herself from the periphery to the center of the literary world. Indeed, she later noted that publishing in the *Athenaeum* "gratified a wish which had haunted [her] very dreams." In June 1841, her poems appeared in the *Athenaeum* under the initials "F. B.," but in January 1842, her full name and home location, Stranorlar, were appended to her contributions, thus marking her as an Irish woman poet. "From that period," she later notes, "my name and pretentions have been more before the public – many poems of mine having appeared in the pages of that publication, in Mr. Hood's *Magazine*, and in the *Keepsake* edited by the Countess of Blessington."[24]

Publishing in an English metropolitan journal was essential for building a poetic career, but highlighting her status as a provincial Irish woman poet enabled her to create a unique brand in a crowded marketplace. Her first poem published under her signature in the *Athenaeum*, "Weep Not for Him That Dieth," appeared on January 15, 1842. The title was most likely taken from Caroline Norton's widely reprinted poem by the same name that had been published in the *New Monthly Magazine* in 1830. While Norton's poem focused on the transcendence of grief after loss of a loved one, Brown's emphasized the broader social meanings of spiritual healing:

Or mourns our land the brave and just,
    – Her sword and shield laid low –
For hearts in whom the nations trust?
    The true, the faithful, go.
But glory to the eagle's home,
    Though clouds around it spread,
For tempests never reach the tomb: –
    Weep not our fearless dead.[25]

The references to "our land" and "nations" seem to signify Great Britain and its empire. Indeed, Brown subtly signaled her Britishness by changing her surname from the more Irish "Browne" (listed on her official documents) to the Anglicized "Brown" (used for most of her signed publications). Yet the "Stranorlar" also listed at the foot of the poem flags a more specifically Irish geographical affiliation and thus alludes to her status as a colonized subject located outside the center of imperial power. As Thomas McLean notes, Brown's work as a whole "favored themes of exile and national identity [which] mirrored the major issues facing nineteenth-century Ireland."[26] Indeed, Irish nationalism had been an important theme in her first publications in the *Irish Penny Paper*, and this to some extent carried over into her work for the *Athenaeum*. Brown was thus able to occupy simultaneous niches in the literary marketplace for both British and Irish nationalist poetry.

In 1843, Brown's poem "The First" appeared in the *Keepsake*, edited by another Irish poet, the Countess of Blessington. Publication in a literary annual was a fortuitous step in Brown's career. As Susan Brown notes, the annuals paid well and "fostered a network of women's writing."[27] Blessington not only included Frances Brown in a prestigious community of writers but also participated in the construction of her public identity. In an editorial footnote to "The First," Blessington identifies Brown as "resident in a small town in a remote part of Ireland; one of a numerous family of humble fortune; and further, suffering under the heavy infliction of total loss of sight." This, she notes, gives Brown's work "double value" – as verse that is both aesthetically beautiful and personally poignant.[28] Blessington's editorial invites readers to interpret the poem's final stanza not only as a reflection on the power of early experiences and impressions but also as commentary on Brown's childhood loss of sight:

> And thus, whate'er our onward way,
>   The lights or shadows cast
> Upon the dawning of our day
>   Are with us to the last.
> But ah! the morning breaks no more
>   On us, as once it burst,
> For future springs can ne'er restore
>   The freshness of the first.[29]

In addition to offering Brown's blindness as a key to unlocking the poem's meaning, Blessington also references her Irishness and her impoverished circumstances – intersecting markers of difference that deepen the poignancy of the poem's melancholy meditation on loss.

The "double value" of Brown's poetry – aesthetic and biographical – was instrumental in her subsequent rise to fame. When her first book of poetry, *The Star of Attéghéi*, appeared in 1844, it included a lengthy biographical preface that told the story of her childhood struggles, persistence, and literary triumph. This narrative was frequently reprinted in literary monthlies and magazines of popular progress, which often profiled working-class heroes, presenting them as models of industry and moral virtue. *Ainsworth's Magazine*, for example, quoted liberally from Brown's biography and referred to her as a "writer of no common powers, of extremely uncommon experiences; and a poet little short, in her own personal history, of a personified romance."[30] While the emphasis on Brown's biography undoubtedly deflected attention from her poetry, it also had the positive effect of constructing her as a memorable persona – the "Blind Poetess of Ulster" (Figure 8).[31] Building upon biographical and critical characterizations of her as an impoverished poet, Brown reinforced her sympathy and identification with working-class struggles in her poetry.[32] Brown's growing reputation as an exemplary working-class poet enabled her to find work writing for popular periodicals aimed at an artisan and lower-middle-class audience. In 1843, she began contributing to Cook's "Facts and Scraps" column in the *Weekly Dispatch*, and four years later she and her sister moved to Edinburgh, where she worked as a contributor to *Chambers's Edinburgh Journal*. By her own accounting, she published 178 articles (excluding reviews) in periodicals and newspapers between 1846 and 1866.[33]

In 1848, Brown published a second volume of poetry, *Lyrics and Miscellaneous Poems*, which included verse that had originally been published in periodicals. In the preface, she justifies republishing these "scattered" works due to the "risk of controverted authorship" actuated by the frequent reprinting of her work in newspapers and periodicals, sometimes without attribution.[34] However, the publication of a new book of poetry, even when added to her extensive prose and poetry publications in newspapers and periodicals, was not enough to keep her afloat financially. In 1852, she moved to London and in 1855 received a £100 grant from the Marquis of Lansdowne, but just a year later *Lloyd's Newspaper* described her as "helpless in the stony streets of London" (though she was accompanied by her sister, who for a time worked as her amanuensis).[35] Perhaps hearing of Brown's financial distress, Cook published an article in the September 9, 1854, issue of her journal that repeated the details of Brown's "suffering" and "triumphs" and recommended her collection of poems as a work "full of interest and beauty."[36]

In 1845, reports of Brown's distress led to a pension of £20 per year from the Royal Bounty. Later, she would apply to the Royal Literary Fund on three separate occasions (1860, 1863, 1866) due to financial crises caused by

Figure 8 Portrait of Frances Brown (ca. 1860). Courtesy of Patrick Bonar.

vagaries in the publishing market. Her 1860 letter to the fund directors provides a snapshot of the difficulties women poets faced as they struggled to make a living based on their published work:

> The causes of my present distress are, first, losses by a London Periodical, from which I obtained only half my earnings, and that by legal means. Secondly, a severe illness in the spring of this year, which incapacitated me for work and consumed my small savings. Thirdly, a publisher's delay in issuing a work of mine the profits of which are contingent on the sale, it was to have [been] placed in the printer's hands at the beginning of April last, and is not now half through the press.[37]

Brown was on unstable ground financially because, unlike Cook, she did not come from a prosperous working-class family, and due to her blindness, she was not in a position to edit journals or engage in sophisticated forms of self-marketing. Brown soon turned to writing for the fiction market, publishing her first novel, *My Share of the World*, in 1861. She also wrote a number of works for children, including *Granny's Wonderful Chair*, which first appeared in 1856. In 1860, Samuel Smiles included a profile of Brown in his *Brief Biographies*, and in 1882, *Young Ireland* published a three-part article on her life and work, claiming that she deserved the "bays of a true Irish poetess."[38] But this was not enough to save her from obscurity. Soon thereafter, her work, like Cook's, was set aside as a relic of the past and would not be revived until the late twentieth century.

Conclusion

In 1846, *Fraser's Magazine* published an article titled "The Past and Present Condition of British Poetry," which imagined who might be included in a procession of "rising poets."[39] First came male poets, followed by male dramatists and ballad writers, and then finally a "galaxy of ladies for the gallery, led by Mrs. Norton and Miss Barrett" (p. 713). Soon thereafter followed Frances Brown, Eliza Cook, and a train of several women poets. This imagined procession provides a snapshot of the poetic world in the mid-1840s, with a "gallery" of women assuming a marginalized, secondary role. Significantly, Brown and Cook are next to each other in line, suggesting their affinities as popular working-class women poets. Indeed, both had risen to fame during a time when the expansion and differentiation of print culture made it possible for working-class women poets to achieve widespread fame.

Yet as much as Cook and Brown seemed to occupy a similar niche in print culture, their careers were shaped by distinct markers of difference. Cook's iconoclasm and nonnormative sexuality set her apart from the aestheticized "poetess" ideal and enabled her to fashion herself as a single, independent woman who was both a national bard and influential editor. Brown actively styled herself as the "Blind Poetess of Ulster," whose work and identity were uniquely suited to the emergent magazines of popular progress, which employed her as an anonymous producer of periodical content and celebrated her public identity as a disabled working-class hero. The periodicals that published Cook's and Brown's verse also occupied complex territory in the literary world. Reaching out to diverse and overlapping readerships, they, like Cook and Brown, embodied contradictions within and among the groups they targeted.

It is undoubtedly true that women poets struggled to make their way in a publishing industry largely run by middle-class men, but they experienced marginalization in the literary marketplace in widely different ways due to their unique markers of difference. Some women poets capitalized on the uniqueness of their identities by writing for niche markets and branding themselves as iconoclastic voices in the literary marketplace. In their self-aware negotiation of identity and their strategic use of new media, Cook and Brown anticipated postmodern notions of subjectivity, which similarly rely on an understanding of the intersectional nature of women's roles in the literary marketplace.

Notes

1. Kimberlé Williams Crenshaw, "Mapping the Margins: Intersectionality, Identity Politics, and Violence against Women of Color," in *The Feminist Philosophy Reader*, ed. Alison Bailey and Chris Cuomo (New York: McGraw-Hill, 2008), p. 280.
2. Susan Brown, "The Victorian Poetess," in *The Cambridge Companion to Victorian Poetry*, ed. Joseph Bristow (Cambridge: Cambridge University Press, 2000), p. 184.
3. Linda K. Hughes, "Poetry," in *Routledge Handbook to Nineteenth-Century British Periodicals and Newspapers*, ed. Andrew King, Alexis Easley, and John Morton (New York: Routledge, 2016), p. 125.
4. Ellen Gruber-Garvey, *Writing with Scissors: American Scrapbooks from the Civil War to the Harlem Renaissance* (New York: Oxford University Press, 2013), p. 35.
5. For the complex meanings of "poetess," see Tricia Lootens, *The Political Poetess: Victorian Femininity, Race, and the Legacy of Separate Spheres* (Princeton: Princeton University Press, 2017), p. 12.
6. Dino F. Felluga, "Tennyson's *Idylls*, Pure Poetry, and the Market," *Studies in English Literature* 37:4 (1997), 783–803.
7. Eliza Cook, "The Thames," *Weekly Dispatch*, September 17, 1837, 8, lines 1–9.
8. Eliza Cook, "A Song for Merry Harvest," *Weekly Dispatch*, October 8, 1837, 8.
9. "Miss Eliza Cook," *Sheffield and Rotherdam Independent* 1429 (June 26, 1847), 6.
10. Brown, "The Victorian Poetess," p. 181.
11. See Hilary Fraser, Stephanie Green, and Judith Johnston, *Gender and the Victorian Periodical* (Cambridge: Cambridge University Press, 2003), p. 63.
12. See Kathryn Gleadle, *The Early Feminists: Radical Unitarians and the Emergence of the Women's Rights Movement, 1831–51* (New York: St. Martin's, 1995).
13. Anna Maria Sargeant, "The Poetess," *Eliza Cook's Journal* 3 (July 6, 1850), 147–50.
14. "Song of November (after Eliza Cook)," *Punch Almanack*, January 1, 1846, 11.
15. Eliza Cook, "A Word to My Readers," *Eliza Cook's Journal* 1 (May 5, 1849), 1.

16. D. B. W. Lewis and C. Lee, eds., *The Stuffed Owl: An Anthology of Bad Verse* (1930, rpt. New York: New York Review Books, 2003), pp. 199–200.

17. See "Editor's Preface," *The Star of Attéghéi; the Vision of Schwartz, and Other Poems* (London: Moxon, 1844), p. xvii.

18. "To Our Readers," *Irish Penny Journal* 1 (July 4, 1840), 8.

19. Francesca Benatti, "Irish Patriots and Scottish Adventurers: The *Irish Penny Journal*, 1840–1841," *Canadian Journal of Irish Studies* 35.2 (2009), 37–8.

20. "To Our Readers," 8.

21. F. B. [Frances Brown], "The Pilgrim at the Well," *Irish Penny Journal* 1 (February 27, 1841), line 10, p. 276.

22. "Saint Senan's Well, County of Clare," *Irish Penny Journal* 1 (June 19, 1841), 401.

23. F. B. [Frances Brown],"Songs of Our Land," *Irish Penny Journal* 1 (March 6, 1841), 284.

24. Quoted in "Editor's Preface," *The Star of Attéghéi*, xix–xx.

25. Frances Brown, "Weep Not for Him That Dieth," *Athenaeum*, January 15, 1842, 65.

26. Thomas McLean, "Arms and the Circassian Woman: Frances Browne's 'The Star of Attéghéi,'" *Victorian Poetry* 41.3 (2003), 296.

27. Brown, "The Victorian Poetess," pp. 190–1.

28. Countess of Blessington, "Editorial note to Frances Brown's 'The First,'" *Keepsake* (1843), p. 111.

29. Frances Brown, "The First," *Keepsake* (1843), p. 111.

30. "Progress of Poetry," *Ainsworth's Magazine* 6 (December 1844), 503.

31. See, for example, "Frances Browne," *New Monthly Belle Assemblée* 22 (May 1845), 290.

32. See also "The Poet's Wealth," *Athenaeum*, July 12, 1851, 740–1.

33. Frances Brown, Application to the Committee of the Royal Literary Fund Committee, November 5, 1866, Royal Literary Fund, British Library, Loan 96, RLF 1/1540/38.

34. Frances Brown, introduction to *Lyrics and Miscellaneous Poems* (Edinburgh: Sutherland and Knox, 1848), pp. 7–8; "Editor's Preface," xx.

35. "Recognition of Service," *Lloyd's Weekly London Newspaper*, December 18, 1853, 7.

36. "Frances Brown, the Blind Poetess," *Eliza Cook's Journal* 2 (September 9, 1854), 312.

37. Frances Brown to the Royal Literary Fund Committee, November 6, 1860, Royal Literary Fund, British Library, Loan 96, RLF 1/1540/12–13.

38. John McCall, "Frances Brown, the Blind Irish Poetess," *Young Ireland* 8 (August 5, 1882), 489.

39. "The Past and Present Condition of British Poetry," *Fraser's Magazine* 33 (June 1846), 713.

7

ALISON CHAPMAN

Transatlanticism, Transnationality, and Cosmopolitanism

"I'm a citizeness of the world now, you see, and float loose": so Elizabeth Barrett Browning (EBB) declares her removal from purely British interests.[1] Although Victorian literary culture valued domesticity and patriotism in women's poetry, the recent global turn in literary studies reorientates Victorian women's poetry toward transatlanticism, transnationality, and cosmopolitanism. These interrelated terms all contest the homogeneity of national literature without necessarily needing to relinquish the concept of the nation.[2] Transnationalism, as Lauren M. E. Goodlad and Julia Wright argue, is a movement through geographical borders.[3] Transatlanticism denotes cultural exchange across the Atlantic, especially between America and Britain. Meredith McGill influentially terms transatlantic poetry "the traffic in poems" across conceptual and geographical zones.[4] Cosmopolitanism is a self-conscious liberal practice to cultivate detachment that, in Amanda Anderson's definition, often includes an anxious partiality.[5] Another crucial term in the current debates about kinds of Victorian transnationalism, globalism, is inevitably inflected by the continuing historical contexts of Anglocentrism and imperialism. But recent critics are rethinking assumptions of Western and colonial power to unsettle the "the center-periphery model" of globalism that, in Paul Jay's words, "sees power, commodities, and influence flowing from urban centers in the West to a peripheral developing world."[6] Jay calls for global literary studies to favor hybrid and fluid transnationalism. This approach has particular resonance for decolonizing Victorian literature, particularly for the dominant tradition of Victorian women's poetry that was founded on a fictional transnational poet: the Anglo-Italian Corinne, poet-heroine of Germaine de Staël's profoundly influential French novel *Corinne; or Italy* (1807).[7]

The international network of Victorian women poets emerged in recent years as an important critical project, moving from "a reorientation of literary studies around the network rather than the nation."[8] But it is vital to acknowledge that Victorian women's poetry encompasses writers not born or primarily resident in Britain. Recent criticism has begun to address women's global Anglophone poetry in terms of Priya Joshi's argument that a "migratory practice" is embedded in the very term "Victorian," to relocate Victorian literary studies globally.[9] But much scholarship on British, Indian, Australian, and Canadian Anglophone women writers still largely frames them as a national literary tradition, a project distinct from reevaluating Victorian women's poetry as global and migratory.

As Lauren Goodlad argues, the emergence of Victorian cosmopolitanism often elides the Anglocentrism and imperialism beneath Victorian geopolitics.[10] Likewise, expanding the reach of Victorian women's poetry to encompass a global imaginary and to recover non-British Anglophone writing involves negotiating the unsettled dynamic between local and global as a mobile pairing. Anglophone Victorian women's poetry offers a troubled relationship with nationhood and difference even as it eventually turns to internationalism as an ethical cosmopolitan imperative. This chapter provides an overview of Victorian women's poetry as a transnational practice, bringing into conversation both British cosmopolitan women writers and Anglophone writers from beyond Britain in a series of case studies that uncover their global transactions.

Letitia Landon and Emma Roberts: Rome, London, Bengal

Letitia Landon (L.E.L.), one of the first Victorian women poets, helped establish the intrinsic transnationalism of the Victorian woman poet through her engagement with the fictional Anglo-Italian poetess Corinne. Landon did the metrical translations of Corinne's improvised poetry for Isabel Hill's 1838 translation of de Staël's novel, and she also wrote poetry about Corinne.[11] Corinne was also formative for later women's poetry, notably EBB's *Aurora Leigh*. But L.E.L.'s transnationalism also included orientalism, and her little-known collaboration with the Anglo-Indian writer Emma Roberts affords a potent example of a transnational network predicated on professional status, print culture, and sociability.

Roberts wrote about England for an Indian audience and about India for an English audience. She moved from England to India in 1828, lived in several cities in Bengal, and issued her first volume of poems in 1830 while living at Cawnpore.[12] In 1831, Roberts moved to Calcutta and began writing for the periodical press in India and London, as well as editing and contributing to *Oriental Observer*.[13] She returned to London in 1832, continuing her career as a prolific Anglo-Indian writer, including contributions to the *Asiatic Journal*, a London edition of her poems, an 1835 travel account of picturesque scenes, and a posthumous memoir of Landon.[14] In 1839, she returned to India and died in Poona a year later.

Roberts navigated expectations of British women poets' interaction with non-English cultures. Like L.E.L., Roberts had a successful career as a professional woman writer, and like L.E.L. her poetry engages with transnationalism, but with a more overt politicized tension between London and the colonies. Roberts's first poetry volume included an ambitious preface that heralds the book as "the first production of the kind, emanating from a female pen, which has issued from the Calcutta Press," as "an auspicious omen of the advancement of literature in the East." The book will "stimulate my country women in India to cultivate those intellectual pursuits which have raised so many female writers to eminence at home."[15] This tribute launches *Oriental Scenes* as a new female Anglo-Indian literary tradition. The 1830 volume contains an initial section, "Oriental Scenes," with ten poems on Indian subjects, and the remaining poems address a variety of English and European picturesque scenes. The 1832 London edition is refashioned as entirely Indian by expanding the earlier volume's Indian section, removing the other poems and the title words *with Other Poems*, and adding a dedication to L.E.L. As an Anglo-Indian poet publishing in Calcutta, Roberts forges an overtly new transnational female poetic tradition. But as an Anglo-Indian poet publishing in London two years later, Roberts re-invents herself as wholly an oriental poet in the tradition of L.E.L. and in the empire's London center. This re-invention came after a period of working and living with Landon in London (1832–8), until Landon left for Ghana with her new husband, tragically dying there on October 15 in mysterious circumstances. If anyone performed the transnational poetess to the end, it was L.E.L.

This colonial poetic exchange between two successful women poets involves an uneasy negotiation between India and London. Mary Ellis Gibson, in *Indian Angles: English Verse in Colonial India from Jones to Tagore*, considers Landon's relationship with Roberts as part of the negotiation with colonial bardic nationalism. As Gibson notes, Roberts's poem on the Taj Mahal exemplifies the affective power of the Indian landscape for the colonial English poet, which Gibson argues is ultimately treated with scepticism as well as imperialism by Roberts.[16] But the poem also offers a case study of the transnational exchange of Roberts and Landon, which shapes Roberts's career as a bifurcated English and Anglo-Indian poet. Roberts's notes to the poem "The Taaje Mahal" (the famous palatial mausoleum and gardens that the Mughal Emperor Shah Jehan built in Agra, Bengal, between 1631 and 1648, as a tribute to his wife), published in the Calcutta and London editions and presumably written when she lived in Agra, recast the iconic exemplar of Muslim art as a celebration of a Western spousal devotion.[17] Roberts adds that the emperor engaged European artists and that "there is no prototype [for the monument] in the known world."[18]. Her celebration of the "beauty and splendour" of the Taj Mahal is mediated by the representation of the emperor's implicit embodiment of Western European ideals of courtly love. The implication is that Roberts's poem, and her volume, is also offered as a prototype with no imitators, a daring move given that the Taj Mahal was often the subject of colonial poetry.

Roberts's poem begins by voicing the emperor's devotion to his dying wife, offering a catalogue of her peerless beauty (line 10) tinged by Christian as well as Indian imagery: she is a "Cashmerian rose" but also "pure as heaven-born seraphim" (line 15). The emperor describes his architectural tribute as a shrine for "pilgrims . . . from many a distant clime" to "gaze upon the work sublime" (lines 49–51). The fact that his elegy has a well-known European stanzaic form, the sesta rima, most associated with Shakespeare's *Venus and Adonis* (1593), a poem based on the Greek myth origin story for doomed romantic love, again mediates the origin of the Taj Mahal through a European frame. The second narrative section of the poem, in a third-person voice, begins with a sesta rima but then interlaces rhyming couplets with quatrains. Here the poem offers a mixed response to the Taj Mahal: a symbol for faded Muslim glory now that "strangers from a foreign strand / Rule unopposed the conquered land" (lines 69–70); an exemplar "of love's idolatry" (line 86), transforming ideal spousal devotion into danger-ous un-Christian excess; and an enchanting place still resplendent for the "stranger's . . . eye" (line 84) of superlative aesthetic delight. The "stranger" who visits the Taj Mahal is overcome by its timeless dream-like enchantment, "the light work of fairy wands" (line 95) that lifts the mausoleum out of its colonial context, to praise its sublime visual delight: the Taj Mahal's unique-ness is ultimately contingent on erasing its orientalism. This doubleness is underscored by the poem's conclusion, which imagines visiting lovers kneel-ing at the tomb of the empress, lifted out of a sense of mortality through the tale "That strong affection may endure / In human hearts beyond the grave" (lines 123–4). The ending transforms the poem's competing meanings into a conventional poem in the tradition of the English poetess, repeating the characteristic trope of the grave as a place of appropriate affect, and eliding the poem's tensions between oriental and colonial.

L.E.L. wrote a poem on the same topic, "The Taj-Mahal, at Agra. The Tomb of Muntaza Zamani," for her 1831 *Fisher's Drawing Room Scrap-Book*, as a "poetical illustration" to a sketch of the monument by Robert Elliott, whom Gibson identifies as a friend of Roberts, whose sketchbook Roberts used in her own prose writings about India, and whose plates, in turn, influenced Landon.[19] The colonial exchange on the Taj Mahal has several phases: Landon's 1831 poem was published in the year between the two editions of Roberts's poetry; Roberts reused Elliott's sketch of the monument in her 1835 descriptive entries for *Views in India, China, and on the Shores of the Red Sea*, a book that was issued by the same London publisher as the *Scrap-Book*, H. and R. Fisher; and *Views in India* was itself a revised publication of an 1832 edition that contained descriptive text by Elliott. Landon's poem begins, as Roberts's does, with the words of the emperor but adds a footnote on the monument's vanity as well as artistry.[20] Landon's poetic illustration of Elliott's facing page sketch underscores the moral lesson, repeated in a prose note that vanity overrides "this most exquisite specimen of Mahommedan architecture." An Italian artist, she claims, "regretted there was not a glass-case to cover it."[21] Landon's expensive and lavishly illustrated annual is in fact that "glass-case," offering a picturesque view of the Taj Mahal alongside the poetic lesson on oriental hubris. Roberts's revised London edition published one year later adds a new note to the end of the poem that echoes Landon's criticism on the emperor's failure in his vision: before he could erect a tomb for himself on the other side of the Jumna River, he suffered misfortunes that meant he ended up buried beside his wife.

In 1835, Roberts returned again to the Taj Mahal, writing the descriptive commentary for the reissue of Elliott's 1832 *Views in India, China, and on the Shores of the Red Sea*, which replaced Elliott's original text but kept his sketches, including the Taj that L.E.L. used in her 1831 annual. In this travel account, Roberts repeats much of the representation of the Taj Mahal in her earlier poem, such as the language of Western Christian piety and the superlative beauty of the mausoleum. But she also emphasizes the tourist site as a safe space for the "European," termed in the poem a "stranger" who will find the garden an "Eden," a Romanticized place of such "melancholy sublimity" that their eyes will "involuntarily gush out with tears." Her description focuses on the importance of vantage point, which angle the Taj Mahal is best viewed from: how the excess of the scene "arrests the eye," but also how the European tourist and reader of the book must imagine this oriental gem. She suggests that the Taj Mahal exceeds oriental/European binaries in its beauty but also places the Taj Mahal safely within Western representational axioms, even reminding the reader that the British government has now taken an "especial protection" of the site by spending a significant amount of money in repairs, and also keeping it "always open to European and native visitors."[22] Roberts could not have foreseen that during the 1857 Indian Uprising, the mausoleum would be raided by the British.

Toru Dutt and Sarojini Naidu: Hastings, London, India

Toru Dutt has recently emerged as a prominent Victorian Anglo-Indian poet, and yet her poetry puts pressure on each of those terms. Dutt is celebrated in the Indo-European literary tradition as the first published Anglophone woman poet, but as her editor Chandani Lokugé points out, her multilingual cosmopolitan writing "resists both conservative Indian and conventional British identities."[23] Gibson argues that Dutt's cosmopolitanism – her complex engagement with European and Indian literary traditions, her translations, her education at Newnham College, as well as her family's controversial conversion to Christianity – is evidenced by her ability to "radically remake" both Christian religious and Indian literary tropes "in an incipient cosmopolitan poetics." Gibson, along with Tricia Lootens, terms Dutt's Anglo-European poetry a triangulation between "metropolitan/colonial relations" and French, English, and Indian literary cultures.[24]

Whereas Roberts's and L.E.L.'s poems on India focus on oriental tourist sites, Dutt's Anglo-Indian poetry offers a more complex transnationalism, such as her translations from Hindustan and France, and her poems that uneasily translate Indian locations into European literary forms ("Sonnet – Baugmaree," "Sonnet – The Lotus," "Our Casuarina Tree").[25] In "Near Hastings," for example, Dutt places the speaker and her companion by several boundaries: a coastline near but not at Hastings (a popular English seaside resort), the "blent" mixture of sea and sky, the transition between day and night, and the contrast between the speaker and the passing elderly lady (who thought she was French).[26] Hastings was the site of the only successful foreign invasion of the British Isles in 1066, and, beneath the blending of boundaries, the topography of "Near Hastings" encodes an ironic thrust at British colonial rule, in a wry move typical of Dutt's poetry. In Dutt's poem, the lady's unexpected gift of red roses is compared to Indian lotus: "Sweet were the roses, – sweet and full, / And large as lotus flowers / That in our own wide tanks we cull / To deck our Indian bowers."[27] The remainder of this penultimate stanza leans the poem toward a Christian meaning: "I think that He who came to save / The gift a debt will own." While the beauty of the roses recalls her home flowers, the poem makes another swerve toward a Wordsworthian tradition of the consolation of memory: "Still bloom her roses in my heart! / And they shall never fade!"[28] The poem shifts from the uneasy boundaries to the recollection of home, then to Christian and finally Wordsworthian restorative interiority, positioning the speaker as a stranger twice over (Indian, mistaken as French) whose sense of difference from the location is compensated by the rose metaphor. The poem's form, in the literary ballad's alternating tetrameters and trimeters, recalls Wordsworth in genre as well as theme to appropriate but also destabilize his English balladic tradition.

While Dutt is often labeled by critics as an Indo-European cosmopolitan poet, this poem's cosmopolitanism is uncertain as well as joyful. After her death, Dutt was reclaimed as a foremother of the Indian national literary canon. A later poet, Sarojini Naidu (1879–1949) occupied both positions at once: a cosmopolitan Indian national poet. Naidu, like Dutt, attended Cambridge University (in her case, Girton College) and became part of 1890s London literary circles. Arthur Symons published her poem "Eastern Dancers" in *The Savoy*.[29] This poem was renamed "Indian Dancers" for her 1905 poetry volume *The Golden Threshold*, perhaps because Edmund Gosse advised her to leave 1890s decadent poetics for a more "genuine" Indian poetic identity.[30] The poem in *The Savoy* adopts dactylic heptameter, in the fashion of long-lined poems of the 1890s, winding the lines down the *mise-en-page* (or layout) in the manner of the rapturous "wild and entrancing" music and dance: "And exquisite, subtle and slow are the tinkle and tread of their rhythmical slumber-soft feet." Gibson claims that the poem offers an uneasiness between the speaker/viewer and the dancers, although the form of the poem disrupts that tension by mimicking the dance.[31] Gibson also notes that Naidu's poem in the *Savoy* engages with Symons's earlier poem "Javanese Dancers."[32] Symons's poem also captures the sensual rhythms of the dance yet represents the women as "inanimate," other, and disembodied. Naidu's poem heightens the eroticism of the dancers, presses rhythm into the service of replicating the "wild" dance, and insists on the embodiment of the women as the dancers blend with the dance.

Naidu's poetry, like Dutt's, is located at the intersection between European and Indian literary culture, but while Dutt's poetry often presses uncomfortably at this juncture to remake European poetic forms for Indian literature, Naidu makes this location politically active by incorporating her poetic identity with nationalist politics. The year that *The Golden Threshold* was published, 1905, was also the year that Naidu entered Indian politics following the partition of Bengal. Naidu became a prominent politician, advancing her principles of "communal harmony" in her poetry and politics, promoting intersectional coalitions in India as a Hindu nationalist allied with Muslims, and working to empower women.[33] Her literary cosmopolitanism allowed her to engage with English literary culture, and in particular 1890s poetics, while also writing as an Indian poet: in the context of Indian literary culture in the nineteenth century, such a mediation was, rather than a simple paradox, an integral part of the complex and ambivalent transnational networks of Anglophone Indian poetry.

Elizabeth Barrett Browning: England, Florence, Boston

The relationship between Victorian women's poetry and transatlantic literary exchanges largely depended on the absence of an international copyright agreement until the Chace Act of 1891. Before then, British authors were commonly subject to literary piracy. Some prominent Victorian women poets, with their marketability as leverage, secured authorized American publication, such as EBB's arrangement with C. S. Francis to publish an American edition of *Aurora Leigh*. But EBB was still frequently the target of literary piracy as well as posthumous repackaging of her works. For example, Charles Scribner issued an 1870 edition of "Lady Geraldine's Courtship," which originally appeared in Elizabeth Barrett's 1844 *Poems*, and which EBB viewed as a poetic origin of *Aurora Leigh*.[34] Scribner's volume was a gift book, with gold decoration on a maroon cover, gilt edging, and thick paper. This edition also presented the ballad in the style of a novel: the generous number of illustrations depicted key dramatic moments of the plot as in an illustrated novel; the prefatory two-page list of illustrations read like a series of chapter titles; and the line breaking in Scribner's edition split each poem line earlier than the Moxon 1844 edition, which made the *mise-en-page* resemble prose.

This poem, like *Aurora Leigh*, gained an American following because it represented the kind of British narrative poems that, as Mary Loeffelholz argues, "are inextricably part of the substance *and* the structure of the post–Civil War American cultural field."[35] This is certainly clear in Scribner's *Lady Geraldine's Courtship*. But Scribner's also had an investment in EBB as an iconic British poet presented for their American magazine (*Scribner's Monthly*) and book readership. In November 1873, Edmund Clarence Stedman published "Elizabeth Barrett Browning" in *Scribner's*, a celebratory essay that established Scribner's investment in her literary capital and Stedman's definition of Victorian women's poetry. Stedman claimed that EBB was the leading Victorian woman poet in the Anglophone world:

> The Victorian era, with its wider range of opportunities for women, has been illumined by the career of the greatest female poet that England has produced, – nor only England, but the whole territory of the English language; more than this, the most inspirational woman, so far as known, of all who have composed in ancient or modern tongues, or flourished in any land or time.[36]

For Stedman, an American who first defined Victorian poetry as "Victorian," EBB is the epitome of the women poet in any land and in any language. While he laments "commonplaces" that mar "Lady Geraldine's Courtship," he praises it "as her first open avowal, and a brave one in England, of the democracy which generous and gifted spirits, the round world over, are wont to confess" (107). EBB represents for Stedman democracy, freedom, and an implicit exemplar for American women's poetry. Indeed, many American women poets attested EBB's influence, and often her poetry functioned as a trope for their negotiations with the British poetic tradition, particularly in the case of Emily Dickinson, Anne C. Lynch Botta, and Helen Sarah Whitman.

EBB exploited her importance as a transatlantic poet for political reasons, particularly in her contributions to the abolitionist *The Liberty Bell*. EBB was invited by the Boston Female Anti-Slavery Society to submit to their annual, and "The Runaway Slave at Pilgrim's Point" was published in the 1848 issue, followed by "A Curse for a Nation" in 1856. EBB sent her second poem to the editor, Maria Weston Chapman, who was then resident in Paris, by passing a copy to her sisters as they visited the poet in Florence in December 1854, and in fact the poem also overlays transatlantic literary politics with European contexts.[37] Not only did EBB end the poem with the byline "Florence, Italy, 1854," but reviewers of the later volume that reprinted the poem, *Poems before Congress* (1860), assumed the curse was directed at England for failing to overtly support Italian Unification, rather than at America for failing to abolish slavery.

The *Liberty Bell* version of "A Curse for a Nation" highlights the performative aspect of the poem in two ways, suggesting that transatlanticism enables women's poetic and political agency. First, the initial page of the poem has an illustration of the Liberty Bell from which the gift book derived its name, engraved with the words "PROCLAIM LIBERTY TO ALL THE INHABITANTS." The bell, a potent symbol for American independence, stands as a synecdoche for the poem, and vice versa. The poem is structured as a prologue in which an angel appears to the speaker imploring her to "'Write! / Write a nation's curse for me, / And send it over the western sea,'" followed by the curse itself. The entire poem curses America for enchaining the freedom of its people and asserts the especial authority of a woman writer to issue the written curse from "over the western sea." The illustration of the bell above EBB's poem conveys a visual reminder that her poem chastises America for not holding to the promise of the Declaration of Independence for all people. The ringing bell in the illustration legitimates, if ironically, the poem's performative speech act. Second, this version of the poem differs from the publication in the 1860 *Poems before Congress* in its use of the exclamation mark as a rhetorical reminder of the urgency, affect, and expressive power of the poem, such as in the refrain "This is the curse – write!" (compared with the 1860 version, the more restrained "This is the curse. Write."). That performativity enacts the triangular relationship among America, England, and Italy: the abolitionist cause is supported by an English writer, writing from Florence, at the center of the Italian Unification, which was commonly compared to abolitionism as another movement for liberty of the Italian people metaphorically enslaved. When the British press condemned EBB's curse, as the last poem in *Poems before Congress*, by misreading the poem as an unpatriotic attack on England for failing to unify Italy, EBB confessed that parts of the poem "do 'fit' England 'as if they were made for her.' Which they were *not* though!"[38]

A. Mary F. Robinson: London, France, Italy

Europe was often central to Victorian women poets' transnationalism, even triangulating colonial, imperial, and transatlantic poetry. One of the most prominent Anglo-European writers was A. Mary F. Robinson, who published aestheticist poetry, often on French and Italian subjects and literary forms, as well as literary criticism in French and English. Robinson married the French translator of her first poetry book, *A Handful of Honeysuckle*, the scholar and translator James Darmesteter, in August 1888, after which she moved to Paris and hosted a prominent literary salon. Darmesteter died in 1894, but Robinson stayed in Paris, eventually marrying the French biologist Pierre Emile Duclaux in 1901. Robinson's publications, from her poetry volumes in English to her essays in English and French on European literature, history, and culture cultivated a cosmopolitan European aestheticism.

Robinson's Eurocentric transnationalism was especially significant for its experimentation with ancient European poetic forms, particularly in *An Italian Garden: A Book of Songs*.[39] Robinson's poetics of place are markedly different from a volume published the previous year, *Roadside Songs of Tuscany* (1885) by the American expatriate Francesca Alexander (1837–1917), which locates the songs and the singers firmly in a rural Tuscan setting, signifying their place of origin.[40] For Robinson, the old Italian folk forms are not preserved as an antiquarian exercise or gathered to signify rural culture but rather are integrated into her aestheticist poetics to gesture to a cosmopolitan relationship between poetic form and geographical place, because the history of the shape of the poem was so closely and dynamically embedded with its topographical origins. *A New Arcadia* (1884), Robinson's previous volume, was judged harshly by critics for its political engagement in the specificities of English rural poverty, which they determined to be at the expense of her poetry.[41] *An Italian Garden* represents Robinson's return to lyric aestheticism, relocating her poetics to European poetic forms and places and experimenting with the ability of Anglophone poetic form to signify another place at all. Robinson's carefully researched experiments with form and place tease at the limits of poetry's ability to adhere to specific national identity, implying that a transnational poetics erases any certainty of representation tied to geographical affiliations.

Robinson bonds ancient poetic forms with place through what she terms in the preface to her 1902 *Collected Poems* the "patina" of time, or historical layers, through the poems' working and reworking of old forms, especially popular Italian folk songs, the stornello and rispetto.[42] The poetics of patina represents geographical location through Paterian impression, or aesthetic association, rather than verisimilitude. Her poems in *An Italian Garden* refuse completely to naturalize or Anglicize the forms, maintaining the Italian rhyme, meter, and assonant sounds despite the difficulties of adopting them in English. Robinson's poems revivify ancient Italian forms while maintaining their difference and foreignness, an uncanny poetics influenced by Vernon Lee's theories of form as ghostly, "shift[ing] between something and nothing,"[43] a phrase that also serves as a definition of aestheticist cosmopolitanism.

In the preface to her 1902 *Collected Poems*, Robinson compares her poems to the folk forms usually made by women: "We have always been the prime makers of ballads and love songs, of anonymous snatches and screeds of popular song."[44] She reminds her readers "that the beautiful rispetti of the Tuscan hills, the ballads of Scotland and Piedmont, have all at one moment lacked the admirable patina which age and time alone confer."[45] These comments, made at the end of her preface, intrinsically link her poems to folk forms that are intimately connected with specific places (Tuscany, Piedmont, Scotland). While her poems are not themselves adapted and circulated in and through indigenous place, like the oral culture from which she takes the poetic forms, her poems already signify the performative process she asks of the readers, to give them an authentic patina of time through their fluid movement between specific place and nonspecific space.

The impressions of places in *An Italian Garden* are symbolically arranged in the volume through the subsections entitled "Nocturnes," "A Garland of Flowers," "Tuscan Cypress," "Songs and Dreams," and "Vestigia" (vestiges). The collection moves through a series of associations of places real, mythological, and imagined, beginning with night poems (conventionally enigmatic place poems based on imaginative reveries), and ending with vestiges (a word meaning a trace or sign of something that no longer exists). This last section is prefaced by a quotation from Baudelaire's "Harmonie du Soir" (from *Fleurs du Mal* [1857]) that implicitly offers Robinson's poetic manifesto: "*Un cœur tendre qui hait le néant vaste et noir / Du passé lumineux recueille tout vestige*" ("A tender heart that hates the vast, black void / Gathers up every shred of the luminous past!").[46] Baudelaire's "vestiges" is a trace that shadows Robinson's Vestigia section, implying that her poetry is the tender heart that gathers the remains of light from the darkness. Robinson's epigraph to the *Collected Poems* version of *An Italian Garden* includes this citation from Baudelaire after a Tuscan stornello that suggests the source of the darkness is the end of a love affair: "*M'affaccio alla fenestra e veggo il mare / E mi ricordo che s'ha da morire: / Termineranno le speranze eare!*" ("I look out of the window and view the sea / And I remember she has died: / My cherished hopes are gone!"). In the original 1886 volume, Tuscan rispetti and stornelli are included as epigraphs and adaptations to signify vestiges of the *passé lumineux*, traces of the memory of place, as an Italian garden interiorized. For Robinson, transnationalism is a poetic, linguistic, historic, and geographic practice that intricately performs the associations of poetry and place as an interiorized sensation, not a realistic depiction.

The entire volume resonates with echoes, memories, dreams, ghosts, moonlight, seemings, and glimmers. While they are not the only ancient European forms in *An Italian Garden*, stornelli and rispetti run like a refrain throughout the poetry performing the same poetic work as the aestheticist vocabulary. Rispetti are deployed as epigraphs to the entire volume: "A Rifiorita" (24) reworks the conventional closure to the stornello form, the collection's middle section "Tuscan Cypress" (33–50) begins with an epigraph of two Tuscan stornelli followed by a collection of sixteen rispetti, the section "Songs and Dreams" has a Tuscan rispetto as an epigraph (53), and the sequence "Stornelli and Strambotti" (63–4) includes two sections that each contain two stornelli with a strambotto (originally an Italian eight-line stanza of hendecasyllables, a variant of the rispetto).[47] "To a Rose Dead at Morning" (28) revises Robinson's version of the rispetto by moving the two concluding couplets to the start of the poem (rhyming aabbcdcd). The historical moment in which Robinson's volume was published coincided with a fashion for Italian folk forms, as well as a turn in poetics toward difficult closed forms based on old European poetic genres.[48] Many poets turned to the villanelle, the sonnet, the ballade, the triolet, and other old European forms, as explorations of poems whose very form was conceived as an aesthetic transnational object.

As the last poem in the volume, "Pulvis et Umbra" (100–102) exclaims, playing on the allusion to Horace's *pulvis et umbra sumus* (all is dust and shadows):

> In vain I think. O moon-like thought of Death,
> All is unreal beneath thee, uncertain all,
> Dim moon-ray thrown along a world of shades!   (102)

For all its poems of places and associations and memories, the strongest pull in the collection is toward the uncertainty of place and even no place at all, somewhere "Out of the world" desired by the speaker in the tenth rispetto of "Tuscan Cypress" (33–50). For a volume of poems that exhibits such a profound investment in Tuscany as a location expressed through its ancient forms, whose associations are recalled through the speaker's memory, *An Italian Garden* wonders whether other places can ever be apprehended as tangible in this "transient world" ("Pulvis et Umbra" 100). Augusta Webster's review of this volume identifies its distance from "the living workaday world of men and women."[49] But Webster's invitation to Robinson, her urge that she leave behind her sense of the world as "a fanciful land of lotus-eaters" and "come into the real world", misses the point of the volume: can aestheticist cosmopolitan poetry apprehend the real world at all?

Victorian women poets navigated other cultures through their literary, social, and political networks, and mapping these exchanges offers a new geography of women's literary traditions, replete with connections and dis-connections as the poetry mediates the uneasy relations between center and periphery. The combination of a local engagement and global imaginary suggests that Anglophone women's poetry of the Victorian era assumed that their international and cosmopolitan practice was a cross-cultural nego-tiation of zones, recalling Mary Louise Pratt's concept of the "contact zone," specific locations of cross-cultural contact where complex structures of power collide. Victorian women's poetry represents such contact zones but also offers its own formal poetic space as a contact zone that redefines what makes women's poetry "Victorian" in the first place. The field of global Victorian women's poetry is impossible currently to map and in fact may need to elude easy homogenous critical overviews; it is nonetheless clear that international women's Anglophone poetry of the Victorian era is a poetry of networks, exchange, mediation, and dislocation. If not a utopian "floating loose" (in the manner of EBB), nor a lotus-eating aesthetic play devoid of any material referentiality (as Webster termed it), moving beyond specifically *British* women's poetry involves an uneasy yet productive exchange between the rose and the lotus, the metropole and the colony, that redraws the boundaries of the conventional literary canon and challenges our under-standing of the way cultures, poetic forms, and power interconnect.

Notes

1. Elizabeth Barrett and Robert Browning, *The Brownings' Correspondence*, 25 vols., ed. Philip Kelley et al. (Winfield, KS: Wedgestone Press, 1984), 17.70.
2. See Lauren M. E. Goodlad and Julia M. Wright, "Introduction and Keywords," Victorian Internationalisms special issue, *Romanticism and Victorianism on the Net*, 48 (November 2007), parag. 1.
3. Ibid., parag. 2.

4. Meredith McGill, ed., *The Traffic in Poems: Nineteenth-Century Poetry and Transatlantic Exchange* (New Brunswick, NJ: Rutgers University Press, 2008).
5. Amanda Anderson, *The Powers of Distance: Cosmopolitanism and the Cultivation of Detachment* (Princeton: Princeton University Press, 2001).
6. Paul Jay, *Global Matters: The Transnational Turn in Literary Studies* (Ithaca: Cornell University Press, 2010), p. 3.
7. Germaine de Staël, *Corinne; or, Italy*, ed. and transl. Sylvia Raphael (Oxford: Oxford World's Classics, 2009).
8. Caroline Levine, "From Nation to Network," *Victorian Studies*, 55 (2013), 649.
9. Priya Joshi, "Globalizing Victorian Studies," *The Yearbook of English Studies* 41.2 (2011), 20–40; Mary Ellis Gibson, *Indian Angles: English Verse in Colonial India From Jones to Tagore* (Athens: Ohio University Press, 2011).
10. Lauren M. E. Goodlad, *The Victorian Geopolitical Aesthetic: Realism, Sovereignty, and Transnational Experience* (New York: Oxford University Press, 2015).
11. Germaine de Staël, *Corinne; or, Italy*, transl. Isabel Hill, with metrical translations of the odes by L. E. Landon (London: Richard Bentley, 1833).
12. Emma Roberts, *Oriental Scenes, Dramatic Sketches and Tales, with Other Poems* (Calcutta: P. S. D'Rozario, 1830).
13. "Memoir," Emma Roberts, *Notes of an Overland Journey Through France and Egypt to Bombay* (London: Wm. H. Allen, 1841), pp. xvi–xvii.
14. Emma Roberts, *Oriental Scenes, Sketches, and Tales* (London: Edward Bull, 1832); *Views in India, China, and on the Shores of the Red Sea*, illus. Robert Elliott, descriptions by Emma Roberts, 2 vols. (London: H. Fisher, R. Fisher, and P. Jackson, 1835); "Memoir," in Letitia Landon, *The Zenana and Minor Poems* (London: Fisher, 1839).
15. Roberts, *Oriental Scenes* (1830), pp. iii–iv.
16. Gibson, *Indian Angles*, pp. 87–8.
17. Emma Roberts, "The Taaje Mahal," *Oriental Scenes* (1832), pp. 32–8; "Notes," p. 170.
18. Ibid., p. 170.
19. Mary Ellis Gibson, ed., *Anglophone Poetry in Colonial India, 1780–1913: A Critical Anthology* (Athens: Ohio University Press, 2011), p. 122.
20. Letitia Landon, "The Taj-Mahal, at Agra. The Tomb of Muntaza Zemani," *Fisher's Drawing Room Scrap Book, with Poetical Illustrations by L. E. L.* (London, Fisher, Son, and Jackson, 1831), p. 20.
21. Ibid.
22. Roberts, "The Taj Mahal," *Views in India, China, and on the Shores of the Red Sea*, 1.21–4.
23. Chandani Lokugé, ed., *Toru Dutt: Collected Prose and Poetry* (New Delhi: Oxford University Press, 2006), p. xiii.
24. Gibson, *Indian Angles*, pp. 209, 213; Tricia Lootens, "Bengal, Britain, France: The Locations and Translations of Toru Dutt," *Victorian Literature and Culture*, 34 (2006), 573–90.
25. *A Sheaf Gleaned from French Fields* [1876], *Ancient Ballads and Legends of Hindustan* [1882].
26. Lokugé, *Toru Dutt*, pp. 206–7.
27. Ibid., p. 206.

28. Ibid., p. 207.
29. Sarojini Chattopâdhyây [her maiden name], "Eastern Dancers," *The Savoy*, No. 5 (September 1896), 84.
30. Sarojini Naidu, "Indian Dancers," *The Golden Threshold* (London: Heineman, 1905), pp. 71–2; Gibson, *Anglophone Poetry*, 364.
31. Gibson, *Indian Angles*, p. 248.
32. Arthur Symons, "Javanese Dancers," *Silhouettes*, 2nd ed. (London: Leonard Smithers, 1896), p. 33.
33. Gibson, *Anglophone Poetry*, p. 365.
34. Elizabeth Barrett Browning, *Poems*, 2 vols. (London: Edward Moxon, 1844), 1.209–50.
35. Mary Loeffelholz, "Mapping the Cultural Field: *Aurora Leigh* in America," in *The Traffic in Poems*, p. 140.
36. E. C. Stedman, "Elizabeth Barrett Browning," *Scribner's Monthly*, 7 (November 1873), 102.
37. *The Brownings' Correspondence*, 21.38.
38. Elizabeth Barrett and Robert Browning, *Florentine Friends: The Letters of Elizabeth Barrett Browning and Robert Browning to Isa Blagden 1850–1861*, ed. Philip Kelley and Sandra Donaldson (Winfield, KS: Wedgestone Press and the Armstrong Browning Library of Baylor University, 2009), p. 321.
39. A. Mary F. Robinson, *An Italian Garden: A Book of Songs* (London: T. Fisher Unwin, 1886).
40. Francesca Alexander, transl. and illustr., and John Ruskin, ed., *Roadside Songs of Tuscany* (Orpington: George Allen, 1885).
41. A. Mary F. Robinson, *The New Arcadia and Other Poems* (London: Ellis and White, 1884).
42. A. Mary F. Robinson, *The Collected Poems Lyrical and Narrative* (London, T. Fisher Unwin, 1902), p. x.
43. Angela Leighton, *On Form: Poetry, Aestheticism, and the Legacy of a Word* (New York: Oxford University Press, 2007), p. 110.
44. Robinson, *Collected Poems*, x.
45. Ibid.
46. Translation from William Aggeler, *The Flowers of Evil* (Fresno, CA: Academy Library Guild, 1954), http://fleursdumal.org/poem/142 (accessed June 28, 2017).
47. See J. G. Fucilla and C. Kleinhenz, "Strambotto," *Princeton Encylcopedia of Poetry and Poetics*, ed. Roland Greene et al., 4th ed. (Princeton: Princeton University Press, 2012), p. 1360.
48. See especially Edmund Gosse, "A Plea for Certain Exotic Forms of Verse," *Cornhill Magazine*, 36 (July 1877), 53–71.
49. Augusta Webster, review of *An Italian Garden: A Book of Songs*, *Athenaeum*, April 17, 1886, 51.

8

KIRSTIE BLAIR

Dialect, Region, Class, Work

In October 1844, the *Northern Star*, Britain's leading Chartist newspaper, printed "The Auld Aik Tree," an unsigned poem by the "Irish girl" reprinted from the Scottish *Ayr Advertiser*. She was "the" (rather than "an") Irish girl because she was already known to readers of both papers. The *Northern Star* had reprinted her verses on the Burns Festival of August 1844, again first published in the *Ayr Advertiser*, and in September featured a column giving readers more information. The "Irish Poetess of Ayr," they were informed, was "poor but virtuous and clever" and in need of charitable assistance; the *Northern Star* had "received through the medium of a friend of the poetess two poetic pieces in manuscript" and printed one of them, "My birth-place is in Erin's isle."[1] The editor was not particularly complimentary about the poetry, which he believed did not deserve "our highest praise," though it did "contain much simple sweetness": "Allowance must be made" for the poet's lack of education, and she was worthy of someone's help. A headnote to "The Auld Aik Tree" just over a month later noted with satisfaction that she had received help from Ayr merchant David Auld and praised Auld for his "patronage and generous aid given to the humble and struggling living."[2]

Though the *Northern Star* either did not note or did not know this in September, "My birth-place is in Erin's isle" was dedicated to Auld. "Lines Most Respectfully Inscribed to David Auld, Esq" recalls the poet's happy pastoral childhood in Newry, County Down, with particular attention to her transformational encounter with Robert Burns's poems:

> And I remember well the first
>   First book of poems I perused,
> Was Burns': and my young heart nurst,
>   The glow of feeling they diffus'd.
> Then would I sit with book in hand
>   And read to my companions young
> With accent of the Scottish land,
>   As that had been my native tongue.

I dream'd not then that e'er my feet
  The very land of Burns should tread
I dream'd not then I e'er should meet
  The offspring of the gracious dead.   (lines 49–60)[3]

The "Irish girl" was twenty-year-old Sarah Parker, though it was more than three years before a poem under her full name rather than pseudonym or initials appeared in the *Northern Star*, and she continued to use this pseudonym throughout her poetic career. Parker worked in domestic service: Florence Boos reports her appeal to the Royal Literary Fund seeking assistance to return to Scotland from London, where she had hoped to find "a situation as companion to a Lady."[4] In later years, her husband, unemployed due to illness, tried to support them by selling Parker's poetry door to door; she died in poverty. This poem to Auld gratefully commemorates a visit from two of Burns's sons, who thanked her for her Burns poem and, more importantly, gave her a cash gift.

Parker's appearance in the *Northern Star* indicates how this radical paper presented one of the comparatively few working-class women poets it printed. The column on the "Irish Poetess of Ayr" appears immediately after an account of William Thom, a working-class weaver poet from Northern Scotland, partly drawn from his autobiography. The editorial motive for discussing these two poets is clear. In the aftermath of the enormous Burns Festival, directed by Lord Eglinton and ostensibly designed to bring the poet's sons and other relatives together in Ayrshire, the *Northern Star* sought to highlight that Scotland's self-reproach for allowing Burns to die in poverty had not translated into support for her living poets. While huge expense and effort were lavished on commemorating Burns, Thom and Parker languished, thus demonstrating the hypocrisy of the wealthy toward the poor. These poets nicely illustrated two recurring themes in the newspaper and wider Chartist discourse: the injustice experienced by the working class and the existence of numerous intelligent, cultured, and ambitious men and women within it.

The two poets, however, are represented very differently. Thom – admittedly a more skilled writer than Parker – is praised as a model for working men: "Wherever a reading club, or working men's society exists, it should be the work of the members to procure as speedily as possible the poems and songs of William Thom."[5] Parker, in contrast, who remains anonymous, is primarily significant for her "virtue" and "cleverness." Her "sweet," simple poems are printed to show that she is worthy of the patronage granted by better-off men. Specifying that her poems were supplied by a friend suggests her modesty as an author (also emphasized in "To David Auld"), implying she did not seek publication. Irish and Scottish nationalism and Burns's radical poetics were of considerable interest to Chartism and Chartist poets in the mid-to-late 1840s, yet there is no sense in editorial comments that Parker, an Irish emigrant poet in Burns's Ayrshire, might speak to these interests or be part of a specifically Chartist poetic tradition.

"Lines Most Respectfully Inscribed to David Auld" is significant, however, when we consider the intersections of regional and linguistic identities and how these play out in Victorian poetry, especially when we assess the modes of publication and self-presentation available to working-class women poets. In Parker's poem, reading Burns in Ulster foreshadows her adoption of Scottish loyalties. Scots is not her "native tongue," but she innately understands and can operate as reader and writer within it. Most of her poems are, however, written in Standard English. In "The Auld Aik Tree," the titular refrain is the only Scots phrase; nor are there linguistic identifiers of Irish or Ulster-Scots speech in her poems. Parker's relationship to Burns's poems is, in some respects, highly cynical. Representing herself as a passionate Burns fan who embodied Burns's continued appeal beyond Scotland successfully brought her publication in Ayr in 1844, patronage by businessmen and newspaper editors, and financial reward. On the other hand, the first encounter with Burns is a foundational scene in numerous radical working men's autobiographies from this period, and Parker makes a bold move in claiming Burns for the woman reader and poet. Her "Irish Girl" persona, preserved through many years in Scotland, is also intriguing. "Girl" was often adopted by women poets in this period, as in Ellen Johnston's "Factory Girl" pseudonym, because it suggests youth, insouciance, and romantic possibilities, and it is less a marker of class status than "lady." By identifying herself as "Irish," Parker connects herself to, and to some extent counteracts, discourses that presented Irish immigrants as uneducated, threatening, and far less respectable than the Scots and English working classes. She produced a very marketable set of poems about nostalgia for her homeland, which hint at economic reasons for emigration without making this explicit, and which appeal to long-standing connections between Ulster and Scotland, particularly in Ulster-Ayrshire cultural and physical links. She doubtless also recognized that her pseudonym could attract a wider readership of Irish emigrants in Scotland, as well as lending her a romantic, youthful tinge.

When reading writers like Parker, we must appreciate that they are shaped by the need to earn money from poetic production if at all possible, by the demands of the marketplace, and by available publishing contexts, which tended to be more restrictive for women poets. By far the most important publishing venue for working-class writers was local or regional newspapers, followed next by periodicals, especially those designed for working-class readerships (including, for instance, *Eliza Cook's Journal*, Cassell's *Working-Man's Friend*, *Ben Brierley's Journal*) and national newspapers for working readers, like the *Northern Star*. Many working-class women poets achieved volume publication because they had formed a productive relationship with the editor of a regional newspaper or periodical, as Parker did with Thomas Gemmell and the *Ayr Advertiser*, who then published a series of their poems in the newspaper and often assisted in printing them in book form. Other better-known examples include Fanny Forrester and *Ben Brierley's Journal*, Ellen Johnston and the *Penny Post*, and Marion Bernstein and the Glasgow *Weekly Mail*. Very few working women from backgrounds like Parker's could have printed books without this assistance.

Despite the outstanding efforts of recovery made by scholars, we still know far fewer British working-class women poets than male poets. This is undoubtedly in large part because women were more likely to have domestic duties or child care in addition to paid employment, leaving them with even less time than working men to read and write. But it is also because newspapers and periodicals were public spaces, in which women who ventured into print exposed themselves to criticism and potentially censure. The condescending attitude of the *Northern Star* toward Parker is typical. Editorial commentary, though it was equally hard on male and female aspiring poets, did tend to signal the poet's gender: so, in the Dundee *People's Journal* correspondents' column, Isa is informed that she "writes well, but we would advise her to give up that nasty scrawling lady's hand, which is, to us at least, a great hindrance to the intelligent reading of her verses"; "The Village Girl" is told "to give her sole attention to reading, writing and spelling until she is a woman, and then we shall be happy to look at her effusions"; and a fifteen-year-old is informed that she is unlikely to be published, but "We would not dissuade her from making farther attempts, since the exercise may prove highly beneficial to her as a mental discipline."[6]

To escape editorial sarcasm and meet recognized standards, much newspaper poetry by working-class women is highly conventional, usually falling into familiar genres of love poem, elegy, pastoral, and poems on family and domestic life. We should not therefore dismiss it: originality was not a meaningful criterion of value for Victorian working-class poets, and an ability to follow conventions should itself be recognized as a deliberate signal of cultural literacy. Yet we should acknowledge that it was harder for women to publish poems on some themes than it was for men. If a working woman wanted to publish, say, a fierce verse indictment of the local town council (not uncommon in Victorian newspapers), it is highly probable that she would do so anonymously or pseudonymously.

What this chapter particularly explores is the intersection among non-Standard English, class, and regional identity in working women's poems, suggesting that they show us the vitality of local voices and the function of poetry in addressing particular communities from within. The importance of "local" verse, ubiquitous in Victorian media in Britain's "four nations" and in every country with an English-language press, is underestimated in studies of Victorian poetry. It is important to recognize and recover this genre in accounts of women's poetry, since women tended to have less independent mobility and personal income than men and could not always choose to live and work close to metropolitan literary circles and publishing houses. Many women participated in poetic cultures that were not city or London based, and in which the "canon" of established women poets was less likely to include a highly educated and sophisticated poet like Christina Rossetti, and more likely to feature Eliza Cook, Frances Brown, Jessie Morton, and other poets who were staples of the provincial press.

Dialect literature, if not the most common mode for women poets, supplies a way to consider how provincial, regional, and local poetic identities were constructed and manipulated. Throughout the Victorian period, male poets from Alfred Tennyson to William Barnes, Edwin Waugh, or even William Butler Yeats adopted Lincolnshire, Dorset, Lancashire, and Irish dialect words and phrasing for both humorous and serious ends. Few women followed their lead. For Irish and Scottish women writers, particularly those active around the turn of the century, poems alluding to or using Irish and Scottish language and legend fed into growing nationalist literary traditions: poets Kathleen Tynan, Florence Wilson, Rachel Annand Taylor, and many others can be situated in relation to the Scottish Renaissance and Celtic Revival. As Catherine Brennan documents, Welsh English-language women poets, including Maria James, Sarah Williams, and Emily Pfeiffer, also reflected significantly on Welsh national identity and on the implications of writing in English (usually, as in Tynan, Wilson, and Taylor, Standard English, with only the occasional Welsh phrase or word) when most people living in Wales spoke only Welsh.[7]

James, for example, one of the earliest of these Welsh poets, and the only one from a working-class background, emigrated to the United States at age seven, at which point she spoke no English. The opening poem of her only collection, "Wales," reflects on her memory of hearing the Bible first "In Cymry's native tongue" (line 54). Immediately succeeded by "Ode: Written for the Fourth of July, 1833," this pairing of poems signifies James's transferral from Wales to America and from Welsh to the "purest English" she claimed to have gained through service in educated households.[8] "Purest" here reflects both on Welsh and

American English, and the assumption that poetry worth publishing will be written in respectable and recognizable English, irrespective of the poet's location and background. Like many emigrant and settler poems of this period, by men and women, James's "Wales" reflects transnational loyalties, including loyalty to literary norms established in England.

For some women writers, dialect writing gained impetus as a result of wider cultural interests in preserving and reviving folk traditions. Mabel Peacock, part of a family of pioneer folk collectors in Lincolnshire, wrote dialect prose and verse to assist efforts to preserve distinctive Lincolnshire speech, especially "women's talk," as did Mrs. G. M. Tweddell in her *Rhymes and Sketches to Illustrate the Cleveland Dialect*.[9] Both writers focus on touching tales, comic and tragic, of rural village life and customs. Tweddell's "T' Yamless Lad," for instance, recounts a familiar moral tale of the childless elderly couple who adopt a homeless orphan who arrived at their door – in a terrible storm, rather predictably – and are rewarded by his or her gratitude and care:

> "Pour bairn! sed Ah, "thou sud gan yam
>   Thou'll git de death te neet;
> It isn't fit for bairns like thou
>   Te be tonnd out i' t' street."
>
> "Ah hev neea yam," he sed to me,
>   "Faythere an' mudher's deead;
> Neeabody cares a bit fer me,
>   An' Ah's foorst te beg me bread." (lines 5–12)[10]

In fact, this clichéd narrative might help the reader understand the unfamiliar dialect terms, such as "yam" for home and "neet" for night, since the direction and details of the story can be easily guessed. Tweddell adopts the persona, very common in dialect verse, of an older, married working-class woman. Her preface, however, explains that this is ventriloquism rather than a representation of her own speech:

> The rules of grammar have not been attended to, as it has been the writer's wish to give the words in the way they would have been spoken by the people who constantly use the dialect. Had any other person in the district been writing in the Cleveland dialect at the present time, the following pieces would not have been published.[11]

Tweddell carefully separates herself from dialect users and reassures readers that she herself understands grammatical conventions. Her collection manifests her pride in local customs and was sponsored by a long list of local subscribers, but she herself expresses some anxiety about publishing non-Standard English.

Perhaps due to fears that dialect writing would make the author seem uneducated or uncouth – particularly among working-class women who wished to display their educational credentials by producing publishable verse – it was very unusual for English working-class women to write dialect poems. Forrester wrote nothing in Lancashire dialect even while she published in one of its primary vehicles, *Ben Brierley's Journal*. Anglo-Irish writer M. R. Lahee (who published as M.R.L.) is, as Taryn Hakala shows, a rare exception to the lack of dialect literature by Lancashire working women, but Lahee published nearly exclusively in prose.[12] No working-class women poets have yet been identified as significant in any English dialect verse tradition. This does not mean that no working-class women dialect poets existed, but that they either published anonymously or still await recovery within local periodical cultures. Many anonymous dialect poems are presented from a woman's perspective, but it is usually difficult to read such poems as "authentic." What should we make, for instance, of a northeast dialect poem like "Hoora! For the strikes," published in the *Alnwick Mercury* in 1872, which is distinctly cynical and anti-strike:

> A' folks gane striking, aw think they're maist mad,
> Ald folks and young folks, and my ain honest lad;
> Wey they tell me they'll get ony money they like
> If they only diven't work, but gan on the strike.
> My sangs! but I think it maun be grand fun;
> They like striking sae weel when they get it begun:
> Wey they gan about drest wi' a' their best claes on,
> And strike till they get what they've set their minds on.

* *

> Then hoora! aw'll strike tee! aw'm a stoot ranting hussy,
> Aw can dee ought or nought and always be busy
> Aw carena if only aw get plenty of money,
> Aw'll dress like my leddy and gan off wi' my mannie.[13]

The poem is unsigned and fits a satirical newspaper poetry tradition in which an ignorant working-class woman, young or old (often a maidservant, as here), reflects on a wider political situation from a personal, self-centered perspective, which then highlights misguided or hypocritical actions and beliefs of working men. Here, the point is that the speaker's reductive view of the strikers' rationale is actually correct. For this unidentified author, the strike is simply about greed. It is highly unlikely that a working-class woman poet would refer to herself as a "stoot ranting hussy." This and similar poems help explain why working-class English women poets may have viewed dialect writing as problematic, since they risked locating themselves in a tradition in which male poets, in female-voiced poems, either represented women as comic figures (as in Tennyson's "The Spinster's Sweet-Arts") or paragons of sentimental domesticity (as in Waugh's "Come Whoam to thi Childer an Me").

If this was so in England, it was emphatically not the case in Scotland, and to a lesser degree in Ulster (which had a small group of Ulster-Scots women poets, especially late in the period) and Ireland. Scotland is the principal focus of this chapter because it provides such rich sources for working-class women's poetics and Scots poetry and boasted the two working-class women writers now most anthologized and discussed, Ellen Johnston and Janet Hamilton. In Boos's seminal anthology cited earlier, more poets are included from Glasgow than from all of southern and central England. Among factors that might account for this are the presence in Scotland of particularly strong, highly respected oral cultures of song and recitation in which women had always participated and Scotland's greater opportunities for female education (especially prior to England's 1870 Education Act) due to a system of affordable parish schooling for both boys and girls. Most significantly, the enormously popular novels of Sir Walter Scott and the still more popular poems of Burns had ensured that Scots had a status in "literary" culture that English dialect did not. Whether or not accurate, Victorian Scottish commentators invariably represented Scotland, post-Burns, as unique in its encouragement of working-class writers – "the Peasant Poetic Queen of Nations," as poet Henry Shanks put it – creating a self-fulfilling prophecy in that this national self-image inspired Scottish working-class men and women to try their hand at verse.[14] Scottish working-class women poets are thus the primary female contributors to a tradition of non-Standard English. Scotland of course also supplied major Gaelic poets: though Gaelic literature is beyond this chapter's scope, the working-class Gaelic poet Mary MacPherson (Màiri Nighean Iain Bhàin/Màiri Mhòr nan Oran), "Big Mary of the Songs," is one of the most important and politically active Victorian women poets.[15]

The use of Scots by women poets parallels its use by male poets. It often signals an appeal to a shared regional or national identity, a sense of local pride and community. It is particularly likely to feature in satirical and political poems (again following Burns's example), humorous poems, poems on domesticity, and love poems drawing on ballad and song traditions. Dialect poetry is also strongly associated with a pose of plain-speaking honesty, even on delicate topics. In 1865, for instance, Johnston decided to intervene in a reported local scandal through a newspaper poem. According to "The Lasses of Lochend" in Glasgow's *Penny Post* in March 1865, a newborn had been found drowned in Loch Ness; in response, the authorities required that all local women in the small town of Lochend undergo medical inspection to check if they had recently given birth.[16] The poets of the *Penny Post* were divided over how to treat this incident. Johnston's poem is strongly critical of a fellow-writer whose "doggrel rhyme," published previously in the newspaper's poetry column, had been, in her view, "biggot'd" against the women of Lochend.[17] Pointedly titling her riposte (under her early pseudonym "Nelly") "The Maidens of Lochend," she opened:

> Mony a time I ha'e heard tell,
> O' maidens that frae virtue fell,
> But never since my name was Nell
>   Did I hear penn'd
> A tale that did for shame excel
>   That o' Lochend.
>
> I've been in France, I've been in Spain,
> In London toon, that bears sic fame,
> And on my honour I'll maintain,
>   Through a' their strife,
> I ne'er heard sic a scand'lous shame
>   In a' my life.   (lines 1–12)[18]

This is in habbie stanzas (aaabab, where the "a" lines are four-beat and the "b" lines two), an older form popularized by Burns and particularly used by Scottish poets writing on political and social issues. Johnston moved fluently between Scots and Standard English, and her choice of Scots here, plus her most informal pseudonym (she also used "E. J.," "Ellen Johnston," and "The Factory Girl") signals that she is, like the threatened women, a Scottish maiden. Her argument is that any shame or scandal associated with an illegitimate child is dwarfed by the scandal of forcing women to submit to intimate inspection against their will. Whether Johnston might have in mind the Contagious Diseases Acts, also to become notorious for subjecting working-class women to forcible medical inspection, is uncertain: the first act was passed in 1864, but opposition from women did not spread extensively until later in the decade. Johnston had never visited France, Spain, or London. The listing of destinations that compare favorably or unfavorably with something happening in the speaker's location is a staple of broadside verse and popular song, an accepted poetic exaggeration rather than authentic fact. As readers would later discover from Johnston's autobiography, she had an illegitimate child herself and was not inclined to adopt standard attitudes of horror toward fallen women, but readers of

"The Maidens of Lochend" did not have this knowledge. What they would see is a Scottish woman factory worker, since Nelly's signature includes the location "Chapelshade Factory, Dundee," standing up for women who were being badly treated by male authorities and by male poets, and representing herself as one of them.

From a different perspective, though also on the topic of fallen women, the Dundee *People's Journal* of 1886 published "Out of the Depths" by Georgina Courtenay, whose given address was a rehabilitation or "Magdalen" home, "The Home, Paton's Lane, Dundee." This poem was republished as a broadside and probably distributed for free, which strongly suggests it was authored, whether or not by a "real" fallen woman, as an advertisement for "The Home" and its Christian mission. The poem opens:

> I want to write a line or twa to some lassies that I ken,
> Ye'll oblige me, Mr Editor, if a corner ye can len'
> O' yer paper, for I'm thinkin' when I lie doon ilka nicht
> If I could only say a word to gar them do what's richt.
>
> A word to them wha, like mysel', hae dune sae very wrang,
> An' feel they'll never do what's richt, they hae been bad sae lang.
> An' winna gie themsel's a change, nor ony time to think,
> But try to droon the "wee still voice" in anither spate o' drink.

(lines 1–8)[19]

The use of Scots, epistle verse format, and the author's implication that she knows the audience she addresses render the poem informal, conversational, and persuasive – even colloquially translating the King James Bible's "still small voice" into a "wee still voice." This makes it far more effective propaganda for the Home's reforming mission to help working women escape alcoholism and prostitution than an exhortation in Standard English addressed "from above" to fallen women. Although the first five verses call women to repentance, the poem takes a more radical turn in its sixth stanza:

> Weel, maybe I am far frae richt, but this indeed I ken –
> They ca' us fallen women – there's nae word o' fallen men;
> Yet *they* were those wha temptit us an' robbed us o' oor fame,
> An' helpit us to lead a life o' infamy an' shame.

This is not an atypical sentiment, given the growing women's movement in the 1880s around the issue of sexual double standards for men and women, but it is pithily and strongly expressed. The poem also ends by telling repentant women not to be ashamed if people remind them of their past, because "Christ sympathises wi' yer griefs, for He has felt the same," a potent comparison between Christ and the fallen woman.

For Johnston and Courtenay, positioning themselves as part of a Scots-speaking community shows that they are members of the group of women they discuss, and thus entitled to speak for and about them. Scots signified a *local* perspective, which could be leveraged by working-class women to enable more distinctive and assertive poetry than is necessarily found in their Standard English works. Speaking for and from their community gave working-class women writers a viable poetic identity and the potential for a public voice. For a poet like domestic servant Tina Galbraith of Airdrie in Lanarkshire, for instance, about whom we know very little, the defense of her neighborhood became a means to participate in newspaper debates: "she was ever jealous of Airdrie's good name, and never lost the opportunity of castigating those 'Wha' daured meddle wi' her.'"[20] When a Sheriff Mair described Airdrie as "the most benighted town in Scotland," "Tina" wrote to the papers in verse to express her indignation and support for "her" town:

> I will you back through thick or thin,
> It may be even to a sin;
> I hate to hear the like o' him
>   Misca'in' you;
> It is like middlin' kith and kin,
>   And country too.
>
> Altho' I whiles misca' you sare
> For morals or polluted air,
> I'm like a mither: none else dare
>   To thro' a blame;
> And so I'll no' let Sheriff Mair
>   Spread your ill name.[21]

Speaking on behalf of her town meant that Galbraith could assert her views in opposition to a male authority figure. In the small selection of her poems that are anthologized, she seems to have consistently presented herself via this "motherly" persona as a long-term local resident who had gained the right to speak her mind, and who was a staunch believer in the values of home and domesticity. Whether this genuinely reflects her poetic output, as opposed to the bias of the anthologizer James Knox, is unclear. Knox cites a letter he received about "Tina" stating, "Her output of poems must have been enormous as most of her correspondence was conducted in verse. Unfortunately very few copies have been kept, so most of her works are probably lost," which serves to show the ephemerality of much verse by working women.[22]

Galbraith lived in the same area and published in the same period and with a similar persona as did Janet Hamilton. Hamilton was well known in her time and is an important figure for scholars of working-class poetics today. For Victorian critics and commentators, she was an attractive example of the Scottish working class because of her devotion to the cause of temperance (vital for working-class poets since Scottish newspapers were very pro-temperance and welcomed verse on the evils of drink), her history as a hardworking wife and mother, and her status as a beacon of self-improvement and good moral character despite becoming disabled by blindness. She had pursued her love of reading throughout her working life and taught herself to write in old age. Most of her poems were dictated to her son James, who emphasized her desire that they should be useful to "some of her class in a social, moral, and spiritual sense."[23] It also helped that she was from the "rough and fiery" region of Coatbridge in industrialized Lanarkshire, known for its ironworks, collieries, pollution, noise, and sense of lawlessness.[24] Hamilton was a model, upstanding Lanarkshire citizen and a living link, as she herself highlighted repeatedly, between Lanarkshire's rural past and industrial present. Her age and blameless life meant that she could be celebrated without reservation, in contrast to a poet like Johnston, whose youth and checkered family and romantic history, as well as her factory labor outside the home, rendered her suspect.

For twentieth- and twenty-first-century critics of Victorian poetry, Hamilton is important because, despite her often conservative attitudes toward women's position within society, she was a champion of radical causes and wrote trenchantly about the realities of industrial Scotland. As I have discussed elsewhere, the majority of her poems are in Standard English and proudly display a high level of allusiveness and literary knowledge, but it is those written in Scots that have been most anthologized, and which tend to adopt the most outspoken positions on current affairs.[25] Several poems offer passionate defenses of Scottish culture and language. "Auld Mither Scotland" opens with very standard statements of love for the Scottish people and landscape, but the third stanza turns to an attack on England's cultural and political dominance:

> Nae, mither! nae; we maunna pairt!
>   E'en tho' they say thou's deein';
> That speech is gaun, they say thy face
>   We'll sune nae mair be seein'.
> But oh! I fear the Doric's gaun,
>   For, mang baith auld an' young,
> There's many noo that canna read
>   Their printit mither tongue.

> I like the English tongue fu' well
>   In writin' an' in readin'
> But 'tween the English an' the Scotch
>   There's lack o' truth an' breedin'
> It's England's meteor flag that burns
>   Abune oor battle plains;
> Oor victories, baith by sea an' lan',
>   It's England aye that gains.   (lines 17–32)[26]

The poem has a specific religious grievance, as later verses outline, against the "English" introduction of organs into Presbyterian churches, of which Hamilton strongly disapproves. It also probably references, in lines 25–32, a felt perception that Scottish regiments were not given full credit for their bravery in British overseas campaigns. In the better-known "A Plea for the Doric," Hamilton highlights the tendency of Scotland's (male) writers to move south to London, "I'm wae for Auld Reekie; her big men o' print /To Lunnon ha'e gane, to be nearer the mint" (lines 29–30), meaning that Scots is abandoned.[27] In contrast, she implicitly argues, she is part of a local literary tradition rooted in provincial Scotland, which seeks to preserve the speech of William Wallace, the Covenanter martyrs, and Burns. Although Hamilton was not a Scottish nationalist in the sense of advocating separation from England, her poems show a strong sense of a Scottish national identity under threat from English literature as well as English politics and religion.

In her own location, the subject of her most anthologized poem, "Oor Location," Hamilton would have been well aware of Scotland's increasing diversity and international connections: Lanarkshire was home not simply to large numbers of English and Irish Catholic immigrants (Coatbridge was the scene of sectarian riots during Hamilton's lifetime), but also to Polish miners and other workers from Europe and farther afield. She herself wrote extensively on European and international political causes. Much of her work reflects on the coming of "modernity," as in "Rhymes for the Times IV – 1865," published in the *Airdrie Advertiser*, a poem in a newspaper subgenre of December verses reflecting on the year gone by:

> Juist noo there are mony wha rin to an' fro,
> An' knowledge increases, abune an' below;
> The yird's like a riddle, pits, tunnels, an' bores,
> Whaur bodies, like mowdies, by hunners an' scores
> Are houkin', an' holin', an' blastin' the rocks;
> An' droonin's an' burnin's, explosions an' shocks,
> An' a' ither meagries, amang us are rife;
> Oh, mony's the slain in the battle o' life!
> It's Mammon we worship, wi' graspin' an' greed,

Wi' sailin' an railin' at telegraph speed,
Get gowd oot the ironstane, an' siller frae coal,
An' thoosan's on thoosan's draw oot o' ae hole.
Wi' oil shale aneath us, an' fire-warks abune,
I think we'll tak' lowe, an' bleeze up to the mune.[28]

Hamilton's Scots gives a sense of the energy devoted to Lanarkshire industry, with her driving couplets and long sentences representing the rapidity and mobility she describes. She gives a sense of the literal instability of her location, as it is mined below and developed above ground, changing beyond recognition. The language in these Lanarkshire poems might be read as Hamilton's defiant use of Scots in the face of new developments encroaching around her, yet her Scots also seems to fit graphic descriptions of physical labor: if dialect is crude, then it suits poems about work.

What such dialect poems show us are some reasons why women poets chose to code-switch between Standard and non-Standard English according to the suitability of theme, intended audience, and publication venue. It is clear that this was a choice. In another poem to a patron, by the late Victorian and early-twentieth-century poet Isa Forrest of Keith (in Moray, in northeast Scotland), Forrest uses the switch mid-poem to signal her varied capacities. Telling her addressee about her poetic ambitions, she writes:

I do not covet ermine robe,
　　Nor seat in gilded ha',
An honest, independent mind
　　I coont afore them a'.

As Hogg and Burns hae tuned their lyre
　　In mony a homely lay,
To heights like these my thoughts aspire,
　　They bloom but to decay.

But why should I to heights aspire
　　That never can be mine?
Or why vain hopes my bosom fire,
　　Then leave me to repine?

Poor and obscure, I must endure
　　The pinch of want and woe,
While fate denies to me the gifts
　　She does on some bestow.[29]

This self-deprecating stance about the difficulty of writing as an uneducated poet is very common throughout working-class poetry. What stands out in Forrest's poem is the change from Scots to English. Scots in the first six stanzas of the poem shows an allegiance to working-class Scots verse, especially Burns and his assertions of pride and independence despite poverty. The Standard English beginning on "To heights like these my thoughts aspire," in contrast, highlights that Forrest is not uneducated, and that she understands the language and conventions of English poetry. Her volume, particularly in two striking poems on mutual improvement dedicated to the teacher of her "continuation" (adult education) classes, emphasizes the importance of both poetry and education for "poor and obscure" women.

Forrest is an example of a poet who has never been anthologized or discussed in twentieth- or twenty-first-century criticism. Although she identifies herself as working-class in her poems, there is nothing to signal to a researcher that her volume is a significant addition to our knowledge of working-class women's literature. Without the personal history passed down via her descendants in Australia, Forrest could only have been tentatively identified via detailed, time-consuming, and speculative research into the surviving editions of the *Banffshire Journal*, her publisher, and other local newspapers.[30] There are unquestionably many more women poets like her, whose fame was purely local. Whether retrieving their works from the archives will change our views of Victorian women's poetry is doubtful, since all these writers consciously aimed to meet the standards and conventions expected from women poets; thus, their poems are likely to seem familiar rather than novel. Yet such writers should help us perceive that there were rich, diverse regional and local verse cultures for British women poets, operating outside known literary establishments and London-centric poetic society, deploying different versions of English, and enabling women with little formal education to participate in literary communities that shaped readers' everyday experience of Victorian poetics.

Notes

1. "The Irish Poetess of Ayr," *Northern Star*, September 14, 1844, 3. See Parker's *Northern Star* contributions in Appendix B, Michael Sanders, *The Poetry of Chartism: Aesthetics, Politics, History* (Cambridge: Cambridge University Press, 2009), pp. 230–85.
2. "The Auld Aik Tree," *Northern Star*, October 26, 1844, 3.
3. Sarah Parker, *Miscellaneous Poems* (Glasgow: Bowie & Glen, 1856), p. 80.
4. Florence S. Boos, ed., *Working-Class Women Poets in Victorian Britain: An Anthology* (Peterborough, ON: Broadview, 2008), p. 33.
5. "William Thom, the Poet of Inverury," *Northern Star*, September 14, 1844, 3.
6. "To Correspondents," *People's Journal*, March 1, 1862, 2; October 31, 1865, 2; February 13, 1864, 2.

7. Catherine Brennan, *Angers, Fantasies and Ghostly Fears: Nineteenth-Century Women from Wales and English-Language Poetry* (Cardiff: University of Wales Press, 2003), p. 5 and passim.

8. Maria James, *Wales, and Other Poems*, intro. A. Potter (New York: John S. Taylor, 1839), pp. 49, 36.

9. *The Peacock Lincolnshire Word Books 1884–1920*, ed. Eileen Elder (Scunthorpe: Scunthorpe Museum Society, 1997), p. 11; Mrs. G. M. Tweddell [Florence Cleveland], *Rhymes and Sketches to Illustrate the Cleveland Dialect* (Stokesley: Tweddell and Sons, 1875).

10. Tweddell, *Rhymes and Sketches*, p. 15.

11. Ibid., Preface, n.p.

12. Taryn Hakala, "M. R. Lahee and the Lancashire Lads: Gender and Class in Victorian Lancashire Dialect Writing," *Philological Quarterly* 92.2 (2013), 272.

13. "Hoora! For the Strike," "Original Poetry," *Alnwick Mercury*, September 7, 1872, 2.

14. Henry Shanks, *The Peasant Poets of Scotland and Musings Under the Beeches* (Bathgate: Gilbertson, 1881), p. 167.

15. See Donald E. Meek, *Tuath Is Tighearna/Tenants and Landlords: An Anthology of Gaelic Poetry of Social and Political Protest from the Clearances to the Land Agitation (1800–1890)* (Edinburgh: Scottish Gaelic Texts Society, 1995).

16. "The Lasses of Lochend," *Penny Post*, March 11, 1865, 1.

17. Donald McPherson, untitled extract, "To Correspondents," *Penny Post*, April 1, 1865, 4.

18. "The Maidens O' Lochend," "To Correspondents," *Penny Post*, April 15, 1865, 4.

19. Georgina Courtenay, "Out of the Depths." Broadside. Dundee Central Library, Lamb Collection 125.14; *People's Journal*, November 27, 1886, 2.

20. James Knox, *Airdrie Bards, Past and Present* (Airdrie: Baird and Hamilton, 1930), p. 232.

21. Reprinted in Knox, pp. 232–3.

22. Letter from Fergus B. Graham, cited in Knox, p. 234.

23. Preface to *Janet Hamilton, Poems, Sketches and Essays* (Glasgow: James Maclehose, 1885), p. vii.

24. Alexander Wallace, "Janet Hamilton," *Poems, Sketches*, p. 15.

25. Kirstie Blair, "'He Sings Alone': Hybrid Forms and the Victorian Working-Class Poet," *Victorian Literature and Culture* 37 (2009): 523–41.

26. Hamilton, *Poems, Sketches*, p. 144.

27. Ibid., p. 162.

28. Ibid., p. 225.

29. Isa. [Isabella] Forrest, "Respectfully Dedicated to Mr Watt, Solicitor, Gowanpark, Banff," *Islaside Musings* (Banff: Banffshire Journal, n.d. [1926]), p. 14.

30. I am grateful to the poet's great-granddaughter Katrina Giebels in Australia for alerting me to Forrest's history.

9

MARJORIE STONE

Politics, Protest, Interventions
Beyond a Poetess Tradition

"Poor little FACTORY SLAVES – for YOU these lines complain!"[1] In her anonymously published *A Voice from the Factories: In Serious Verse* (1836), Caroline Sheridan Norton boldly intervened in Parliamentary debates on child labor. Addressing Lord Ashley in her "Preface," she explained her desire "to *join* my voice to that of wiser and better men," along with her choice of form: "as poetry is the language of feeling, it should be the language of the multitude." While Norton's Spenserian stanzas are not written in the multitude's "language," she does skillfully employ poetry to convey the sensations of factory children as they toil

> [w]here the air thick and close and stagnant grows,
> And the low whirring of the incessant wheel
> Dizzies the head, and makes the senses reel:
> There, shut for ever from the gladdening sky,
> Vice premature and Care's corroding seal
> Stamp on each sallow cheek their hateful die,
> Line the smooth open brow, and sink the saddened eye. (Stanza 10)

Norton evokes the suffocating air and unremitting factory noise through clotting consonants ("thick and close and stagnant"), throat-constricting vowels ("low whirring"), the hissing of the "incessant wheel," and the sonic circling of "wheel" back to "whirring" and the rhyme of "reel." Other industrial metaphors ("corroding seal[s]," the dies of the tool and die industry) convey the premature age "stamp[ed]" on the bodies of the child laborers, even as the falling cadences of the closing alexandrine underscore their annihilated humanity – "sink the saddened eye."

Norton's *A Voice from the Factories* not only mobilizes multiple motifs pervading Victorian factory poems; it also exemplifies patterns and paradoxes in interventions by women poets through the century in various causes and controversies. Dominant concerns shifted from factory reform, class divisions, slavery, and the "Irish question" in the 1830s and 1840s, to the "woman question" and war debates (Italian liberation, the Crimean War) at mid-century, then to additional women's causes (prostitution laws, suffrage), socialism, and anti-vivisection, among other issues. If the causes engaging women poets shifted, however, they were also intricately interwoven: in part because many women poets were involved in multiple movements, simultaneously or successively, in part because these movements were animated by shared or sometimes conflicting discourses of rights or "liberty."[2] Mary Howitt, for example, worked at the nexus of working-class and abolitionist activism in the 1840s: writing poems on child labor, collaborating with her husband William in editing journals for the people, and hosting the American fugitive slave Frederick Douglass during his 1845–6 British speaking tour. Howitt also advocated for Catholic religious rights and, after mid-century, for women's rights and animal rights. Norton's *A Voice from the Factories* reflects the intersecting causes common in protest poetry by comparing child factory labor to slavery (abolished in British colonies in 1833) and to exploited child actors, Italian street boys, and chimney sweeps (St. 3, 8, 10). In denouncing "men" in the "British Senate" for defending "the unalienable RIGHT OF GAIN" and blaspheming British "Freedom" (St. 17–19), Norton furthermore connects factory reform to European political reform, presenting Britain as a "refuge" for "the melancholy sons of Spain" and the "Enthusiast Pole!" dreaming of "Liberty" (St. 25).

Like numerous works by Victorian women poets, *A Voice from the Factories* is contradictory in its Anglocentrism and problematic in its class and race politics. Thus Norton ironizes "'[t]he happy homes of England!'" (St. 32) saluted by Felicia Hemans;[3] yet her own presentation of the idyllic father-centered family that factory children lack overshadows the labor conditions she critiques, just as apostrophizing Britain's "glorious Past" (St. 24) distracts the reader from its industrial present. Alluding to Britain lifting "the curse from SLAVERY'S dark domain," Norton asks, "What is it to be a slave?" (St. 17–18); however, like other white Victorian writers, she ignores the racial and legal underpinnings of chattel slavery. Nor, despite her title, does Norton present an actual voice "from" a factory worker, even though there were "large-scale demonstrations of factory children" featuring "texts of children's addresses."[4] Instead, she focuses on child laborers as pitiable spectacles, like the "pale Orphan" among "half-seen objects" with "its hot, trembling, languid little hands" (St. 46). She also alternates between pity and warning that "[u]ntaught, unchecked," such children "yield as vice invites" (St. 14), describing "each visage wan, and bold, and base" (St. 45). Her "Preface" to Lord Ashley reveals her reliance on aristocratic structures of patronage to promote social change. At the same time, her own position was complicated by her gender and the fact that, like Letitia Landon (L.E.L.),

146

who in "The Factory" (1835) similarly protested the "low appalling cry" of children destined to "sicken and to die," Norton wrote in part to support herself.

The contradictions in *A Voice from the Factories* are illumined by the paradoxes Tricia Lootens and others explore in the growing body of "poetess" scholarship.[5] This work has investigated the complexities of a figure who is "less a heroine than a heritage," in Lootens's words: generically female yet also normatively white; private yet performative and often political; lyrical yet highly rhetorical; a vessel of nationalist ideologies yet also, as Alison Chapman argues, an agent with transnational "mobility."[6] While poetess studies enhance understanding of aspects of Victorian women's protest poetry, they risk obscuring others, including the cross-gender alliances often integral to advancing political causes. The poetess model also fits some works and poets better than others: Norton's "The Picture of Sappho," for instance, rather than *A Voice from the Factories*, and Hemans and L.E.L. rather than Elizabeth Barrett Browning (EBB), Augusta Webster, Mathilde Blind, or Eliza Cook and working-class women poets more generally. The focus in poetess studies on lyric expressive forms and "representing public concerns as if they were private"[7] does not capture the generic hybridity and polemicism of *A Voice from the Factories*. Albeit under a male mask, Norton addresses public suffering and debates in "the British Senate" (St. 16), dramatically portrays arguments in defense of child labor ("'T is their parents' choice'"), and joins her "voice" to less radical parties refuting them ("We grant their class must labor ... Not against TOIL, but TOIL'S EXCESS we pray," St. 20–1). As for the "class" that "must labour," Florence Boos demonstrates that a Sapphic poetess tradition is less important to most working-class poets than bardic and oral traditions – as in Ellen Johnston's "The Last Sark" (1859), a monologue in Scottish dialect by a starving mother grieving her dead "bairn."[8]

Women poets across classes employ diverse genres in their political interventions – ballads, dramatic monologues, elegies, odes, satire, meditation, reportage, polemic, and prophecy; they also hybridize genres in innovative ways. One feature cutting across genres is the emphasis on voice and being heard: "My Lord, I confess myself anxious to be *heard*," Norton states in her "Preface." Another is the use of dramatic speakers, both incorporated in various genres and in dramatic monologues that focus as much on political or social critique as on character revelation, as in EBB's "The Runaway Slave at Pilgrim's Point." Indeed, protest poems teem with diverse speech acts, as EBB's poem suggests through its address to the Pilgrim fathers ("I speak to you!," line 8), multiple curses, and a call for a slave insurrection ("lift your hands, / O slaves ... !" (lines 230–1)).[9] Speech acts similarly pervade the titles of political poems. The "cry" – with its range of meanings from lament to outcry to indictment – is especially frequent, most famously in "The Cry of the Children," but also in works like Mary Howitt's "The Cry of the Animals" ("They brand us, and they beat us") and Henrietta Tindall's "The Cry of the Oppressed."[10] Grace Aguilar chooses the polemical appeal in "The Hebrew's Appeal": protesting an 1843 decree by the Russian czar resettling Jews ("thousands are cast out, to exile and to death"), Aguilar urges English readers to hear "the voice of suff'ring."[11] Perhaps most ubiquitous is the "song": more often a communal song or ballad of protest or testimony than the lyrical gush and "musical chord" of an affective "expressive aesthetic" that Isobel Armstrong subtly delineates in a female tradition more aligned with poetess conventions.[12]

Eliza Cook (see Chapter 6 in this volume) produced one of the largest number of political "songs" in Victorian women's poetry. Works such as "A Song for the Workers," "A Song for the Ragged Schools," and "Song of the City Artisan," written in the voice of a male worker, helped to make Cook's name "as popular in America, India, and Australia" as in the "industrial districts of England," according to the *Illustrated News* in 1871.[13] Cook's "A Song: To 'The People' of England" supports the third Chartist petition and mobilization of 1848, the year when revolutions shook Europe. "Ye shall soon have wider Charters! / England hears the startling cry," Cook writes, alluding to the Chartist demand for universal male suffrage and urging readers to "[m]eet Oppression ... [n]ot with weapons red and reeking" or "Anarchy's wild flame," but through "open speaking / In 'The People's' Mighty Name.'"[14] The same year, in *Letters to the Mob* published under the pen name "Libertas" in the *Morning Chronicle,* Norton denounced the Chartist "dream of equality," linking Chartists to Irish repealers and a mob crying, "'We want Liberty! Equality! Fraternity!'"[15] Cook's class identity was complicated by her upward mobility, however. On the one hand, an 1866 article on "The Factory Poetess" Ruth Wills in *The Working Man* groups her with EBB as "female votaries of the Muse" and then asks, "where are our working women singers?"[16] On the other hand, both EBB and Christina Rossetti distanced themselves from Cook in class-based terms: EBB noted Cook's *"talent"* in "putting verses together," joking about her name as *Punch* did (see Chapter 6), while Rossetti joked with her brother William Michael Rossetti that "he should just call her 'Eliza Cook' if he thought her verses were quite that bad."[17]

Nevertheless, as a more outspoken poet than Rossetti, EBB uses the polemical "song" for political purposes as Cook does, though with more force and literary allusion. Thus in "A Song for the Ragged Schools of London" (1854), EBB invokes Percy Bysshe Shelley's political ballads, most notably "The Masque of Anarchy." "As I lay asleep in Rome," Shelley begins. EBB opens with the more assertive, "I am listening here in Rome"; satirizes "speakers" vaunting England's "empire" (line 25); and tells her English readers you "have ruins worse than Rome's / In your pauper men and women":

> Women leering through the gas
> (Just such bosoms used to nurse you),
> Men, turned wolves by famine – pass!
> Those can speak themselves, and curse you.
>
> But these others – children small,
> Spilt like blots about the city,
> Quay, and street, and palace-wall –
> Take them up into your pity! (lines 39–48)[18]

Influenced by the work of EBB's sister Arabella Moulton-Barrett with street girls, the poem portrays these city "blots" with more variegation (lines 49–75) than Norton portrays factory children, and with a realism anticipating Blind's socialist depiction of "[c]hildren mothered by the street" in "The Street-Children's Dance" (1881).[19]

EBB's earlier appeal for "pity" on behalf of children in factories and mines in "The Cry of the Children" (1843) stood in for Victorian women's political poetry generally through the twentieth century, when the poem epitomized the view – expressed even by Angela Leighton in 1995 – that such "protest poems" were written in a "compulsively sentimental style."[20] Elsewhere, Leighton terms "The Cry of the Children" "propagandistically tear-jerking," despite incisively analyzing its anatomy of patriarchal systems and contrasting it with the pious conclusion of Cook's "Our Father" (1849), which also echoes the 1843 Royal Commission reports.[21] Critics have since reframed the "sentimentality" of "The Cry of the Children" as allusive artistry (Peaches Henry) and analyzed its strategic disruption of social formations and metrical conventions (Caroline Levine, Herbert Tucker).[22] Like Norton, EBB employs the motif of dizzying wheels, but Stanza 7 of her poem with its turning trochaics ("Turns the sky ... Turns the long light ... Turn the black flies") captures the mechanical rhythm of the Commission reports – as in the Eliza Field deposition, "*Wórks* at pressing washers; *wórks* with an iron machine."[23] EBB's public cry to "brothers" in industry, government, church, and her own family (see later) to "hear" the children "weeping" also contrasts with Norton's anonymous publication and male impersonation in *A Voice from the Factories*. EBB's unpublished fragment "My sisters!" – drafted in the same notebook as "The Cry of the Children" and more in a poetess vein – reveals the struggle she experienced in boldly speaking out to men in the political sphere. In the fragment, addressed to "Daughters of this Fatherland," she implores her "sisters": "Do confirm my voice – lest it speak in vain."[24]

"The Cry of the Children" gathers power from dramatizing the collective voice of the children to explore the psychological effects of industrial systems – as Norton does not do, but William Blake does. Blakean echoes are particularly evident in the children's story of envying "little Alice" asleep in "the pit" in death (St. 4), reminiscent of little Tom Dacre in the first "Chimney Sweeper" lyric in *Songs of Innocence and Experience,* among works EBB transcribed in 1842.[25] In "The Dying Child" (1846), Mary Howitt similarly dramatizes the psychology of an exploited child by adapting Hans Christian Andersen's monologue of the same title, depicting a generic child addressing his mother and "kissed" at the close by an angel with "white wings." Howitt makes the child a millworker grappling with "thoughts, like spectres" in a double-voiced poem haunted by the voice of the "unseen Angel of Death." Although the Angel releases this "slave of hunger, want, and cold" into "bliss," its menacing approach dominates the poem, reinforced by unrelenting rhyme:

> It is my voice within that calls;
> It is my shadow, child, that falls
> Upon thy spirit, and appals,
> That hems thee in like dungeon walls.[26]

The "hunger" enslaving this child is another frequent theme in women's political poetry, especially in the "hungry forties," when the Corn Laws raised the price of bread, and when, in Ireland, there was apocalyptic famine. A passage EBB added to "The Cry of the Human" (1842) in revising it for *Poems* (1844) critiques the Corn Laws:

> The rich preach 'rights' and future days,
>   And hear no angel scoffing, –
> The poor die mute – with starving gaze
>   On corn-ships in the offing.   (lines 50–3)

This passage probably contributed to the request EBB received in January 1845 from the Leeds' Ladies Committee of the Anti-Corn Law League for a poem raising money for the cause. Describing herself to Mary Russell Mitford as a free-trade woman, "leagues before" the rest of her family "in essential radicalism," EBB was keen to write "an agricultural-evil poem" to complete her "Factory-evil poem into a national evil-circle." However, her father and brothers shouted down the idea that "a woman's verses" could do any good.[27] In any event, the Corn Laws were repealed in

1846. The causes of the Irish famine precipitated the same year by the potato blight were more systemic and devastating, like the epidemics that followed in 1845–9. The 1851 census, compiled by William Wilde, the man Jane Francesca Wilde or "Speranza" married the same year, documented an "'excess mortality'" of more than a million, with two million more estimated to have left the country in "coffin ships."[28]

Lady Wilde's "The Famine Year," published in *The Nation* as "The Stricken Year" (1847), echoes EBB's critique of the Corn Laws in "The Cry of the Human" while also indicting the colonial structures compounding the famine, "Weary men, what reap ye?" Wilde asks and answers, "Golden corn for the stranger . . . Fainting forms, hunger-stricken, what see you in the offing? / Stately ships to bear our food away, amid the stranger's scoffing" (lines 1–4).[29] In "The Exodus" (1864), Wilde takes retrospective toll of the colossal human and national losses:

> "A million a decade!" – of human wrecks,
>   Corpses lying in fever sheds –
> Corpses huddled on foundering decks
>   And shroudless dead on their rocky beds;
>   Nerve and muscle, and heart and brain,
>   Lost to Ireland – lost in vain.   (lines 7–12)[30]

Fannie Forrester, the working-class daughter of Irish immigrants, further testifies to the reverberating effects of the famine in "The Poor Man's Darling. A Tale of Hard Times" (1870), a dramatic monologue in which the Irish speaker laments his daughter's death from starvation.[31] Poets of Irish origins aside, however, many Victorian women poets expressed little awareness of the Irish "holocaust"[32] or of the racist Irish stereotypes that creep into even works for children like Menella Bute Smedley's (1820–77) "The Irish Fairy" (1869), in which the fairy "liked . . . an Irish pig / And just a dhrop of whiskey" and "had no call to work."[33] Other poets contested such attitudes, as Emily Hickey does in *Michael Villiers, Idealist* (1891) by portraying Villiers, a socialist and supporter of Home Rule, debating a college friend who dismisses the Irish as "dirty, lazy priest-rid loons."[34]

The Irish famine was also eclipsed in England by revolutionary convulsion throughout Europe in 1848–9, especially the Italian liberation movement that deeply engaged EBB and other expatriate English and American women discussed in Alison Chapman's *Networking the Nation*. EBB's *Casa Guidi Windows* (1851) addresses or elegizes principal agents in the *Risorgimento*, most notably, its charismatic theorist Guiseppe Mazzini, the "most influential revolutionary in Europe."[35] In three apostrophes, EBB invokes Mazzini as a potential leader of a liberated Italy but also cautions him to avoid terrorist assassination (2.441–5, 526–36, 566–73). These apostrophes, like her calls for "lands of Europe" (1.1104) to advance Italian liberty, are acts of cultural diplomacy in a poem that began as a "meditation" on Tuscan politics and expanded into a generically hybrid work (in a semi-Italian verse form) mixing history, satire, religion, reportage, prophecy, and politics. Within England, too, poets such as Blind, Smedley, and Harriet Eleanor Hamilton King engaged with the "Italian question," sometimes like Blind directly influenced by Mazzini.[36] In King's elegiac ode, "The Execution of Felice Orsini" (1869), Mazzini figures as the central figure of the 1849 Roman Republic, the climax of the First War of Italian Independence:

> Then arose that dawn sublime,
> That short, glowing, glorious time,
> The third Rome in her bridal prime;
> When Mazzini's words of fire
>   Rang through the halls of Rome.   (lines 478–81)[37]

As in *Casa Guidi Windows*, where EBB describes Tuscan hopes for constitutional reform crushed by Austrian troops flowing into a subjugated Florence – "cannons rolling on, / Like blind slow storm-clouds" (2.301–3) – the third Roman Republic that King depicts was "short," as Guiseppe Garibaldi's valiant volunteers were crushed by the armies of Austria and Louis Napoleon of France. In 1849, then-president of the French Republic, Louis Napoleon intervened in Italy on behalf of Austria and the Papal States; in 1859, as Emperor Napoleon III he intervened in alliance with Italian nationalist forces, resulting in the Second War of Italian Independence and the creation of the Kingdom of Italy in 1861.

EBB's response to this second war in *Poems before Congress* (1860) resulted in one of the most politically controversial works of the period, generating an "extraordinary sensation," in the words of Odo Russell, England's diplomatic observer in Rome. Modern criticism has emphasized controversies over the poem concluding the book, "A Curse for a Nation." However, its opening ode "Napoleon III in Italy," casting the French emperor as Italy's "Sublime Deliverer" (line 94), provoked more widespread debate, shaped by differing nationalities and "conflicting political affiliations."[38] Thus Charles Synge Christopher Bowen in the Tory *Saturday Review* denounced the book's "dilettante Liberalism" and support of "democracy and socialism," whereas Edmund Ollier in the *Atlas* defended EBB's portrayal of Louis Napoleon, the "man whom demagogues and Tories over all the globe have conspired to stamp with odium."[39] English working-class agitation prior to the Second Reform Bill made the opening of "Napoleon III in Italy" especially inflammatory, since EBB defended the

1851 plebiscite confirming popular support for Louis Napoleon's *coup d'etat* and instituting universal manhood suffrage as "eight millions" exercising "their manhood's right divine" (lines 4–5). Her refrain in the ode thus salutes Louis Napoleon as "Emperor Evermore" in part because "the people's blood runs through him" (line 301). However, many disagreed, even among working-class sympathizers like William Howitt, or poets supporting the *Risorgimento* like King. In "The Execution of Felice Orsini," King presents Orsini as a martyr and his 1858 attempt to assassinate Louis Napoleon as "[t]yrannicide" (line 337) after many, including EBB, dismissed Orsini as a terrorist. King's ode can thus be seen as a counter-text to EBB's "Napoleon III in Italy," much as the earlier ode writes back against Tennyson's "Ode on the Death of the Duke of Wellington."[40]

While women poets expressed diverse views on both the Italian wars and the Crimean War, one common thread is conflict between dedication to patriotic or nationalist ideologies and the sacrifice of human life. In *Casa Guidi Windows*, EBB reversed her support of "free trade" in the Corn Law debates and attacked the "cry up in England" that "for ends of trade . . . We henceforth should exalt the name of Peace" (2.373–6). In contrast, she militantly maintains that better "dying men and horses, and the wave / Blood-bubbling" than a peace written on "gibbets," "upon chain-bolts," or "beneath the freeman's whip" – peace at the cost of "Annihilated Poland, stifled Rome . . . Hungary fainting" (2.388, 393, 395, 404–5, 416–17), she adds, strategically linking causes. Part I of *Casa Guidi Windows* ends on a similar bellicose note, as EBB alludes to "Rows of shot corpses" in Naples uprisings and exclaims, "So let them die! . . . Heroic daring is the true success" (1.1205, 1210–15). At the same time, however, the more somber Part II dwells on the suffering that free trade and heroic causes alike ignore or entail. The limits of trade are addressed in the indictment of the 1851 Exhibition as "Imperial England" drawing people and commodities from the "ends of the earth," but leaving its "poor" uneducated and its "women, sobbing out of sight / Because men made the laws" (2.578–9, 635, 638–9).[41] The suffering involved in heroic causes is addressed through EBB's elegy for Anita Garibaldi dying pregnant in the aftermath of the Roman Republic, the comrade-in-arms

> who, at her husband's side, in scorn,
> Outfaced the whistling shot and hissing waves,
> Until she felt her little babe unborn
> Recoil, within her, from the violent staves
> And bloodhounds of the world.   (2.678–82)

This elegy is followed by a more Anglocentric conclusion, in which the poet addresses her own child with his "brave blue English eyes" as a "blue-eyed prophet" of a better future (2.747–57). Nevertheless, the Anita Garibaldi memorial anticipates EBB's later grappling with the suffering integral to "the birth-pangs of nations" (line 93) in "Mother and Poet" (1862), with its speaker's stunned grief: "Dead! both my boys!"; "When one sits quite alone! . . . / God, how the house feels!" (lines 3, 28–30). Although the poem portrays the Italian patriotic poet Laura Savio, it also surely registers EBB's reflection on her earlier response to the Naples "corpses": "So let them die!" As the "agonized" speaker recalls, *she* taught her boys "a country's a thing men should die for . . . I prated of liberty, rights, and about / The tyrant cast out" (lines 20–5).

Some Crimean War poems similarly wrestle with the collision between maternal nurturing and sacrificial support of what Dinah Mulock Craik terms the "God of battles" in "By the Alma River." As Lootens asks in subtly analyzing Craik's poem, "Can the Gods of (future) soldiers and of mothers be the same?"[42] No, the Gothic undercurrents of "By the Alma River" suggest, insistent as the return of the title in the refrain, insistent as the mother's buried fears that Willie's father may be dead beside the Alma River, not burying those who died. Willie's mother tells him, "Let it drop, that 'solider' toy," and pray that God's will "be done," yet she is caught up in "Chance-poised victory's bloody work" (lines 2, 15, 54). The parallels between Craik's poem and EBB's "Mother and Poet" are at first striking, yet Craik's poetess verse more exclusively focuses on private suffering; "Rights of nations" are mentioned only to be disregarded (line 14). In contrast, in "Mother and Poet" the political imperatives of Italian nation building and "rights" are pervasive and unquestioned, despite the mother's grief.

"The Crimean War" by working-class poet Elizabeth Duncan Campbell[43] similarly contrasts with Craik's "By the Alma River" in its attention to class and power, beginning with its opening: "I think it's a pity that kings go to war, / And carry their murd'rous inventions so far." God figures in these hierarchies, first as "King of kings," then in unspecified relation to the "God of War, in Heaven's car," who cries "Go, kill, kill, kill!" (lines 21, 25–7). Campbell alludes to Tennyson's "The Charge of the Light Brigade" but stresses British "blunders" more, describing "iron-nerved British" falling "hundreds bleeding" as they run "in confusion" at Sebastopol (lines 59–62), not gallant troopers between cannons volleying symmetrically to left and right. She furthermore expresses maternal sympathy even for deserters, saying that while "many a mother's tears" were saved by "those that found a grave" and escaped "a flogging," "Neath Britain's boasted Freedom's flag, / Deserters out their life must drag, / White fear their footsteps dogging" (lines 85–92). In "The Lesson of War" (1855), Adelaide Anne

Proctor claims that all ranks have "the same great stake" in the Crimean War; those who "toil and suffer" should not "envy" the more fortunate (lines 38–51).[44] Campbell implies that the stakes differ depending on class. As she writes in "The Death of Willie, My Second Son," Willie survived the Crimean War only to die mangled in an "insufficiently covered" machine from "gory wound[s]."[45]

Preoccupied with the composition of *Aurora Leigh* from 1853 to 1856, EBB did not engage poetically with the Crimean War, apart from a reference to the "Czar" in "A Song for the Ragged Schools" (line 3). In 1853, "the social question" was her primary focus, embodied in her depiction of Aurora's philanthropic cousin Romney Leigh, his attempt to stage a cross-class marriage with the seamstress Marian Erle, and his failed phalanstery on the model of French socialist Charles Fourier. By the mid-1850s, the "woman question" was also an increasingly dominant concern for EBB and many other women writers, including Norton in *English Laws for Women in the Nineteenth Century* (1854), as activists fought for rights to higher education; more employment opportunities; and legal, political, and economic "personhood." *Aurora Leigh* speaks to all of these issues, as the most multi-faceted poetic intervention on the "woman question" in the Victorian period. Key dimensions include the satire of Aurora's young lady's education (and Marian's lack of any education), the representation of a professional woman writer, and the exposé of working-class women's wrongs. Marian flees the battered mother who would sell her to the squire's lust, starves as a seamstress in London, is trafficked across the Channel, raped, and impregnated; yet she still asserts her selfhood to those who would shame her or, like Romney, marry her to rescue her. EBB's interventions in the social question and the woman question were debated for decades, as they are again today. Some, like John Nicholl in the *Westminster Review* (1857), condemned the portrait of Romney as biased against socialism; others, like Harriet Waters Preston, editor of the 1900 Cambridge edition of EBB's works, dismissed *Aurora Leigh* as "distinctly socialistic" – possibly reacting against a new wave of socialism inspired by Karl Marx and William Morris influencing poets like Blind or Louisa Bevington in her anarchist *Liberty Lyrics* (1895).[46]

The multiple dimensions of the woman question in *Aurora Leigh* resonate more in women's poetry from the 1860s through the 1890s than the social question, although many authors also portray the two as intertwined. Augusta Webster's dramatic monologue "A Castaway" (1870) echoes *Aurora Leigh* in its critique of women's education (lines 365–76) and economic opportunities ("More sempstresses than shirts," line 266) but also presents prostitution more realistically in portraying a professional sex-trade worker (Eulalie) who gains her living as men "feed on the world's follies, vices, wants" (line 93) in occupations from law to medicine to commerce. Which of their "honourable trades ... All secrets brazened out, would shew more white?" than hers, Eulalie asks (lines 97–8).[47] "A Castaway" intervenes in battles led by Josephine Butler against the Contagious Diseases Acts (CD) of 1864, 1866, and 1869, which empowered police to lock up and medically inspect all suspected prostitutes, using criteria such as a woman's going "to places of public resort." This campaign stimulated mobilization for suffrage, as women noted that such acts "'could never have been ... sanctioned by a Parliament in which women were represented.'"[48] Webster was immersed in suffrage activism in the 1870s and approached Christina Rossetti to "lend her name to the campaign" too, although Rossetti declined.[49] Rossetti did, however, explore the sexual double standards the CD acts epitomized, not only in "Goblin Market" (1862) but also in "The Iniquity of the Fathers Upon the Children" (1866), written in the voice of an illegitimate girl who forgives the "Lady" mother who patronizes her without owning her as her daughter, while repudiating the father who loads both women with shame.

Webster's "A Castaway" and Rossetti's "Iniquity" are among numerous poems employing dramatic speakers to critique sexual double standards, prostitution, illegitimacy, and the laws they shape, while also exploring the psychological conflicts they create. Fannie Forrester's "The Bitter Task" (1873) portrays the reflections of a mother as she rocks her child, sews the wedding apparel for the bride of the man who impregnated her, and plots to hold her child up for him to see at his wedding.[50] EBB's earlier "Void in Law" (1862) similarly depicts the embittered thoughts of a mother rocking her illegitimate child in a dramatic monologue adapting the traditional ballad "Lady Bothwell's Lament" to throw more attention on "law." Forrester seems to echo both EBB's poem and, more directly, Webster's "A Castaway": the unnamed speaker terms herself a "castaway toy," and like Eulalie, she spurns her lover's offer to "*pay*" her but then yields to a "vile tempter" she longs to "curse" in order to support her son (lines 32, 65, 70). Significantly, however, the working-class Forrester implies that her speaker moves in and out of sex work as need demands, not earning a comfortable living: the poem ends with the speaker's "fingers ... toiling" at her needlework for her child (line 80).

Blind's "The Russian Student's Tale" (1891) exposes male complicity in economically driven sexual exploitation by combining the myth of Philomela with the dramatic voice of a male student as in D. G. Rossetti's earlier poem "Jenny" (1870). Blind's speaker recalls overflowing in passion for a girl with the face "of a little child" whom he rows to "a student's haunt" along the river Neva in St. Petersburg (lines 41, 56), his sexual excitement conveyed by the refrain lyricizing the "Neva's surge and swell" and the "amorous ecstasies and throes" of a nightingale's "love-song" (first sounded in lines 35–8). Learning from the girl that as a "weary semptress, half a child," she "barter[ed]" her innocence for "gold," he can see only a "murdered virgin" (lines 89–93, 111) whom he abandons, as a "blankness overspread[s] her eyes" and, above the "Neva's surge and swell," he hears the "last sob of a nightingale" (lines 134, 154, 158).[51] Blind's poem resonates with the controversy over "five pound virgins" provoked by W. T. Stead's 1885 article "The Maiden-Tribute of Modern Babylon" in the *Pall Mall Gazette,* in a period when Butler and others involved in the CD acts campaign mobilized again to counter sexual traffic in women, girls, and children.[52] The poem that Butler repeatedly invokes in these later campaigns is not *Aurora Leigh* but "The Cry of the Children," as, like Blind, she underscores the violated innocence of the traffic's younger victims.

Among many poems on abandoned mothers and illegitimate children, May Probyn's "The End of the Journey" (1883) stands out in portraying the effects of cross-racial relationships in an age of imperialism. Its protagonist speaks an "Indian tongue" (line 40) and travels long distances with "small uncovered head" on "naked feet" leaving "a track of red" (lines 9–11) to confront the white man who left her with the baby at her breast. Crouching among "snakes," she observes the "shadow" of a "fair white woman" within his dwelling (lines 25–8), then approaches the man as he exits, only to have him spurn her as she clings to his knees with "a dog's dumb, patient look" and finally takes his "knife into her heart" (lines 49–52).[53] The woman's smallness, the bloody "track," the comparison of her to a cruelly mistreated "dog" (resonating with anti-vivisection discourse), and the closing metaphor of penetration all imply a sexual union involving a violent act of colonial subjugation.

Other Victorian women poets, like the white woman who casts a "shadow" on this Indian woman's life, show less sensitivity than Probyn to the experiences of women doubly subjugated by gender and race, or triply subjugated if class and caste are also involved. Rossetti's "In the Round Tower at Jhansi – June 8, 1857" responds to the Indian Mutiny by portraying an English captain and his wife as besieged martyrs who "kiss and die" (line 14) and the Indian rebels as "swarming howling wretches below" (line 3). This racializing rhetoric obscures much, including the fact that "the Jhansi rebel leader" was the woman "Rani of Jhansi, who had deeply resented British annexation of her territory."[54] Similar imperial discourse pervades Frances Ridley Havergall's "An Indian Flag," with its celebration of the Christian conversion of Punjabi citizens; Emily Pfeiffer's portrayal of the battle against Zulu warriors in "The Fight at Rorke's Drift" (1882); and the feminist orientalism in her paired sonnets, "Peace to the Odalisque" (1873).

Still, like Probyn, other Victorian women poets resisted Anglocentric imperialism – especially Irish poets like "Speranza," Scottish women poets, or writers with cosmopolitan backgrounds like the German-Jewish Blind. Mixing epic tale with pastoral and tragedy in *The Heather on Fire: A Tale of the Highland Clearances* (1886), Blind portrays the resistance of the crofter's wife Mary expelled from their torched cottage, as she nurtures a dying child and her husband's aged parents. While Mary is fictional, women and their poetry were central in protests against the Clearances of Highland Scots that began in the mid-eighteenth century and continued into the nineteenth. Boos notes that when "the Voting Act of 1884 widened the franchise to include many crofters," the songs of poet-midwife Mary Macdonald MacPherson "helped to elect Land Law Reform Association candidates throughout the Highlands" (173). Reflecting the vitality of oral bardic traditions in an age of print, "Big Mary" held thousands of lines of verse in her memory, learned to read but not write, and produced "highly sarcastic and dramatic set-pieces" like "Incitement of the Gaels," in which she fired up crofters and mocked the evictors who told them they would "'get honey on the grass-tops / in Manitoba,'" in effect offering the Highlanders "a bare hook and no fish" (lines 63–7).[55] As MacPherson's songs remind us – fortunately preserved in print – satire often featured among the diverse generic registers of Victorian women's political poetry, and there may be many examples of voices raised in protest that have gone unrecorded.

Notes

1. Stanza 9. For Norton's works, see the Brown Women Writers Project: http://webapp1.dlib.indiana.edu/vwwp/view?docId=VAB7191.xml
2. Linda K. Hughes, *The Cambridge Introduction to Victorian Poetry* (New York: Cambridge University Press, 2010), p. 216.
3. Ibid., p. 123.
4. Kathryn Gleadle, "'We *Will* Have It': Children and Protest in the Ten Hours Movement," in *Childhood and Child Labour in Industrial England: Diversity and Agency, 1750–1914*, ed. Nigel Goose and Katrina Honeyman (London: Routledge, 2013), pp. 149, 152.
5. Tricia Lootens summarizes poetess scholarship in *The Political Poetess: Victorian Femininity, Race, and the Legacy of Separate Spheres* (Princeton: Princeton University Press, 2017), pp. 1–19.
6. Lootens, *Political Poetess*, p. 3; Alison Chapman, *Networking the Nation: British and American Women Poets and Italy, 1840–1870* (New York: Oxford University Press, 2015), p. 99.
7. Yopie Prins, qtd. in Lootens, *Political Poetess*, p. 12.

8. Florence S. Boos, ed., *Working-Class Women Poets in Victorian Britain: An Anthology* (Peterborough: Broadview Press, 2008), pp. 208–9.
9. Sandra Donaldson, gen. ed., Rita Patteson, Donaldson, Marjorie Stone, and Beverly Taylor, vol. eds., *The Works of Elizabeth Barrett Browning*, 5 vols. (London: Pickering and Chatto, 2010), 1.409–30.
10. Angela Leighton and Margaret Reynolds, eds., *Victorian Women Poets: An Anthology* (Oxford: Blackwell Publishers, 1995), pp. 24, 215–16.
11. *The Occident and Jewish Advocate*, 2.6 (September 1844). Available at www .jewish-history.com/occident/volume2/sep1844/hebrews_appeal.html
12. Isobel Armstrong, *Victorian Poetry: Poetry, Poetics, and Politics* (London: Routledge, 1993), pp. 323, 339.
13. Qtd. in Shu-chuan Yan, "'When Common Voices Speak': Labour, Poetry and Eliza Cook," *Women's Writing*, 22 (2015), 431.
14. Qtd. in Yan, 435–6.
15. Norton, Letter 1, *Letters to the Mob* (London: Thomas Bosworth, 1848), pp. 4–5.
16. Ruth Wills, in Boos, *Working-Class Women Poets*, p. 231.
17. Qtd. in *Victorian Women Poets*, pp. 175–6.
18. *The Works of Elizabeth Barrett Browning*, 5.32.
19. *Nineteenth-Century Women Poets: An Oxford Anthology*, ed. Isobel Armstrong and Joseph Bristow, with Cath Sharrock (New York: Oxford University Press, 1996), pp. 653–6.
20. Leighton, "Introduction II," *Victorian Women Poets*, p. xxxviii.
21. Angela Leighton, *Victorian Women Poets: Writing Against the Heart* (Charlottesville: University Press of Virginia, 1992), pp. 92–6.
22. Peaches Henry, "The Sentimental Artistry of Barrett Browning's 'The Cry of the Children,'" *Victorian Poetry*, 49 (2011), 535–56; *Works of Elizabeth Barrett Browning*, 2.435–6.
23. *Elizabeth Barrett Browning: Selected Poems*, ed. Marjorie Stone and Beverly Taylor (Peterborough, ON: Broadview Press, 2009), p. 327 (emphasis added).
24. *Works of Elizabeth Barrett Browning*, 5.642.
25. Ibid., 1.432.
26. Mary Howitt, in *Victorian Women Poets*, pp. 21–3.
27. Qtd. in *Works of Elizabeth Barrett Browning*, 1.432–3.
28. Chris Morash, ed., *The Hungry Voice: The Poetry of the Irish Famine* (Dublin: Irish Academic Press, 2009), pp. 15–16.
29. Ibid., p. 221.
30. Ibid., p. 219.
31. Qtd. in Boos, *Working-Class Women Poets*, p. 240.
32. Ibid., p. 16.
33. Menella Bute Smedley, in *Victorian Women Poets*, p. 258.
34. Emily Hickey, in *Victorian Women Poets*, p. 483.
35. D. M. Smith, qtd. in *Works of Elizabeth Barrett Browning*, 2.484.
36. James Diedrick, *Mathilde Blind: Late-Victorian Culture and the Woman of Letters* (Charlottesville: University of Virginia Press, 2017), pp. 22–5.
37. Harriet King, *Nineteenth-Century Women Poets*, pp. 625–51.
38. Qtd. in Denae Dyck and Marjorie Stone, "The 'Sensation' of Elizabeth Barrett Browning's *Poems before Congress* (1860): Events, Politics, Reception,"

BRANCH: Britain, Representation and Nineteenth-Century History, ed. Dino Felluga. Web. www.branchcollective.org.

39. Qtd. in Dyck and Stone, Section IV.

40. Hughes, *Cambridge Introduction*, pp. 51–2.

41. See Beverly Taylor, "Elizabeth Barrett Browning and Transnationalism: People Diplomacy in 'A Fair-going World,'" *Victorian Review*, 33 (2007), 59–83.

42. Lootens, *Political Poetess*, p. 93; Craik, in Lootens, *Political Poetess*, pp. 91–2.

43. Elizabeth Duncan Campbell, in Boos, *Working-Class Women Poets*, pp. 128–30.

44. Adelaide Anne Procter, in *Nineteenth-Century Women Poets*, pp. 473–4.

45. Campbell, line 16 and Campbell's note, in Boos, *Working-Class Women Poets*, pp. 126–7.

46. Nicholl and Preston, qtd. in Stone, "The Advent of *Aurora Leigh:* Critical Myths and Periodical Debates," *BRANCH*, ed. Felluga; Hughes, *Cambridge Introduction*, pp. 228–9.

47. *Portraits and Other Poems*, ed. Christine Sutphin (Peterborough, ON: Broadview Press, 2000), pp. 192–213.

48. Qtd. in Susan Brown, "Economical Representations: Dante Gabriel Rossetti's 'Jenny,' Augusta Webster's 'A Castaway,' and the Campaign Against the Contagious Diseases Acts," *Victorian Review*, 17 (Summer 1991): 78–9, 90.

49. Patricia Rigg, *Julia Augusta Webster: Victorian Aestheticism and the Woman Writer* (Madison, NJ: Fairleigh Dickinson University Press, 2009), pp. 167–71.

50. Fanny Forrester, in Boos, *Working-Class Women Poets*, pp. 247–9.

51. Mathilde Blind, in *Nineteenth-Century Women Poets*, pp. 660–3.

52. W. T. Stead, "The Maiden Tribute of Modern Babylon," *Pall Mall Gazette*, July 6–10, 1885 (five installments, each begun on the front page).

53. May Probyn, in *Victorian Women Poets*, pp. 532–3.

54. Hughes, *Cambridge Introduction*, p. 199.

55. Mary Macdonald MacPherson, in Boos, *Working-Class Women Poets*, pp. 175, 181.

10

CHARLES LAPORTE

Religion and Spirituality

Religion and spirituality were arguably Victorian women poets' paramount concerns. Any sustained treatment of the era's two most influential female poets, Elizabeth Barrett Browning (EBB) and Christina Rossetti, must acknowledge their work's central religious element.[1] But this element also inheres in Victorian women's poetry more generally, down to anonymous or initialed poems in popular periodicals. Male poets often shared this religious preoccupation, to be sure, and attitudes toward the poet as *sacer vates* pervade what William McKelvy calls the era's "cult of literature."[2] Nonetheless, Victorian women's poetry has special claims to attention because secularization has blunted the force of its religious expressions and thereby contributed to its subsequent devaluation.

Historians now agree, for instance, that nineteenth-century Britain was deeply religious and that women maintained much higher levels of fidelity to organized religion than men – in perception as in reality.[3] In retrospect, such religious allegiance poses questions for feminism as well as literary aesthetics, for our scholarly mores presume a level of distance from devotional attitudes. As F. Elizabeth Gray points out, our inclinations and experiences (if not our prejudices) can prevent us from sympathizing with what Victorian women were trying to do in their poetry:

> [A] real lack persists in our understanding of Victorian women's devotional writing and its cultural contribution. To ignore or 'read past' the overwhelmingly Christian tenor of most Victorian women's poetry is to marginalise or violate its chief perspective; to abstain from engaging critically with Christian-themed poetry is to surrender the most salient literary position from which women could speak.[4]

Gray's point bears repeating: religion and spirituality are not merely two themes among many in Victorian women's poetry. They may be said to furnish "its chief perspective." When we fail to give religious culture its due or recognize it in the first place, we refuse to meet Victorian women poets where they actually were. Gray focuses upon Christian-themed poetry as comprising the overwhelming majority of religious verse (statistically true), but poetry remains central to other faith expressions as well, including Judaism and religious movements such as Spiritualism and Theosophy.[5] Religion informs the whole meaning of the genre in this period.

This chapter begins with evangelical verse liable to alienate twenty-first-century readers (represented by Charlotte Brontë). Subsequently, I turn to theologically ambitious sentimental verse (EBB) and the role of liturgical forms (Rossetti). I then consider explicitly political poetry (Grace Aguilar) and poetry from non-Western traditions (Toru Dutt). Owing to space limitations, I reluctantly omit freethinking, atheist, and agnostic poetics and minority traditions including Roman Catholicism. However, our scholarship has usually done better with expressions of iconoclasm than with expressions of devotion, and one way of deepening our understanding of such minority poetries is to appreciate better the robust Protestant culture surrounding them.

Evangelical Poetry (Brontë)

Some poetic forms lend themselves to the hermeneutics of modern literary criticism better than others. We often celebrate EBB's feminist theology, for instance, albeit more for the feminism than the theology. We likewise celebrate Rossetti's measured and musical devotions, albeit more for the measures than the devotion. But we struggle to engage with more starkly evangelical poems. Take Charlotte Brontë's extraordinary "The Missionary," a dramatic monologue from *Poems by Currer, Ellis, and Acton Bell* (1846). This lyric, a sort of dry run for the St John Rivers plot of *Jane Eyre* (1847), depicts a shipbound cleric travelling to an Indian mission:

> Yes, hard and terrible the toil
> Of him who steps on foreign soil,
> Resolved to plant the gospel vine,
> Where tyrants rule and slaves repine;
> Eager to lift Religion's light
> Where thickest shades of mental night
> Screen the false god and fiendish rite;
> Reckless that missionary blood,
> Shed in wild wilderness and wood,
> Has left, upon the unblest air,
> The man's deep moan – the martyr's prayer.
> I know my lot – I only ask
> Power to fulfil the glorious task;
> Willing the spirit, may the flesh
> Strength for the day receive afresh. (lines 107–21)[6]

The poem is straightforward enough: a young clergyman vacillates between trepidation and resolve on leaving his homeland and asks divine assistance "to fulfil[l] the glorious task" of his mission. But no twenty-first-century scholar, however partial to Christianity, can sympathize with the speaker's depiction of devotees of Hinduism (or Jainism, Sikhism, Parsi Zoroastrianism, etc.) as "slaves" practicing "fiendish rite[s]" in "thickest shades of mental night." We no more sympathize with this speaker's motivations than with Alfred Tennyson's "St Simeon Stylites" or Robert Browning's "Johannes Agricola," though these earlier figures were drawn unsympathetically on purpose.

Victorian dramatic monologues often feature such religiously alienated and alienating speakers who illuminate thorny philosophical issues by espousing repugnant points of view. Brontë's monologue, however, actually takes for granted our sympathy with the speaker's evangelical zeal and, as Miriam Elizabeth Burstein observes, locates its drama in his heroic sacrifice of loved ones and homeland.[7] There is even a proto–Rosamond Oliver character, named for the famous beauty of antiquity, whom he has left behind: "Helen! thou mightst not go with me, / I could not – dared not stay for thee!" (lines 53–4). "The Missionary" thus confronts us with the limits of our own historical sympathies, with our (admittedly paradoxical) intolerance of intolerance. Intellectually, we grant the speaker to have admirable qualities: devotion to what he conceives to be the greater good, disregard for personal comforts, sublime indifference to possible martyrdom. Yet these cannot bring us past his ideas of India as "Hell's empire," peopled by "pagan-priests, whose creed is Wrong, / Extortion, Lust, and Cruelty" (lines 67–8). And crucially, it is evolving cultural attitudes about religion that make the missionary's views about Indian religions so unacceptable today. To frame this question as we do reflects a sea change in modern thinking that he would himself reject. For "religion" as we use the term emerges as a modern concept when other people's error and heresy become alternative forms of devotion: private matters that may (who knows?) be good for them.[8] By contrast, Brontë's character uses "Religion" and "Christianity" as coextensive categories in his phrase about lifting "Religion's light" before benighted peoples. To him, Indian religions are no religion at all.

Brontë seems to have anticipated the challenge that "The Missionary" poses for readers who do not share her form of evangelicalism (including evangelical readers today). When she recycles this missionary plot in *Jane Eyre*, she removes his slanders toward practitioners of other faiths, though adding nothing to suggest that St John feels differently, and gives him a raft of charming additional attributes: he becomes stunningly handsome, conspicuously intelligent, accomplished, and scholarly, with perfect hair, a perfect nose, and "polished, calm, and gentlemanlike" manners, none of which appear in this monologue.[9] Such additions speak to Brontë's ongoing belief in the good of British missionary efforts; to doubt this belief is to misunderstand both works. Readers today struggle with the circumstance that Brontë gives St John the final words of *Jane Eyre*, but this ending more or less repeats the conclusion of "The Missionary": "Then for my ultimate reward – / Then for the world-rejoicing word – / The voice from Father–Spirit–Son: / 'Servant of God, well hast thou done!'" (lines 156–9). Like the St John plot of *Jane Eyre*, this is a spiritual drama written from and for another era.

Theology and Sentiment (EBB)

The scholarly imagination that we must bring to Brontë will serve us well when we consider Victorian women's verse more generally, which often resists being read against the grain. Poetic hermeneutics developed in the academy have often struggled with sentimental verse, for instance. Consider EBB's "The Cry of the Human" (1842) first printed in the *Boston Miscellany of Literature and Fashion*, an extended gloss on the Biblical psalms that begin "The fool hath said in his heart, *There is* no God" (Psalms 14.1, 53.1):

> 'THERE is no God' the foolish saith,
>   But none 'There is no sorrow.'
> And nature oft, the cry of faith,
>   In bitter need will borrow:
> Eyes, which the preacher could not school,
>   By wayside graves are raisèd,
> And lips say, 'God be pitiful,'
>   Who ne'er said, 'God be praisèd.'
>   Be pitiful, O God!   (lines 1–9)[10]

Despite its opening line, "The Cry of the Human" does not rehearse the Psalms' invective toward atheists. Instead, it looks for common ground for believers and unbelievers in the universal fact of human sorrow (lines 1–2) and reflects that religious life generally derives from pragmatic needs and relational life rather than from abstract theology. "Eyes, which the preacher could not school" may arrive at the gist of the preacher's sermon all on their own. Perhaps they uncover its most important lessons, as the poem suggests when capping each of its thirteen stanzas with a final *kyrie eleison*: "Be pitiful, O God!"

EBB, of course, wrote much religious verse that today finds only an academic readership (and some of it hardly that). Twentieth-century anthologies overlooked such verse even after second-wave feminism inspired a sustained effort to reconsider women's poetics. Today's readers are more likely to recognize Arthur Hugh Clough's untitled 1849 parodic rewriting of EBB's poem, which begins as follows:

> 'THERE is no God' the wicked saith,
>   'And truly it's a blessing,
> For what he might have done with us
>   It's better only guessing.'
>
> 'There is no God' the youngster thinks,
>   'Or really if there may be,
> He surely didn't mean a man
>   Always to be a baby.'
>
> 'Whether there be,' the rich man thinks,
>   'It matters very little,
> For I and mine, thank somebody,
>   Are not in want of victual.'   (lines 1–12)[11]

Clough reworks EBB's initial line, her psalmic allusion, and her ballad measures. As she does, he plays with a feminine ending on the second and fourth lines. But his poem arrives at a very different tone, for he cuts off each building stanza at line 5, and just where she begins to vary and enrich her rhythm ("**Eyes**, which / the **preach-** /er **could** / not **school**" or "**not school**"), he begins afresh, returning abruptly to the opening measures for the comic potential of those feminine rhymes. Likewise, Clough drops EBB's final *kyrie* refrain, with all of its pregnant authority, opting instead for mildly ridiculous anticlimax.

Together, Clough and EBB enact a lopsided conversation about pragmatic religious impulses. He repeats her argument that the needy and beleaguered, not the wealthy and self-possessed, tend most often to lean upon God. But he reduces her ideas about the universality of suffering to a truncated, humorous pronouncement:

> And almost every one when age,
>   Disease, or sorrow strike him;
> Inclines to think there is a God,
>   Or something very like him.   (lines 29–32)

The lines are irreverent but not dismissive, playful but sincere, typifying Clough just as EBB's earnestness typifies her. Clough's final rhyme (strike him / like him) leaves readers with the incongruous notion of "something very like" a nineteenth-century God whose foremost attribute was His divine incomparability with anything else. God is a funny paradox, and so are people. Such anticlimax could hardly be further from EBB's conclusion, an ardently expressed exposition of Trinitarian theology:

> And soon all vision waxeth dull –
>   Men whisper, 'He is dying:'
> We cry no more 'Be pitiful!'
>   We have no strength for crying.
> No strength, no need. Then, soul of mine,
>   Look up and triumph rather –
> Lo, in the depth of God's Divine,
>   The Son adjures the Father,
>   BE PITIFUL, O GOD!   (lines 118–25)

For EBB, the poem's initial idea of faith as a relational life also lives at the heart of Christian theology in the divine interrelationships of the Triune God. Christ intercedes with God the Father on our behalf and echoes our very language in doing so. EBB wrote "The Cry of the Human" shortly after translating for the *Athenæum* the poetry of St. Gregory of Nazianzus (329–90 C.E.), the foremost theologian of the Trinity in the ancient Church, renowned for his ideas about movements between the three individual persons of the Christian God.[12] Although her lyric begins by setting aside abstract theology and Church tradition as practically irrelevant, it then returns to these with a passion, arguing that the ancient teachings matter, that our voices are also God's, that our interpersonal needs are mirrored by divine love at the core of God's very being. The sentimental nature of this poem should not disguise the reach of its ambition as an exposition of the *perichoresis* (the movement between persons of the Trinity) of Nazianzus, upon whom EBB's scholarly researches had made her a real and rare authority. (The *Athenæum* published her scholarship anonymously, but she made no secret of her authorship.) And if EBB's Congregationalist tradition gave her no professional opportunity to become the "preacher" who appears in line 5, yet everywhere she presents her poetic vocation as a higher religious calling. Such poetry presents her as a veritable scribe for God, recording which "word is being said in heaven," as she puts it in *Aurora Leigh* (1.875).[13] Her poem thus aims infinitely higher than Clough's; she aspires to redeem nonbelievers with the divine truths of ancient theology, to confirm believers in the mysteries of their beliefs.

I compare these two lyrics to demonstrate how much more scholarly effort Victorian women's poetry can require. Today Clough's poem may be found on websites like PoemHunter.com and poetrybyheart.org.uk, but it is hard to imagine such websites showcasing EBB's lessons in the Trinitarian theology of St. Gregory Nazianzus. Clough's ironic humor makes his poem more legible to us. Victorian women poets could employ iconoclastic humor, of course; think of Constance Naden, Amy Levy, May Kendall, A. Mary F. Robinson, even George Eliot. Nonetheless, if we have a set of scholarly hermeneutics that teaches us to prize irony, heterodoxy, and rebellion against established rules (as we do), and we study a culture in which religious mores were far more often flouted by men (as we do), we will end up with a general bias against Victorian women's verse (as we have done). In her defense of the Greek Christian poets, and Nazianzus in particular, EBB wrote, "It is, too, as religious poets, that we are called upon to estimate these neglected Greeks."[14] But the same holds true of our ability to estimate these neglected aspects of EBB and her contemporaries; Victorian religious culture furnishes an essential context for the reach of their poetics.

Formal Restraint (Rossetti)

A related challenge of our scholarly vantage is that many Victorian religious cultures valued restraint and conformity, qualities that we tend to oppose to authentic art. As Kirstie Blair spells out, "it is both more difficult and, for formally engaged criticism, inherently less interesting, indeed less fun, to discuss poetry that militantly sticks to conventions and that takes its faith for granted."[15] Literary scholars tend to prize revolt over piety, subversion over conformity, variation over regularity. Even at the level of affect, we look first for disruption and agitation. Victorian poets themselves recognized the paradoxes inherent to their wedding of poetic and religious cultures. Literary affect may escape, exceed, or fail religious constraints; religious affect may seem at odds with formal literary constraints.

Take Christina Rossetti's "Good Friday," first published in Orby Shipley's *Lyra Messianica: Hymns and Verses on the Life of Christ, Ancient and Modern* (1864), which wrestles openly with this conundrum. "Good Friday" dramatizes a believer who feels insufficiently moved by scriptural and liturgical traditions surrounding Christ's passion:

> Am I a stone, and not a sheep,
>   That I can stand, O Christ, beneath Thy cross,
>   To number drop by drop Thy blood's slow loss,
> And yet not weep?
>
> Not so those women loved
>   Who with exceeding grief lamented Thee;
>   Not so fallen Peter, weeping bitterly;
> Not so the thief was moved;

Not so the Sun and Moon
    Which hid their faces in a starless sky,
    A horror of great darkness at broad noon –
I, only I.

Yet give not o'er,
    But seek Thy sheep, true Shepherd of the flock;
    Greater than Moses, turn and look once more
And smite a rock.   (lines 1–16)[16]

Good Friday is of course the day of Jesus's crucifixion and burial as represented in the Paschal Triduum of the Church calendar. In Rossetti's Anglo-Catholic tradition, its observance entails fasting, liturgy, and prayer. But in the poem, a rehearsal of Christ's passion has failed to inspire commensurate emotion. The speaker acknowledges the significance of the divine event and emotive models in scriptural characters. But she feels no passion herself and begs to be moved, literally to be beaten, to feel the divine event. The Biblical Moses had created springs of fresh water by striking a rock with his staff; this speaker asks Christ likewise to strike her that she might better feel his still greater pain.

Thematically, "Good Friday" presents the inverse of EBB's and Clough's meditations on the pragmatic, human sources of religious devotion, which arise spontaneously or in relation to life circumstances, such as "when age, / Disease, or sorrow strike" us. By contrast, Rossetti urges the importance of forms themselves, forms divorced from personal circumstances. The Church calendar's days of fasting and feasting cannot correspond to any one believer's personal bearings. Outside of Church tradition, they must seem arbitrary. For Rossetti, the challenge is to realize the mystery of the Atonement on the day dictated by the Church and in communion with other believers. J. A. Froude once described such a moment in John Henry Newman's Church of St Mary's during the heady days of the Oxford Movement:

> Newman described closely some of the incidents of our Lord's passion; he then paused. For a few moments there was a breathless silence. Then, in a low, clear voice, of which the faintest vibration was audible in the farthest corner of St Mary's, he said, 'Now, I bid you recollect that He to whom these things were done was Almighty God.' It was as if an electric stroke had gone through the church, as if every person present understood for the first time the meaning of what he had all his life been saying.[17]

Rossetti's speaker longs for just such a wedding of intellectual recognition and feeling as Froude describes of his youth at Oxford: "an electric stroke." In this poem, assent to church dogma provides a condition for the stroke of insight. The stroke must come from God, yet the poem anticipates its arrival in the arresting final line.

As always in her poetry, Rossetti guards relentlessly against complacency and cheap emotion. Matthew Arnold's sister once described him, uncharitably, as "stretched out full length on one sofa, reading a Christian tale of Mrs. Gaskell's, which moves him to tears, and the tears to complacent admiration of his own sensibility."[18] The speaker of "Good Friday" might be "stretched out full length" on the stone floor of a church, but never on the Arnold family sofa. Indeed, the lyric's beauty lies in the stonelike austerity of its appeal. Its very reticence gives it heft: the foreshortened final line of the first, third, and fourth quatrains conveys an abruptness, a severeness of self-evaluation that culminates in Stanza 3, where the chiasmic dimeter of "I, only I" lingers isolated after the "horror" of line 11 (and in close visual proximity to it). This abrupt and apparently isolated line then finds a companion in the dimeter of line 13 before the syntax reestablishes the pentameter of the interior lines. The rhyme, too, has altered at the crisis marking the third stanza, such that the final appeal, "And smite a rock," echoes now a line that had been (in Stanzas 1 and 2) part of an interior couplet: "true Shepherd of the flock." The poem thus mourns a state of emotional stasis but suggests nonetheless the stirrings of movement, and the promise of more. She waits upon her shepherd still, but something, at least, is on the way.

Betty S. Flowers reminds us that "The temptation to read Rossetti's verse as morbid or depressed must be tempered by these biblical allusions that speak of other realities beyond the merely personal reality of the moment."[19] "Good Friday" might exemplify how Rossetti's verse can spurn mere personal reality as almost unworthy of consideration. For Rossetti, the Church calendar ought to shape the vicissitudes of ordinary life, rather than the other way around. Rossetti demonstrates few of EBB's grand ambitions. But like her American contemporary Emily Dickinson, Rossetti took EBB as a negative example (however much admired) and shows us the alternative power of severe restraint.

Religious Politics (Aguilar)

To consider ambition in Victorian women's religious poetry is also to render visible its politics. Here again EBB stands out preeminently, with *Aurora Leigh*, "The Cry of the Children," "The Runaway Slave at Pilgrim's Point," and "A Curse for a Nation" all now staples of the university classroom that speak to her various social and religious commitments. But EBB participates within a tradition of religiously informed social protest poetry that ranges across denominations and across religions. Consider Grace Aguilar's verse, directed toward both Jewish and Christian readerships. "The Hebrew's

Appeal: On Occasion of the Late Fearful *Ukase* Promulgated by the Emperor of Russia" (1844), for instance, responds to the pogroms of Czar Nicholas I in the mid-1840s:

> O God, that this should be! that one frail man
> Hath power to crush a nation 'neath his ban.
>
> Will none arise! with outstretch'd hand to save!
> No prayer for pity, and for aid awake?
> Will SHE who gave to Liberty the slave,
> For God's own people not one effort make?
> Will SHE not rise once more, in mercy clad,
> And heal the bleeding heart, and Sorrow's sons make glad?
>
> Will England sleep, when Justice bids her wake[?]   (lines 23–31)[20]

Aguilar requests sanctuary for the persecuted Russian Jews from her nation, personified as Mother England. In this respect, her appeal resembles Anna Letitia Barbauld's "Epistle To William Wilberforce, Esq., on the Rejection of the Bill for Abolishing the Slave Trade" (1791), a poem that addresses Mother England in less admiring terms: "She knows and she persists – Still Afric bleeds, / Uncheck'd, the human traffic still proceeds; / She stamps her infamy to future time, / And on her harden'd forehead seals the crime" (lines 15–18).[21] Barbauld's England, indeed, seems to be stamped on the forehead, like the lost souls of Revelation 13.17. But Aguilar writes after Wilberforce's efforts had culminated in the Slave Trade Act of 1807 and the Slavery Abolition Act of 1833. She looks to England as a heroic liberator, urging it once more to arise to meet this new crisis of human rights: "Will SHE who gave to Liberty the slave, / For God's own people not one effort make?" (lines 27–8).

The interreligious politics of such a poem are, perforce, complex. It remains uncertain whether Aguilar intended "The Hebrew" of her title to represent Russian Jewry or her own Sephardic ancestry. Ordinarily, Aguilar would refer to herself as an English Jew. But Jews here are "Hebrews," "Israel's race" (line 1), "Israel" (line 4), "God's own people" (line 28), and "His chosen race" (line 45). Such language asks its readers to recall the earliest parts of their shared Biblical heritage. By contrast, Aguilar here avoids the terms "Jew," "Jewess," and "Jewish," possibly fearing that these might provoke anti-Semitic responses. Her account of the poem's print history clarifies such lexical decisions:

> The above poem was written nearly six months ago, when the Russian *ukase* was first made public, and sent to the only paper in England devoted to Jewish interests – the *Voice of Jacob*, – the writer wishing to prove that at least one

female Jewish heart and voice were raised in an appeal for her afflicted brethren. The Editor of the V. of J. did not insert it, on the plea of having so much press of matter as to prevent giving it the required space. The *Christian Lady's Magazine* not only accepted and inserted it, but in bold and spirited prose appealed to her countrymen on the same subject. Still a Jewish paper is the natural channel for the public appearance of the poem, and therefore the writer sends it to the *Occident*, believing that though somewhat late, it will not there be disregarded.[22]

The poem's initial appearance in Charlotte Elizabeth Tonna's *The Christian Lady's Magazine*, we see, is owing to its prior rejection by *The Voice of Jacob*. Tonna added a brief promotional blurb (the "bold and spirited prose") appealing to readers: "The following touching stanzas are by a Jewish lady; – may they move many hearts to a practical response!"[23]

The poem's place in that evangelical publication should not surprise us. While interdenominational and interreligious suspicions ran high in the nineteenth century, poetry often generated common causes across religious lines. Barbauld had been a Unitarian, for instance, raised Presbyterian, writing in support of Wilberforce, an evangelical member of the Established Church. Likewise, Tonna, an Orangeist Protestant, promoted her "Jewish lady" amid articles inveighing against Catholic "Popery." Then again, Aguilar's poem follows an article discussing the Russian pogroms as an apocalyptic event presaging the final (and, for Tonna's readers, happy) conversion of the Jews. Aguilar naturally resented Christian conversionist efforts, and this may explain her subsequent decision to republish the poem in *The Occident*, "a Jewish paper."[24] The poem's print history thus involves multiple awkward compromises. Tonna encourages material aid for Russian Jewry ("a practical response!") but also espouses the prior article's millenarianism. In turn *The Occident*, an American publication, had no investment in a self-congratulating myth of English abolitionism. The conflicting religious, denominational, and national allegiances that always underlie Victorian poetics thus become especially vivid in a case like Aguilar's.

Global Contexts (Dutt)

The Bengali poet Toru Dutt's posthumously published *Ancient Ballads and Legends of Hindustan* (1882), finally, extends these issues to non-Western traditions in a set of translations representing her Sanskrit scholarship and stories she knew from childhood. Dutt does not write as a Hindu, for her family converted to Christianity when she was six; she renders into English the beauties and lessons of her ancestral faith, mostly in sympathetic terms.

In response, Edmund Gosse, Dutt's foremost Victorian promoter, racializes her in the English edition as perfect for such verse:

> She was pure Hindu, full of the typical qualities of her race and blood, and, as the present volume shows us for the first time, preserving to the last her appreciation of the poetic side of her ancient religion, though faith itself in Vishnu and Siva had been cast aside with childish things and been replaced by a purer faith.[25]

Plainly, Gosse's introduction involves self-contradiction. He aligns religion with "race and blood" and turns Dutt into an uncertain hybrid: "pure Hindu" Christian. His dismissal of Dutt's ancestral "faith in Vishnu and Siva" as "childish" recalls Brontë's description of the same faith as "fiendish." He cannot intend to link her family's conversion to her adolescence (as she was only six). Additionally, his language echoes St. Paul's disquisition on the Christian understanding of divine love: "When I was a child, I spake as a child, I understood as a child, I thought as a child: but when I became a man, I put away childish things" (1 Corinthians 13.11). Coming from a fervent evangelical, such a reference might be taken as an affirmation of the superiority of Christian faith. Yet Gosse was nothing of the kind. He himself had "put away" the faith of his father, and his autobiography *Father and Son* (1907) made him one of the era's most famous apostates. Like Tonna's championing of Aguilar, then, Gosse's championing of Dutt puts both figures into ideologically curious positions.

Dutt also sometimes betrays a mixed attitude toward her source materials, as Tricia Lootens has suggested.[26] Consider "The Royal Ascetic and the Hind," a ballad that recounts the story of King Bharata from the Vishnu Purana. The most pious of men, Bharata fled from the world to reside as a holy anchorite at Sálagráma and there witnessed an extraordinary zoological mishap: a pregnant deer, startled by a lion, leapt into a river, gave birth, and died. Bharata took home the newborn fawn in a feeling of "tenderest pity" (line 43) and raised it as a pet. The Vishnu Purana uses Bharata's story to illustrate how difficult it is for humans to forgo all earthly connections in the quest for sainthood. As Dutt records, "Though a kingdom he had left, / And children, and a host of loving friends, / Almost without a tear, the fount of love / Sprang out anew within his blighted heart" (lines 59–62). Bharata's mundane affections ultimately distract him from his austere devotions. He fails to reach a higher level of enlightenment, and upon his death is reincarnated as a deer (later to be reborn as a holy Brahmin before his story ends).

By utter contrast to the Vishnu Purana, Dutt interrupts "The Royal Ascetic and the Hind" to inveigh against the king's asceticism as irreligious and misguided. After recounting the story of his (initial) death, with its caution

about pious reflections diverted by his beloved pet, she interjects the
following:

> Thus far the pious chronicle, writ of old
> By Brahman sage; but we, who happier, live
> Under the holiest dispensation, know
> That God is Love, and not to be adored
> By a devotion born of stoic pride,
> Or with ascetic rites, or penance hard,
> But with a love, in character akin
> To His unselfish, all-including love.
> And therefore little can we sympathize
> With what the Brahman sage would fain imply
> As the concluding moral of his tale,
> That for the hermit-king it was a sin
> To love his nursling. What! a sin to love!
> A sin to pity! Rather should we deem
> Whatever Brahmans wise, or monks may hold,
> That he had sinned in *casting off* all love
> By his retirement to the forest-shades;
> For that was to abandon duties high,
> And, like a recreant soldier, leave the post
> Where God had placed him as a sentinel.   (lines 100–19)

In this extraordinary passage, Dutt denounces her source ("the pious chronicle") and entirely inverts the lesson of the original narrative. Dutt suggests
that "the Brahman sage" who recorded the Purana mistook the value of love,
and that Bharata, far from sinning in love for his hind, had first sinned by
abandoning his throne and family to take up an anchorite's lifestyle. Dutt
seems to imply the superiority of Christianity to Hinduism in this respect; her
first-person pronoun abruptly introduces our modern selves as readers of the
Christian scriptures: "we, who happier, live / Under the holiest dispensation,
[and] know / That God is Love." Dutt here quotes "He that loveth not
knoweth not God; for God is love" (1 John 4.8), a scripture central to
virtually all Christian teaching. Nonetheless, any apparent Hindu vs.
Christian dichotomy belies the importance of both familial affections in
Hindu writings and also Christian traditions of asceticism. The first finds
warrant from Dutt's own collection, as in her opening poem, "Savitri,"
about the devoted wife from the Mahabarata. Equally important, Christian
saints like Francis of Assisi or Catherine of Sienna unquestionably rival
Bharata at his most ascetic.

Dutt's poem thus wonderfully captures not just the complexities of
Victorian religious culture but also the ways in which it was always evolving,

contested, and renegotiated. Asceticism inspired endless debate among Victorian Christians, both inter- and intra-denominationally. The friends to whom Tennyson first read "St Simeon Stylites" had no idea whether or not he was joking, partly because while Simeon remained canonized in Anglican tradition, his mortifications had become entirely *outré*. Protestants cast aspersions at Catholicism but practiced asceticism in their own ways. (Gosse writes poignantly in *Father and Son* of a Christmas plum pudding being condemned by his Plymouth Brethren father as an "accursed thing.") Even Catholics balked at extreme instances like St. Rose of Lima, whereas Victorian Protestants still revered saints like Francis.[27] Secularism too had its severer forms, so that G. K. Chesterton could champion his "beef and beer" Catholicism against the austerity of his freethinking friend George Bernard Shaw. Rhoda Nunn, the self-denying New Woman activist and secularist reformer of George Gissing's *The Odd Women* (1893), remarks approvingly that "Christianity couldn't spread over the world without help of the ascetic ideal, and this great movement for woman's emancipation must also have its ascetics." Her collaborator responds cautiously that asceticism seemed unlikely to come back into fashion altogether: "I can't declare that you are wrong in that. Who knows? But it isn't good policy to preach it to our young disciples."[28] Dutt's Christianity likewise allows for no unhealthy immoderation and imagines itself marked by good taste, familial bonds, and ordinary compassion. "The Royal Ascetic and the Hind" thus captures ways that Victorian religion, though ubiquitous, was forever being renegotiated by poets who wrestled with it. Dutt's expressions of faith are scripturally grounded but also capricious, for they select modern emphases within Christianity as representative of the whole faith.

The closest religious precedents to Dutt's philosophy might bring us full circle to EBB's sentimental poetic Christianity, or even to Brontë. Dutt's interjections – "What! a sin to love! / A sin to pity!" – advocate the very modern attitudes that we find expressed in something like Brontë's *Shirley* (1849), where the heroines craft their own feminist theologies. "[L]ove! no purest angel need blush to love," cries Caroline Helstone, "And when I see or hear either man or woman couple shame with love, I know their minds are coarse, their associations debased."[29] Shirley, the eponymous heroine, rejoins, "Thou art right, Lina. And in their dense ignorance they blaspheme living fire, seraph-brought from a divine altar" (p. 301). Here, Brontë rejects a patriarchal Christian poetic tradition (explicitly represented in *Shirley* by John Milton) and demands new poetic theologies. Shirley's intimate second-person pronoun, characteristic of Yorkshire dialect, equally evokes the second-person of Anglican prayer. Gail Turley Houston calls such expressions "Victorian alternative religion," but Brontë was a member of the established Church her entire life, and Houston's "alternative" turns out to be a capacious category even within orthodox traditions.[30] Nor can we forget that *Shirley*'s religious polemics come from the author of "The Missionary," the dramatic monologue with which we began.

Religion and Secularization

Religion is not a static category against which secular culture moves, but an evolving discourse that moves with culture. This makes its place in literature more challenging to study, but also more interesting. During much of the twentieth century, under the auspices of what is now called "the secularization narrative," religion's most remarked-upon trait was its presumed incompatibility with the modern world. Scholars habitually viewed any (usually male) poet's interrogation of faith as a forward-thinking anticipation of our own iconoclastic modernity. For many reasons, this paradigm no longer holds water: its teleology, its Eurocentricity, its perverse disregard for the fact that religion has not yet disappeared even from the West. For us, what matters is that Victorian literature continues to bear the fruits of religion's complex legacy. Recent years have seen an enormous amount of exciting work on Victorian literature and religion – far more than I can acknowledge here – largely because we have learned to see Victorian religion not as "a subtraction narrative," in the words of Canadian philosopher Charles Taylor, but as a "spiritual super-nova": an explosion of existential vantages and possibilities.[31] I here treat varying poetic perspectives – evangelical Anglican, Congregationalist, Anglo-Catholic, Jewish, (theoretically) Hindu – to show that in every instance, throughout Victorian women's poetry, the stakes remain exceedingly, sometimes breathtakingly, high.

Notes

1. Kirstie Blair, *Form and Faith in Victorian Poetry and Religion* (Oxford: Oxford University Press, 2012); Karen Dieleman, *Religious Imaginaries: The Liturgical and Poetic Practices of Elizabeth Barrett Browning, Christina Rossetti, and Adelaide Procter* (Athens: Ohio University Press, 2012); Donald S. Hair, *Fresh Strange Music: Elizabeth Barrett Browning's Language* (Montreal: McGill-Queen's University Press, 2015); Constance W. Hassett, *Christina Rossetti: The Patience of Style* (Charlottesville: University of Virginia Press, 2005); Michael D. Hurley, *Faith in Poetry: Verse Style as a Mode of Religious Belief* (London: Bloomsbury, 2017); Joshua King, *Imagined Spiritual Communities in Britain's Age of Print, Literature, Religion, and Postsecular Studies* (Columbus: Ohio State University Press, 2015); Elizabeth Ludlow, *Christina Rossetti and the Bible: Waiting with the Saints* (London: Bloomsbury, 2014); Emma Mason, *Christina Rossetti: Poetry, Ecology, Faith* (New York: Oxford University Press, 2018).

2. William R. McKelvy, *The English Cult of Literature: Devoted Readers, 1774–1880* (Charlottesville: University of Virginia Press, 2007).
3. Hugh McLeod, *Religion and Society in England, 1850–1914* (Basingstoke: Macmillan, 1996).
4. F. Elizabeth Gray, *Christian and Lyric Tradition in Victorian Women's Poetry* (New York: Routledge, 2010), p. 26.
5. See, e.g., Cynthia Scheinberg, *Women's Poetry and Religion in Victorian England: Jewish Identity and Christian Culture* (New York: Cambridge University Press, 2002); Richa Dwor, *Jewish Feeling: Difference and Affect in Nineteenth-Century Jewish Women's Writing* (London: Bloomsbury, 2015).
6. Thomas J. Collins and Vivienne Rundle, *The Broadview Anthology of Victorian Poetry and Poetic Theory* (Peterborough, ON: Broadview, 1999), p. 537.
7. Miriam Elizabeth Burstein, "The Religion(s) of the Brontës," in *A Companion to the Brontës*, ed. Diane Long Hoeveler and Deborah Denenholz Morse (Oxford: Wiley, 2016), pp. 433–51.
8. Talal Asad, *Formations of the Secular: Christianity, Islam, Modernity* (Stanford: Stanford University Press, 2007).
9. Charlotte Brontë, *Jane Eyre*, ed. Richard Dunn, 3rd ed. (New York: W. W. Norton & Co., 2001), p. 376.
10. Elizabeth Barrett Browning, *The Works of Elizabeth Barrett Browning*, vol. 2, ed. Marjorie Stone and Beverly Taylor (London: Pickering & Chatto, 2010), p. 232.
11. Arthur Hugh Clough, *Clough: Selected Poems*, ed. J. P. Phelan (London: Longman, 1995), p. 197.
12. Elizabeth Barrett Browning, *The Works of Elizabeth Barrett Browning*, ed. Sandra Donaldson, vol. 4 (London: Pickering & Chatto, 2010), pp. 347–442.
13. Ibid., vol. 3, p. 23.
14. Ibid., vol. 4, p. 371.
15. Blair, *Form and Faith in Victorian Poetry and Religion*, p. 4.
16. Christina Rossetti, *Christina Rossetti: The Complete Poems*, ed. R. W. Crump (New York: Penguin Classics, 2001), pp. 180–1.
17. James Anthony Froude, *Short Studies on Great Subjects* (London: Longmans, Green and Co., 1907), pp. 206–7.
18. Leonore Davidoff and Catherine Hall, *Family Fortunes* (London: Psychology Press, 2002), p. 111.
19. Rossetti, *The Complete Poems*, p. xl.
20. Grace Aguilar, *Selected Writings* (Peterborough, ON: Broadview Press, 2003), pp. 200–202.
21. Anna Letitia Barbauld, *The Poems of Anna Letitia Barbauld*, ed. William McCarthy and Elizabeth Kraft (Athens: University of Georgia Press, 1994), p. 114.
22. Aguilar, *Selected Writings*, p. 200.
23. Grace Aguilar, "The Hebrew's Appeal," *The Christian Lady's Magazine*, ed. Charlotte Elizabeth [Tonna], 21 (1844), 163.
24. Aguilar, *Selected Writings*, p. 34.
25. Toru Dutt, *Ancient Ballads and Legends of Hindustan*, ed. Edmund Gosse (London: Kegan Paul, Trench & Co., 1885), pp. xi–xii.

26. Tricia Lootens, "The Locations and Dislocations of Toru and Aru Dutt," in *A History of Indian Poetry in English*, ed. Rosinka Chaudhuri (New York: Cambridge University Press, 2016), pp. 82–97.

27. Gareth Atkins, ed., *Making and Remaking Saints in Nineteenth-Century Britain* (Manchester: Manchester University Press, 2016), pp. 13–17.

28. George Gissing, *The Odd Women*, ed. Patricia Ingham (Oxford: Oxford University Press, 2008), p. 70.

29. Charlotte Brontë, *Shirley*, ed. Jessica Cox (New York: Penguin, 2006), p. 301.

30. Gail Turley Houston, "Alternative Victorian Religion and the Recuperation of Women's Voices," *Literature Compass* 13.2 (February 1, 2016), 98–107.

31. Charles Taylor, *A Secular Age* (Cambridge, MA: Harvard University Press, 2007), pp. 26ff., 300.

PART III

Nurturance and Contested Naturalness

11

LAURIE LANGBAUER AND
BEVERLY TAYLOR

Children's Poetry

Nineteenth-century poetry for youth by women poets provides an exciting area of literary and cultural research. Critics such as Angela Sorby in her *Schoolroom Poets* (2005) have turned to the poetry of established nineteenth-century women poets who wrote poems not intended for young people but avidly read by them and institutionalized within schools and children's anthologies: Felicia Hemans, Elizabeth Barrett Browning (EBB), and Christina Rossetti. Other critics foreground the few poems these poets actually wrote for children, especially Rossetti's *Sing-Song* (1872). To modern scholars, their poems *about* children seem to resist categorization as children's poetry due to their emphasis on adult subjects: politics, sex, or mortality. At the time, formal qualities such as short lines and simple diction warranted their selection by adults for children's anthologies nonetheless.

In "Self-Culture for Girls" (in an 1899 *Girl's Own Paper*), the Religious Tract Society writer Lily Watson (1849–1932) encourages her young audience to read and love poetry, but the only woman poet she mentions is Mrs. Browning.[1] By pointing child readers to established poets who did not actually write for them, Victorians obscured the host of women who did. Current children's poetry scholars such as Morag Styles suggest the surviving children's canon culled from old anthologies only lists celebrated poets who ignored children as an audience, thereby hiding the lively tradition of (supposedly) minor women poets who wrote expressly for them.[2]

Popular sources provide a different picture. The girls' magazine *Atalanta* (1887–98) cites EBB and Rossetti as the only women allowed to "rank high" but notably itself finds the well-known children's storyteller Jean Ingelow as equally distinguished; indeed, *Atalanta* published both Rossetti *and* Ingelow. In fact, the author "Maxwell Gray" (Mary Gleed Tuttiett [1846–1923]) asserts that other "women poets are certainly making a brave show in these days," herself among them.[3] Such claims defend the overlooked poets, bravely producing the largest part of children's poetry, against the barbs of cultural gatekeepers. For instance, at the beginning of the twentieth century, the *Cambridge History* did mention Ingelow but considered her one of the lesser poets of the time, guilty of "gush" – and it decreed Menella Bute Smedley and Adelaide Proctor to be lesser poets too, poets who merely wrote "books[s] that used to belong to a fellow's sisters."[4]

Recognized by other women writers even while disparaged by the establishment, these women poets for young people (especially for girls) remain little known today. Recovering this forgotten women's heritage opens up important research directions. It corroborates Lynn Vallone's insight that the tradition of nineteenth-century children's literature "is also the history of women's writing."[5] It also rewrites the cultural history of the time by emphasizing what mattered to readers. This reevaluation takes seriously women's writing for youth that the *Cambridge History* dismissed as sentimental and feminine, at best merely popular.[6] It points attention to a new group of writers – unrecognized women poets but also girl writers – and changes how poems should figure in today's literary canon.

Some neglected women poets for young people are receiving recognition. Styles's wide-ranging study *From the Garden to the Street: An Introduction to 300 Years of Poetry for Children* (1998) mentions Catherine Ann Dorset (c. 1753–1817), Dorothy Kilner (1755–1836), Sarah Catherine Martin (1768–1826), Elizabeth Turner (1775–1846), Adelaide O'Keeffe (1776–1855), Ann and Jane Taylor (1782–1866, 1783–1824), Mary Howitt, and Jane Euphemia Browne [Aunt Effie] (1811–98). In *British Children's Poetry in the Romantic Era* (2014), Donelle Ruwe expands Styles's list to include Charlotte Smith (1749–1806), Mary Ann Kilner (1753–1831), Maria Montolieu (c. 1765–?), Arabella Rowden (c. 1780–c. 1840), Mary Belson Elliott (c. 1794–1870), Agnes Strickland, and Sara Coleridge (1802–52). Ruwe's reconstruction of long misattribution of *Original Poems for Infant Minds* that elided O'Keeffe's contributions reveals the complex suppression of women's poetic agency against which these studies conduct their careful recoveries.[7] Other recent books redirect attention to the actual publication venues of now-unknown women writers; in *Over the River and Through the Wood: An Anthology of Nineteenth-Century American Children's Poetry* (2013), Karen L. Kilcup and Angela Sorby salvage many of their writers from the pages of periodicals.

Recovering women poets for young people demands this mining of periodicals. Nineteenth-century book anthologies of children's poetry deliberately passed over these poets, who nevertheless enjoyed a large audience within magazines for youth. Children's magazines played a central role in the mass print culture that proliferated over the nineteenth century, so that by 1900 around 160 children's magazines had been launched in Britain.[8] Researching magazines prompts formal reconsideration since they published children's hymns, secular and scientific poems, humorous verse, and so on, revealing poetry's "hybridity."[9] This poetry imagines the child variously, pointing to a heterogeneous understanding of childhood, neither fixed nor universal. "Children's poetry" actually addresses a range of implied ages, from nursery poetry geared to infants to more allusive verse meant for adolescents (styled on the school prize poem or "poetess" poetry). Lorraine Kooistra's careful location of Eliza Cook, Proctor, and Ingelow within the larger multimedia publication industry of the time, for instance, exemplifies the particular formal and historical knowledge necessary fully to understand such poetry and its value in culture.[10]

Tracing poetry aimed at adolescents in girls' magazines such as the late-Victorian *Atalanta* reveals a long-standing tradition of poetry for girls going back to the gift books and annuals that burgeoned in the 1820s (dwindling away by the 1860s).[11] Single volumes published around Christmas, their lavish pictures often prompting their poetry, these annuals predated the more frequent periodical magazines soon to follow. Illustration was part of this tradition, as it was to Rossetti's children's writing and would be to children's magazines. Because magazines became commercially practical in the second part of the nineteenth century due to reductions of taxes on newspapers, advertising, and paper, they flourished and supplanted annuals and book publication in the preponderance of poetry produced for young audiences.[12] Moreover, girls not only read, they also wrote this magazine poetry. The vibrancy of female writing for youth is directly connected to a dynamic juvenile tradition that literary criticism has also begun to see flourishing in the nineteenth century. Recognizing that young women wrote children's poetry redefines the category "children"; it implies not just babies or Romantic innocents but adolescent youth who were active agents with something to say.

Reconfiguring children's poetry through girls' magazines addresses another critical hurdle: a lack of theory surrounding children's poetry.[13] Until recently, most literary criticism refused children's poetry serious analysis, presuming commercial expediency as the only rationale for its existence and ubiquity: though women wrote thousands of children's poems, they only "wove their verses by the yard to clothe a market," Donald Hall assumes in *The Oxford Book of Children's Verse in America* (1985).[14] Modern critics base such dismissal on Victorian dis-regard – few leading articles or reviews of the time treat children's poetry *per se*, and those that do determinedly avoid the women poets who expressly wrote it. Yet, rather than lack a sense of worth or an explana-tory system for its own importance, poetry for youth demonstrates its seriousness in its practice. The consensus in girls' magazines such as

Atalanta that poetry for youth mattered was so deeply shared by its writers and readers as almost to go without saying. The poetry and essays within those magazines provide a treasure-house of material implicitly but firmly engaged with the importance of writing for children.

Established Poets

Although Felicia Hemans died two years before Victoria became queen in 1837, her poetry remained central to Victorian experience for much of the century. Her *Hymns for Childhood* (1834) combined detailed observations of nature with devotional praise, producing poems celebrating the skylark and the nightingale, for example, as manifestations of divine love. Hemans's works written for a general audience, not specifically for children, became well known to young readers as favorite schoolroom recitation pieces (most especially "Casabianca,"[15] "Evening Prayer, at a Girl's School," and "The Stately Homes of England"), and volumes of Hemans's poetry were frequently presented as school prizes, mostly for girls. Hemans herself was initially celebrated as a girl poet (as Felicia Dorothea Browne), publishing her first volume at age thirteen. The prominence of her work among memorization pieces and book prizes led to the 1847 publication of a *Hemans Reader for Female Schools.*

Hemans's popularity with young readers was soon matched by the popularity of Elizabeth Barrett Barrett (after 1846, Barrett Browning), even though EBB never published poems especially directed to young readers, a reminder that the line between poetry for adults and for young audiences remained uncertain. Also a precocious poet, EBB had begun composing verse by the time she was six. While her earliest piece, four lines on the subject of naval impressment, anticipated the political preoccupations evident in much of her late poetry, many of her earliest childhood writings were jocular pieces teasing family members, memorializing family travels or notable events on her family's estate, or describing the trying experiences of fictional children who defied parental instructions or otherwise violated social taboos or boundaries. EBB's childhood writings remained unpublished until well into the twentieth century, however, and her publications for adult readers – available in periodicals and annuals such as *Finden's Tableaux*, as well as in her poetry collections – account for her popularity with young readers, a phenomenon memorialized by Emily Dickinson's tribute poem remarking her own adolescent discovery of EBB. "I think I was enchanted," she wrote about first reading "that Foreign Lady" when she was just "a sombre Girl." In EBB's "Tomes of solid Witchcraft," young Dickinson heard "the meanest Tunes" "murmured" by Nature as "Titanic Opera."[16]

Just a year after EBB, celebrated as Victorian England's "Queen of Song," died, Christina Rossetti emerged as her successor, publishing the very successful volume *Goblin Market and Other Poems* (1862). Although the title poem was not written for children, it has frequently appeared in collections and publications for young readers, beginning with Mary A. Woods's anthology *A Second School Poetry Book* (1887), designed for readers aged eleven through fourteen (thirteen through fifteen in a later edition).[17] The poem's delightful diction and rhythm and its fantasy elements – primarily the Goblin men (Rossetti originally intended to use the title "A Peep at the Goblins") – would seem purposefully contrived to attract young readers.[18] Although Rossetti insisted she intended no allegorical meaning, modern critics have interpreted the poem from multiple complex, sophisticated perspectives, many of them ill suited for young readers. Persuasive analyses include Marxist and other economic interpretations, and Freudian and other sexual discussions. Critics have foregrounded topics including temptation and salvation; female agency and critique of Victorian gender roles; and erotic desire, transgression, and moral and social redemption. The poem's attention to the "Fallen Woman," encapsulated in references to Jeanie, "Who should have been a bride; / But who for joys brides hope to have / Fell sick and died" (1.19, lines 313–15), conspicuously violates Victorian propriety. Laura's speaking to her young daughters and nieces at the poem's end may frame the work as an address to girls, advising that "there is no friend like a sister ... To lift one if one totters down, / To strengthen whilst one stands" (1.26, lines 562–7). Even so, the poem's lessons urging wariness of "goblin men" and of sensory (erotic) appetites weigh heavily against the formal qualities and sound effects that might commend the poem to children: elements including short lines, varying and compelling rhythms, repetition, witty rhymes, abnormal syntax, frequent puns, repetition, oxymorons, and catalogues of exotic fruits continue to attract anthologists targeting young readers. Victorian reviewers noted this tension between the aggressively adult subject matter, on the one hand, and the imaginative and auditory appeals to young readers, on the other. An American, Mrs. Charles Eliot Norton (née Sarah Sedgwick, 1838–72), reviewing in *Macmillan's Magazine*, observed the poem's hybridity, calling it "a ballad which children will con with delight, and which riper minds may ponder over."[19]

Like both Hemans and EBB, Rossetti was a precocious writer. Her earliest recorded poem, composed before she turned six and before she could write, demonstrates sprightly imagination: "Cecilia never went to school / Without her gladiator."[20] Rossetti's poetic play as a child writer soon yielded to a serious commitment to formal development. She wrote more than fifty poems before she turned sixteen, experimenting with ballads, hymns, and

LAURIE LANGBAUER AND BEVERLY TAYLOR

sonnets. She and her brothers competed in writing *bouts rimés* sonnets, working against the clock and one another to compose in the Petrarchan pattern using predetermined rhyming words in a prescribed order.

Perhaps because of reactions to "Goblin Market," Rossetti a decade after its publication compiled a collection specifically addressed to children, *Sing-Song: A Nursery Rhyme Book* (1874), becoming the first major Victorian woman poet to write specifically for children. She wittily dedicated *Sing-Song* to an unnamed baby ("Rhymes dedicated without permission to the baby who suggested them," 2.19), the nephew of longtime friend Charles Cayley, at one time her suitor. Even so, Rossetti did not manifest strong interest in educating or entertaining children with her verse. In 1862 she declined to contribute to a poetry collection for children, because "*children are not amongst my suggestive subjects.*"[21] She assembled *Sing-Song,* and two years later a volume of three prose fantasy tales entitled *Speaking Likenesses* (1874) to capitalize on the lucrative market for children's Christmas books.[22] Gratifyingly enthusiastic reviews of her poetry collection did not produce especially strong sales, though a new edition of *Sing-Song,* for which Rossetti rearranged poems, lengthened six, and added five new ones, appeared in 1893. The first edition collected 121 brief poems. Most are only one or two stanzas long, with short lines, simple syntax, simple diction, and imagery familiar from nature. Recurring imagery suggests that mother's loving embrace is but one element in a child's physical nurturance. Nature imagery reinforces this general view with lots of references to soft lambkins, happy birds, and flourishing flowers. Some recurring motifs and preoccupations may seem emotionally challenging for young auditors and readers, however, since they emphasize the abiding shadow of death.

Mortality becomes an overarching theme of the collection from first to last. Poems admonish children not to harm animals, referencing "cruel boys" who rob birds' nests, leaving parent birds desolate (2.22). Such gestures toward dangers and death reinforce preoccupations with human mortality evident from the collection's beginning. Whereas the first poem presents a "pretty babe" in its cradle, "like a curly little lamb" treasured and protected by angels (2.19), and the second lyric represents a doting mother singing lovingly to her baby, the third poem opposes the "poor little baby" who has neither father nor mother to the "rich little baby!" who has both (2.19). The fourth poem of the volume imagines a baby who has died but anticipates its being reunited with "Mamma" in heaven (2.20). This poem expresses the faith that undergirds abundant references to death throughout the collection: the dead go to Heaven, where love engulfs them and mirrors the warm love that enfolds children on earth, love lavished by parents and reflecting love that permeates Nature and emanates from God.

The final poems in the collection echo sentiments of the first four. The third from last poem depicts a lovely baby who requires to be cuddled and loved; the penultimate poem, a lullaby, croons a baby to sleep – with flowers, lambs, and birds; and the collection's last poem speaks of putting the baby in its cradle, ending the poem and the volume with "Baby, sleep." But the fourth from the last poem admonishes about a dead baby: "Kiss her once and leave her" (2.50). If the poems about cherished babies at the collection's beginning and end create a reassuring frame, the dead baby poems just inside this frame constitute a kind of visual mat setting off the picture within, highlighting mortality to point up the collection's religious faith underlying the quiet drama of the everyday.

Given the volume's belief in elevation to celestial joy and love, the suggestions of danger, loss, and bad weather (especially winter's cold) create a stoic understanding that life will mix pleasure with pain, love with loss. The brilliant rose that "sets the world on fire" with her "glowing heart" will soon wilt, leaving only thorns (2.43). Stormy seas may engulf a loved one; winter's cold may devastate. But sunshine returns, and spring comes again. Insistent reminders of death awaiting all mortal creatures pulsate steadily beneath the poems' abundant celebrations of all that is charming, joyful, and beautiful in Nature. A brief litany of the language of flowers (rose for delight, honeysuckle for love, heliotrope for hope, pansies for memory, etc.) culminates in "violets of fragrant breath, / For death" (2.40). The next poem juxtaposes bells gaily memorializing a wedding with bells sighing "for a funeral" (2.40). Elsewhere "Three merry sisters" in Stanza 1 become "Two mournful sisters" hearing a "tolling knell" in Stanza 2 (2.36). In sum, the collection's overarching lesson for its child audience is to appreciate the joys of this world fully and gladly while accepting their ephemerality, for joy and love also await us in Heaven.

Some of the poems serve explicitly pedagogical ends: they teach fundamentals for understanding time (sixty seconds in a minute, sixty minutes in an hour [2.30]), currency (how much is in a pound, a shilling, a penny [2.30]), sums (from 1 plus 1 to 12 plus 12 [2.29–30]), and months of the year (2.30). Other poems teach more abstract life lessons, such as the value of persistence and patience: a young girl bemoaning how very many stitches she must sew to hem her handkerchief learns that by just setting to work she will accomplish the seemingly impossible and be rewarded, liberated to "play" (2.28). Another verse prompts that a cold person will prize a lump of coal more highly than a diamond (2.42). Other examples in Nature offer life lessons: a toadstool springs up overnight, but while an oak may take a hundred years to grow, it will finally be an oak, not a mere toadstool (2.28). Numerous poems model the culture's gender roles without overtly

187

interrogating them. Money will pay the tariff for a ferry ride whereas
a female's blue eyes will not, despite her pride in them (2.41). A "wee
wifie" must ask her husband for money to stock the cupboard, but he may
not provide it (2.44–5). When doling out cherries, the speaker has one each
for her mother and her siblings, but six for father, who will come home from
work "hot and tired" (2.31–2). "If I were a Queen," muses a girl, "I'd make
you King, / And I'd wait on you." "If I were a King," he replies, "I'd make
you Queen, / For I'd marry you" (2.26).

Although Lewis Carroll's *Alice in Wonderland* (1865) may have influenced the fantasy elements of Rossetti's prose *Speaking Likenesses*,[23] the
poems of *Sing-Song* do not consistently express what Julia Briggs has called
"the high spirits, free-floating imagination, and anarchic feelings so characteristic of childhood." Instead, the poems recall Briggs's point that children's
books are written by adults for the adults who will purchase them.[24]
Nonetheless, Constance W. Hassett makes a compelling case for *Sing-Song*'s
clever artistry, attractiveness to children, and contributions to the tradition
of poetry for youths.[25] The poems of *Sing-Song* are frequently amusing and
playful. In linking colors to things in Nature, Rossetti concludes, "What is
orange? why, an orange" (2.31). Sometimes clever play of language animates
absurd situations: "If a pig wore a wig, / What could we say?" "If his tail
chanced to fail, / What could we do?" Finding a "tailoress" to make a new
tail will solve the pig's problem (2.28–9). Several poems play with oddities of
language: "A dumb-bell is no bell, though dumb" (2.21); "A pin has a head,
but has no hair"; "Needles have eyes, but they cannot see"; "A timepiece
may lose, but cannot win"; a wineglass has a stem but no root (2.32);
"The peacock has a score of eyes / With which he cannot see" (2.34). One
poem depends on the pleasure of saying the word "pancake" four times in
six brief lines (2.38). Another makes a riddle of linguistic oddity, asking
what has "an eye without a head," hinting that "the answer hangs upon
a thread" (2.36).

Arthur Hughes's illustrations in the text constituted an important feature
of the poems. Rossetti initially proposed that her friend Alice Boyd be
contracted to illustrate the works, for she would execute the drawings with
"fun and zest."[26] Hughes, a well-known painter and book illustrator, produced images more sentimental than fun or zesty. Usually the illustration
heading each poem neatly complements its text, but occasionally the illustration shapes a surprisingly acute interpretive context by supplying details not
evident in the poem. To illustrate the observation that when the speaker's one
rose dies, only thorns will remain, Hughes connects the metaphor directly to
the collection's preoccupations with children and mortality by depicting
a child sick in bed, nursed tenderly by its mother. He similarly accentuates

a metaphor's link to human behavior when he illustrates a verse about the blushing rose that hangs her head while the white lily stands upright: Hughes images a lady tending flowers while a man leans over her garden gate, thereby turning the poem's essentially innocuous floral contrast into a lesson about maidenly virtue. Elsewhere Hughes's image emphasizes the full meaning of the text: for the poem "Motherless baby and babyless mother, / Bring them together to love one another" (2.50), he draws a baby being handed across a grave into a new guardian's keeping.

The didactic element conspicuous in many of Rossetti's poems and in some of Hughes's illustrations continues an instructional dimension inherent in children's literature from its beginnings. This aspect of the literary tradition for children was evident, for example, in *Pretty Lessons in Verse for Good Children* (1834) by Sara Coleridge, daughter of Samuel Taylor Coleridge, who explained the framework of economic colonialism in "Good Things from Distant Places" ("Tea is brought from China; / Rice from Carolina, / India and Italy – / Countries far beyond the sea"), and who tailored behavioral advice to her son in "Mama's Advice to Herbert."[27] Later in the century, the popular novelist and poet Jean Ingelow broke with this conventional didactic and moralizing strain, including in her story *Mopsa the Fairy* (1869) some oddly quirky, imaginative poems that seem at least superficially unconnected to the story. Rossetti's *Sing-Song* represents a pivotal collection for the nursery – what Debbie Pullinger calls "a landmark" in children's literature because it joins three strands that had previously been treated separately in writing for young audiences: the oral tradition of legends, tall tales, and the supernatural; moral and religious verse; and Romantic poetry that draws heavily on elements of nature to illustrate concepts and connect to the transcendent.[28] The volume also illustrates the challenges of defining children's poetry: what ages are encompassed in the word "children," and who mandates what they will find interesting, understandable, and meaningful?

Redefining Poetry for Youth

Over the course of the century, women writers expanded the reach of children's poetry by increasing the age of its audience. Pullinger argues that though readers assumed children's poetry was simple, it never actually was; nevertheless, the pervasive sense it ought to be also reveals the assumption of a particular audience – very young readers. As Kooistra suggests, the simplicity of diction and meter in Rossetti's *Sing-Song* was supposed to mirror "the special grace of little children." Ruwe traces this emphasis on simplicity to the preface of *Original Poems for Infant Minds* (1804) by the Taylor sisters and O'Keeffe and notes that foregrounding plain words, often of just one or two syllables, short lines, and straightforward syntax became hegemonic in children's poetry at the beginning of the century.[29] Certainly the similarly uncomplicated illustrated rhymes in John Harris's Cabinet series – such as Martin's *The Comic Adventures of Old Mother Hubbard and Her Dog* (1805) or Dorset's *The Peacocks "At Home"* (1809) – were obviously meant for young children (Cabinet Books were one of the miniature libraries designed for small hands). Such books remained popular through mid-century; their emphasis on simple diction and meter continued to century's end in the verse of Kate Greenaway (1846–1901). By the time of Victoria's ascension, however, this nursery poetry had come to share the bookstall with a new vogue addressing girls, not babies – ornamental literary annuals, miscellanies of stories, poems, and illustrations, which, given advances in steel engraving, had become cost-effective. Annuals were overwhelmingly popular for readers of all ages, but especially for women, their families, and their daughters in particular. Frederick Faxon's early bibliography lists at least ten British annuals in the 1830s entitled some variant of "Juvenile," with other titles addressing "Young Ladies."[30]

Such poetry aimed far beyond the nursery. Lily Watson claims "there is scarcely a more favourite subject for the delineation by the poet or artist than the period when childhood is just melting into womanhood."[31] *The Juvenile Forget-Me-Not* annual of 1836 (published 1828–38 and 1862, edited after 1829 by "Mrs. S. C. Hall" [Anna Maria Fielding, 1800–81]), has poetry by women poets Letitia Landon (L.E.L.), Mary Howitt, and Sarah Stickney [Ellis] (1799–1872), each of whom edited the adult literary annual *Fisher's Drawing Room Scrap-Book* (1832–54); Ellis also edited *Fisher's Juvenile Scrap-Book* (1836–50). Although their poems in the *Juvenile Forget-Me-Not* were aimed at young children – L.E.L.'s "The Lesson" addresses a "mother's darling" who has to learn his alphabet before he can run off to play[32] – the writers' presence in both markets underscores that "the division between children's and adult literature didn't exist as sharply as it does today."[33] L.E.L.'s poem appeals perhaps more to the young women who read such poems aloud to younger siblings than to the small boys it purports to address (but depicts as only interested in playing outside). Such young ladies, occupying the liminal space between women's and children's poetry, operated as the audience for both: scholars argue that publishers selling poetry assumed that women and children were the same market.[34]

Young ladies were also poets. L.E.L., first published at age seventeen, was touted by her impresario William Jerdan as a girl prodigy, simultaneously a woman writing for children and a child writing for adults. Recent criticism has explored a tradition of young poets, recognized and reviewed at the time, writing out of a common sense of youth. Even the *Cambridge History* grudgingly admits, "Some, mainly younger, poetesses . . . obtained, and one or two of them deserved, reputation as such."[35] In addition to Hemans, EBB, Rossetti, and L.E.L., other writers mentioned here published before they turned twenty-one: Rowden (probably), the Taylor sisters, Elliott, Howitt, Coleridge, Cook, Procter, Rossetti, L. T. Meade (1844–1914), Harriet Prescott Spofford (1835–1921), and Mary E. Wilkins [Freeman] (1852–1930), most in periodicals, and – by the century's end – especially in juvenile magazines. Such magazines were explicitly interested in juvenile writing. *Atalanta* discusses Louisa May Alcott's and EBB's and even printed lines from Robert Browning's juvenile *Pauline*. Margaret Oliphant (1828–97) asserted about *Atalanta* that "this magazine is not without responsibility in having encouraged and guided the early footsteps of some who are entering that profession."[36]

From their eighteenth-century beginning, periodicals, needing free copy, encouraged juvenile publication. Juvenile journals ran competitions for young readers to encourage their contributions, including girls as well as boys.[37] *Atalanta* even improved on this practice; its Scholarship and Reading Union innovatively asked readers to pay a larger subscription fee to publish writing in its pages. It printed its first prize poem by "Elsie J. Campbell MacLachlan (aged 18)" (c. 1869–1903?) and included others in its "Brown Owl" editorial columns.[38] As Oliphant observed, some contributors did go on to literary careers. Sally Mitchell notes that Angela Brazil ("highly commended" in *Atalanta* at age eighteen for her Union essays) became a popular writer of girl's boarding school stories. Steven Holland points out that prizewinner Blanche Oram later published as "Roma White."[39]

A noted teenaged writer, L.E.L. also exemplifies the melding of women's writing and children's poetry within reigning preconceptions about poetic form. Just as nursery poetry was typified by simplicity, poetry for girls was cast in terms of what the *Cambridge History* called adolescent "gush." L.E.L., prominent in the literary annuals in her twenties and thirties, was dismissed by cultural gatekeepers because of that placement as perpetually juvenile – a "poetess." Supposedly artless and jejune, poetess "gush" was associated with purported childish simplicity; Laura Mandell's stylistic analysis of poetess poetry parallels Ruwe's analysis of children's nursery verse,[40] explaining why some L.E.L. verses could seem to contemporaries equally infantile and geared to young ladies. But Tricia Lootens finds in supposed gush an overt politics, and Isobel Armstrong redefines it formally as self-aware, arguing that L.E.L's writing is not naïve but rigorous and intricate.[41] L.E.L., Hemans, and other so-called poetesses directly reflect on their own writing in terms of power and agency, exploring its relation to juvenility.[42]

In "The Little Mountaineer," another of L.E.L.'s poems in the *Juvenile Forget-Me-Not*, the speaker strongly identifies with her child protagonist – "A poet's world is in her heart" – who provides an emblem for the implied depths within this writing: "a pensiveness beyond its years / Is in her childish grace."[43]

Meta-reflection was actually widespread within a periodical press that modern critics find not just self-aware but endlessly interested in itself as an important subject.[44] As *Atalanta* asserted: "This is assuredly the day of periodical literature."[45] Every issue of *Atalanta* demystified some aspect of publication. Considering "Literature" as a possible occupation for *Atalanta* readers, Gray presents writing as hard practical work: "poetry will pay only when very bad or very good, possibly not then; for poetry is seldom read these days." In "From the Editor's Standpoint," L. T. Meade concurs and advises girls how dispassionately to regard and pragmatically to sell their writing. Women (including Gray) offer wry accounts of their naïvety in their first publications. Male writers (E. Conder Gray [Alexander Japp]) contribute comic stories about young men's romanticizations of "The Lady Poet."[46]

Atalanta – aimed at girls in their teens and early twenties of the upper-middle classes but carried by libraries so that it also reached the middle and working classes[47] – demonstrates that poetry for young people was complex and serious. Meade tirelessly solicited an array of women writers: Oliphant and Mary Louisa Molesworth serialized novels, contributed to its editorial column, and wrote essays and reviews. Its women's poetry mixed well-known literary or popular writers – Anna Letitia Barbauld (1743–1825), Christina Rossetti, Marion Buchanan (1840–?), Katharine Tynan (1861–1931) – and celebrities – Caroline Blanche Elizabeth (née FitzRoy), Lady Lindsay (1844–1912), Violet Hunt (1862–1942) – as well as established children's writers including E. Nesbit and Graham R. Tomson (Rosamund Marriott Watson), who was a major contributor to E. Nesbit's children's anthology *Night-Songs and Sketches* (1890), and the Americans Clara Doty Banks (1837–95), Spofford, and Freeman. By and large, the women poets it frequently printed remain unresearched – Ella Fuller Maitland (1857–1939), Mary MacLeod (fl. 1890s), and Mary Gorges (fl. 1890s) are just a few of those most published who are still little known.[48]

Poetry for youth was so popular, its audience so committed to the magazines that carried it, that we need to rethink its status, recognizing it as a shaping force for a generation of young women: Sally Mitchell found that most girls entering the 1900 *Girl's Realm* competition on "My Ambition" wanted above all to be famous writers.[49] Whether or not they went on to publish in magazines or anywhere else, magazine readers agreed that magazine writing for youth was vital. Periodicals depended on getting readers so involved they became fans – as any letters' section attests – a loyal base necessary to keep these publications afloat.[50] But their readers' investment also rested in the potential for agency, literary opportunity, and even cultural influence that children's poetry promised. Sorby argues that women had more editorial control over children's poetry than any other publication sphere, as all the editors of juvenile magazines – Fielding, L.E.L., Howitt, Ellis, and Meade – in this chapter indicate. Since assumptions of the time sanctioned women as children's poets, paradoxically that role provided a kind of authority for them, a position at odds with the minor or sentimental role to which we modern readers might relegate children's poetry. Wielding that authority meant these women wrote poems that were sometimes "more barbed and transgressive" than poems for adults.[51] Sorby cites Emily Dickinson, who transformed simplicity of form into devastating cultural critique, as did Rossetti in *Sing-Song* when her speakers lay out gender inequity as simply as children laying out their blocks: Kings marry (and in that way create) Queens; Queens simply "wait on" Kings.

Such new frameworks make children's poetry a rich and lively field for modern research. A new generation of scholars now addresses poetry for youth with the same understanding Gray takes to literature as an occupation for young women, understanding that it is a field that women have already "entered, unsummoned and unheralded," and one in which they have "borne themselves gallantly." "Do they realise – does anyone realise," she concludes, "the greatness and glory of that" charge?[52]

Notes

1. Lily Watson, "Self-Culture For Girls," *Girl's Own Paper*, August 5, 1899, 706.
2. Morag Styles, *From the Garden to the Street: An Introduction to 300 Years of Poetry for Children* (London: Cassell, 1998), p. 188.
3. Maxwell Gray, "Occupations of Gentlewomen. III. Literature," *Atalanta*, 8 (1893–4), 289.
4. William Thackeray, qtd. in *The Cambridge History of English Literature*, vol. XIII: *The Nineteenth Century II*, eds. Adolphus William Ward and A. R. Waller (New York: Cambridge University Press, 1916), pp. 177–8.
5. Lynne Vallone, "Women Writing for Children," in *Women and Literature in Britain 1800–1900*, ed. Joanne Shattock (Cambridge: Cambridge University Press, 2001), p. 276.
6. Ward and Waller, *Cambridge History*, p. 178.
7. Donnelle Ruwe, *British Children's Poetry in the Romantic Era: Verse, Riddle, and Rhyme* (London: Palgrave Macmillan, 2014), pp. 74–82.
8. Linda K. Hughes, *The Cambridge Introduction to Victorian Poetry* (Cambridge: Cambridge University Press, 2010), p. 177; Claudia Nelson, "Children's

Writing," in *The Cambridge Companion to Victorian Women's Writing*, ed. Linda Peterson (Cambridge: Cambridge University Press, 2015), pp. 260–1. Nelson cites Diana Dixon for the figures.

9. Vallone, "Women," p. 277.

10. Lorraine Janzen Kooistra, *Poetry, Pictures, and Popular Publishing: The Illustrated Gift Book and Victorian Visual Culture, 1855–1875* (Athens: Ohio University Press, 2011), p. 177.

11. A. Bose, "The Verse of the English Annuals," *Review of English Studies*, n.s. 4 (1953), 38.

12. Kristine Moruzi, *Constructing Girlhood through the Periodical Press, 1850–1915* (Burlington, VT: Ashgate, 2012), p. 5.

13. Debbie Pullinger, *From Tongue to Text: A New Reading of Children's Poetry* (London: Bloomsbury, 2017), p. 5.

14. Donald Hall, "Introduction," *The Oxford Book of Children's Verse in America* (New York: Oxford University Press, 1985), pp. xxxii, xxxv.

15. See Catherine Robson, *Heart Beats: Everyday Life and the Memorized Poem* (Princeton: Princeton University Press, 2012).

16. Emily Dickinson, "I think I was enchanted," *The Poems of Emily Dickinson: A Variorum Edition*, ed. R. W. Franklin, 3 vols. (Cambridge, MA: Harvard University Press, 1998), Fr627.

17. Lorraine Janzen Kooistra, "Goblin Market as a Cross-Audienced Poem: Children's Fairy Tale, Adult Erotic Fantasy," *Children's Literature*, 25 (1997), 185.

18. Christina Rossetti, *The Complete Poems of Christina Rossetti: A Variorum Edition*, ed. R. W. Crump, 3 vols. (Baton Rouge: Louisiana State University Press, 1979), 1.234. Subsequent quotations from Rossetti's poetry follow this edition, with volume and page numbers noted parenthetically.

19. Mrs. Charles Eliot Norton [Susan Ridley Sedgwick], review of Patmore's "The Angel in the House" and Rossetti's "Goblin Market," *Macmillan's Magazine*, 8 (1863), 402; cited in U. C. Knoepflmacher, *Ventures into Childland: Victorians, Fairy Tales, and Femininity* (Chicago: University of Chicago Press, 1998), p. 321.

20. Christina Rossetti, *The Poetical Works of Christina Georgina Rossetti with Memoir and Notes*, ed. William Michael Rossetti (London: Macmillan, 1904), p. xlix.

21. Christina Rossetti, *Letters of Christina Rossetti*, ed. Antony H. Harrison, 4 vols. (Charlottesville: University Press of Virginia, 1997–2004), 1.159.

22. Nelson, "Children's Writing," p. 262.

23. Rossetti, *Letters*, 2.12; see also 1.257.

24. Julia Briggs, "Women Writers and Writing for Children: From Sarah Fielding to E. Nesbit," in *Children and Their Books: A Celebration of the Work of Iona and Peter Opie*, ed. Gillian Avery and Julia Briggs (Oxford: Clarendon, 1989), pp. 222–3.

25. Constance W. Hassett, *Christina Rossetti: The Patience of Style* (Charlottesville: University of Virginia Press, 2005), pp. 117–53.

26. Rossetti, *Letters*, 1.343–4.

27. Sara Coleridge, *Pretty Lessons in Verse for Good Children*, 4th ed. (London: John W. Parker, 1845), pp. 14–16, 20–1.

28. Pullinger, *Tongue to Text*, p. 17.
29. Pullinger, *Tongue to Text*, p. 3; Kooistra, *Christina Rossetti and Illustration: A Publishing History* (Athens: Ohio University Press, 2002), p. 108; Ruwe, *British Children's Poetry*, pp. 20–1.
30. Frederick Faxon, *Literary Annuals and Gift Books; A Bibliography with a Descriptive Introduction* (Boston: Boston Book Co., 1912), pp. 99–100, 112.
31. Lily Watson, "Girlhood," in *The Girl's Own Outdoor Book*, ed. Charles Peters (London: Religious Tract Society, 1889), p. 13.
32. L.E.L., "The Lesson," *The Juvenile-Forget-Me-Not*, ed. Mrs. S. C. Hall (London: Ackermanns, 1836), p. 151.
33. Monika Elbert, "Review of *Over the River*," *Legacy*, 32 (2015), 318; Anne Lundin, "Victorian Horizons: The Reception of Children's Books in England and America, 1880–1900," *Library Quarterly*, 64 (1994), 40–2.
34. Barbara Onslow, *Women of the Press in Nineteenth-Century Britain* (London: Macmillan, 2000), p. 130.
35. Ward and Waller, *Cambridge History*, p. 181.
36. Edward Salmon, "Miss L. M. Alcott," 448, Mrs Humphrey Ward, "English Men and Women of Letters of the 19th Century: Elizabeth Barrett Browning," 709, *Atalanta* 1 (1887–8); L.T.S., "The Brown Owl," *Atalanta*, 5 (1891–2), 308, 372; Mrs. Oliphant, "The Brown Owl: Things in General," *Atalanta*, 7 (1893–4), 732.
37. Laurie Langbauer, *The Juvenile Tradition: Young Writers and Prolepsis, 1750–1835* (New York: Oxford University Press, 2016), pp. 60, 129–30.
38. Elsie J. Campbell MacLachlan, "Historical Subject: After the Battle of Hastings," *Atalanta*, 1 (1887–8), 298; for possible contributors' poems, see "The Brown Owl," *Atalanta*, 4 (1890–1), 541, 670, 734, and *Atalanta*, 10 (1896–7), 262, 430, 485, 542–3, 654.
39. Sally Mitchell, *The New Girl: Girls' Culture in England, 1880–1915* (New York: Columbia University Press, 1995), p. 16. Steven Holland, "British Juvenile Story Papers and Pocket Libraries Index," www.philsp.com/homeville/bjsp/t9.htm#TOP
40. Laura Mandell, "Introduction: The Poetess Tradition," *Romanticism on the Net*, 29–30 (February, May 2003) www.erudit.org/en/journals/ron/2003-n29-30-ron695/007712ar/ paras 26–36; Ruwe, *British Children's Poetry*, pp. 20–35.
41. Tricia Lootens, *The Political Poetess: Victorian Femininity, Race, and the Legacy of Separate Spheres* (Princeton: Princeton University Press, 2017), p. 200; Isobel Armstrong, "The Gush of the Feminine," in *Romantic Women Writers: Voices and Countervoices*, eds. Paula Feldman and Theresa Kelley (Hanover: University of New England Press, 1995), pp. 26, 32.
42. Langbauer, *Juvenile*, pp. 187–228.
43. L.E.L., "The Little Mountaineer," *The Juvenile-Forget-Me-Not*, ed. Hall (London: Ackermanns, 1836), p. 32.
44. Onslow, *Women of the Press*, p. 6.
45. L. T. Meade, "The Brown Owl," *Atalanta*, 4 (1890–1), 414.
46. Gray, "Occupations," 287; Meade, "From the Editor's Standpoint," *Atalanta*, 6 (1892–3), 839; A. Fleming, "My Editors," Mrs. Cooke, "Our First Publisher," and E. Conder Gray, "The Lady Poet," *Atalanta*, 7 (1893–4), 81–2, 385–9, and 511–13; Maxwell Gray, "My First Success," *Atalanta*, 9 (1895–6), 32–5.
47. Mitchell, *New Girl*, p. 11.

48. For Macleod, see Raya M., "Mary Macleod and the Poetry of Religious Surrender," *Victorian Poetry Network* http://web.uvic.ca/~vicpoet/2013/03/mary-macleod-and-the-poetry-of-religious-surrender/
49. Mitchell, *New Girl*, p. 147.
50. Onslow, *Women of the Press*, pp. 132, 131.
51. Angela Sorby, *Schoolroom Poets: Childhood, Performance, and the Place of American Poetry, 1865–1917* (Durham: University of New Hampshire Press, 2005), p. 176.
52. Gray, "Occupations," 290.

12

EMILY HARRINGTON

Marriage, Motherhood, and Domesticity

Victorian women's poetry represents a variety of competing experiences, ideals, and problems with marriage, motherhood, and domesticity, which generally exist in an uneasy alliance. Whereas marriage plot novels often presume domestic bliss in marriage as a goal, poetry has license to evoke the conflict, instability, and dissatisfaction within it. Often, social conventions obstruct the love that might form domestic bliss, while allegiances to family and nation defy the union of erotic and maternal love. I open with a gift book collection and a poem in which marriage, motherhood, and domesticity appear to be fractured within and between one another. Because poets often address these experiences individually, I also discuss them separately thereafter.

Fractured Homes

Home Thoughts and Home Scenes (1864) seems primed to reinforce conventional domestic ideology. One of the many annuals and Christmas-release publications marketed as gift books, handsomely bound collections of pictures and poems that constituted one of the most conventional and popular means of circulating women's poetry in the nineteenth century, *Home Thoughts and Home Scenes* contains pictures depicting child life by Arthur Boyd Houghton and poems commissioned from popular women poets Jean Ingelow, Dora Greenwell (1821–92), Amelia B. Edwards (1831–92), and Caroline Norton to accompany the engravings. Such books were domestic and familial in their target markets and object status, for they were meant to be of intergenerational interest, given as gifts that would occupy a prominent place in the drawing room. By virtue of their gender, women were deemed ideal authors of poems on children and home, though most poets in *Home Thoughts* were single and childless, save Norton.[1]

Together, the poems and pictures create a vision of childhood experience that goes beyond the domestic. The children in the poems and pictures often imaginatively project themselves outside the home, pretending to be on a stage coach, doing the rough work of haymaking, or even executing Mary Queen of Scots. Fathers make no appearance and grandparents make a couple of cameos; even mothers are far from central, and a mother's perspective hardly ever appears, except in "The Queen of Hearts" by L. W. T., when the speaker instructs the mother to enjoy fully the baby's affection:

> Happy mother! Closer, nearer,
>   Revel in that velvet kiss –
> Take your fill – for nothing dearer
>   Life can offer you than this.[2]

Both the structure of the book and most of its contents reinforce a domestic ideology in which childrearing constitutes the pinnacle of a women's experience. Yet here the idea comes not from the mother herself, but from another family member who idealizes the experience from the outside. So while a book with the repeated "home" in its title might seem to offer visions of domestic completeness, it is notable for representing the way children imagine themselves outside of home, and for its absences and exclusions, particularly of the perspectives of grown women. Although other poets discussed in this chapter consider women's experiences with great nuance, this book, created for the popular market, seems largely uninterested in them, with the exception of the final poem.

Implicit, perhaps unintentional absences in most of the collection give way to a story of deliberate exclusion from the domestic ideal in the final poem of *Home Thoughts*, Caroline Norton's "Crippled Jane," which opens as follows:

> They said she might recover, if we sent her down to the sea,
> But that is for rich men's children, and we knew it could not be:
> So she lived at home in the Lincolnshire Fens, and we saw her, day by day,
> Grow pale, and stunted and crooked, till her last chance died away.[3]

With these opening lines, Norton exposes the conditions of class, gender, and ability on which the assumptions of all the other poems rely. The poem's long lines, hexameters that depart from the lilting tetrameters of other selections, advertise that this poem takes on comparably serious topics, ones that require a meter of drama, tragedy, or epic. In the phrase "rich men's children," she notes that in this society both money and children belong to men, a condition that Norton knew personally, since she lost both money and custody of her children when she separated from her abusive husband, and one that she successfully worked to amend, taking an instrumental role in lobbying for the Custody of Infants Act of 1839 and the Matrimonial Causes Act of 1857.[4]

In "Crippled Jane," disability is a condition of the poor, who cannot afford resources for recovery. Jane is disabled, but it is not clear from the poem or the picture what her disability is. She has trouble walking; she is "dwarfish" and has headaches; yet another line casts almost anything that departs from the merry tempers, mildness, and piety of other children as a disability: "But Jane will be weird and wayward; fierce, and cunning, and hard." The "we" of these first few lines, presumably Jane's parents or family, dwindles to an "I," presumably Jane's mother, the only mother of *Home Thoughts* who speaks for herself. Jane's mother is dying and wonders how her daughter will be provided for: "How will strangers bear with her, when, at times, even I felt tired?" "Crippled Jane" expresses the heartache of a mother who has limited financial and emotional resources to care for her daughter, both for her physical ailments and her exhausting waywardness. In doing so, the poem exposes how the domestic ideal relies on men's wealth. Closing with this striking work and its implicit lacunae, *Home Thoughts and Home Scenes* reminds us that even works designed explicitly to honor a traditional domestic ideology can unintentionally disrupt it, suggesting the instability of the domestic triumvirate.

Two decades later, E. Nesbit, an active Socialist who wrote prolifically in poetry and prose for both children and adults, offered a story in verse that shows explicitly how marriage, domesticity, and motherhood might not coincide. In "The Moat House," from the 1886 collection *Lays and Legends*, these three elements are central but never overlap. The narrative tells of a young woman who grows up in a convent and then steals away with her lover. When her lover proposes that they find a priest to sanction their relationship, the woman, skeptical of the nuns who wanted to suppress her erotic life, responds, "'He would divide, not join us, dear. / I am mine – I give myself to thee.'"[5] So without marrying her, he takes her to his estate, called the "Moat House," where they row boats and frolic in the woods, fields, and house until the following spring. "Lady Ladybird," as the woman is called by the servants of the Moat House, has love but not marriage or a home. Her lover is then needed by a sick relative in the city and departs with assurances that he will soon be back. She replies that home is in (or near) their bodies: her heart will be "at his side," while his will beat against her "lace bodice." The moat house is alienating to her, rather than protective, haunted with ghosts, alive with anthropomorphized voices; the garden and sundial tell her that his love will fade like a flower, while the house and the dog call out for their "master." This house is not her home.

While her lover is away, Lady Ladybird has a baby, to whom she sings one of Nesbit's most frequently anthologized songs, "Oh baby, baby, baby dear," celebrating the cozy, affectionate dyad of mother and child:

> We are so tired, we like to lie
> Just doing nothing, you and I,
> Within the darkened quiet room.
> The sun sends dusk rays through the gloom,
> Which is no gloom since you are here,
> My little life, my baby dear.[6]

These lines simultaneously represent fatigue and joy, enclosure and exclusion of the world outside this dyad. The baby's father is not present, but there are no "questions, longings vain" because "you need but me." Motherhood, Nesbit acknowledges, can push aside the erotic coupling that created it, within marriage or without it.

Marriage in "The Moat House" rests not on mutual affection, respect, and love but a set of social rituals divorced from emotion. The request to visit his sick relative was merely a ruse to get her lover away and to introduce him to an eligible young woman of similar class and station, Lady May. He resists awhile, insisting on his fealty to Lady Ladybird, but eventually gives in, marrying Lady May. "The Moat House" depicts rich, emotionally satisfying experiences of love and motherhood, but never in the context of marriage or domesticity, both of which are alienating social conventions. The man's engagement with Lady May consists of "Concerts, flower shows, garden parties, balls and dinners, rides and drives, / All the time-killing distractions of these fashionable lives."[7] As the wedding entourage rolls up to the Moat House, Lady Ladybird jumps out from the welcoming crowd and the carriage runs her over, killing her. The "old nurse," that frequently invisible mainstay of domesticity on which middle- and upper-class Victorian motherhood so often relies, who cared for Lady Ladybird at the moat house, runs to the woman's body and chastises the man, telling him that God will condemn him but will be kinder to Lady Ladybird, "With your babe's milk in her bosom, your horse-hoof marks on her hair."[8] The poem elevates the nurse from a figure of invisible drudgery to one of authority and conscience who delivers judgment and a benediction. In this moment, Lady May takes the baby with her and rides away, leaving the man after declaring that she never wants to see "your dastard face again."[9] Lady May, too, will have motherhood, but without marriage, without erotic love, and without the estate the baby might otherwise inherit. "The Moat House" deliberately disarticulates marriage, motherhood, and domesticity to show how emotions and affections are separate from social conventions and could, given the chance, thrive apart from those conventions.

Domesticity

In Nesbit's 1886 narrative, affections are deeply personal and, she implies, should be kept separate from social conventions. By comparison, Felicia Hemans portrays domesticity – the sense of home in a place – as both a social convention and a feeling. Writing between the high Romantic and Victorian periods, Hemans figures domestic affections as both internal and national, in the sense that home is not just about family but about geographical belonging. Hemans was immensely popular and prolific until her death in 1835, and many of her poems addressed domesticity, motherhood, or marriage, from her encomium to the "Homes of England" to her declaration in "National Lyrics" that a "minstrel" shall "find a theme":

> Where'er a blessed Home hath been,
>   That now is Home no more:
> A place of ivy, darkly green,
>   Where laughter's light is o'er. (lines 17–20)[10]

Similarly, the title poem of Hemans's 1812 collection *The Domestic Affections* tells us that home is not a physical place but is "Most fondly cherish'd, in the purest mind." Protected from the wars that threaten nations, domestic bliss remains "unruffled": "Her empire, home! – her throne, affection's breast!" Hemans presents home as an emotional state analogous to empire but neither directly supportive nor destructive of it. The "day-light dreams" of home can "cheer the soldier's breast," providing an internal mental respite. But like empires, the domestic affections are fragile, and subject to perpetual destruction and rebuilding. Presented initially as an idealized abstraction, home must also always be imaginatively reconstructed, for in addition to the soldier, "The Domestic Affections" offers the figure of the Siberian exile, who loses not only home as a place but also the friends and family that constitute the emotional bonds of it, and a "sad emigrant" whose home has been ruined by revolutionary violence. Home, for them, is the lost, the absent, the unattainable people and places to which these exiles were rooted. Though Hemans conceives of domesticity as a mind-set rather than as a place, as Herbert Tucker notes, and in distinction from the hearths and houses readers often find in Victorian poetry, Tricia Lootens quite rightly asserts that "Victorian culture tells soldiers that they fight for home, and it often does so in the voice of Felicia Hemans."[11]

In contrast, Adelaide Anne Procter emphasizes home as a place, frequently framing her poems in vivid domestic settings, as in the story told by the hearthside in "True Honors." Since she was a frequent contributor to Charles Dickens's journal *Household Words*, and her poems were often set to music and sung in at-home concerts around the family piano, Procter's poems were written to be read, as were gift books like *Home Thoughts*, or sung in domestic familial settings. Procter was a fierce defender of women's rights, a member of the Langham Place group that published the *English Women's Journal*, and a member of the Society for Promoting the Employment of Women. Keenly aware that domestic bliss was a middle-class privilege, she authored such poems as "Homeless," which criticizes the concern for shelter that animals, criminals, and even saleable goods receive over and above the poor, and "Cradle Song of the Poor," in which a mother who can't feed her baby almost wishes that the baby would die rather than eke out a starvation existence.

Procter also, perhaps inadvertently, presents the domestic ideal as particularly white and European in "Homeward Bound." The male speaker is shipwrecked off "red Algiers" and spends years as a slave with the "black Moors of Barbary." Whether Procter was asserting the whiteness of the domestic ideal or inviting readers to imagine a European enslaved to better sympathize with the very real black slaves in America whose families were consistently torn apart cannot be answered here. Suffice it to say that the poem raises the question of how the domestic ideal might be racialized. Taking a page from Hemans, figuring the home as both a household and a nation, Procter's speaker insists that a "tender vision" of his wife and child praying for him at home is the only thing that sustains him through his years of forced servitude. After being rescued by crusaders, on the voyage home he imagines the moment of his return:

> I would picture my dear cottage,
>   See the crackling wood-fire burn,
> And the two beside it seated,
>   Watching, waiting my return.[12]

He arrives home twenty-six years after his departure to almost that very picture: his wife sitting by the fire holding a small child. But since so much time has passed, that child is not his, and his wife is smiling up at her new husband, his "ancient comrade." The wife can be forgiven, the poem suggests, for assuming that her husband was dead and for remarrying. The three of them weep together (the speaker also learns, parenthetically, that the son he left behind has died), and the speaker leaves, "in silence passed away." The poem ends ambiguously, with his declaration that he will "reach a haven":

> I, too, shall reach home and rest;
> I shall find her waiting for me
> With our baby on her breast.[13]

Is this haven actually a "heaven," an afterlife where he can relive his domestic ideal? A repetition of his previous life with a new wife? Either way, Procter seems to be saying that more than the cottage, the fire, the wife and children, a man's ideal of home requires a return. Home is a fantasy of a place where nothing changes, where one can always come back to an imagined ideal, one in which women are passive and men are active, in which women stay put and wait. For the woman in this story, however consistent and even hackneyed the visions of home and hearth are, the particulars and the people within that common fantasy are subject to change. Whereas in the speaker's imagination, she is always sitting and mostly pining away for him, female readers in particular would have known that such a woman would rarely have had an opportunity to sit down and that her domestic experience would be just as characterized by action, motion, and change as the speaker's experience of adventure abroad.

Other poets include work as part of the domestic experience, for instance, Christina Rossetti's "Goblin Market," a poem about two sisters who are tempted by goblins selling delicious magical fruit that, once eaten, can never be eaten again and slowly poisons the consumer. Within this story of sin (Laura's consumption of the fruit) and redemption (Lizzie's antidote of pulp from fruit that the goblins press against her) lies a female-centered domestic existence that requires work that is pleasurable rather than burdensome.

> Laura rose with Lizzie:
> Fetched in honey, milked the cows,
> Aired and set to rights the house,
> Kneaded cakes of whitest wheat,
> Cakes for dainty mouths to eat,
> Next churned butter, whipped up cream,
> Fed their poultry, sat and sewed. (lines 202–8)[14]

Home requires maintenance, but the work seems pleasurably varied and the women enjoy the products (not fruits) of their labor. Presumably this condition does not change after the women marry and have children. No mention is made of husbands, but the sisters are together as they gather their children around to tell the story of the fruit-selling Goblins.

Work is also central to a sense of home for working-class Scottish poet Ellen Johnston. In her tribute "My Mother," industry and her trials and sorrows compose her mother's generosity of heart.[15] Furthermore, as Susan Zlotnick argues, since homes are often not safe havens but can be places of danger and abuse, as in "The Drunkard's Wife," factories offer a stronger feeling of family loyalty.[16] In her sole collection, *Autobiography, Poems and Songs*, Johnston pens a number of tributes to factory foremen, which cast workers as sons and daughters of the factory. In "The Factory Girl's Farewell," the speaker bids goodbye to the factory as she is about to marry a man who will take her to London. The poem captures her mixed feelings about the emotional ties to the factory and her life transition:

> Farewell, my honour'd masters two,
>   Your mill no more I may traverse;
> I breathe you both a fond adieu;
>   Long may you live lords of commerce.
> Farewell unto my native land,
>   Land of the thistle and blue bell;
> Oh! Wish me joy with heart and hand:
>   So Galbraith's bonnie mill, farewell![17]

Because the poem describes the truest friends of the mill as well as the "works around, / The glad mill, foundry, cooperage too," her "native land" might be read as the industrial city as well as Scotland. Work is clearly central to a sense of belonging to place in Johnston's poetry. Her representation of home as national extends to Johnston's love poem to her daughter, about whose out-of-wedlock birth Johnston wrote publicly and unashamedly as the "sweet offspring of false love." She closes "A Mother's Love" with the declaration that this love song "swells forth like the stern patriot's hymn," comparing a mother's devotion to a soldier's, and extending the connection of family attachment and national pride so central to Hemans.[18] Johnston, like Nesbit after her, argues that marriage need not precede motherhood, and that a sense of home may well precede them both and be independent of them. It may also be derived variously from personal attachments or living and working in a house, land, or nation.

Marriage

Poems addressing life after marriage are few and far between in the period, and those that do are often troubled. A number of poems anticipate marriage, as does Elizabeth Barrett Browning's (EBB) *Aurora Leigh*, as well as her *Sonnets from the Portuguese*. In both of these works, EBB confronts the potential lack of autonomy in a marriage while articulating the need for mutual understanding to see the beloved as he is and not as she imagines him to be: "I will not have my thoughts instead of thee!"[19] Still other poems by women look forward to the prospect of marriage with dread, anticipating heavy emotional demands from a husband that will compete with a woman's other priorities. In Augusta Webster's ironically titled dramatic monologue "The Happiest Girl in the World," a young woman worries that her own love for her fiancé is insufficient but articulates her unrealistic ambition to be "So much to him, so almost everything." She even declares that although she loves "innocent fond eyes of little ones," she wants no children because "I would be all for him, / Not even children coming 'twixt us two."[20]

In Procter's "A Woman's Question," a woman makes the same kinds of demands of her husband-to-be, declaring that she needs to know "Before I peril all for thee" whether "thou hast kept a portion back, / While I have staked the whole," and asking him, "Is there within thy heart a need / That mine cannot fulfil?"[21] "A Woman's Answer," a companion poem, articulates the opposite fear, that a husband will not be able to acknowledge his wife's other commitments and interests: "Dearest, although I love you so, my heart / Answers a thousand claims besides your own." This poem offers a solution to the problem by integrating the things she loves with her love of a man: the summer, the winter, the stars, the flowers, all remind her of him, and she loves people who also love him. She also declares her heart to have room for books, for "The Poets that you used to read to me." Most importantly, in line 43 she names EBB's *Aurora Leigh* for reasons that remain between herself and the beloved: "Because – because – do you remember why?" This question is not merely rhetorical; she is asking whether their shared experiences matter as much to him as to her, and whether he can accept two characters who follow arduous individual paths to be able to anticipate a marriage of equals. This poem posits that a husband and wife can look outward from each other to love the same things together. Reading "A Woman's Answer" in isolation does not reveal whether the speaker and her beloved are married or only courting. Yet a third poem in the series, "A Woman's Last Word," implies that the marriage never took place because "the links are broken."

Procter can posit both fears and ideals in anticipation of marriage, but when she writes a rare poem that depicts life after marriage, "Philip and Mildred," the relationship turns into a passionless, disconnected cohabitation. The betrothed spend years apart while Philip builds his career as a scholar in London and across Europe. When he finally amasses enough wealth, he marries Mildred and brings her to London, but the years of solitary waiting rob her of her joy in him, while he develops ideas and interests that he cannot share with her, so that their marriage is a "peace so cold and bitter, that we almost welcome strife" and she comes to understand "That he gave her home and pity, but that heart, and soul, and mind / Were beyond her now."[22] She fears he married her merely out of obligation to "pay her for the patience of her youth," and she dies, presumably withering from lack of emotional attention.

"Philip and Mildred" asserts that the failure of the relationship stems not only from extended absence but also from the way that Mildred is expected to take on the role of moral guide to him: "Philip's young hopes of ambition, ever changing, ever altering, / Needed Mildred's gentle presence even to make successes sweet." Given the opportunity to pursue his fame and fortune, Philip "bade her take the burden of decision," whereupon she finds she cannot "doom him to inaction." Having forced her to sanction his departure under the guise of giving her the choice, he installs her in a role of a passive angel guardian unable to live her own independent life, as the poem exhorts her to do in a brief direct address: "Live thy life: not a reflection or a shadow of his own."

The term "reflection" in "Philip and Mildred" resonates with "Any Husband to Many a Wife" in which Emily Pfeiffer (1827–90) represents a husband's need to see his best self mirrored in his wife's eyes: "Whereby I shape the fond endeavour / To justify your faith at last."[23] In these poems, the wife exists to shore up her husband's sense of self. Although Procter and Pfeiffer suggest this is a vacuous, corrosive option for women, earlier poetry from Felicia Hemans suggests that women can take pride in being the real heroes, without whose encouragement men could not defend their territory. In "The Switzer's Wife," adapted from Friedrich Schiller's play *William Tell*, a husband comes home despondent and defeated because conquering armies are about to invade. Having none of it, the wife spurs him to go from house to house to gather a defensive force, and he credits her encouragement for his bravery:

> "My bride, my wife, the mother of my child!
> Now shall thy name be armour to my heart;
> And this our land, by chains no more defile,
> Be taught of thee to choose the better part!" (lines 103–6)[24]

The moral, mental force of men, and by extension, the integrity of national boundaries, Hemans suggests, depends on the fortitude of soldiers' wives. From Hemans to the end of the century, however, the idea of wife as stalwart supporter of her husband's bravery seems to erode.

From Procter on, many poems show that a husband's need for a wife as a moral compass, anchor of home, or domestic servant impoverishes wives' experiences. A few decades later, Amy Levy's dramatic monologue "Xantippe," in the voice of Socrates's widow, traces a trajectory from her youthful hope that she would share his intellectual life to bitter disappointment at being contemptuously dismissed and treated as a "goodly household vessel." Xantippe turns to that classic women's domestic labor, spinning, to numb the pain of Socrates's rejection of her mind and heart: "I spun until, methinks, I spun away / The soul from out my body."[25] If Socrates neglects Xantippe, in "The Farmer's Bride" by Charlotte Mew (1869–1928) the farmer outright abuses his wife. After she tries to run away, presumably because he sexually assaulted her and "she turned afraid / Of love and me," he locks her in the house, where "She does the work about the house / As well as most, but like a mouse." When she is not working, she hides in the attic, while her husband steadfastly refuses to try to understand her fear and fantasizes about the "soft young down of her."[26] In the scenarios drawn by Procter, Levy, and Mew, the husbands' impositions reduce marriage to imprisonment within a place rather than wives' ownership of it, emptied of rather than infused by love and affection.

Perhaps the most ideal vision of marriage in Victorian women's poetry comes not in the fraught heterosexual pairings typical of poems on marriage, but from the lesbian couple who published under the name Michael Field: Katharine Bradley and Edith Cooper. Although Bradley and Cooper could not be legally married, they considered themselves to be "closer married" than the Brownings because they collaborated and published under the same pseudonym, rather than writing separately.[27] They provide an account of their vow in one of their most famous poems, "It was deep April": "My Love and I took hands and swore, / Against the world, to be / Poets and lovers evermore."[28] Although the phrase "against the world" certainly describes the way a same-sex couple would defy the norms of heterosexual marriage, it also describes their unconventional mode of collaborative writing and determination to continue writing and publishing poetry following a downturn in their critical fortunes after the real identities behind their pseudonym became well known in literary London. They continued to represent their relationship within the tropes of marriage, as in this lyric from the 1908 *Wild Honey from Various Thyme*: "I love you with my life – 'tis so I love you; / I give you as a ring / The cycle of my days till death." As their diaries and poetry attest, they considered their relationship to model marriage as a shared enterprise focused on a joint artistic and poetic life together as both producers and consumers of art.

Same-sex couples were not the only ones for whom legal recognition of devoted romantic partnership was unavailable. In "The Runaway Slave at Pilgrim's Point," EBB tells the story of an escaped slave who bears, and murders, her white rapist's baby "to save it from my curse." Before this point, she falls in love with a man she cannot marry because they are both slaves:

> We were black, we were black,
>   We had no claim to love and bliss,
> What marvel if each went to wrack?
>   They wrung my cold hands out of his, –
> They dragged him – where? I crawled to touch
> His blood's mark in the dust.   (lines 92–7)[29]

"The Runaway Slave at Pilgrim's Point" speaks to the power of slavery and racism to distort the natural progression of erotic and familial love. Marriage, motherhood, and domesticity are presumably founded on and perpetuate an ethos of mutual care. The love story within "The Runaway Slave" begins when "tender and full was the look he gave," and progresses through a vow of love "As he carved me a bowl of the cocoa-nut / Through the roar of the hurricanes" and "I sang his name instead of a song."[30] Although this relationship is forbidden, these details of romance participate in the Victorian ideal of companionate marriage, one that rises out of mutual attraction and affection rather than social necessity. The fissures in the marriage-motherhood-domesticity triumvirate bring about violence in "The Runaway Slave," the cruelties of slavery destroying personal attachments. In "The Runaway Slave," slavery and racism violently undermine the speaker's erotic attachment to her would-be husband and impair her experience of motherhood to murderous results. The combination of her own enslavement, the child's prospective enslavement, and his existence as the product of her white rapist interrupt the affection, love, and care seen in poems about more secure white women, so that grief, fear, and panic dominate her experience. Repeatedly, social and political structures founded on class and race instead of love destroy an ethos of care in Victorian women's poetry and force women especially to live by social dictates rather than to determine their own emotional, romantic, and familial course.

Conclusion: Motherhood

I have been arguing thus far that marriage, domesticity, and motherhood are frequently at odds with one another, and sometimes exclude one another; in the poems discussed thus far, a variety of mothers suffer from this conflict. Often, conflicting affections shut out the very motherhood the union of affections and social conventions is meant to enable, as in Webster's "The Happiest Girl." The mother in Norton's "Crippled Jane" is shut out from a sense of home and safety because she lacks the money to treat her daughter's affliction and the support of her community. The most tender expressions of maternal feeling seen so far, in Johnston's "A Mother's Love" and Nesbit's song in "The Moat House"

("Baby, baby, baby dear"), appear in mothers who have their children out of wedlock, supposedly a chief Victorian sin. Yet these poems firmly defend the care and affection of single mothers as virtues. In fact, these poems form a category one might call the "tender dyad poems" about Victorian motherhood, which focus on the mother-child dyad to such an extent that whether the mother is married makes very little difference to the representation of the mother's experience.

These dyad poems often depict fierce love together with ambivalence, in moods that range from humorous in "A Natal Address to My Child, March 19th, 1844" by Eliza Ogilvy (1822–1912), which begins "Hail to thy puggy nose, my Darling," to the near-tragic in Alice Meynell's "The Modern Mother," in which "This mother, giver of life, death, peace, distress, / Desired ah! Not so much / Thanks as forgiveness."[31] Augusta Webster's sonnet sequence "Mother and Daughter" constitutes one of the most nuanced depictions of motherhood in Victorian women's poetry. Webster's use of the sonnet form, associated with unrequited erotic love, reinforces the mother-child dyad as an exclusive pair rather than part of a domestic family group. Webster's own daughter, like the daughter in the sonnets, was an only child, a choice that Webster defends in precisely the terms of romantic love: "Since first my little one lay on my breast / I never needed such a second good," and "she is one, she has the whole."[32] She need not divide her love, and her daughter need not share her mother's time and affection. Yet Webster also focuses on the loss that is central even to ideal experiences of motherhood. The simple passage of time and the very growing up that mothers enable ensure that the dyad cannot persist:

> Dearer she is to-day, dearer and more;
>   Closer to me, since sister womanhoods meet;
> Yet, like poor mothers some long while bereft,
> I dwell on toward ways, quaint memories left,
>   I miss the approaching sound of pit-pat feet,
> The eager baby voice outside my door. (lines 9–14)[33]

Webster at once celebrates and mourns the way that the mother-child relationship constantly evolves. As her daughter grows up, they can share mutual understanding in sister womanhoods, but the speaker loses the child whose eagerness for shared frolic centered on her mother. Webster extends her contemplation of loss to her own life-span and her daughter's. While she can understand her own and her husband's deaths as part of the natural order of things, "To know she too is Death's seems misbelieve / . . . Life is Death begun: / But Death and her! That's strangeness passing grief."[34]

Felicia Hemans's "The Indian City" centers on the loss of a child. While cruel, violent social conventions replace love with grief in "The Runaway Slave," in "The Indian City" the murder of a child transforms that grief into intercultural destruction. In this poem, Muslims making a pilgrimage to Mecca stop to rest in a Hindu village. While there, a boy sees an inviting pool and decides to take a swim, without realizing that it is a sacred pool. The villagers murder the boy for befouling their sacred space, and his mother, in her grief, tells her fellow pilgrims and calls for the city to be destroyed. While Webster cannot quite imagine the feeling that would accompany her daughter's death, even from natural causes, the mother in "The Indian City" cannot quite get to grief ("not yet I weep") until she calls for revenge: "Not till yon city, in ruins rent, / Be piled for its victim's monument."[35] The violation of a mother's protective love turns into ruinous conflict. The Hindus hear the approach of the Muslim army and, misunderstanding the conflict as stemming from religious animus, cry out "War! 'tis the gathering of a Moslem war!" As the soldiers lay waste to the Indian city, the mother herself dies and is buried next to her son. The sacred principle violated here is, of course, not from either religion but is the mother's bond with her son, as the closing lines make clear:

> Palace and tower on that plain were left,
> Like fallen trees by the lightening cleft;
> . . .
> And the jungle grass o'er the altar sprung –
> This was the work of one deep heart wrung![36]

For Hemans, mother love is a force that shapes civilizations, here, destructively.

In Mathilde Blind's epic poem on evolution, *The Ascent of Man* (1889), motherhood, marriage, and domesticity are a civilizing force. The poem features a scene of motherhood and domesticity at a key turning point. Here, Blind seems to suggest, are motherhood and domesticity at their most basic:

> They raise a light aërial house
>   On shafts of widely branching trees,
> Where, harboured warily, each spouse
>   May feed her little ape in peace,
> Green cradled in his heaven-roofed bed,
> Leaves rustling lullabies overhead. (lines 106–11)[37]

In my discussion of poems such as Nesbit's "The Moat House," I showed how poets valued authentic feeling over familial structures and social convention. In *The Ascent of Man*, Blind prioritizes mere survival. Yet that very instinct for survival establishes this primitive version of domesticity, marriage, and motherhood embodied in her rhyme of "house" with "spouse" and trees that create shelter and safety in which the mother affectionately feeds her baby in peace. For Blind, domesticity precedes humanity, creating conditions for its evolution. This is a female-centric version of evolution, in which feminine care, rather than masculine force, makes development possible. In contrast with the marriage plot novels associated with the nineteenth century, in this poem marriage, motherhood, and domesticity are united at the beginning of the story, rather than at the end.

Notes

1. Lorraine Janzen Kooistra, "*Home Thoughts and Home Scenes*: Packaging Middle-class Childhood for Christmas Consumption," in *The Nineteenth Century Child and Consumer Culture*, ed. Dennis Denisoff (Aldershot: Ashgate, 2008), pp. 151–72.
2. *Home Thoughts and Home Scenes*, ed. The Brothers Dalziel (London: Routledge, Warne and Routledge, 1864), poem XXV, n.p.
3. Ibid., p. xxxv.
4. Diane Atkinson, *The Criminal Conversation of Mrs. Norton: Victorian England's Scandal of the Century and the Fallen Socialite Who Changed Women's Lives Forever* (Chicago: Chicago Review Press, 2013).
5. E. Nesbit, *Lays and Legends* (London: Longmans, Green and Co., 1886), p. 20.
6. Ibid., pp. 38–9.
7. Ibid., p. 49.
8. Ibid., p. 55.
9. Ibid., p. 56.
10. "National Lyrics," in *Felicia Hemans: Selected Poems, Prose, and Letters*, ed. Gary Kelly (Peterborough, ON: Broadview Press, 2002), p. 393.
11. Tricia Lootens, "Hemans and Home: Victorianism, Feminine 'Internal Enemies,' and the Domestication of National Identity," *PMLA* 109 (1994), 239; see also F. Tucker, "House Arrest: The Domesticization of English Poetry in the 1820s," *New Literary History* 25 (1994), 521–48.
12. "Homeward Bound," in *The Complete Poetical Works of Adelaide Anne Procter, with an Introduction by Charles Dickens* (New York: T.Y. Crowell, 1903), p. 35.
13. Ibid., p. 37.
14. "Goblin Market," in *Christina Rossetti: The Complete Poems* (New York: Penguin, 2005), p. 10.
15. Ellen Johnston, "My Mother," in *Autobiography, Poems and Songs* (Glasgow: William Love, 1867), p. 12.
16. Susan Zlotnick, "'A Thousand Times I'd Be a Factory Girl': Dialect, Domesticity, and Working-Class Women's Poetry in Victorian Britain," *Victorian Studies* 35 (1991), 23.

17. Johnston, "The Factory Girl's Farewell," *Autobiography, Poems and Songs*, p. 95.
18. Johnston, "A Mother's Love," *Autobiography, Poems and Songs*, p. 45.
19. *Elizabeth Barrett Browning: Selected Poems*, ed. Marjorie Stone and Beverly Taylor (Peterborough, ON: Broadview Press, 2009), p. 223.
20. Augusta Webster, *Portraits and Other Poems*, ed. Christine Sutphin (Peterborough, ON: Broadview Press, 2000), pp. 190, 192.
21. Adelaide Anne Procter, "A Woman's Question," in *Victorian Women Poets: An Anthology*, eds. Angela Leighton and Margaret Reynolds (Oxford: Blackwell, 1995), p. 306.
22. Procter, "Philip and Mildred," in *Victorian Women Poets*, p. 335.
23. Emily Pfeiffer, "Any Husband to Many a Wife," in *Victorian Women Poets*, p. 342.
24. "The Switzer's Wife," *Felicia Hemans: Selected Poems, Prose, and Letters*, p. 322.
25. Amy Levy, "Xantippe," in *Victorian Women Poets*, p. 597.
26. Charlotte Mew, "The Farmer's Bride," in *Victorian Women Poets*, pp. 647–8.
27. Michael Field, *Works and Days, From the Journal of Michael Field*, eds. T. and D. C. Sturge Moore (London: John Murray, 1933), p. 16.
28. Michael Field, *Michael Field, The Poet: Published and Manuscript Materials*, eds. Marion Thain and Ana Parejo Vadillo (Peterborough, ON: Broadview Press, 2009), p. 128.
29. Elizabeth Barrett Browning, "The Runaway Slave at Pilgrim's Point," in *Elizabeth Barrett Browning: Selected Poems*, eds. Marjorie Stone and Beverly Taylor (Peterborough, ON: Broadview Press, 2009), pp. 196–7.
30. Ibid., p. 196.
31. Eliza Ogilvy, "A Natal Address to My Child," and Alice Meynell, "The Modern Mother," in *Victorian Women Poets*, pp. 300–301, 521.
32. Webster, "Mother and Daughter," in *Portraits and Other Poems*, pp. 350–1.
33. Ibid., p. 347.
34. Ibid., p. 345.
35. Felicia Hemans, "The Indian City," in *Records of Woman* (Oxford: Woodstock Books, 1991), pp. 90–1.
36. Ibid., p. 96.
37. Mathilde Blind, from "The Ascent of Man," in *Victorian Women Poets*, p. 468.

13

JILL R. EHNENN

Sexuality

Readers of nineteenth-century verse face at least three challenges when they set out to examine representations of sexuality in the work of Victorian women poets: (1) the problem, for Victorians, of the very idea of a female Poet; (2) the problem, for Victorian women writers, of an essentialist, binary gender ideology that overdetermined the parameters within which they and their contemporaries were supposed to understand and represent female sexuality and desire; and (3) the problem, for scholars today, of thinking about sexuality in the past, when it is likely that our subjects may have understood sexual desire in ways that exceed our present concepts. Given these challenges, this chapter seeks to complicate reductive narratives of Victorian women's sexuality by examining a range of verse that depicts female sexuality across a continuum of practices. *Aurora Leigh* (1856) by Elizabeth Barrett Browning (EBB) and "Goblin Market" (1862) by Christina Rossetti will serve as touchstones and points of departure as the following discussion addresses these three problems in turn.

The Poetess: Victorian Gender Ideology and the Creative, Embodied Self

Well into the nineteenth century, literary tradition held that women *were* the poem, not the poet; they were the desired object of the gaze, not the desiring, speaking subject. If women were to write, what would they possibly write about? Such notions present scholars with a familiar set of historical and literary obstacles: female absence, female silence, and the "inappropriateness" of women's desire, including women's desire to be a Poet (not a *poetess*) on par with writers who are men. In essence, before we can analyze how Victorian women represented sexuality in verse, we must acknowledge nineteenth-century thinking about the inappropriateness of women strongly desiring *anything* (including a writing vocation), except perhaps loving in very specific and limited ways.

As Dorothy Mermin observes, "Since women had appeared in poetry almost exclusively as amatory objects, it was generally assumed that when they wrote poems themselves love should be their theme."[1] If love was to be their theme, nineteenth-century sex-gender norms presuming female passionlessness dictated that women's writing should be about "properly" feminine objects of desexualized love: God, country, children, and (chastely) their husbands. Notably, *desexualized* does not necessarily mean *disembodied*; eyes, lips, and other body parts as well as the notion of bodily sensations that accompany the expression of emotion do appear prominently in Victorian women's verse – as long as they function in the service of nonsexual love.

Consider Cecil Frances Alexander's famous hymn, "All Things Bright and Beauteous" (1848). After describing many pleasurable sights, Alexander concludes:

> He gave us eyes to see them,
> And lips that we might tell,
> How great is GOD Almighty
> Who has made all things well.[2]

The sensing body and full heart also appear in women's poems about the pleasures of motherly love and the intensely embodied sorrow of losing a child. Ellen Johnston's "A Mother's Love" (1857), for instance, documents profound emotional and physical pleasure in "gaz[ing] on thy fairy form," and "that sweet angel face on this heart-burning breast; / Thy last parting kiss lingers on my chin."[3] Mary Howitt's "The Dying Child" (1847) overflows passionately with sorrow: "My heart is very faint and low / My thoughts like spectres come and go; / I feel a numbing sense of woe."[4] Similarly, Charlotte Brontë's verses on the deaths of her sisters are insistently embodied; she writes of "grinding agony," "crushing truth," and how "the galled heart is pierced with grief, / Till wildly it implores relief, / But small relief can find."[5]

Such content and sentimental tone are perhaps what the public expected of a poetess; certainly, they reinforce notions that Victorian women were not sexually desiring subjects, except for the purpose of pleasing husbands and producing children. Adelaide Anne Procter's "Philip and Mildred" (1858), for instance, celebrates Mildred's gentle, patient loyalty as she awaits Philip's return, then focuses upon Philip's sense of honor and Mildred's quiet resignation when the couple finally marry, even though his love has waned.[6] Despite the long history of love's metonymic association with sex, in this and similar examples, the heart's association with sympathy trumps its association with erotic love and sexuality.

Some female poets employ a similarly dispassionate tone on the topic of authorship, in stark contrast to the ardent masculine voices of Shelley,

Wordsworth, Tennyson, or Browning. Felicia Hemans's "Women and Fame" (1839) calmly says of Fame, "A hollow sound is in thy song, / a mockery in thine eye" because for women, Fame pales compared to "Sweet waters from affection's spring."[7] Likewise, in "To My Lyre" (1870), Eliza Cook describes her creative efforts with modesty and moderation: "Let the bright laurel-wreath belong / To prouder harps of classic song."[8] If these and similar poems can be interpreted as the female poet's ironic pose behind a mask of false humility, they can just as easily be understood literally, as reinforcing middle-class ideology about the gentle, retiring nature of woman, even when she succeeds at authorship. Such verse posits the poetic self as an embodied self, but only modestly so.

In contrast, some Victorian women's poetry expresses a passionate desire to write that *does* seem to emanate from an embodied, erotic self. In EBB's *Aurora Leigh*, Aurora ponders the connection between her poet's fame and

> our quick sense of love
> Our very heart of passionate womanhood,
> Which could not beat so in the verse without
> Being present also in the unkissed lips.[9]

"If woman's poetry acts as a container for the woman poet's sexual desire," Patricia Pulham argues, "then both poetry and the woman poet are eroticized in the process."[10] Indeed, Aurora continues, "To have our books / Appraised by love, associated with love / While *we* sit loveless! is it hard you think?" (5.473–5). Here Aurora is not dispassionate; she bluntly makes known her intense desires: "We're hungry" (5.487). In "Sappho's Song" (1824), Letitia Landon (L.E.L.) similarly asserts the connection between passionate love and authorship: "It was not song that taught me love, / But it was love that taught me song."[11] The speaker in Fanny Kemble's "Lines on Reading with Difficulty some of Schiller's Early Love Poems" (1883) concedes that, despite her personal unfamiliarity with "the maiden's guilt, the mother's woe / And the dark mystery of death and shame," because of her shared writerly affinity with Schiller "these strains of thine need no interpreter. / Ah! tis my native tongue!"[12] These examples represent writing as a deeply libidinal exercise of desire. Some critics even read the verbal excesses of Christina Rossetti's "Goblin Market" as guilty pleasure about writing, an instance when the usually reserved Rossetti indulges in the sensuous abandon of a poet lost in the moment, savoring the erotic roll and dance of words on her tongue.[13]

As Isobel Armstrong asserts, the Victorian poet's project is "to renegotiate a content to every relationship between self and the world."[14] As this section has illustrated, female Victorian poets, *as poets*, employed a range of approaches when depicting the creative self as an embodied self. While some poetesses represented themselves as mere sentimental scribbling sisters of Coventry Patmore's "angel in the house," others perceived themselves as much more. As demonstrated here, Victorian female poets embodied, and indeed could be said to channel, the sexualized, desiring legacy of the original poetess Sappho, who embraced the strong urge to write for the sensual joy of writing and unabashedly celebrated her sexual love for both men and women.

The Female Poet and the Fallen Woman

A challenge for nineteenth-century women poets was middle-class ideology that essentialized women's nature, desires, and embodiment in dichotomous poles of passionless domestic angels versus fallen women. According to Angela Leighton, "the fallen woman is a type which ranges from the successful courtesan to the passionate adulteress, from the destitute streetwalker to the seduced innocent, from the unscrupulous procuress to the raped child. To fall, for women, is simply to fall short."[15] Through depicting multiple types of fallenness and adopting a wide variety of moral postures, Victorian women poets left verse documentation of their thinking about women's sexuality.

For example, one common interpretation of "Goblin Market" is that Christina Rossetti was influenced by her charity work among fallen women in Magdalen homes, and that "Goblin Market" warns that danger, violence, and death can ensue when women associate with men.[16] Lizzie counsels Laura, "Twilight is not good for maidens; / Should not loiter in the glen / In the haunts of goblin men."[17] In this reading, Laura falls into sexual sin by giving of her body, trading her "precious golden lock" (l. 126). Having learned Jeanie's sad fate, the reader recognizes that Laura's extreme pleasure in the goblin men's forbidden fruit has dire consequences. In this interpretation, the Christ-like sacrifice of her sister saves Laura, along with eventual assimilation into woman's normative domestic role. Laura herself need not be portrayed literally as a prostitute for the wages of sin and the path of redemption for fallen women to be clear.

EBB's depiction of Marion Erle in *Aurora Leigh* provides a more extended and complex opportunity to ponder the figure of the ruined woman. Aurora is initially disgusted when she sees Marion and her child:

> Small business has a cast-away
> Like Marion, with that crown of prosperous wives
> ....
>   it means, with her,
> Instead of honour, blessing, merely shame. (6.346–7, 353–4)

Here, Aurora's stance echoes Victorian gender ideology: fallen women simply do not deserve to be mothers. "She is no mother but a kidnapper, / And he's a dismal orphan, ... not a son" (6.636–7). Even Marion thinks herself abominable, having internalized contemporary notions about motherhood. As the rest of the verse-novel unfolds, Marion holds fast to her assertion that she is unworthy of Romney's marriage proposal – of any man's love, and that she is forever ruined and should be shunned by society.

The traditional fallen woman narrative reinforces binary notions of femininity: seduction and loss of virtue lead inevitably to prostitution; the domestic angel's pure sweetness can save the fallen woman; the prostitute, although redeemed, must die because she cannot return to a "normal" womanly role and taint society. Yet in "Goblin Market" and *Aurora Leigh*, depictions of fallen women are not wholly straightforward. Rather, they, and so many other examples of Victorian women's poetry, are what Isobel Armstrong calls *double poems*. For Armstrong, Victorian poetry, contra Bakhtin, is not monologic but instead seems deliberately to invite multiple interpretations.[18] As a prime example, Rossetti's Laura does not meet the tragic fate generally reserved for fallen women. Armstrong characterizes such verse as "repeatedly redefining the terms of a question and contending for its ground."[19] Women poets put this technique to good use when addressing female sexuality, especially fallenness. It enables the poetess to express compassion for the fallen woman and to create complex textual environments that reflect complex social realities. By Book Seven, Aurora makes Marion a radical proposal:

> 'Come – and henceforth, thou and I
> Being still together, will not miss a friend,
> Nor he a father, since two mothers shall
> Make that up to him.   (7.122–5)

Here, Aurora's eventual sympathy and love for Marion expand her perception of the fallen woman and (as in "Goblin Market") a future for her that does not necessitate an unending downward spiral, isolation, and death.

Granted, other ruined women are not so lucky. The speaker in Amy Levy's "Magdalen" (1884) tells her story while dying in a Magdalen house. Although her tale of seduction, abandonment, and death is stereotypical, Levy permits the woman to speak frankly about sexuality. She is unselfconscious about the erotic pleasure she shared with her lover: "(And life was very sweet that tide) / ... / With one great pulse we seemed to thrill."[20] She regrets only that she did not foresee her lover's self-interest and inevitable betrayal. In contrast to the passion she felt in their intimate moments, now she reflects upon her fate with dispassionate irony and concludes that, although outcast and dying, "I am free; / ... you, through all eternity, / Have neither part nor lot in me" (lines 83–5). Levy's speaker does not leave the reader condemning the unrepentant and agnostic Magdalen. Rather, the dramatic monologue delivers two complementary messages: it demonstrates a course of events that could lead any woman into this Magdalen's situation and firmly holds the male partner accountable for his part in what society deems a sin, even though only she is suffering the consequences.

Laura, Marion, and Levy's Magdalen are not prostitutes; although to varying degrees, they only narrowly escape that fate. However, sympathy and a complex stance toward prostitutes can frequently be found in Victorian women's verse. One of the earliest dramatic monologues told in the prostitute's voice is Dora Greenwell's "Christina" (1867), whose speaker resides, like Levy's, near death in a Magdalen refuge. Contra Levy's poem, this speaker is wholly repentant, thanks to her childhood friend, Christina, whose goodness brings the speaker back to faith in God and His forgiveness. Greenwell crafts a weighty cautionary tale in blank verse:

> Mine is a common tale, and all the sadder
> Because it is so common: I was sought
> By one that wore me for a time then flung
> Me off; a rose with all its sweetness gone.[21]

After being spurned, she turns to other men to support herself and "So I lived on in splendour, lived through the years / Of scorning, till my brow grew hard to meet it" (lines 73–4). Conservative in its viewpoint, "Christina" does not stray from the standard fallen woman narrative; after being saved by Christina, the speaker lives in a Magdalen hospital and gratefully awaits death. Although Greenwell humanizes the prostitute by providing economic details about her past, her message seems primarily about sympathy and Christ's saving grace, rather than challenging double standards of sexuality.

Mathilde Blind's "The Message" (1891) similarly reinforces feminine stereotypes while voicing, like Levy's "Magdalen," some social critique. In "The Message," Nellie Dean, a hardened prostitute, refuses spiritual help in the Magdalen home with "savage spleen"; but then a young girl "Passed like sunbeam through the place," bringing flowers that work a miraculous transformation.[22] Nellie Dean has visions of her mother, repents, and peacefully dies, forgiven. This is one of Blind's less subversive poems; it features extremely regular meter and rhyme and employs familiar tropes – innocent maidenhood, Nature's pure beauty, and the loving mother – to simultaneously contrast and save the fallen woman. Yet, although it seems to reify gender ideology, "The Message" does mention the social problems of male drunkenness and a sexual double standard:

> Was she a wicked girl? What then!
> She didn't care a pin!
> She was not worse than all those men
> Who looked so shocked in public, when
> They made and shared her sin. (lines 66–70)

Blind's critical gestures in "The Message" are voiced in a more complex and scathing way in her "The Leading of Sorrow" (1889).[23] This remarkable, metrically intricate poem places the prostitute in a comprehensive context where all of Nature – human and nonhuman life, landscape, cosmos, and Time – interacts, strives, and suffers in a chaotic, evolutionary struggle. Blind makes clear that the prostitute is no different from any other fallible human, subject to fate and social ills; ultimately, she does seek and find forgiveness, but here, the transcendental signifier is not so much the traditional idea of God but a mystic, Eternal power of universal communion.

Less mystic, more informally conversational, but similar in complex social outlook is Augusta Webster's dramatic monologue, "A Castaway" (1870), wherein the speaker, Eulalie, constructs a fierce defense of female subjectivity and sexuality. Eulalie presents moral arguments against hypocrisy, double standards for male and female sexual behavior, and the folly of blaming women for making sinful sexual "choices" in the context of harsh economic realities. She ponders her past and present self, "the silly rules this world / makes about women," and her hatred of men; then she closes thinking about her brother who married for money, and how shocked his wife would be to admit "we exist, we other woman things."[24] The speaker's tone is at times cavalier, at times movingly reflective, always direct; as the poem nears its end with the observation that as far as laughing and crying are concerned, "there's not much difference / between the two sometimes," Eulalie implies that there's also not much difference between a woman selling herself sexually for money versus anyone – male or female – marrying for money (lines 622–3). Thus Webster argues that the prostitute should not be viewed as an unusually sinful woman, but as merely human.

Victorian women's verse, especially toward the fin de siècle, also features women whose romantic and erotic desires are acknowledged with no reference to prostitution. Violet Fane's "The Siren" (1896) provides a particularly interesting case: a beautiful yet dangerous mythical creature with a human reason – jealousy – for killing a sailor she loves. The siren's strong, possessive, carnal mode of loving is more like a stereotypical man's than the heart-centered sympathy associated with Victorian women's love. Indeed, resonating with tropes found in male-authored verse, the poem's opening blazon catalogues the siren's own sensual beauty, in her own voice. After killing her beloved, the siren seeks to understand why he said, "You cannot understand / Or love your love as the maidens do / That live upon the land."[25] She discovers that land girls often make men unhappy; the poem suggests sexual withholding is the reason:

> I made far merrier than they
> The moon that I was wed!
> And he was mine, – my very own!
> I clasped him firm and fair. (lines 55–8)

In creating a space where women can desire as men do and act upon those desires, Fane's "The Siren" provides an example of what Talia Schaffer calls "fantasias" by late-Victorian female aesthetes that "permitted new sorts of gender politics. Writers situated women's desire in the unreal space of 'dream' and 'fantasy' thereby preventing the reader from criticizing the character according to everyday nineteenth-century sexual norms."[26]

Women's sexual desire is also articulated throughout EBB's *Sonnets from the Portuguese* (1846). "Love is fire!" the speaker proclaims in sonnet 10; love "taught her the whole / of life in a new rhythm."[27] As Beverly Taylor and Marjorie Stone argue, erotic metaphor in manuscripts from EBB's honeymoon indicate that her conjugal relations inspired a new phase in her work;[28] this, in turn, supports identifying allusions to carnal love in the sonnet sequence. Sonnet 21 celebrates love's excesses; and Sonnets 22 and 23 posit embodied love on earth as preferable to spiritual love in heaven. Thus, through close readings of fantasy and metaphor, readers today can begin to glean how the ideal married woman might have thought about her life's more intimate moments.

Victorian women's verse sometimes even portrays adulterous women thoughtfully and sympathetically, thereby complicating the fallen woman narrative. Desire and erotic love are illustrated as complex experiences not always confined to the institution of marriage, while marriage sometimes brings misery for wives. Although radically feminist critiques of marriage tend to be associated with fin-de-siècle women writers, we also see evidence of such ideas earlier in the period. In Caroline Norton's "Marriage and Love" (1833), a sympathetic maiden, Laura, is pressured to make a sensible marriage to a man she later discovers is "Cold, harsh, unfeeling, proud" who "Changed his will to show *he* had the power."[29] She falls in love with his cousin Francis; they are discovered and run away. But eventually Francis's love wanes as both are affected by Laura's loss of reputation; Laura repents, then dies. The last three quatrains of "Marriage and Love" critique gendered double standards for sexual behavior. Francis ends up happily married to an angel in the house, "a gentle bride / . . . / Unused to grief, and impotent to chide"; in contrast, the last lines portray poor dead Laura with ambivalence: "She sinned – she wept – and is no more ashamed" (lines 147–9, 157).

Violet Fane's "Lancelot and Guinevere" (1872) also depicts an adulterous woman, one who strongly identifies with Guinevere's complex emotions. When she confesses, "I share the cross of Guinevere / Like her my guilty secret hide," the reader has already learned of her great capacity for sympathy, tenderness, and willingness to sacrifice for her love.[30] Fane also implies that, like Guinevere's Arthur, the woman's husband has become neglectful: "Her husband did not seem to hear / Or, if he heard, he heeded not" (lines 9–10). Thus, between religious connotation and emotional rationale, Fane makes it difficult for the reader to unequivocally condemn the adulterous wife.

Depictions of female sexual desire *before* marriage also indicate that women poets knew female stereotypes were overdetermined. Contrary to the notion that most women were uninterested in sex until marriage (if ever), poems like Felicia Hemans's "Italian Girl's Hymn to the Virgin" (1839) illustrate how a maiden could be very aware of her "earthly love's excess" and "wild idolatory."[31] As the maiden prays for her absent love to be kept safe at sea, her embodied reflections about "trembl[ing]," "feverish strife," and "Too much o'er *him* is poured / My being's hope" convey her keen awareness of her sexuality (lines 33, 39, 29–30).

Mathilde Blind similarly explores unmarried women's sexual agency in "The Song of the Willi" (1871), inspired by a Hungarian folktale about betrothed girls, deceased before marriage, whose spirits rise to visit their beloveds. The dead maiden croons,

> I hold thee, I hold thee, I drink thy caresses,
>> O love, my love!
> Round thy face, round thy throat, I roll my dank tresses,
>> My love!
> I hold thee, I hold thee![32]

Verbal lovemaking gives way to unceasing sensual dance, which, according to legend, results in the young man's death. Although this might seem simply another example of Victorian representations of dangerous femininity safely set in a foreign land, in the hands of a woman poet we can read Blind's Willi as a female fantasy of sexual expression and fulfillment: at the poem's end the lovers die (literally and in the Renaissance sexual sense) locked in an eternal embrace.

All of this section's examples denaturalize marriage as the sole state, and the home as the sole place, for women's sexuality to manifest only as the adjunct of romantic, marital love. Further, in the imagination of the Victorian woman poet, even the most respectable option for the fallen

woman – the convent – can articulate a complex message about female
sexuality. Adelaide Anne Proctor's "A Legend of Provence" (1861) tells
a typical tale of ruin and forgiveness: a girl raised in a convent falls in love
with a patient and runs away with him, descending into shame. But eventually she returns to the convent where she is welcomed, reminding readers
that "*our place is kept*, and it will wait / ready for us to fill it, soon or late."[33]
The speaker in Christina Rossetti's "The Convent Threshold" (1862)
recounts how her family discovered her with her lover and sent her to
a convent, where she now resides on the threshold of life and death, thinking
of her beloved and the "pleasant sin" they shared, and hoping he will "repent
with me, for I repent."[34] Both these examples illustrate how, especially for
Protestant England, the convent disrupts woman's place in the home. Yet, in
both "A Legend of Provence" and "The Convent Threshold," the convent
does not restrain or erase women's sexuality. In Proctor's poem, the cloistered maiden finds sexual awakening while performing her convent duties;
and in Rossetti's, the fallen woman repents and her faith grows in the
convent, but her desire for her beloved continues to flourish. She hopes
they will meet in heaven where he will "lift [her] veil" and "love with old
familiar love," which, the speaker's story makes clear, was sexual (lines
144–8).

Victorian Women Poets and Queer Sexualities

Although fallen women in their seemingly infinite variety created a dominant
mode for Victorians to talk about women's sexuality, women's verse indicates many were aware of a wide range of what we today would term
antiheteronormative, or queer, desires. For example, Mathilde Blind's
"The Mystic's Vision" (1891) transforms the conventional genre of the
poetess's devotional lyric into a flagrantly erotic dramatic monologue
about a nun, in bed, eagerly awaiting her heavenly Spouse. When she feels
God's presence,

> My heart is hushed, my tongue is mute,
>   My life is centred in your will;
> You play upon me like a lute
>   Which answers to its master's skill,
> Till passionately vibrating,
> Each nerve becomes a throbbing string.[35]

Whether we understand the poem as a moment of autoeroticism with elements of masochistic fantasy or as "real" spiritual vision, the speaker's
intense desire is articulated with traditional tropes of love and sex: the

maiden awaiting her beloved, orange blossoms and roses, and repeated exhortations to "die in you" (line 47). The speaker is "drowned in your love which flows o'er me," and as "You take possession of your Bride" she repeatedly begs to be penetrated, literally to the point of annihilation:

> Ay, break through every wall of sense,
> > And pierce my flesh as nails did pierce
> Your bleeding limbs in anguish tense,
> > And torture me with bliss so fierce,
> That self dies out. (lines 5, 44, 55–60)

Notably, the poem's conclusion asserts that fulfillment of the speaker's desire will release her from "the noisy world's inanities" (line 65). Whether inside the convent walls or after death, this passion will not find its release within marriage or any other relationship with men.

Such representations, of course, are not without precedent. Religious devotion has long been eroticized – and in ways that evade heteronormativity – from the sensual medieval visions of Julian of Norwich and Margery Kempe to the homoeroticism of male fin-de-siècle Aesthetes who converted to Catholicism, with their cult of Saint Sebastian. Lovers and coauthors Katharine Bradley and Edith Cooper, who wrote as "Michael Field," produced many comparably erotic devotional lyrics after their conversion to Catholicism. "A Crucifix" (1913), for example, opens as follows:

> Thee such loveliness adorns
> On Thy Cross, O my Desire–
> As a lily Thou art among thorns,
> As a rose lies back against his briar.[36]

Devotional and homoerotic desire become intertwined in this lyric, with reclining floral images giving way to a vulvular conceit: "Thou art as a welcoming opening fruit" (line 7). As the poem progresses, Cooper's willowy form seems to haunt Bradley's admiration of Christ's feminine limbs, "so fine so long," especially as the speaker invokes feminine genital imagery as she rhapsodizes, "Thy body maketh a solemn song / As a stream in a gorge confined" (lines 13, 15–16).

The sensual language and eroticized fervor of Victorian women's poetry expressing antiheteronormative desire prompts consideration of whether our twenty-first-century concepts adequately describe gender and sexuality as it was conceived of in the past, especially vis-à-vis what we today call queer sexualities. A persistent interpretive conundrum exists, for example, regarding the insistently lesbian overtones permeating the Eucharistic imagery between the sisters of "Goblin Market":

> "Did you miss me?
> Come and kiss me.
> Never mind my bruises,
> Hug me, kiss me, suck my juices
> Squeez'd from goblin fruits for you,
> Goblin pulp and goblin dew.
> Eat me, drink me, love me;
> Laura, make much of me." (lines 465–74)

Some literary historians contextualize such affectionate outbursts within notions of female passionlessness and label them nonsexual romantic female friendship (which has no place among our concepts of sexuality today). Intensely romantic and often homoerotic language appearing in women's verse honoring female authors and friends has often been understood this way, such as A. Mary F. Robinson's references to experiences shared with Vernon Lee. Similarly, in Amy Levy's "To Lallie" (1884), the speaker's "poet-heart went pit-a-pat" in seeing Lallie enter a museum with a mutual friend, and "all my blood was flame / O Lallie, Lallie!"[37]

Yet, beyond the category of romantic friendship, which really does not disturb the binary of fallen woman versus domestic angel, and despite society's strongly patriarchal, heteronormative expectations, Victorian women's poetry is replete with instances of sexual desire for other women. Eliza Cook's "To Charlotte Cushman" (1870), for example, exceeds the parameters of romantic female friendship; Cushman (who is widely presumed to have been Cook's lover) is praised for her acting skills, but in so doing, Cook eroticizes the feminine mode of sympathy and expressiveness:

> I did not think thou couldst arouse a throb
> Of deeper, stronger beating in my heart;
> I did not deem thou couldst awake the sob
> Of choking fulness, and convulsive start.[38]

"Let crowds behold and laud thee as they will," Cook concludes, combining flattery and seductive promises, "But this poor breast, in shunning what they seek, / May yield, perchance, a richer tribute still" (lines 26–8).

While Cook is quite forward, other women's expressions of queer desire are more subtle. For Sarah Parker, many of Amy Levy's poems represent "homoerotic desire using spectral metaphors that can be explained using [Terry] Castle's theory of the 'apparitional lesbian.'"[39] A glimpse of a familiar face in "In the Mile End Road" inspires a frisson of longing and queer temporality: "For one strange moment I forgot / My only love was dead." Levy's similar "In the Night" also expresses impossible homoerotic yearning:

What ails my love; what ails her? She is paling:
Faint grows her face, and slowly seems to fade!
I cannot clasp her – stretch out unavailing
My arms across the silence and the shade.[40]

Charlotte Mew's "My Heart is Lame with Running After Yours so Fast" is likewise suffused with deferral and longing; it negotiates the difficulty of human connection and, more implicitly, the barriers to love and happiness that are created by society.

Other women use dramatic monologue, literary cross gendering, and various masking devices in the voices of historical figures to articulate queer desires. In Michael Field's "Temptation" (1908), Cooper, inspired by seeing Bradley in a new nightgown, imagines how Zeus lusted after the daughter of Acrisius when he saw her: "Clad in linen, all alone / Clad in linen finely wove / Straight he stared and plotted love."[41] Michael Field also explores gender roles in two poems featuring sex transformations, "Tiresias" and "Caenis Caeneus." And in a volume of lyrics based on Sappho's fragments, *Long Ago* (1889), they celebrate same-sex love through the voice and authority of the original poetess. Michael Field's Sapphics are unapologetic:

Come, Gorgo, put the rug in place,
    And passionate recline;
I love to see thee in thy grace,
    Dark, virulent, divine.[42]

Here, the desiring lesbian gaze is unmistakable, as is their straightforward logic in "Maids not to you my mind doth change" explaining why loving women is superior to loving men: "Between us is no thought of pain, / peril, satiety."[43]

These examples of sexual desire between women suggest that, contra claims by medical men like William Acton about women's innate passionlessness, female emotional expressiveness and inclination toward affection could be linked to natural sexual desire. For some writers, ardent same-sex love and desire became coded within this naturalness, with descriptions of natural objects, especially flowers, standing in for same-sex genital contact, as in Michael Field's "Unbosoming" (1893), in which the speaker declares,

The love that breeds
In my heart for thee!
As the iris is full, brimful of seeds,
And all that it flowered for among the reeds
Is packed in a thousand vermilion-beads
That push, and riot, and squeeze, and clip,

> Till they burst the sides of the silver scrip,
> And at last we see
> What the bloom, with its tremulous, bowery fold
> Of zephyr-petal at heart did hold.[44]

Similarly, "The Sleeping Venus" associates Giorgione's Venus with the land and domestic surroundings. The poem, which opens "Here is Venus by our homes," celebrates women's bodies and desires as beautiful and sacred:

> There is a sympathy between
> Her and Earth of largest reach,
> For the sex that forms them each
> Is a bond, a holiness,
> That unconsciously must bless
> And unite them, as they lie
> Shameless underneath the sky.[45]

As the poem unfolds, the contours of the landscape mirror the curves of Venus's body, with particular focus on the hand resting on her pudenda: "She enjoys the good / Of delicious womanhood," the speaker daringly asserts, suggesting homoerotic and autoerotic possibility for all women (lines 69–70).

Finally, Mathilde Blind depicts multiple, diffuse, libidinal pleasures that anticipate the thinking of Luce Irigaray[46] and other feminist and queer theorists. In "Chaunts of Life" (1889), the speaker sensuously describes the chaotic oneness of the universe, transformed by the messy, amorphous powers of sex and love. For myriad beasts, "The lust of life's delirious fires / Burned like a fever in their blood"; "Voluptuously the leopard lies" and "Stirs with intoxicating stress / The pulses of the leopardess."[47] This amorousness makes no distinction between species or the sexes; although the rhapsodic evolutionary impulses might seem to reify heteronormative sexualities, when we read "Chaunts of Life" alongside "The Orange Peel in the Gutter" (1867), we see how Blind actually advocates something akin to a radically pansexual relation between all elements of the cosmos. The poem begins with a meditation on the unlikely beauty of an orange peel in a dirty London gutter, but Blind muses across time and to other places where,

> Heart melts with heart, and kiss with kiss,
> In holy night, in holy bliss,
> As in the wondrous sunset skies
> Hues melt with hues and dyes with dyes
> Till all in one vast glory lies.[48]

The language of science and evolution collapses into the language of erotic abandon as Blind catalogues all the aspects of nature that "Revealed the throbs of mutual love, / Ensphered by kindling stars above!" (lines 167–8). Completely non-ironic in tone, such *jouissance* is made possible only because of Blind's sensuous connection with the whole wide world, realized through a castoff orange peel.

These varied illustrations of antiheteronormative sexual expression remind us that the angel in the house, fallen women, and romantic female friendship are not the only recorded permutations of Victorian female sexuality. Jack Halberstam advocates that "perverse presentism" can usefully deploy "present-day insights to make sense of the complexities of other eras; we can see that multiple modes of variance exist in both contemporary society and nineteenth-century society."[49] Such insights provide space for thinking about poetic expressions of sexuality that do not "fit" with our sexual terminology. In addition to considering Blind's relationship with nature and evolution as belonging to the libidinal, such a queer reading of sexuality, intentionally anachronistic, would be useful to readers of a poet like Michael Field, whose writing demonstrates their complex relationship to the pleasures of power and desire, and their strategic inhabiting of a fluid array of sexually dissident positions such as bisexual, non-monogamous desire within a long-term same-sex relationship, intergenerational erotics, role play, and cross-gender identification. Future critics may find it useful to categorize these and other Victorian women writers not as lesbian, queer, or trans as the terms are used today, but perhaps as belonging to a category of gender variation and/or sexuality that exceeds our present concepts. As we denaturalize what we think we know about essentializing narratives of nineteenth-century sexuality, we would do well to deliberately employ the term "sexuality" broadly and thereby more accurately reflect the complexities of Victorian women poets' lived sexual experience.

Notes

1. Dorothy Mermin, *Godiva's Ride: Women of Letters in England 1830–1880* (Bloomington: Indiana University Press, 1993), p. 75.
2. Cecil Frances Alexander, "All Things Bright and Beauteous," in *Victorian Women Poets: An Anthology* (*VWP*), ed. Angela Leighton and Margaret Reynolds (Oxford: Blackwell, 1995), p. 217, lines 25–9.
3. Ellen Johnston, "A Mother's Love," *VWP*, pp. 408–9, lines 10, 14–15.
4. Mary Howitt, "The Dying Child," *VWP*, p. 22, lines 1–3.
5. Charlotte Brontë, "On the Death of Emily Jane Brontë," *VWP*, pp. 166–7, lines 2, 8, 10–13.
6. Adelaide Procter, "Philip and Mildred," *VWP*, pp. 331–6.

7. Felicia Hemans, "Woman and Fame," *VWP*, pp. 7–8, lines 19–20, 8.

8. Eliza Cook, "To My Lyre," *VWP*, pp. 184–5, lines 17–18.

9. Elizabeth Barrett Browning, *Aurora Leigh and Other Poems*, ed. John Bolton and Julia Holloway (London: Penguin, 1995), pp. 150, 5.441–4.

10. Patricia Pulham, "Victorian Women Poets and the Annuals," in *Victorian Woman Poets*, ed. Alison Chapman (Cambridge: D. S. Brewer, 2003), p. 17.

11. L.E.L., "Sappho's Song," *VWP*, p. 42, lines 11–12.

12. Frances Anne Kemble, "Lines on Reading," *VWP*, pp. 148–9, lines 5–6, 16–17.

13. Steven Connor, "'Speaking Likenesses': Language and Repetition in Christina Rossetti's 'Goblin Market,'" *Victorian Poetry* 22 (1984), 439–48.

14. Isobel Armstrong, *Victorian Poetry: Poetry, Poetics and Politics* (New York: Routledge, 1993), p. 7.

15. Leighton, "'Because men made the laws': The Fallen Woman and the Woman Poet," in *Victorian Women Poets: A Critical Reader*, ed. Angela Leighton (Oxford: Oxford University Press, 1996), p. 217.

16. Mary Wilson Carpenter, "'Eat Me, Drink Me, Love Me': The Consumable Female Body in Christina Rossetti's 'Goblin Market,'" *Victorian Poetry* 29 (1991), 415–34.

17. Rossetti, "Goblin Market," *VWP*, pp. 378–90, lines 144–6.

18. Armstrong, *Victorian Poetry*, p. 14.

19. Ibid., p. 15.

20. Amy Levy, "Magdalen," *VWP*, pp. 602–4, lines 37, 40.

21. Dora Greenwell, "Christina" *VWP*, pp. 277–86, lines 67–70.

22. Mathilde Blind, "The Message," in *Dramas in Miniature* (*DM*) (London: Chatto & Windus, 1891), pp. 18–31, lines 81, 108.

23. Mathilda Blind, "The Leading of Sorrow," in *The Ascent of Man* (*AM*) (London: Chatto & Windus, 1889), pp. 85–110.

24. Augusta Webster, "A Castaway," *VWP*, pp. 433–48, lines 377–8, 615.

25. Violet Fane, "The Siren," *VWP*, pp. 474–5, lines 38–40.

26. Talia Schaffer, *The Forgotten Female Aesthetes* (Charlottesville: University of Virginia Press, 2000), p. 51.

27. EBB, *Sonnets from the Portuguese*, in *Aurora Leigh and Other Poems*, p. 381, line 5, p. 380, lines 6–7.

28. Marjorie Stone and Beverly Taylor, "Elizabeth Barrett Browning's Unpublished Honeymoon Poem, a Poetics in Transition, and Petrarch's Vaucluse: 'Wilder ever still & Wilder!'" *Victorian Poetry* 57.1 (Spring 2019).

29. Caroline Norton, "Marriage and Love," in *Poems by the Honble Mrs. Norton* (Boston: Allen & Ticknor, 1833), pp. 135–40, lines 60, 68.

30. Fane, "Lancelot and Guinevere," in *Nineteenth-Century Women Poets* (*NCWP*), ed. Isobel Armstrong and Joseph Bristow (Oxford: Clarendon Press, 1996), pp. 665–8, lines 86–7.

31. Felicia Hemans, "Italian Girl's Hymn to the Virgin," in *The Works of Mrs. Hemans* (Edinburgh: Blackwood, 1839), pp. 22–4, lines 26, 36.

32. Mathilde Blind, "The Song of the Willi," *Dark Blue*, 6 (August 1871), 741–5, lines 129–33.

33. Procter, "A Legend of Provence," *VWP*, pp. 309–16, lines 327–8.

34. Rossetti, "The Convent Threshold," *VWP*, pp. 373–6, lines 51–2.

35. Blind, "The Mystic's Vision," *DM*, pp. 12–16, lines 31–6.

36. Michael Field, "A Crucifix," in *Mystic Trees* (London: Eveleigh Nash, 1913), p. 36, lines 1–4.
37. Levy, "To Lallie," *NCWP*, pp. 778–89, lines 10, 2.
38. Cook, "To Charlotte Cushman," *VWP*, pp. 188–9, lines 16–20.
39. Sarah Parker, "Urban Economies and the Dead Woman Muse in the Poetry of Amy Levy and Djuna Barnes," in *Economies of Desire at the Victorian Fin de Siècle: Libidinal Lives*, ed. Jane Ford et al. (New York: Routledge, 2015), p. 97.
40. Amy Levy, "In the Mile End Road," "In the Night," in *A London Plane Tree and other Verse* (London: Fisher Unwin, 1889), p. 50, lines 7–8, 41, lines 13–16.
41. Michael Field, "Temptation," in *Wild Honey from Various Thyme* (London: Fisher Unwin, 1908), p. 57, lines 16–18.
42. Field, "Come Gorgo, put the rug in place," *VWP*, p. 490, lines 1–4.
43. Field, "Maids not to you my mind doth change," *VWP*, p. 490, lines 6–7.
44. Field, "Unbosoming," in *Underneath the Bough* (London: George Bell, 1893), p. 100, lines 1–10.
45. Field, "The Sleeping Venus," *NCWP*, pp. 704–7, lines 21–6, 1.
46. Luce Irigaray, *This Sex Which Is Not One* (Ithaca: Cornell University Press, 1985).
47. Blind, "Chaunts of Life," *AM*, pp. 7–58, 2.31–2, 44, 47–8.
48. Mathilda Blind, "The Orange Peel in the Gutter," in *Poems* (London: Alfred Bennett, 1867), pp. 47–57, lines 74–8.
49. Jack Halberstam, *Female Masculinity* (Durham: Duke University Press, 1998), p. 59.

14

ANA PAREJO VADILLO

Poets of Style: Poetries of Asceticism and Excess

A year before the publication of Christina Rossetti's *Goblin Market and Other Poems* (1862), Max Müller argued in one of his *Lectures on The Science of Language* (1861) that "what we are accustomed to call languages, the literary idioms of Greece, and Rome, and India, of Italy, France, and Spain, must be considered artificial, rather than natural forms of speech."[1] This materialist understanding of language, language estranged from biology and defined instead as an artificial national and social construct, facilitated in the late nineteenth century newly imagined mythologies – quite literally the creations of worlds of words. But Müller's theory, as Linda Dowling has argued, also brought about a deep existential linguistic crisis, for if languages were constructs they could also be deconstructed.[2] In England, Müller's theory was interpreted in relation to the perceived weakening of the British Empire: just as the fall of Rome had provoked the death of Latin, the English language could too decay. How to energize the English language became the key question of the period. One of the effects of such questioning, through the discourse of the art for art's sake movement, was a profound period of linguistic experimentation, most notably in poetry.

Beginning with Christina Rossetti, this chapter traces the ways in which women poets styled their poetics through artifice. It unfolds the rich variety of poetic practices that began to deal with questions concerning the ontology of poetry. If the poetry of the period is traditionally framed within the discourses of the sensual and phenomenological, this chapter also suggests that formal experimentation was an attempt at generating questions about the independence of art, an issue particularly important for women, who saw in the notion of art for art's sake a form of social and political revolution. I distinguish two main poetic responses to the linguistic challenges of the fin de siècle, both produced by obsession with language's materiality that was at the heart of decadence: first, an ascetic style based on disciplining the word; second, an aesthetics of excess, bathed in historicism and characteristically animated by luxurious language. To illustrate, I discuss the ascetic lyric poetry of Alice Meynell, and the poetics of excess in the verse dramas of Michael Field.

Styling Artifice, Christina Rossetti

To begin our discussion of women poets cultivating artifice, it is helpful to start with Christina Rossetti's "Winter: My Secret" (1862). Two aspects of this poem are especially important. The poem is paradigmatic of Rossetti's style and shows Rossetti at her most playful with language. Additionally, the poem allows us to think of Rossetti's poetic practice as influenced by the aesthetics of earlier nineteenth-century poets *and* as influencer of the poetic innovations of women poets in the late nineteenth century. For Rossetti's experimental poetics influenced a new generation of fin-de-siècle poets, including Alice Meynell, Michael Field, and Amy Levy, all of whom, though younger, were Rossetti's contemporaries. Rehearsing Rossetti's textual materiality can provide a wider vision of women poets' experiments with artifice in the later nineteenth century, of their construction of artificial worlds and realities that existed through their writings' style.

"Winter: My Secret" is a foundational poem of aestheticism and decadence. The enigma and opacity of this poem are the direct consequence of Rossetti's experimentation with language. It was published in *Goblin Market and Other Poems* (1862), which marked Rossetti as a Pre-Raphaelite poet and crowned her as the foremost female poet of her time (Elizabeth Barrett Browning had died in 1861). "Winter: My Secret" shares with "Goblin Market," another foundational poem, the sense of secrecy and luxuriousness of language that would be the stamp of her poetics. Originally entitled "Nonsense," it entices the reader to play a guessing game: "I tell a secret? No indeed, not I." "You want to hear it? well: / Only, my secret's mine, and I won't tell." The game has only begun, but as we reach the second stanza the speaker turns a corner on us:

> Or, after all, perhaps there's none:
> Suppose there is no secret after all,
> But only just my fun.
> Today's a nipping day, a biting day;
> In which one wants a shawl,
> A veil, a cloak, and other wraps:
> I cannot ope to everyone who taps,
> And let the draughts come whistling thro' my hall;
> Come bounding and surrounding me,
> Come buffeting, astounding me,
> Nipping and clipping thro' my wraps and all.
> I wear my mask for warmth.[3]

In the third stanza, we are led to believe that perhaps the expansiveness of Spring may bring her to disclose her secret. The ending of the poem is intriguingly ambiguous: "some languid summer day," "Perhaps my secret I may say, / Or you may guess" (lines 28, 33–4).

Yopie Prins's argument is that the poem "playfully responds to new ways of telling meter by refusing to 'tell' a secret."[4] Her analysis demonstrates that the riddle can be solved by focusing on meter: the variable number of accents and lines are reminiscent of Edmund Spenser's *The Shepherd's Calendar* (1579), in which each month follows a different measure. As Prins shows, Rossetti's metrical pattern echoes the verses of Spenser's February. The secret is thus February, and the voice is not the voice of a speaker but the voice of temporality: time is materialized in poetic language through prosody. This is one aspect of Rossetti's experimentation with material textuality: meter produces signification through sound.

But the poem on the page also has signification. The month of February is the last in the winter season. The secret was thus out from the start, printed in black and white, "Winter: My Secret." The second stanza simulates the reality of winter. The speaker wants a shawl, a veil, a cloak, and other wraps. Clothes are here *both* material objects and metaphorical entities, for the guarding of a secret often requires covering it up. If prosody intones the secret, style then works to conceal, adorn, but also to reveal it. As Constance Hassett suggests, the poem "manages to be simultaneously flagrant and reserved, to withhold a secret even as it enfolds the hope of a poetry that is sensuous, expansive, and self-revealing."[5] As Hassett further remarks, "Winter: My Secret" enacts "the paradox of [Rossetti's] authorship, the impulse to write what is lyrically private, countered by the sure knowledge that words do and do not reveal the poet's 'inward laughter'" (p. 63). "Winter: My Secret" thus speaks of and displays the high degree of artifice and formal sophistication inherent in Rossetti's poetic practice. The poem simultaneously hides, tells, creates, and simulates thought (and the *absence* of thought) through an exercise in rhetoric. But it also styles a simulacrum of winter, Rossetti's winter, *her* secret. The poem in this sense theorizes its own construction by bringing attention to the materiality of its rhetoric. Her poetry clothes words with words, projecting the poem as an object with graphic and oral existence.

Artifice is the game and the poem signals Rossetti's poetic practice as a masquerade. Significantly, Rossetti's stylization of poetry shows her indebtedness to two different schools of poetries: the tradition of the poetess and metaphysical poetry. As Hassett notes, Rossetti's self-mockery can be traced to the influence of *The Golden Violet* (1827) by Letitia Landon (L.E.L.), a poem concerning the difference between public mask and private face. "Never let an envious eye / gaze upon the heart too nigh," L.E.L. intones in *The Golden Violet*.[6] There is rebellion in Rossetti's use of this poem: she rejects biological readings of femininity to highlight Landon's style and artifice. Rossetti later paid homage to Landon in her poem "L.E.L" (1866), which included an epigraph taken from EBB. Rossetti studied closely Landon's use of voice and was particularly influenced by Augusta Webster's dramatic monologues, both crucial in Rossetti's construction of poetic voice and simulations of realities.

To this immediate background, Rossetti extended her exploration of historical poetics to the playful, precious language of seventeenth-century metaphysical poets. Aestheticism owes much to metaphysical poetry, for its mysticism was appropriated and re-invented to mean the worship of the beautiful and/or religious mysticism. In "The Metaphysical Poets" (1921), T. S. Eliot would describe Rossetti's poetry as an echo of seventeenth-century poets George Herbert, Richard Crashaw, and Henry Vaughan. Both Eliot and Alice Meynell, the two most insightful critics of metaphysical poetry in the twentieth century, placed Rossetti within the nineteenth-century school of metaphysical poetry. Meynell writes that "mystery and mysticism" are the characteristics of metaphysical poetry, adding that metaphysical poets "are allowed to hide themselves in very truth."[7] For Eliot suggested that metaphysical poetry, though undefinable, is one that can "clothe the abstract ... with the painful delight of flesh."[8] Cloaks, veils, spring, birds, fruits – they all form part of Rossetti's poetic world. They are the "flesh" of her poetic artifice. After all, perhaps we have guessed that Rossetti's secret is her artifice, for it reveals that her world is wholly made out of language, her secret broken down into a mystic empowerment of the word. Just for fun.

In Waves

Inspired by Rossetti and attracted to aestheticism's emphasis on language and style, women poets consciously began to think of poetry as a meta-discourse on poetic artifice, a poetry for poetry's sake. Literary decadence, Dowling argues, "represents a moment when the linguistic artificiality and autonomy of the written language are mirrored in a mode of curious stylistic opacity."[9] Consider, for example, Margaret Veley's "A Japanese Fan" (1876), a distant refraction of Rossetti's "Winter: My Secret."[10] Veley's dramatic monologue is presented as a conversation taking place in an aesthetic home. Alternating in long and short lines, Veley's meters locate the poem at a midpoint between embracing the house beautiful movement and comically rendering the cult for all things Japanese.

Home and poem are full of stuff and the poem reads like an inventory of aesthetic decorative objects, but the focus is the fan. The speaker recounts the story behind this "Japanese fan," which is printed, in Japanese, on the fan: "You don't understand the language? / I'll translate."[11] The "translation" of an ill-fated love, however, takes more than seventy lines, and the auditor ends up doubting the story's veracity. The impossibility of seventy verses being a translation of a few lines implicitly brings into view two issues. First, for a non-speaker of Japanese, the language in the scroll can only be an image, a letter-type. Second, the impenetrability of the foreign language transforms that language into a signifier and, disrobed of meaning, it gets refashioned into the story of the speaker.

Dowling has compellingly suggested that "decadence in the English literary experience always represents less a program than a perception about the materiality and autonomy of its own linguistic medium."[12] With Rossetti's poetry as a model, women poets began to use a variety of genres (dramatic monologues, narrative poems, sonnets, poetic dramas) as they experimented with methods of composition based on craft, artifice, and languages. Many women poets worked with translations to find in classical languages and/or modern foreign languages ways of enriching their poetries to create their own styles. Examples include Augusta Webster's *Medea of Euripides* (1868) or *Yu-Pe-Ya's Lute. A Chinese Tale in English Verse* (1874); A. Mary F. Robinson's *The Crowned Hippolytus* (1881); Amy Levy's *Medea* (1881); Michael Field's *Long Ago* (1889); or Graham R. Tomson's edition of *Selections from the Greek Anthology* (1889). Mathilde Blind used Scots in *The Heather on Fire: A Tale of the Highland Clearances* (1886). All these poets fashioned a cosmopolitan style, which showed the breadth of their artifice and marked their poetries as "learned." An example of such cosmopolitan writing is Margaret L. Woods's *Lyrics and Ballads* (1889), with poems such as "L'Envoi," "Gaudeamus Igitur," "The Death of Hjöward," or "Rameses." The cultivation of languages as artifice stuffed fin-de-siècle poetry with novelty and innovation.

But there is more to say about how the new generation of poets appropriated Rossetti's artistry for their own aims. In perhaps the best review of Rossetti during her lifetime, Amy Levy re-appreciated the poet in 1888 for her generation. Younger women poets, whose contemporaries were also D. G. Rossetti, A. C. Swinburne, and Walter Pater, were keen to find contemporary poetic models of poetry by women that escaped biological readings and empowered their own development of aesthetic style. As Levy writes,

> The quaint, yet exquisite choice of words; the felicitous *naïveté*, more Italian than English; the delicate, unusual melody of the verse; the richness, almost to

excess, of imagery – all are apparent in these first-fruits of her muse. And not less apparent are the mysticism and the almost unrelieved melancholy which we associate with Rossetti's better-known poetry. Indeed, there is here to be found that youthful exaggeration of sadness, the perverse assumption of the cypress.[13]

Astonishingly, Levy signifies Rossetti as a decadent poet: "quaint," "richness of imagery," "excess," "melancholy," "mysticism," even perversity. Michael Field once described her as the fin-de-siècle La Gioconda of women poets: "Christina Rossetti, in her brother's drawing, looks as if she could murder happiness in cold blood."[14] Levy highlights the foreignness of Rossetti's poetics too, "more Italian than English." Levy dares not predict if Rossetti's poetry could resist the "waves of Time," but her most curious assessment of the poetry comes at the end of her review: "From the branches of a wondrous tree, transplanted by chance to our clime, we pluck the rare, exotic fruit, and the unfamiliar flavour is very sweet."[15] Levy's chosen metaphor strategically links Rossetti to the decadent passion for the exotic, to the perversions of des Esseintes, the character of Huysman's 1884 decadent novel, À rebours. More significantly, Levy implies that Rossetti's poetry tastes like the luscious, decadent fruits of the "Goblin Market," which were both addictive and deadly. And yet, in "Goblin Market," in the eating of fruits, Rossetti enabled a utopian sisterhood outside the goblins' tyranny. One might discern something of that utopian fantasy in Levy's review, with Rossetti as the strong link in the chain of modern decadent poetry by women.

In understanding Rossetti's reappropriation, we can begin to chart models of poetic artistry that emerged in the 1870s. The experiments with artifice, language, and style in the late nineteenth century enabled a spectrum of poetries ranging from the precious and precise to the excessive and exotic, from the lyrical to the dramatic, from the religious to the Dionysian. These paired responses became in effect the two sides of the same movement: on one hand ascetic poetry, often colored with a metaphysical mysticism, and on the other a poetry of excess. The first is founded on measure and moderation, the second is saturated with extravagance and artifice. Women poets moved freely within both aesthetics, but I will concentrate on the two poets who best represent each aesthetic, Alice Meynell and Michael Field.

Ascetic Style: The Composure of Alice Meynell

In 1893, Alice Meynell published simultaneously two books with Elkin Mathews and John Lane, the book of essays *The Rhythm of Life* and *Poems,* a reprint – with new poems – of her first book, *Preludes* (1875). Reading *The Rhythm of Life* alongside *Poems* offers striking insights into

Meynell's poetic theory. One key aspect of those essays is Meynell's theorization of prosody. The book's first sentence signals from the outset her devotion to meter: "If life is not always poetical, it is at least metrical."[16] Recently critics have begun to reveal the soundscapes of her poetry. Here, however, I want to dwell on another radical aspect of her work, the textual materiality of her poetics. For she is a language poet, and her language-centred poetic theory is central to assess the ascetic style she came to represent.

In the 1890s, Meynell was often compared to Walter Pater, even though, perhaps too disingenuously, she claimed never to have read him. At the core of their writings was Paul Bourget's definition of decadence as an aesthetic of decomposition: "a style of decadence is one in which the unity of the book is decomposed to make way for the independence of the page, the page is decomposed to make way for the independence of the sentence, and the sentence makes way for the independence of the word."[17] As I argue elsewhere, Meynell and Pater turned Bourget's definition around.[18] Both envisioned a recomposed sentence through composition, from the root of the word up, not just down, to one's own style of composition. Of Ruskin, Meynell would say that decomposition is death and that composition is natural life.[19] Writing was, for Meynell, an imprint of man. This is what she meant by "composure," the title of one of the essays in *The Rhythm of Life,* which ends with the following lines: "Shall not the Thing more and more, as we compose ourselves to literature, assume the honour, the hesitation, the leisure, the reconciliation of the Word?"[20]

Meynell's poetics were philological, focused on language as a human-made construct with a material existence both aurally and on the printed page. She was obsessed with refining language. She actually signed letters as "Johnson" (a reference to the eighteenth-century lexicographer Samuel Johnson). Her short poetic oeuvre responds to a poetics of measured composition, which included the combination of Latin and Anglo-Saxon words to produce controlled rhythms. Notice, for example, in the poem "Future Poetry" the line "Who knows what musical flocks of words," where the word "musical" from the Latin *musica* breathes time into the verse as a counterpoint to the quickness of the Anglo-Saxon.[21] Nothing is superfluous in her poetry, the topic of another essay, "Superfluous Kings" (on Shakespeare).[22] Rejecting the poetics of excess of the eighteenth century (though not its satirical tinge, which predominates in her essays), Meynell constructed a style based upon the word as she disciplined it to produce art that was rooted on the measure of her thinking, her precious poetry governed by austerity of expression and compression of thought.

In "Pocket Vocabularies," Meynell fiercely attacked the misuse and over-use of decadent language, which produced marketed, prefabricated poetry:

> A serviceable substitute for style in literature has been found in such a collection of language ready for use as may be likened to a portable vocabulary. It is suited to the manners of a day that has produced salad-dressing in bottles, and many other devices for the saving of processes. Fill me such a wallet full of "graphic" things, of "quaint" things and "weird," of "crisp" or "sturdy" Anglo-Saxon.

She goes on to describe what it means to write with style:

> "The man is style" . . . The literature of a man of letters worthy the name is rooted in all his qualities, with little fibres running invisibly into the smallest qualities he has . . . Certain poets, a certain time ago, ransacked the language for words full of life and beauty, made a vocabulary of them, and out of wantonness wrote them to death. To change somewhat the simile, they scented out a word – an earlyish word, by preference – ran it to earth, unearthed it, dug it out, and killed it.[23]

Killing words by overuse is one of Meynell's strongest critiques of modern writing.

Oscar Wilde rightly called her "the new sibyl of style."[24] Perhaps the essay that best exemplifies her ascetic style is "Rejection," for her writings theorized as they produced an ascetic regime of discipline and linguistic rigor. And her gendering of her poetic theory was not incidental; it emphasized her vision that woman is style: "Simplicity is not virginal in the modern world. She has a penitential or a vidual singleness. We can conceive an antique world in which life, art, and letters were simple because of the absence of many things; for us now they can be simple only because of our rejection of many things." Editing out the superficial and superfluous is thus required: "We are constrained to such a vigilance as will not let even a master's work pass unfanned and unpurged."[25]

In *Poems* (1893), we see Meynell's poetic theory and her artistry at work. I focus on ten poems of this collection, which she later grouped together as a sequence entitled "A Poet's Fancies" in *Collected Poems* (1913).[26] I work with the 1913 re-ordering because it better illuminates her theories of composition and shows the continuity of her asceticism. The 1913 reordering of "A Poet's Fancies" is as follows:

> "I. The Love of Narcissus" (1893 ed. "Sonnet. The Love of Narcissus," p. 46);
> "II. To Any Poet" (1893 ed. "To A Poet," pp. 3–5);
> "III. To One Poem in a Silent Time" (1893 ed., "Sonnet. To One Poem in a Silent Time," p. 62);
> "IV. The Moon to the Sun. The Poet sings to her Poet" (1893 ed. "The Poet Sings to her Poet. The Moon to the Sun," p. 65–6);

"V. The Spring to the Summer. The Poet sings to her Poet," (1893 ed. "Song of the Spring to the Summer. The Poet Sings to her Poet," p. 6–7);

"VI. The Day to the Night. The Poet sings to his Poet" (1893 ed. "Song of the Day to the Night. The Poet Sings to His Poet," pp. 28–9);

"VII. A Poet of One Mood" (1893 ed. "Sonnet," p. 55);

"VIII. A Song of Derivations" (1893 ed. "The Modern Poet. A Song of Derivation," pp. 68–9);

"IX. Singers to Come" (1893 ed. "Future Poetry," pp. 63–4); and

"X. Unliked." (1893 ed. "A Poet's Sonnet," p. 67)

The sequence is a meditation on the art of writing poetry. Although an obvious point, it matters that its title, "A Poet's Fancies," is made up of two Greek words: poet, from *poiein* "create," and "fantasy," from *phantazein* "make visible." A poet is one who creates. Fantasy signifies not intellect but the faculty of imagination; it means invention, artistry, artifice. "Fancies" *is* a decadent word, but the genitive case marks here that the poet is in possession of her fancy, that artifice is mastered by the poet. The title of each poem within the sequence announces a progression in Meynell's materialization of this poet's fantasy. But the fantasy is precise without the melodrama or stridencies of decadence: the simplicity of a diamond.

The sequence rests on seeing "the poet" as both speaker and auditor: the poet speaking to his imagined poetic selfhood. Thus, in Poem I, "The Love of Narcissus," the poet "trembles at his own long gaze."[27] Poem II, "To Any Poet," reflects on the poet's writing methodology, which is waiting (waiting for nature to reveal its secret, which ultimately for Meynell, the Catholic poet, is God). Waiting is central to the art of writing poetry because waiting produces what she calls a poetry of silence: "Silence, the completest / of thy poems, last, and sweetest" (p. 57). Poem III, "To One Poem in a Silent Time" is an echo of Rossetti's "Winter: My Secret." Quietness, reflection, and the art of poetry making are its subject matter, as the poet talks to the poem to "divine" the ontology of poetry:

Who looked for thee, thou little song of mine?
This winter of a silent poet's heart
Is suddenly sweet with thee. But what thou art,
Mid-winter flower, I would I could divine. (p. 57)

In the next three poems, Meynell adopts the voice of the Moon, the Spring, and the Day. "All thy secrets that I treasure," she writes, "I translate them at my pleasure" (p. 58). And thus in the next sonnet "A Poet of One Mood," the poet discloses her power: "I make the whole world answer to my art" (p. 61). This message is reinforced in poem VIII, "A Song of Derivation," where the poet is positioned as part of a long chain of past poets. This idea is continued in poem IX, "Singers to Come": "Something of you already is ours; / Some mystic part of you belongs /To us." But the poem hammers its point home by ending with an identification of the woman poet with style, which Meynell sees as the future of poetry. Like the maid of Orpheus, she bears the lyre within her arms:

> For I, i' the world of lands and seas,
> The sky of wind and rain and fire,
> And in man's world of long desire –
> In all that is yet dumb in these –
> Have found a more mysterious lyre. (p. 64)

The last poem, "X. Unlinked," is an extraordinary sonnet about owning poetry. If the poet were to unlink herself from poetry, what would she do with her art? She "shall live a poet waking, sleeping" and she "shall die a poet unaware." But her poetry cannot unlink itself from her: "And I, a singer though I cease to sing, / Shall own thee" (p. 65). The poem ends with the suggestion that her poetry would be unconsciously immersed in her linguistic world.

It is appropriate to end this discussion of Meynell's ascetic style with "To Silence." Written toward the end of her life, the poem is an ode to the poetics of quietness that dominated her career as a poet: "Man's lovely definite melody-shapes are thine, / Outlined, controlled, compressed, complete, divine."[28] Outlined, controlled, compressed but complete and, for the Catholic poet, divine too: these are the qualities of Meynell's silent, ascetic poetry.

Poetry of Excess: Michael Field's Revolution in Poetic Language

"Aunt & niece – why this is more like a fairy tale than ever," exclaimed poet and critic Theodore Watts when he met Katharine Bradley and Edith Cooper in 1891.[29] Watts was surprised that a fantasy in the manner of the sisterhood of Rossetti's "Goblin Market" could actually be possible. Michael Field was an artificial poetic construct, and in that artificiality rested their originality, for it enabled the poets to think of poetry and language in radical ways. Yet their revolutionary poetry, more evident to us today in the lyric poetry, began and ended with the genre of poetic drama. Verse drama dramatically exposed that poetic voice was a construct, too, and therefore need not be written as normal speech (unlike the realistic drama of Ibsen and others). It also distinctively animated the formation of abstraction through simulations of realities, freeing the poets from the corset of a masculine vision of women poets and liberating them to the possibilities of the word.

The poets experimented with this Romantic genre and modernized it as they evolved it from the dramatic monologues of Robert Browning and Webster, and the historical poetic dramas of Swinburne. But, as I have argued elsewhere, the central modernizing force was the theories of music and poetry of Wagner and Nietzsche.[30] Histrionic in their approach to the genre, Michael Field's verse plays created new mythologies as they used classical Greek drama to revive the myths of Bellerophon and Dionysus (*Bellerophôn*, 1881; *Callirrhoë*, 1884); Latin texts to recreate the fall of the Roman Empire (*Brutus Ultor*, 1886, or *The World at Auction*, 1898); or English Renaissance plays to construct their own vision of an English female Renaissance in *The Tragic Mary* (1890).

In reviewing *Long Ago* (1889), a series of verses that translated and expanded Sappho's poems, John Miller Gray welcomed Michael Field's turn to the discipline of lyric poetry:

> But what she has hitherto done, amid all its splendour, was often marred by extravagance, by want of measure and of balance, and by want of finish; and these faults were fostered by the freedom of dramatic form in which most of her earlier work was embodied. She has been wise to turn to the finer, firmer, lyric measure, and to submit herself to the straighter discipline which it affords.[31]

In contrast, Michael Field's poetic dramas were described as being "marred by extravagance." When they were preparing for publication *The Tragic Mary*, which recounted the fall of Mary, Queen of Scots, Cooper wrote in their diary: "all is settled ... we can have our own extravagant way for once again."[32] In his review of the play, the poet Lionel Johnson called it an "Elizabethan extravagance with Elizabethan force," showing "a dangerous love of daring phrases."[33] Jarring metaphors, histrionic plots, outmoded use of language, a queen involved in several sexual relationships, and who dressed as a man – the *Athenaeum*'s verdict was "some of these things are only extravagant, others approach insanity."[34]

Sensational excess has been the distinctive feature of decadence literature, and Michael Field's dramas abounded in excess. Robert Browning, a strong supporter of the women's dramas, suggested that at a second reading, Michael Field's artificialities did not feel superfluous but rather inherent to the work of art: "I did not, at the first hasty reading of the first part of Callirrhoe, do justice to the originality of the poem: and certain abruptnesses – (shall I say?) in artificialities of contrivance in the fitting together of scene with scene, – these even disappeared on better knowledge of the whole."[35] Michael Field's discourse on excess was key to their vision of poetry rather than destroying the beauty of poetry – the underlying criticism in all these reviews. They aimed to reactivate language, stretch it, and reform it. There is no doubt that they could discipline poetry, as Bradley once noted in her diary: "as for rhymes I can always force them to obey me like slaves."[36] But this comment shows precisely Michael Field's poetic rebellion: not to submit to laws of meter, but rather to make the laws serve their poetic theories.

What does excess mean in the context of Michael Field? First, it meant an outflow of poetic language, which made their plays long, unbound by the acts that contained the action. It also meant overuse of metaphors; rich, luxurious ornamentation; a language of color. A reviewer of Michael Field's *Stephania: A Trialogue* (1893) noted with disdain, "there is so much of decking of hair, of unrobing and of robing, of crucifixes and crusaders, of jewels and of ornaments and of vestments, throughout the romance before us, that the meaning is overlaid by the ornament."[37] Against the iaconic poetry of writers such as Meynell (Michael Field called it "most beautiful & restrained Art"[38]), they cultivated extravagance. Like Nietzsche, Michel Field conceived poetry in the struggle between the Apollonian and the Dionysian principles, one the principle of form, rationality, and restraint; the other rapture, rupture, the world of excess. It is no coincidence that their first drama as Michael Field was *Callirrhoë,* a play about the beginning of the Dionysian cult in Greece.

Michael Field indulged in the language and history of the past to produce outmoded recreations that further highlighted the estrangement of modern poetic language. Swinburne, for instance, would declare that their work vividly reminded him of Robert Landor, and of the dramatists of the Shakespearean age.[39] When Arthur Symons defined decadence in 1893 as the product of a "civilization grown over-luxurious, over-inquiring," he could well have been thinking of Michael Field's dramas.[40] In their diaries, "Works and Days," they listed not only the books they had used for their research but also their visits to the places their historical characters had been or lived. The linguistic and historic estrangement that the genre allowed enabled Michael Field to create not one but multiple texts at once. The plays were scholarly but also poetical; they felt old, and yet they were radically new; the poetic voices were those of the past, often quoted *verbatim* from the chronicles they studied, but Michael Field's poetic speech infused them with new signification and meaning so that the plays felt removed from the real, only existing in the realm of art.

Perhaps the work that best highlights Michael Field's poetics of excess is *The World at Auction* (1898). Based on Edward Gibbon's *The History of the Decline and Fall of the Roman Empire* (1776–9), Michael Field described it as an "essentially Latin" play.[41] It begins with the following stage directions: "A hall in the house of Didius. Cornelius & Abascantus watch while a number of Slaves arrange objects of art and luxury in full light."[42] The material page does matter for our analysis. The book was beautifully designed by Charles Ricketts, with a green cover decorated with peacocks. The stage directions are printed in red on the first page. But the page is so heavily illustrated that it is unclear if the directions are actually part of the play or simply ornamentation. The play actually begins from the central image, the large black letter "A," from the word "All. " The "A" is decorated with baby fauns, with the two letters "l" in red but in a smaller font size. From the start, the reader is made aware that language is materiality but also that language is image:

> All brought from Pertinax?
> ABASCANTUS But secretly.
> The Emperor, it was rumoured, set a trap
> To catch our men of substance by the sale
> Of every luxury dead Commodus
> Left treasured in the palace: those who bought
> Would be accounted shamefully inclined
> To softness and expense. (vi)

Didius's lust for ornament drives the plot. For Didius, the rich collector who would in due course buy the Roman Empire, cares not for power, but for beautiful things. He buys the Empire as a gift to his daughter Clara, whose voracious desire for things is as intense as her passion for the court dancer Pylades.

One of the key moments of the play comes after Didius has bought the Empire and is about to be crowned emperor. Clara starts getting dressed for the event:

> PYLADES: And this opal . . .
> CLARA: You see, it is a hazel-nut in size.
> PYLADES: A world of sky in variance.
> CLARA: An estate
> In price. You touch the beryls: they are fair.
> PYLADES: Deep-sea-like in their strangeness.
> CLARA: And neglect
> My emeralds, these from the mine of Egypt,
> These from the Ural mines. And look! My robe!
> The finest wool of Po, the deepest purple
> Of Tyrian murex; owned by Commodus,
> A thousand deniers bought it, and perchance
> It once was worn by Marcia. (cxlix)

Clara wants her jewelry and clothes to signify that she is the powerful daughter of the emperor and an aesthete. Her dress is of the deepest purple of Tyrian murex. The choice of color was both historical and literary. In the Roman period, purple was the color emperors wore, but it was also the color of the 1890s. Holbrook Jackson, for example, famously defined the decadent style as "Purple Patches."[43]

But perhaps where we see the poetics of excess most at work is in Pylades, the court dancer, whose wild rhythms bring ecstasy to his audience. To achieve that, Michael Field used the dithyramb, a wild choral hymn of ancient Greece, dedicated to Dionysus. The following quote is the end of a long chorus in which Pylades dances as a reveler. The chorus and the crowd are getting wilder and wilder:

> We are revellers, for revel
> Strikes the sky from our array;
> We are revellers, the ground
> Shakes behind us, red with leas,
> Strewn with foliage and the shreds
> Of the rended flock and herd.
> We are just a feast to look on;
> We are terrible to know–
> Every withy hides a spear-point;
> Every voice rails high, and Pan,
> Leader of our dread parade,
> Blowing from his pipe, defeats
> Courage in a mortal's blood.   (lxviii)

The World at Auction ends with the murder of Didius. People die, but beauty and beautiful things continue to reign.

Toward the end of 1898, Katharine Bradley reflected with sadness that she had not written much that year, noting in their diary: "The language of crisis, when the volcano tosses the flowers of its florid heart."[44] Not a silent poem, then, but the eruption of a revolution in language.

Notes

1. F. Max Müller, *Lectures on the Science of Language* (London: Longman, 1861), p. 47.
2. Linda Dowling, *Language and Decadence in the Victorian Fin de Siècle* (Princeton: Princeton University Press, 1986), p. 67.
3. Lines 7–18, in Christina Rossetti, *The Complete Poems*, ed. R. W. Crump, notes and introduction by Betty S. Flowers (London: Penguin, 2001), p. 41, and *passim*.

4. Yopie Prins, "Victorian Meters," in *The Cambridge Companion to Victorian Poetry*, ed. Joseph Bristow (Cambridge: Cambridge University Press, 2000), pp. 108–9.

5. Constance W. Hassett, *Christina Rossetti: The Patience of Style* (Charlottesville: University of Virginia Press, 2005), pp. 63, 76.

6. L.E.L., "Song," from *The Golden Violet*, in *Letitia Elizabeth Landon: Selected Writings*, ed. Jerome McGann and Daniel Riess (Peterborough, ON: Broadview Press, 1997), p. 101.

7. Alice Meynell, "The Metaphysical Lyric," in *Alice Meynell: Prose and Poetry. Centenary Volume* (London: Jonathan Cape, 1947), p. 325.

8. T. S. Eliot, *Varieties of Metaphysical Poetry: The Clark Lectures at Trinity, Cambridge, 1926, and the Turnbull Lectures at the John Hopkins University, 1933*, ed. Ronald Schuchard (London: Faber, 1993), p. 55.

9. Dowling, *Language and Decadence*, p. 175.

10. Margaret Veley, "A Japanese Fan," in *A Marriage of Shadows and Other Poems* (London: Smith, Elder, & Co., 1888), pp. 69–79.

11. Veley, "A Japanese Fan," p. 70.

12. Dowling, *Language and Decadence*, p. 176.

13. Amy Levy, "The Poetry of Christina Rossetti," *The Woman's World*, 1 (February 1888), 178.

14. Michael Field, *Binary Star. Leaves from the Journal and Letters of Michael Field, 1846–1914*, ed. Ivor C. Treby (Bury St Edmunds: De Blackland Press, 2006), p. 45.

15. Levy, "The Poetry of Christina Rossetti," p. 180.

16. Meynell, *The Rhythm of Life and Other Essays* (London: Elkin Mathews and John Lane, 1893), p. 1.

17. Paul Bourget, "Psychologie contemporaine. Notes et portraits. Charles Baudelaire,"*La Nouvelle Revue*, 13 (Novembre 15, 1881), 413; transl. Havelock Ellis, *Affirmations* (Boston: Houghton Mifflin Company, 1915), p. 180.

18. Ana Parejo Vadillo, "'Gay Strangers': Reflections on Decadence and the Decadent Poetics of A. Mary F. Robinson," *Cahiers victoriens et édouardiens [En ligne]*, 78 Automne 2013, http://cve.revues.org/856; DOI: 10.4000/cve.856

19. Meynell, *John Ruskin* (London: William Blackwood and Sons, 1900), p. 70.

20. Meynell, "Composure," *Rhythm of Life*, p. 59.

21. Meynell, "Future Poetry," in *Poems* (London: Elkin Mathews and John Lane, 1893), p. 63.

22. Meynell, "Superfluous Kings," *The Second Person Singular and Other Essays* (London, H. Milford: Oxford University Press, 1921), pp. 7–11.

23. Meynell, "Pocket Vocabularies," *The Rhythm of Life*, pp. 40, 41.

24. Qtd. in Linda Peterson, *Becoming a Woman of Letters: Myths of Authorship and Facts of the Victorian Market* (Princeton: Princeton University Press, 2009), p. 201.

25. Meynell, "Rejection," *The Rhythm of Life*, p. 79.

26. Meynell, "A Poet's Fancies," in *Poems, Collected Poems of Alice Meynell* (London: Burns & Oates, 1913), pp. 54–65.

27. Meynell, *Collected Poems*, p. 54. Hereafter page numbers are in the text.

28. Meynell, "To Silence," *The Poems of Alice Meynell. Complete Edition* (London: Burns & Oates, 1923), p. 132.

29. Letter, Katharine Bradley to John Miller Gray, August 2, 1891, B.L. Add.MS 45854, fols. 80r-84v.

30. Vadillo, "'This hot–house of decadent chronicle': Michael Field, Nietzsche and the Dance of Modern Poetic Drama," *Women: A Cultural Review* 26.3 (2015), 195–220.

31. John M. Gray, review of *Long Ago, Academy*, June 9, 1889, 389.

32. Michael Field, "Works and Days," BL. Add. MS.46778 (1890), fol. 20r [Edith Cooper].

33. Lionel Johnson, review of *The Tragic Mary, Academy*, August 16, 1890, 123–4.

34. Review of *The Tragic Mary, Athenaeum*, September 20, 1890, 395.

35. Letter, Robert Browning to "Michael Field," May 31, 1884, B.L. Add. MS. 46866, fol. 13r-14v.

36. Michael Field, *Binary Star*, p. 44.

37. Review of *Stephania, Spectator*, February 4, 1893, 163.

38. Michael Field, *Binary Star*, p. 46.

39. Letter, A. C. Swinburne to Michael Field, June 22, 1885, Bodleian Library, MS. Eng. e.32 f. 72–3.

40. Arthur Symons, "The Decadent Movement in Literature," *Harper's New Monthly Magazine* 87 (1893), 858.

41. Michael Field, "Works and Days," B.L., Add. MS. 46787 (1898) fol. 51v [Edith Cooper].

42. Michael Field, *The World at Auction* (London: The Vale Press, 1898), p. v. Hereafter page numbers appear in the text.

43. Holbrook Jackson, *The Eighteen Nineties: A Review of Art and Ideas at the Close of the Nineteenth Century* (London: Grant Richards, 1913), pp. 163–77.

44. Michael Field, "Works and Days," B.L. Add.MS. 46787 (1898), fol. 140r [Katharine Bradley].

PART IV

Reading Victorian Women's Poetry

15

NATALIE M. HOUSTON

Distant Reading and Victorian Women's Poetry

In her landmark essay "Dancing Through the Minefield: Some Observations on the Theory, Practice, and Politics of a Feminist Literary Criticism," Annette Kolodny identified three main tendencies in feminist literary criticism: the recovery of lost writers and texts, the discovery of a distinctive female literary tradition, and the critical examination of the entwined structures of gender and power in literature written by both female and male writers.[1] Each of these strands of feminist criticism has greatly contributed to the study of Victorian poetry. Classroom anthologies of Victorian literature now often include poems by Adelaide Anne Procter, Amy Levy, Michael Field, and Augusta Webster, in addition to Elizabeth Barrett Browning (EBB) and Christina Rossetti. As our canon of women poets has grown, so too has our understanding of the complex intergenerational relationships among women poets, such as those expressed by Letitia Landon (L.E.L.), EBB, and Christina Rossetti in their poetry. Sophisticated critical readings of gender and sexuality within Victorian poems are today probably the most visible of Kolodny's three strands, as the many critical readings of Augusta Webster's "A Castaway," Christina Rossetti's "Goblin Market," and D. G. Rossetti's "Jenny" demonstrate (see Chapter 13). Yet there remains much to be done if we are to continue to challenge the limitations of received canons and evaluations of women's writing. This chapter performs a distant reading of the contents of a late-Victorian poetry anthology to model the possibilities for developing a feminist computational criticism that moves beyond the traditional critical focus on individual authors and exemplar texts.

Even though the impact of feminist recovery projects in the 1980s and 1990s has indeed expanded the critical and teaching canon, the number of Victorian women poets who are routinely the focus of critical study is still quite limited. Five recent anthologies of Victorian poetry aimed at the college textbook market reveal the general contours of the current academic and teaching canon: *The Penguin Book of Victorian Verse* (1997); *The Broadview Anthology of Victorian Poetry and Poetic Theory* (1999); *The Broadview Anthology of Victorian Poetry and Poetic Theory, Concise Edition* (2000); *Victorian Poetry* (Blackwell Essential Literature series, 2002); and *Victorian Poetry: An Annotated Anthology* (Blackwell Annotated Anthologies series, 2004).[2] Although each individual anthology varies in scope and size, from eleven poets in the Blackwell Essential to 140 poets in the Penguin, seventy-eight named poets, plus "Anonymous," are included in two or more of these five anthologies. These seventy-eight poets represent some consensus, some shared notion of the current canon of Victorian poetry; twenty-five of them are women poets.

The ten women poets most frequently included in these anthologies constitute the core concept of Victorian women's poetry as it is currently studied and taught today. Three are included in all five recent anthologies: Emily Brontë, EBB, and Christina Rossetti. Augusta Webster is included in four of the five anthologies and Charlotte Brontë, Eliza Cook, Amy Levy, Charlotte Mew, Alice Meynell, and Adelaide Procter are included in three of the five collections. Women poets constitute, on average, almost a third of the poets included in these anthologies, with volume-specific percentages ranging from twenty-four percent to forty-four percent.[3] Such ratios represent a significant shift in the Victorian canon from the teaching anthologies widely used in the mid- to late twentieth century, such as Jerome Buckley and George Woods's *Poetry of the Victorian Period* and Walter Houghton and Robert Stange's *Victorian Poetry and Poetics*, which included far fewer women poets in their pages.[4] Although choosing women writers as the object of study is perhaps no longer quite as contentious as when Kolodny was writing, it is still a political act with ramifications for the field of Victorian poetry, and Victorian literature as a whole. Feminist criticism today can contribute to the (re)writing of literary history by reflecting on both our process for selecting the texts we study and the methods we use to read them.

Feminist Computational Criticism

Kolodny offers three theoretical propositions that she argues should guide the future development of feminist literary theory and critical practice. These are no less useful today than they were in 1980, as they can guide the development of a computational feminist literary criticism for the coming decades. The first states, "Literary history (and with that, the historicity of literature) is a fiction."[5] Although literary critics have long known that the canonical selection of Victorian texts that are frequently taught and studied is but a small fraction of the literature that was published in the nineteenth century, the new availability of mass digitized archives can help us grapple with what that really means. By changing the scale at which we consider literary history, we change the idea of historicity itself.

The second of Kolodny's propositions states, "Insofar as we are taught how to read, what we engage are not texts but paradigms."[6] Unless we explicitly challenge those paradigms, we are likely to continue valuing those texts that we were first taught to value, and those that are similar: "we read well, and with pleasure, what we already know how to read; and what we know how to read is to a large extent dependent upon what we have already read."[7] Computational criticism offers new paradigms that alter our understanding of what "reading" itself might mean, for both canonical texts and those less familiar.

Kolodny's third proposition states that because the values assigned to texts are not universal, "we must reexamine not only our aesthetics, but, as well, the inherent biases and assumptions informing the critical methods which (in part) shape our aesthetic responses."[8] A critical practice based on close reading will bring with it assumptions about the value of each individual text as an organic whole and as representative exemplar. A feminist computational criticism explores what it would mean to disrupt the norm of close interpretive reading, asking how feminist literary inquiry might proceed without producing a traditional interpretation of a text.

Kolodny's call to examine our literary histories, critical paradigms, and theoretical biases is especially relevant in today's digital environment. After surveying the methods of close and distant reading, the remainder of this chapter presents an example of a distant reading of Victorian women's poetry to suggest how the explicit methodological choices required in distant reading offer the opportunity for the critical self-examination that Kolodny recommends. Feminist computational criticism here thus involves not only the selection of Victorian women's poetry as the object of study but also explicit reflection on the decisions made in constructing the dataset, conducting the analysis, and interpreting the results.

Close Reading

Despite a variety of competing theoretical paradigms in literary studies, the predominant analytical method for literary texts has remained close reading. In the first part of the twentieth century, particular practices for close reading were codified by the New Critics, who sought a formalist approach to literature that could be objective, even scientific, rather than subjective. The New Critics argued that critics should focus on the text itself, rather than on historical context, biographical information about the author, or the critic's personal responses to the text. Identifying rhetorical and linguistic strategies such as irony, ambiguity, and paradox as the hallmarks of good literature, the New Criticism assumed that good works of literature are complex and should be subjected to in-depth formal analysis.

Cleanth Brooks's chapter on Herrick's "Corinna's Going a-Maying" in *The Well-Wrought Urn* takes up the question of the poem's theme or communicated meaning only to find a variety of tensions and complications in its treatment of the natural world and the pagan and Christian viewpoints. Brooks ultimately argues that to ask what a poem communicates is to ask the wrong question:

> It is not that the poem communicates nothing. Precisely the contrary. The poem communicates so much and communicates it so richly and with such delicate qualifications that the thing communicated is mauled and distorted if we attempt to convey it by any vehicle less subtle than that of the poem itself.[9]

Close reading insists on the primacy of the text and the irreducibility of the text to paraphrase.

By focusing on how a poem works rather than what a poem says, close reading has become embedded within literary critical practice as a method for analysis that is used in service of a larger theoretical approach. Thus a feminist critic might closely read passages that reflect or represent gender roles; a psychoanalytic critic might pay close attention to rhetorical structures that mirror the structure of repression. The critic's larger interest or argument typically motivates the selection of passages that are closely read through the identification and interpretation of linguistic, rhetorical, semantic, poetic, or sociohistorical features. The representation of the text and its history are always already circumscribed within the critical paradigm of the argument. Literary critics rarely discuss those aspects of a text that do not fit their interpretive argument.

In literary studies, the term "reading" can even describe all the stages of research and writing, including exploration, hypothesis, collection of examples, analysis, and argument. We choose which texts to read based on a hypothesis; we read to gather information and examples; we analyze texts by performing close readings; and we offer a reading of a text as our final argument. To perform the examination of critical biases and assumptions that Kolodny calls for requires distinguishing more carefully between these different stages of knowledge production. Methods of computational criticism necessarily make these distinctions in the processes of data collection, preparation, and analysis.

Distant Reading

In recent years, the large-scale digitization of nineteenth-century printed materials has transformed both the methods and the objects of literary criticism. Through proprietary databases of periodicals and newspapers, the digital versions of previous generations' bibliographical indices like *Poole's Index* and the *Wellesley Index*, and especially the open access mass digital archives of Google Books and the Internet Archive, we now have access to an abundance of primary texts and evidence of their circulation in Victorian print culture. But the radical increase in scale provided by these resources requires new methods of discovery and analysis. Digitization offers us access to unknown works and also allows us to gain new perspectives on the canonical works we are already familiar with, resituating them within larger, different contexts. As Kolodny suggests, feminist literary criticism should not only focus on expanding or changing the canon but also on interpreting it differently. To do this we need the new methods of exploration and analysis grouped together as distant reading.

Although the term "distant reading" first appeared in 2000, in an intentional opposition to close reading's focus on a small canon of texts, Ted Underwood traces the longer genealogy of distant reading as "a story that stretches back through book history, sociology, and linguistics" and is defined by the use of an experimental method, rather than computation.[10] Underwood defines distant reading as "the practice of framing historical inquiry as an experiment, using hypotheses and samples (of texts or other social evidence) that are defined before the writer settles on a conclusion."[11] For example, Ryan Heuser and Long Le-Khac developed a method for identifying words with similar usage patterns and semantic meaning in the nineteenth century and then charted the use of abstract words and concrete particulars in a corpus of 2,779 British novels to examine how linguistic evidence might correlate with the representation of social space.[12] Distant reading challenges what Andrew Goldstone has identified as the "*doxa* of reading": "the assumption that the primary activity of academic literary study is textual interpretation. Under this assumption, 'reading' includes both the act of reading expertly and the production of expert readings of texts in articles and books."[13] Distant reading aims instead to examine the socio-cultural systems of value that produce the very category of literature itself.

A Victorian Anthology

Kolodny's first proposition for literary studies suggests that feminist critics should examine the ways that literary history has been constructed.

To understand the history of the category of "Victorian poetry," we have to turn to the nineteenth-century American critic Edmund Clarence Stedman. Stedman was the first to use the term "Victorian" to describe the literature produced in Britain after 1837, in a series of essays in *Scribner's Monthly* that were later published as his 1875 book *Victorian Poets*.[14] In this critical study and his 1895 *A Victorian Anthology 1837–1895*, Stedman attempted a comprehensive survey of Victorian poetry. His anthology explicitly does not "offer a collection of absolutely flawless poems, long since become classic and accepted as models" but instead "a truthful exhibit of the course of song during the last sixty years."[15] Stedman's anthology contains 1,284 poems, 199 of which are by women poets. This chapter pursues a distant reading of these poems to answer Kolodny's call for inquiry into the assumptions of our critical methods.

It is in keeping with the feminist goals Kolodny offers that we consider the politics of access to digital materials and tools. One reason I selected Stedman's anthology for this project is that it is available in multiple digital surrogates through the open access mass digital archives of the Internet Archive, HathiTrust, and Google Books, rather than in commercial subscription databases. Stedman's anthology has also been published on the web as a set of HTML texts, which are easily scraped and processed for text analysis.[16] All analysis performed for this project was done using free open access software: Antconc, a corpus analysis tool, and the R programming language and libraries.[17] Finally, the cleaned and processed dataset is available for readers who wish to perform their own analysis of these materials.[18]

Stedman's definition of Victorian poetry is visible in the elaborate structure of his table of contents. He divides the main portion of his collection into three chronological divisions, "Early Years of the Reign," "The Victorian Epoch," and "Close of the Era," with the first two including a number of subcategories by genre, style, or artistic school. "Colonial Poets," the fourth category, contains works by poets from Australia and Canada (and a note about India that cross-references the inclusion of Rudyard Kipling and Toru Dutt in earlier sections). Making the critical categories from his earlier study visible on the pages of his anthology reveals Stedman's goal of analyzing and delimiting the field of Victorian poetry. He does not offer any subcategories for the poets in the most recent group, because he says that he does not yet have sufficient temporal distance from them to assign those categories clearly.

Stedman's anthology provides us with a unique opportunity to examine Victorian poetry as it was first critically conceived. Stedman includes works by seventy-three women poets, far more than the ten poets included in the nineteenth-century volumes (4 and 5) of T. H. Ward's *The English Poets*

(1880).[19] Stedman includes women poets in all four of his major chronological divisions, integrating them into the anthology's critical presentation of Victorian poetry, unlike Alfred Miles's *The Poets and Poetry of the Century* (1892–7), in which women poets are cordoned off (volume 8), although a handful are also included in the subsequently published volume 10, which covers sacred verse.[20] Of his four divisions, Stedman's third chronological category, "Close of the Era," contains the highest percentage of poems by women, at about twenty-four percent (76 of 319 poems). This division includes poems by Mathilde Blind, Michael Field, Amy Levy, Alice Meynell, Dollie Radford (1858–1920), and Rosamund Marriott Watson, as well as poets less frequently reprinted today, such as Alice E. Gillington, Lizzie M. Little (1864–1909), Frederika Macdonald (1845–1923), and Margaret L. Woods (1856–1945).

Poetry anthologies both reflect critical conceptions of the literary field and help to construct that literary field. Because this anthology reflects a late-nineteenth-century critical sensibility, it can help us question the assumptions of our own. For example, Stedman places Augusta Webster in his subgroup of "Dramatists and Playwrights" within "The Victorian Epoch," his mid-century chronological division. He prints only short lyric poems extracted from her verse dramas *Disguises* (1879) and *In a Day* (1882), and from her narrative poem *Yu-Pe-Ya's Lute* (1874). Our modern anthologies and scholarship focus almost exclusively on Webster's dramatic monologues like "A Castaway" and the "Mother and Daughter" series of sonnets, which offer a very different view of Webster's politics and poetics. Examining not only which poets were included in Victorian anthologies but also which texts get reprinted can reveal the changing definitions of Victorian poetry.

Stedman's anthology thus offers us a view of Victorian poetry that can seem both familiar and strange. Because methods of distant reading allow us to compare more texts at once than is possible in close reading, they can help us see more clearly what grounds exist for such critical judgments. Selecting an anthology as the basis for this project underscores Kolodny's first proposition about literary history as a fiction. Any history of Victorian poetry is necessarily incomplete and constrained by ideological blind spots, just as is any corpus of poetry compiled for computational analysis. By using a historical anthology as the dataset, this project makes explicit the boundaries of its particular literary-historical narrative.

Analyzing Texts

Human readers, Kolodny suggests in her second proposition, engage "not texts but paradigms" when we read. By requiring that we identify features of literary texts that can be measured, counted, or otherwise quantified, computational criticism returns our attention in new ways to the text. To translate critical paradigms into code often requires new ways of thinking about the objects of literary study.

There are many different ways that a reader of sonnet 23 from *Sonnets from the Portuguese* by EBB and Christina Rossetti's sonnet "Remember me when I am gone away" might compare these poems: both are sonnets using the Italian rhyme scheme; both are addressed to a beloved; and both contrast the realm of the living with that of the dead:

> Is it indeed so? If I lay here dead,
> Wouldst thou miss any life in losing mine?
> And would the sun for thee more coldly shine
> Because of grave-damps falling round my head?
> I marvelled, my Beloved, when I read
> Thy thought so in the letter. I am thine –
> But ... so much to thee? Can I pour thy wine
> While my hands tremble? Then my soul, instead
> Of dreams of death, resumes life's lower range.   (lines 1–9)[21]

> Remember me when I am gone away,
> Gone far away into the silent land;
> When you can no more hold me by the hand,
> Nor I half turn to go yet turning stay.
> Remember me when no more, day by day,
> You tell me of our future that you plann'd:
> Only remember me; you understand
> It will be late to counsel then or pray.   (lines 1–8)[22]

Examining even just the first few lines of each sonnet reveals some of the stylistic differences typical of EBB's and Rossetti's poetry: EBB's use of enjambment, meter, and syntax creates a more complex tension between the grammatical sentences of her poem and its verse lines, whereas Rossetti's clauses adhere more closely to the structure of the verse lines. By measuring a few simple stylistic features of poetic language, computational criticism provides a more precise way to compare these two poems, the works of these poets more generally, and other texts in Stedman's collection.

As sonnets, both of these poems contain fourteen lines, and they are very similar in the total number of words, or tokens, in the poem (119 for EBB and 111 for Rossetti). Because Stedman's collection is an anthology, it is not surprising to find that 174 of the 199 poems by women are fifty or fewer lines in length, with forty-eight of those (almost twenty-five percent of the women's poems in the collection) consisting of fifteen or fewer lines.

The shortest poems in the dataset include "To February" by Ethelwyn Wetherald (1857–1940), "Love" by Sarah Flower Adams (1805–48), and "Faith" by Frances Kemble. The longest poems include an extract from EBB's *Aurora Leigh* and "The Runaway Slave at Pilgrim's Point" and Jean Ingelow's "The High Tide on the Coast of Lincolnshire."

One marker of stylistic complexity in Victorian verse is the ratio of syntactic sentences to the number of verse lines. Poems with a very high sentence:line ratio tend to have shorter sentences and more end-stopped lines, like Rossetti's "Up-Hill," which has a ratio of 1, because each verse line consists of a sentence:

> Does the road wind up-hill all the way?
> Yes, to the very end.
> Will the day's journey take the whole long day?
> From morn to night, my friend.   (lines 1–4)[23]

The mean sentence:line ratio for all poems in Stedman's collection is .3228, with the mean for the poems by women at .3375 and for poems by men at .32. The mean ratio for Rossetti's poems in the anthology is a bit lower than the general average, at .2839, and the ratio for EBB's poems is higher, at .3866. Examining those poems in the collection with very low or very high sentence:line ratios also highlights sonnet 39 of EBB's *Sonnets From the Portuguese*, which consists of only one syntactic sentence over the fourteen lines of the poem, creating a sentence:line ratio of .0714. Looking at these ratios and the number of lines per poem reveals seventeen other sonnets that also consist of only one syntactic sentence, distributed throughout the chronological divisions of the collection, all of them by male authors. The meaning of such stylistic choices undoubtedly varies across these texts, but this suggests it might be a meaningful pattern in Victorian sonnet writing, and one that would be difficult for a human reader to discern amid the 193 sonnets included in the anthology.

Rossetti's poetic style has frequently been described as "simple," whereas EBB's poetry has often been labeled difficult or obscure.[24] Two features of word usage, type:token ratio and the percentage of repeated words, provide ways to characterize simplicity or complexity in a poem's language. Type:token ratio, often abbreviated TTR, compares the number of types, or distinct words in a text, with the total number of words, or tokens, in a text. Thus a high TTR indicates a text with a more varied vocabulary than a text with a low TTR. Type:token ratio might also be understood as an indicator of how likely a reader is to encounter new or repeated words during the reading process. TTR is widely used as a simple measure for vocabulary richness, or the reading difficulty of a text. In poetry, however, words are often repeated numerous times within a given text to create certain semantic, syntactic, or sonic effects. So for poetic analysis, I have found it useful to calculate both TTR and the percentage of repeated words per poem. Rossetti's eight-line poem "Good-By," for example, contains only twenty types and forty tokens, creating a TTR of .5, which is a mark of relatively simple language. But understanding the poem's language also requires noticing the very high degree of repetition in the poem: .725 of its words are repeated:

> "Good-By in fear, good-by in sorrow,
> Good-by, and all in vain,
> Never to meet again, my dear – "
> "Never to part again."
> "Good-by to-day, good-by to-morrow,
> Good-by till earth shall wane,
> Never to meet again, my dear – "
> "Never to part again."[25]

Rossetti stages the dialogue in this poem and its commentary on the afterlife through the repetition of "good-by," "never," "again," "part," and other words. The mean type:token ratio for all poems in Stedman's collection is .6322, with fairly close scores for the mean for poems by women (.6262) and by men (.6332). The mean TTR for EBB's poems, however, is higher than the overall mean, at .6509, and the mean TTR for Rossetti's poems is slightly lower, at .6290. Rossetti also uses more repeated words (.5446) than the overall mean for the collection (.5112) and EBB uses fewer (.4756). To review the pair of sonnets discussed earlier, Rossetti's "Remember" has a TTR of .5946 and .6218 repeated words, while the more complex vocabulary of EBB's sonnet twenty-three has a TTR of .7227, and only .4118 repeated words. These measures provide a way to compare poetic style in specific terms. A human reader can easily perceive differences in the language of these two poems, but TTR and repetition percentages help make those differences concrete.

Because the organization of Stedman's anthology offers chronological divisions, poetic subgroups, and poets' gender as potential categories for critical analysis, I hoped that this dataset would allow for the comparison of the stylistic signals of these different categories. Would poems from the earliest part of the period be more similar to one another and more different from those from the end of the century? Research in computational stylistics has generally found gender differences to offer a strong signal after that of individual authorial style, so would the poems by women demonstrate marked stylistic differences from those by men?[26]

A useful way to measure distinctive word usage is to compare word frequencies within one set of texts against their distribution in another set of texts to reveal words that are used either significantly more or less frequently.[27] This analysis did reveal one significant distinction between poems by male authors and those by women in Stedman's collection: the pronouns "my," "I," and "me" are far more likely to occur in the set of poems written by women than in those written by men. Of course, this distinction is statistically significant only within the analysis of Stedman's anthology and would need to be tested across larger Victorian corpora. But this finding supports many critical accounts of Victorian women's poetry as displaying significant discursive differences that align with differences in genre, theme, and poetic voice, as well as conceptions of the woman writer and Victorian gender roles. However, other word frequencies were relatively similar across gender categories as well as the chronological categories in Stedman's anthology.

Principal component analysis is an exploratory data analysis technique for examining multiple features of a dataset and projecting them into a lower-dimension graph space to reveal the closeness or distance between the data observations. For textual analysis, the one hundred most frequent words used in the dataset are often used as the features in such analysis. In a dataset with very distinct observations, such as four novels by four authors, for example, principal component analysis will easily distinguish the four novels because of the strength of the authorial signal. However, principal component analyses performed on the Stedman dataset using both word frequencies and the stylistic measures discussed earlier did not reveal any clear distinctions for either the gender or chronological categories. The anthology signal was stronger, in other words, than those of gender or chronology. Further research will be required to discover whether this is something unique to Stedman's anthology, or whether in all anthologies the fact of the poems having been selected by an individual editor tends to smooth over the other distinctions. So, although word usage and stylistic measures can provide valuable means for comparing poems within the dataset, the dataset as a whole may be rather homogeneous as compared to Victorian literature more generally.

Distant reading the formal features and word usage patterns in Victorian poems can help us see them in new ways, beyond our existing critical definitions and paradigms. In particular, distant reading encourages us to think beyond the category of the author. Our critical paradigms tend to privilege authorial intention, political resistance, or aesthetic distinctiveness linked to the writings of an individual poet. Yet many of the formal features discussed earlier, such as type:token ratio, are at the large scale unlikely to be the result of deliberate decisions by the poet. By exploring formal patterns in large sets of texts by multiple authors, we can begin to perceive the general discursive properties of a collection. In this chapter, exploring a dataset constituted by an anthology edited by one individual highlights the fact that any dataset is constructed by a series of decisions about definition and inclusion. The discoveries noted here about Stedman's collection will need to be tested against other collections of Victorian texts, both those derived from anthologies and those constituted by other means, to examine whether they offer useful information about Victorian women's poetry in general. Distant reading opens up the possibility of exploring the contours of Victorian poetic discourse beyond the individual author to perceive larger cultural and historical changes that might be reflected or enacted in formal features.

Reexamining our Critical Assumptions

Kolodny's third proposition for literary studies asks us to reexamine the values we attach to literary texts and the critical methods that produce these aesthetic judgments. Unsupervised methods of machine learning are a form of distant reading that can bypass some biases of human judgments. In the methods applied previously, the features used in the analysis are defined by the researcher. In contrast, unsupervised machine learning algorithms harness the computer's pattern-matching power to reveal semantic patterns in texts, without any predetermined instruction in what to look for or what is significant. Because the results of machine learning approaches often resist human interpretation, they can help us see beyond our existing aesthetics toward a new understanding of textual meaning.

Topic modeling is an approach to understanding large sets of texts using an unsupervised machine-learning algorithm that implements an iterative, probabilistic assessment of word co-occurrences in the documents in the corpus. It sorts through the documents in the corpus numerous times, looking at the words used in each one. As it does so, it gathers information about which words co-occur in the same document, and the probability that those same words would co-occur in another document in the corpus. A basic assumption behind topic modeling is that words that co-occur in documents at a greater than average probability together make up a "topic," a cluster of semantic meaning. Although these "topics" are not as defined or intentional as the themes or topics literary critics traditionally examine, they can offer insight into the semantic content of large sets of documents.

When running this analysis, the programmer selects the number of topics that the algorithm will locate in the corpus. The analytic output of the algorithm assumes that every topic is present in every document in the corpus, to a greater or smaller degree. The algorithm outputs a list of the documents in the corpus, and the percentage of the document that is made up of each topic. Thus the dominant topic of each document can be easily determined. The program also produces a list of the words that make up each topic, ranked by their weight, or importance in the topic.[28]

For greater semantic and interpretive interest, a "stopword" list was applied to the corpus before modeling it, thereby excluding common articles, pronouns, and numbers.[29] The algorithm was programmed to discover fifteen topics. If different numbers of topics are selected when training a model on the same corpus, different results will be obtained, because each parameter that is selected during the analysis affects the output. In the discussion that follows, I refer to the fifteen topics by number, rather than assigning them names, to reinforce the fact that these clusters of words require human interpretation to be meaningful, and that our perceptions of what counts as meaningful are always already shaped by our preexisting critical and aesthetic paradigms.

By running a topic model on all the poems included in Stedman's anthology, we can begin to explore what kinds of discourses or themes are present in the volume. The high-ranked keywords in topic six, for example, suggest a topic related to ships and the sea:

> sea, home, ye, boys, deep, sail, merry, ho, land, ring, shore, back, ship, free, tide, long, town, boat, men, low, foam, maids, fast, sailor, bells, work

In addition to the semantically rich words like "sea," "ship," "sailor," and "boat," the topic also includes the archaic pronoun "ye" and the interjection "ho" that are frequently found in sailor's songs. Not surprisingly, the poem in Stedman's collection containing the highest proportion (seventy-five percent) of topic six is the popular song "Nancy Lee," by Frederic Edward Weatherly:

> Of all the wives as e'er you know,
> Yeo-ho! lads ho! Yeo-ho! Yeo-ho!
> There's none like Nancy Lee, I trow,
> Yeo-ho! lads ho! Yeo-ho! (lines 1–4)[30]

Topic six is also highly represented (fifty-five percent) in Jean Ingelow's "The High Tide on the Coast of Lincolnshire," a ballad describing a deadly flood.

One way to use topic modeling to explore the discourses present in Victorian women's poetry is to calculate the mean percentage each topic represents in poems by female or male authors. Topic eight, for instance, is more strongly represented in poems by female authors than it is in poems by male authors:

> love, sweet, eyes, heart, fair, flowers, rose, lips, flower, day, hair, kiss, face, tears, ah, young, dead, night, joy, dear, soft, sad, beauty, sleep, happy, years, smile

Topic twelve is more strongly represented in poems by male authors than it is in poems by female authors:

> great, men, world, man, england, brave, fight, age, english, battle, land, fame, honor, high, war, noble, doom, crown, people, gods, kings, sword, strife, glorious, freedom, force, path

Topic modeling can help us examine semantic patterns in large sets of texts to see what kinds of discourses are present. In Stedman's collection, the gender separation between these discourses seems to reinforce traditional Victorian ideas about love and emotions being the appropriate territory for female poets, and poems of martial valor being appropriate for male poets. Discovering this statistical confirmation for a familiar critical concept about the gendering of poetry and the poet(ess) can help us explore the extent and limits of such discourse as well as its potential contradictions. In addition to examining the poems by women writers that include a significant percentage of topic eight, such as Caroline Norton's "Love Not" (.4797), Dollie Radford's "If all the World" (.4946), or EBB's sonnet 38 (.3791), we could examine poems by male writers that also include significant percentages of topic eight: Algernon Swinburne's "A Match" (.5322), Alfred Tennyson's "Tears, Idle Tears" (.4719), or Philip Bourke Marston's "After Summer" (.4180). As the example of Tennyson's poem suggests, the algorithm can identify gendered discourse created for a fictional speaker, which might lead to an examination of how the discourse of Victorian women's poetry could be utilized differently by male and female authors.

Other topics defined by the topic modeling algorithm are less clearly thematic. Top keywords in topic ten, for example, include

> wind, sing, white, wild, sea, song, green, hear, long, round, sound, tree, voice, bird, summer, birds, gray, low, wave, high, sings, trees, singing, blow, soft, moon, sky

This combination of natural elements with sound and song might best be understood as marking lyric discourse, rather than a specific theme. Some of the poems with a significant percentage of topic ten include Eliza Cook's "The Sea-Child" (.3523), Amy Levy's "A London Plane-Tree" (.3526), and Alice E. Gillington's "The Rosy Musk-Mallow" (.3747). Written in different styles and decades, these are not poems that a human reader would be likely to compare. In Cook's poem, the mother's human song cannot compete with the fierce wind that soothes the possibly supernatural "Sea-Child":

> No lullaby can the mother find
> To sing him to rest like the moaning wind;
> And the louder it wails and the fiercer it sweeps,
> The deeper he breathes and the sounder he sleeps. (lines 5–8)[31]

In Gillington's poem, the wind is described simply as part of the romantic setting: "The rosy musk-mallow blooms where the south wind blows," and "the south wind's laughter / Follows our footsteps after!" in a "gray sea-town."[32] Levy's "A London Plane-Tree" contrasts the "recuperative bark" of the surprisingly green plane-tree that "loves the town" with its urban setting of "city breezes":

> Among her branches, in and out,
> The city breezes play;
> The dun fog wraps her round about;
> Above, the smoke curls gray.   (lines 9–12) [33]

To read these three poems together goes against traditional critical distinctions between romantic discourses about nature and fin-de-siècle urban symbolism. Close-reading all the poems that contain high percentages of a given topic can provide insights that traditional literary critics might miss, because we would not have thought to read those poems together. It is equally important to recognize, however, that no single poem is adequately described by a single "topic" produced by the topic-modeling algorithm. Close-reading any one of the poems in Stedman's volume inevitably demonstrates semantic range and rhetorical diversity that is not expressed in the topic model.

   Topic models can thus be used to explore sets of texts, to compare corpora, and to point the way to areas for further study. To interpret the results of topic modeling combines the sometimes strange insights of the algorithm with human insight and discovery. The topic model allows us an overview of the 1,284 poems in Stedman's collection that would be difficult for a human reader to perceive, precisely because as we read individual poems we tend to notice their differences rather than the semantic threads that cluster them together. The prevalence of topic ten in Stedman's anthology (forty-seven poems consist of thirty-five percent or more of this topic) raises the question of how and why wind, sea, and song were linked in Victorian poetry more generally. To trace such semantic clusters invites us to see beyond our traditional ways of reading individual poems and authors to develop an associative or networked aesthetic.

Kolodny's call for feminist critics to evaluate the biases and methods that shape literary study should urge us to think beyond the categories of the individual author, selected exemplar texts, and compelling close interpretive readings. These are part of today's received structures of feminist literary study. Computational criticism offers new analytic methods and opens new questions for the decades ahead so that we might continue to reimagine the history and significance of Victorian women's poetry.

Notes

1. Annette Kolodny, "Dancing Through the Minefield: Some Observations on the Theory, Practice, and Politics of a Feminist Literary Criticism," in *The New Feminist Criticism: Essays on Women, Literature, and Theory*, ed. Elaine Showalter (New York: Pantheon, 1985), pp. 144–67.
2. Daniel Karlin, ed., *The Penguin Book of Victorian Verse* (London: Penguin, 1997); Thomas Collins and Vivienne Rundle, eds., *The Broadview Anthology of Victorian Poetry and Poetic Theory* (Peterborough, ON: Broadview Press, 1999); Thomas Collins and Vivienne Rundle, eds., *The Broadview Anthology of Victorian Poetry and Poetic Theory, Concise Edition* (Peterborough, ON: Broadview Press, 2000); Valentine Cunningham and Duncan Wu, eds., *Victorian Poetry* (Malden: Blackwell, 2002); and Francis O'Gorman, ed., *Victorian Poetry: An Annotated Anthology* (Malden: Blackwell, 2004).
3. Natalie M. Houston, "Visualizing the Cultural Field of Victorian Poetry," in *Virtual Victorians: Networks, Connections, Technologies*, ed. Veronica Alfano and Andrew Stauffer (New York: Palgrave Macmillan, 2015), pp. 121–41.
4. Jerome Hamilton Buckley and George Benjamin Woods, eds., *Poetry of the Victorian Period* (New York: Scott, Foresman, 1965); Walter E. Houghton and G. Robert Stange, eds., *Victorian Poetry and Poetics* (Boston: Houghton Mifflin, 1959).
5. Kolodny, "Dancing Through the Minefield," p. 151.
6. Ibid., p. 153.
7. Ibid., p. 154.
8. Ibid., p. 157.
9. Cleanth Brooks, *The Well-Wrought Urn: Studies in the Structure of Poetry* (New York: Harcourt, Brace, 1947), pp. 72–3.
10. Franco Moretti, "Conjectures on World Literature," *New Left Review* 1 (2000): 57; Ted Underwood, "A Genealogy of Distant Reading," *Digital Humanities Quarterly* 11.2 (2017), www.digitalhumanities.org/dhq/vol/11/2/000317/000317.html
11. Underwood, "A Genealogy of Distant Reading."
12. Ryan Heuser and Long Le-Khac, "Learning to Read Data: Bringing out the Humanistic in the Digital Humanities," *Victorian Studies* 54 (2001), 79–86.
13. Andrew Goldstone, "The *Doxa* of Reading," *PMLA* 132 (2017), 637.
14. Michael Cohen, "E. C. Stedman and the Invention of Victorian Poetry," *Victorian Poetry* 43 (2005), 165–9.

15. Edmund Clarence Stedman, *A Victorian Anthology 1837–1895* (Boston: Houghton Mifflin, 1895), p. ix.
16. Edmund Clarence Stedman, *A Victorian Anthology 1837–1895*, in *Great Books Online*, www.bartleby.com/246/
17. Antconc is available from www.laurenceanthony.net/software/antconc/ and R is available from The Comprehensive R Archive Network (CRAN) at https://cran.r-project.org/
18. See https://github.com/nmhouston
19. Thomas Humphrey Ward, *The English Poets* (London: Macmillan, 1880).
20. Alfred Miles, *The Poets and Poetry of the Century* (London: Hutchinson, 1892–7).
21. Stedman, *A Victorian Anthology*, p. 132.
22. Ibid., p. 376.
23. Ibid., p. 377.
24. Jerome McGann, "The Religious Poetry of Christina Rossetti," *Critical Inquiry* 10 (1983), 130; Dorothy Mermin, "The Female Poet and the Embarrassed Reader: Elizabeth Barrett Browning's *Sonnets from the Portuguese*," *ELH* 48 (1981), 351.
25. Stedman, *A Victorian Anthology*, p. 380.
26. John Burrows, "Textual Analysis," in *A Companion to Digital Humanities*, ed. Susan Schreibman, Ray Siemens, and John Unsworth (Oxford: Blackwell, 2004), www.digitalhumanities.org/companion; Matthew Jockers, *Macroanalysis: Digital Methods and Literary History* (Carbondale: University of Illinois Press, 2013), pp. 63–104.
27. Keyness measures and their p-values for statistical significance are easily calculated by corpus analysis software such as Antconc, the open source tool used for this project (www.laurenceanthony.net/software/antconc/). For more information on keyness, see the Log-Likelihood and Effect Size Calculator published by Lancaster University's University Centre for Computer Corpus Research on Language at http://ucrel.lancs.ac.uk/llwizard.html
28. This analysis was conducted using the implementation of Latent Dirichlet Allocation in the *mallet* package for R. See https://cran.r-project.org/web/packages/mallet/index.html
29. The standard English stoplist provided with the MALLET Machine Learning for Language Toolkit (http://mallet.cs.umass.edu/index.php) was used.
30. Stedman, *A Victorian Anthology*, p. 508.
31. Ibid., p. 78.
32. Ibid., p. 609.
33. Ibid., p. 579.

Afterword

ISOBEL ARMSTRONG

Nineteenth-Century Women's Poetry in the Field of Vision

At Harvard in the late nineties I asked my friend Helen Vendler whether she would be able to contribute to the feminist periodical I then edited with Helen Carr and Laura Marcus, *Women. A Cultural Review*. She replied unequivocally, no, and gave an interesting reason for not doing so. She did not think that gender was the defining category of our lives. We had a good correspondence. I think I argued that there were reasons of contemporary history for foregrounding gender. But Helen's unequivocal argument has always remained in my mind. It was highly unusual to take up this position at the time, when gender *was* the defining category in feminist studies and beyond. At one point I wrote, "the category of gender changes our sense of what we know, what we need to know, and how we know it."[1] But I begin with Helen's position because I do not think it would be so unusual today.

Does this mean that a collection of twenty-first-century essays on Victorian women's poetry would have, in comparison with the twentieth century, a rather different rationale today? What would be the modalities of women's writing?

To think about this question requires a return to that founding moment, when women's poetry was almost frenetically extracted from the archive and anthologized. This phase began in the early nineties. Jennifer Breen and Catherine Reilly were first in the field in 1994 with respectively *Victorian Women Poets 1830–1900: An Anthology* and *Winged Words: Victorian Women's Poetry and Verse*.[2] Then followed in 1995 the huge collection edited by Angela Leighton and Margaret Reynolds, *Victorian Women Poets: An Anthology*. The Oxford Anthology edited by Joseph Bristow, Cath Sharrock, and myself, *Nineteenth Century Women Poets*, arrived in 1996. Virginia Blain's *Victorian Women Poets: A New Annotated Anthology* came out in 2001.[3] Editions of individual poets followed rapidly. After William McCarthy's peerless edition of Anna Barbauld's poems appeared in 1994,[4] editions of Joanna Baillie, Charlotte Smith, Amelia Opie, and Letitia Landon subsequently appeared. The Broadview selections from individual poets followed, and it is now possible to find editions from Lucy Aikin and Felicia Hemans to Michael Field in its series. Of course, there were seminal critical books too. Marlon Ross, *The Contours of Masculine Desire* (1989) and Anne K. Mellor, *Romanticism and Gender* (1993) were foundational.[5] For feminist Victorianists, "bliss was it at that time to be alive."

This outpouring could not have happened without the intellectual work of feminist theorists. Juliet Mitchell's *Psychoanalysis and Feminism* (1974) and Mitchell and Jacqueline Rose's absolutely crucial coedited *Feminine Sexuality: Jacques Lacan and the École Freudienne* were massively significant and fundamentally important to feminist thought and activism.[6] Important at the time, with hindsight they are even more significant. Rose's *Sexuality in the Field of Vision* consolidated this work.[7] These books predate the rush of anthologies I have described and prepared the way for them, as the dates of publication indicate.

Despite the popularity, at that time, of now classic essays by Hêlêne Cixous, "The Laugh of the Medusa" (1975), and Julia Kristeva, "Women's Time" (1979), the one deconstructing phallologocentrism with écriture feminine, the other seeking a new signifying space and interiority to challenge male hegemony, Mitchell's and Rose's work seems to me of a different order of significance. Cixous and Kristeva gave feminist thinkers new concepts and a new language, certainly. They articulated and theorized the great surge of protest in second wave feminism, such as Kate Millett's *Sexual Politics* (1970), in a way that no protest writing or feminist history could do. But in elucidating Lacan's thought for their generation, Mitchell and Rose did something else: they moved debate away from biologism, a reading of sexuality through the physical constitution of gender, and away from essentialism; but, much more importantly, their highly philosophical reading of psychoanalysis proposed a *structural* explanation for female abjection and confronted feminists with an intransigent account of phallic power.

This was the symbolic order as Lacan described it, an order entered on necessarily different terms by men and women. Jacqueline Rose's brilliant chapter on Lacan is complex, but she showed that in essence though the symbolic order is a fantasmatic imposture sustained by the culture on both men and women, its force is coercive. The entry of the father into the mother-child dyad is a rupture that brings with it at one and the same time castration, the law, and language – the Name of the Father, as Lacan termed this construct, where the phallus becomes the prime signifier. It is the differential mark creating the androcentric "legislative divide" of sexual difference. Always constructed in relation to the male sign, femininity becomes a masquerade, and though the possession of the phallus is itself a function of the duplicity of the linguistic sign, woman is constructed as a symptom, and in the place of lack. Lacan's famous remark, that the woman does not exist, with the definite article crossed through, sums up the power of the symbolic order.[8]

Of course, this makes for, to use Amanda Anderson's adjective, a bleak feminism. It was challenged in 1990 by the appearance of Judith Butler's *Gender Trouble*.[9] Butler insisted on the pessimism of Lacanian thought and argued for a performative account of gender that recognized the discontinuous and inconsistent nature of gender assignation. She refused the binary underlying Lacanian analysis. Hers was a ludic feminism in which gender was an elective condition and not a predetermined one. Her stress on compulsory heterosexuality released feminism into lesbian and gay discourses. She is an ancestress of LGBT activism.

The elective nature of gender was widely taken up. In many ways this was liberating, but its effect was to dissolve the need for understanding gender through a systemic inequality. A certain individualism was also the consequence of Butler's writing, dissolving the presumption of collective activity. Bleak and deterministic though Mitchell and Rose might seem, their reading of Lacan put gender inequality and phallic power firmly at the center of thinking and, moreover, offered a strenuously philosophical reading of psychoanalysis that had repercussions for writing. Since thinking gender was predicated on the signifier, the centrality of *langue*, how women might write and imagine through writing, was crucial. True, there are aspects of Lacan that can be wearying: his insistence on Love "as the ultimate form of self-recognition," for instance, but his understanding of the symbolic order is crucial.[10]

It is now more than thirty years since this surge of theoretical writing. It would be right to say that the lived experience of feminism and feminist writing has become unmoored from theory. We have forgotten the structural intransigence of the symbolic order. Where psychoanalysis is referenced if at all the important figures are mainly object relations thinkers, Donald Winnicott, Wilfred Bion, and Christopher Bollas. The consequence is that writing about women's poetry tends to follow the dictates of our subject's larger themes and their dialectic – cultural materialism, the turn to affect, to form and prosody, technology and communications – and particularly its drift to the fin de siècle.[11] The fact of systemic inequality is bracketed. A number of other issues are occluded by this eclecticism too: what exactly is a gendered reading of women's poetry? Should there be a kind of separatist criticism that treats of women's poetry on its own in spite of the danger of consolidating the separate spheres to which the woman poet was often doomed? Or should women's and men's poetry be discussed together through intertwined thematic readings? An early example of thematic reading that moves between male and female poets, a trait that is increasing, is Jerome McGann's *The Poetics of Sensibility: A Revolution in Literary Style* (1996). A triumphant recent example of separatist reading is *The Political Poetess: Victorian Femininity, Race, and the Legacy of Separate Spheres* (2017) by Tricia Lootens, who demonstrates the amazing energy of female poets once released from the coercive definitions of the separate sphere.[12]

A recognition of structural inequity might entail the constant reiteration of the same theme of subjection, a kind of repetition compulsion that is ultimately counterproductive. This is the danger of working with oppression as a model and this is why the elective model has been so popular. There is a rather different way of putting this problem, however. If the woman writer is always already the subject of systemic inequity, her *active* negotiation of the symbolic order, her active negotiation of male texts, must not only be structurally necessary but one of the routes to self-affirmation. It is not a situation of choice but one that chooses her. It becomes incumbent on her to create a workable dialogism. This must mean that male and female texts are co-present, both held in play. Such negotiation, I suggest, is empowering. Even when the female writer is not ostensibly "writing as a woman," even when she appears to be participating in a common discourse and on its terms, aesthetic or scientific, historical or philosophical, her position as a writing subject can never be neutral. Not to be neutral does not always entail subjection: because it can be an active negotiation, a negotiation that writes from female cognition, this is exactly what releases her from oppression. But it is a negotiation all the same. I am not arguing that this frees the woman writer from the constraints of the symbolic order: far from it; participation in negotiation is always from the standpoint of the crossed-out definite article.

I end with two examples of feminine negotiation, Lou Andreas-Salomé's reading of Freud's paper on narcissism in a letter of 1915[13] and Alice Meynell's poem to the west wind in *Later Poems* (1901).

When Lou Andreas-Salomé asked Freud to send her his paper on narcissism in 1915, she was already a writer of substance, the author of a study of Nietzsche (1894) and a psychoanalytical work, *The Erotic* (1910): she had written on Ibsen and produced many novels. She was still in correspondence with Rilke, whom she met in 1897. So the deferential tone of her long letter to Freud about his paper is slightly anomalous:

> Dear Professor, This probably somewhat lengthy letter is not intended to intrude as a trouble maker upon one of your working hours. It will be quite content to slip away into some drawer and lie there happily.[14]

But the letter, covering more than three and a half pages of the Norton edition, is anything but self-effacing. She actually writes as an equal and makes a fundamentally revisionary reading of the paper, assuming a reciprocity with Freud. And my point is that it is this assumption of reciprocity that is empowering even if the equity it implies is nonexistent in fact. Her argument is mainly round Freud's assumptions about primary narcissism. She wants to introduce into "the deepest naiveté" of primary narcissism a reflexivity that Freud has not guaranteed to it, to account for the aesthetic, to introduce the body as an active element in narcissism, to consider desire and the experience of pleasure/pain.[15]

What are the Freudian premises she questions? I do an injustice to Freud by reducing the argument of his foundational paper to a few sentences, but I want to give full play to Salomé's ideas. Freud makes a distinction between primary narcissism and secondary narcissism, which is a perverted form of primary narcissism. Primary narcissism has a double movement that accounts almost wholly for the life of the subject. Like the amoeba that can project and retract its cytoplasm, ego-libido and object-libido can be extended and withdrawn, projected onto the other or retracted into the self: "The more one is employed, the more the other is depleted."[16]

To a discussion of these two movements of narcissism, Freud also adds commentary on the sex instincts and the importance of these to biological survival. Scientific positivism is still a powerful aspect of Freud's thinking. We would ultimately find that chemical substances would explain psychical forces.

Lou Andreas-Salomé's letter of January 10, 1915, attempts to complicate the double movement Freud assigns to narcissism in a number of ways, all of which refuse a deterministic psychic economy. First, she wants to distinguish between "the deepest naiveté" of primary narcissism and the moment of "cleavage" when the ego "consciously chooses itself as object." When the cleavage of self-consciousness arises, "one stands as a feeling behind one's feelings, as it were savouring and enjoying them." She distinguishes between the narcissism that takes pleasure in love or fame and the narcissism that enjoys the pleasure itself.[17] Three consequences emerge from her distinction between pleasure in *something* and pleasure for its own sake.

The first is an understanding of the aesthetic and art, which (as it stands in this particular essay) Freud's account would consign to a form of narcissistic ego cathexis or equally narcissistic projection. For Salomé there are two moments to creation: "it would be equally true to say that the frontiers of the ego are totally eliminated, affording in this way an escape from subjectivity and from the opposition of the ego and the external world, as to say that the ego on the contrary relates all desirable features to itself alone."[18]

The ego is the object of the libido only in the return from creative absorption. In the act of creation, narcissism is suspended, or the opposition of the ego and the external world is annulled in the escape from subjectivity. Salomé is attempting to incorporate Freud's "amoeboid" movement of extension and retraction into a dialectic, a dialectic between the dissolution of the ego and the resumption of self-awareness. In this she is also accounting for the free movement of the ego into the world through the act of creation in the making of art. Art is the product of a more profound meeting of the self and world that respects the world's otherness and forgets its own boundaries.

Secondly, Salomé attempts to modify Freud's biological reading of the sexual instincts. The rhythms of pleasure and pain are subject to a form of contradiction, she argues. Positive pleasure, genital pleasure, the primary pleasure, is paradoxical. It becomes a form of unpleasure when it seeks relief. This may be a purely physical state in the first instance, but as a powerful organic experience it affects the whole self. This state requires and desires a great deal more than "mere relief" because from the "overvalued sexual object" is required a union, an affirmation of one as a subject. So genital pleasure is always bound up with complex needs and desires that are other than simple sexual need: "Is not then the great problem of sex that it not only tries to quench the thirst, but that it also consists in the yearning for the thirst itself, that the physical relief of tension, of satiation, at the same time disappoints, because it diminishes the tension, the thirst."[19] The contradictions of sexuality must be seen as more than a problem of instinct.

Her thinking on the erotic acknowledges its more than instinctual power:

> It is nevertheless from here that the whole of the rest of the world opens to us, and this is where our real marriage with life begins, that exteriority of things that we could otherwise never fully incorporate ... Loving, in the most serious sense of the term, means knowing someone whose colors all things must wear if they are to reach us whole.[20]

Where narcissism is an almost universal structural principle for Freud, in which everything comes under its rubric, for her this essentially economic model was displaced by a theory of psychic transformation through reciprocal relations with another.

Finally, her third modification of Freud's essay was to introduce the body as a recalcitrant element that constantly displaced or threw into question a settled narcissism. In illness, we are suddenly hyperconscious of our own body as an object no longer identical with us, alien and hostile. The body even becomes an object of hatred to us. Pain is felt as something independent, acting on the self, and thus drives a wedge between the subject and that within the self, – and is in fact felt as an object: "This state would contrast with the narcissistic pleasure of being at one with one's own body – just as though the aforementioned naïve type of narcissism, which simply feels identical with the whole power of the outer world, contrasts with the self-regarding type; which consciously makes itself its own love object."[21] The body has a double role; it is at one and the same time we ourselves and "the most immediate piece of external reality, to which we are in."[22] With this account of the body as a kind of third term, she had found a way of disrupting the binary of ego-libido and object-libido that trapped the self in an unreflective narcissism. This triangulated the self, the other, the world, so that the inevitability of binary narcissism could be displaced by a mediated state.

Rather movingly, perhaps to mitigate the seeming assault of this letter, Salomé added a PS to say that she had bought a dog – out of "despair at warring mankind."[23] It was, of course, the time of the First World War.

Freud replied on the last day of January 1915, in five paragraphs (the letter takes up half a page of the Norton edition). He acknowledged Salomé's energy and even affirmed that she would make him think further. Nevertheless, Salomé's thoughts are crushed. We have to recognize this and at the same time acknowledge that the fact she did *negotiate* is supremely important. Freud dismissed her thoughts. His work was "metapsychological." He was writing solely about the *unconscious* not *consciousness*: "The cases in which you are interested refer pre-eminently to conditions where this process becomes *conscious*." There speaks the name of the father. His penultimate paragraph ran as follows. In reading it, we must remember Freud's stress and distress – "My eldest son is already in the trenches in Galicia." But he rejects his friend's presumed dialogism: "Nor have I acquired either a dog or a cat; I have enough women-folk in the house as it is. Fortunately, girls are not called up for military service."[24] What a poignant exchange, for both of them, but for different reasons.

My second example is briefer, but it is, importantly, a negotiation of inequity through poetry. Alice Meynell's extraordinary "West Wind in Winter" from *Later Poems* (1901) is a negotiation that presumes reciprocity but encounters inequity. But it's as if her presumption of equity finally surprises the other into recognition:

> Another day awakes. And who –
> Changing the world – is this?
> He comes at whiles, the Winter through,
> West Wind! I would not miss
> His sudden tryst: the long, the new
> Surprises of his kiss.

Vigilant, I make haste to close
With him who comes my way.
I go to meet him as he goes;
I know his note, his lay,
His colour and his morning rose;
And I confess his day.

My window waits; at dawn I hark
His call; at morn I meet
His haste around the tossing park
And down the softened street;
The gentler light is his; the dark,
The grey – he turns it sweet.

So too, so too, do I confess
My poet when he sings.
He rushes on my mortal guess
With his immortal things.
I feel, I know him. On I press –
He finds me 'twixt his wings.[25]

The intense erotics of this poem are all the more intense because of its
setting in the high bourgeois London landscape of park – "tossing park" –
"softened street," and urban houses: "My window waits," where the tension of expectation is transferred to the fabric of the house itself. The body
of the house is alive with expectation as her physicality is transferred to it.
The poem enacts the frankest of erotic unions – "West Wind! I would not
miss / His sudden tryst: the long, the new / Surprises of his kiss." And
although the west wind has the physicality of Shelley's wild west wind,
Meynell's Catholicism would endow the wind as well with the Pentecostal
force of the Holy Ghost.

But there is contradiction at every point. The homogeneity of the A and
B rhyme scheme promises reassuring regularity. (Meynell often used a stanza
form where the A and B rhymes were the same, sometimes throughout
a single poem.) But though the four-beat and three-beat lines alternate
regularly, the unevenness of their alternation in these four hurried six-line
stanzas creates a metrical inequity that is emphasized by the unusually riven
upheaval of the constant caesura. Even the gaps between the stanzas begin to
signify as each presumes a passage of time, a temporal gap, between one verse
and another. It is the same with the vocabulary: a tryst is a mutually prearranged meeting, but here it is a "sudden" occurrence, and the kiss, in the
singular, holds multiple "surprises" – the surprise of orgasm, perhaps, but
unexpected.

Power seems all on the side of the wind. It is the importunate female lover who pursues, the female lover who is in a state of desire, in search of reciprocity, attempting to "close" with the lover. Whenever the word "meet" occurs, a seemingly reciprocal term, the word initiates a strange, uneven sequence of almost missed encounters, of accident, of pursuit and non-convergence, meeting in the act of departure, as the contradictory verbs in the second stanza – come and go – suggest: he "comes my way. / I go to meet him as he goes"; "At morn I meet / His haste." Both the wind and the speaker are in "haste" (a repeated word), but the staccato pauses make this a riven, anxious love affair, an unresolved power relation. It is a poem full of gaps. The wind as spirit is unreachable through the flesh. Indeed, the lover is in pursuit of the intangible, light: "The gentler light is his; the dark; / The grey." Twice the lover needs to "confess" the wind and the poet, the wind's surrogate, and the ambiguity of the verb makes it unclear whether the subject or the object is taken up in the act of confession. Do I make the wind confess or do I confess to the erotics of this importunate encounter with the wind as lover?

The final resting point is one-sided: "He finds me 'twixt his wings" – Meynell thought of the wind as winged, we know from her essays, and through this the wind at least momentarily takes on bodily form that enables a kind of rapprochement, achieved despite the non-convergence of the Pentecostal "rush" of the wind and the "press" of the lover's desire. The lover has been "vigilant" (Stanza 2), but it is her turn to create surprise through bodily presence. In the final stanza, the lover enables the wind to "find" or discover her, "'twixt his wings," a meeting not prearranged or reciprocal but achieved nevertheless. This time the achievement of the female lover has been negotiated through her persistent capacity to imagine the body and circumvent power relations.

These two examples of female negotiation suggest how the inequity of gender power means that negotiation can never be suspended. It can, however, be eased by the *assumption* of equity and dialogism, though this is always problematic and always a postulate, always notional. It is very important that we be self-conscious about this process at this time, when our culture time and again yields evidence of misogyny and violence against women, from the internet to Hollywood abuses. I am impressed by the way these two very different texts raise the same issues – the body, desire, and the underlying theme of art and its power. It is through these topoi that they keep power relations uppermost and escape the narcissism of large differences.

Notes

1. Isobel Armstrong, "The Gush of the Feminine. How Can We Read Women's Poetry of the Romantic Period?" in *Romantic Women Writers: Voices and Countervoices*, ed. Paula R. Feldman and Theresa M. Kelly (Hanover: University Press of New England, 1995), p. 16.

2. Jennifer Breen, ed., *Victorian Women Poets 1830–1900* (London: Everyman, 1994); Catherine Reilly, ed., *Winged Words: Victorian Women's Poetry and Verse* (London: Enitharmon Press, 1994).

3. Angela Leighton and Margaret Reynolds, eds., *Victorian Women Poets: An Anthology* (Oxford: Blackwell, 1995); Isobel Armstrong, Joseph Bristow, with Cath Sharrock, eds., *Nineteenth-Century Women Poets* (Oxford: Oxford University Press, 1996); Virginia Blain, ed., *Victorian Women Poets: A New Annotated Anthology* (Harwell: Longman's, 2001).

4. William McCarthy, ed., *The Poems of Anna Letitia Barbauld* (Athens: University of Georgia Press, 1994).

5. Marlon Ross, *The Contours of Masculine Desire* (New York: Oxford University Press, 1989); Anne Mellor, *Romanticism and Gender* (London: Routledge, 1993).

6. Juliet Mitchell, *Psychoanalysis and Feminism* (London: Penguin Books, 1974); Juliet Mitchell and Jacqueline Rose, *Feminine Sexuality: Jacques Lacan and the École Freudienne* (London: Macmillan, 1982).

7. Jacqueline Rose, *Sexuality in the Field of Vision* (London: Verso, 1986).

8. Mitchell and Rose, *Feminine Sexuality*, pp. 41, 48.

9. Judith Butler, *Gender Trouble* (London: Routledge, 1990).

10. Mitchell and Rose, *Feminine Sexuality*, p. 47.

11. For the turn to cultural materialism see M. A. Favret and N. J. Watson, eds., *At the Limits of Romanticism: Essays in Cultural, Feminist and Materialist Criticism* (Bloomington: Indiana University Press, 1994). For affective reading, see Catherine Maxwell, *Second Sight: The Visionary Imagination in Late Victorian Literature* (Manchester: Manchester University Press, 2009). For prosody-based criticism, see Elizabeth Helsinger, *Poetry and the Thought of Song in Nineteenth-century Britain* (Charlottesville: University of Virginia Press, 2015). For the foregrounding of technology and communications, see Ana Parejo Vadillo, *Women's Poetry and Urban Aestheticism: Passengers of Modernity* (Basingstoke: Palgrave, 2005).

12. Jerome McGann, *The Poetics of Sensibility: A Revolution in Literary Style* (Oxford: Clarendon Press, 1996); Tricia Lootens, *The Political Poetess: Victorian Femininity, Race and the Legacy of Separate Spheres* (Princeton: Princeton University Press, 2017).

13. Sigmund Freud, "On Narcissism: An Introduction" (1914), in *The Complete Psychological Works of Sigmund Freud*, 24 vols. (London: Hogarth Press, 1966–74), 14.73–81.

14. *Letters. Sigmund Freud and Lou Andreas-Salomé*, ed. Ernst Pfeiffer, trans. William and Elaine Robson-Scott (London and New York: W. W. Norton and Company, 1985), p. 22.

15. Ibid., p. 23.

16. Freud, "On Narcissism," 14.76.

17. Andreas-Salomé, *Letters*, p. 23.
18. Ibid., p. 24.
19. Ibid., p. 25.
20. *The Erotic*, trans. John Crisp (New Brunswick: Transaction Publishers, 2014), p. 66.
21. Andreas-Salomé, *Letters*, p. 25.
22. Ibid., p. 26.
23. Ibid.
24. Ibid., p. 27.
25. Alice Meynell, *Later Poems* (London: John Lane, The Bodley Head, 1901), pp. 24–5.

FURTHER READING

Introduction

Armstrong, I., and Blain, V. (eds.) *Women's Poetry, Late Romantic to Late Victorian: Gender and Genre, 1830–1900*, Houndmills, Macmillan, 1999.

Blain, V. (ed.) *Victorian Women Poets: A New Annotated Anthology*, Harlow, Longman, 2001.

Booth, A. "Mid-Range Reading: Not a Manifesto." *PMLA* 132 (2017), 620–7.

Chapman, A. (ed.) *Victorian Women Poets*, English Association Essays and Studies, Cambridge, D. S. Brewer, 2003.

Ledbetter, K. *British Victorian Women's Periodicals: Beauty, Civilization, and Poetry*, New York, Palgrave Macmillan, 2009.

Levine, C. *Forms: Whole, Rhythm, Hierarchy, Network*, Princeton, Princeton University Press, 2015.

Lootens, T. *The Political Poetess: Victorian Femininity, Race, and the Legacy of Separate Spheres*, Princeton, Princeton University Press, 2017.

Martin, M. *The Rise and Fall of Meter: Poetry and English National Culture, 1860–1930*, Princeton, Princeton University Press, 2012.

Vadillo, A. *Women Poets and Urban Aestheticism: Passengers of Modernity*, Basingstoke, Palgrave Macmillan, 2005.

1 Genres

Armstrong, I. *Victorian Poetry: Poetry, Poetics and Politics*, New York, Routledge, 1993.

Billone, A. C. *Little Songs: Women, Silence, and the Nineteenth-Century Sonnet*, Columbus, Ohio State University Press, 2007.

Diedrick, J. *Mathilde Blind: Late-Victorian Culture and the Woman of Letters*, Charlottesville, University of Virginia Press, 2016.

Gregory, M. V. "Augusta Webster Writing Motherhood in the Dramatic Monologue and the Sonnet Sequence," *Victorian Poetry*, 49 (2011), 27–51.

Henville, L. (ed.) Special Issue: Ballads, *Victorian Poetry*, 54 (2016), 411–524.

Markovits, S. "Adulterated Form: Violet Fane and the Victorian Verse-Novel," *ELH*, 81.2 (Summer 2014), 635–61.

Morgan, M. R. *Narrative Means, Lyric Ends: Temporality in the Nineteenth-Century British Long Poem*, Columbus, Ohio State University Press, 2009.

Rigg, P. (ed.) Special Issue: Augusta Webster, *Victorian Poetry*, 55 (2017), 1–124.

Thain, M. "Victorian Lyric Pathology and Phenomenology," in *The Lyric Poem: Formations and Transformations*, M. Thain (ed.), New York, Cambridge University Press, 2013, 156–76.

Tucker, H. F. *Epic: Britain's Heroic Muse 1790–1910*, New York, Oxford University Press, 2008.

2 Prosody

Abbott, R. "George Eliot, Meter, and the Matter of Ideas: The Yale Poetry Notebook," *ELH*, 82 (2015), 1179–211.

Dieleman, K. *Religious Imaginaries: The Liturgical and Poetic Practices of Elizabeth Barrett Browning, Christina Rossetti, and Adelaide Procter*, Athens, Ohio University Press, 2012.

Glaser, B. "Polymetrical Dissonance: Tennyson, A. Mary F. Robinson, and Classical Meter," *Victorian Poetry*, 49 (2011), 199–216.

Houston, N. "Towards a New History: *Fin-de-Siècle* Women Poets and the Sonnet," in *Victorian Women Poets*, A. Chapman (ed.), Cambridge, D. S. Brewer, 2003.

Jackson, V., and Prins, Y. "Lyrical Studies," *Victorian Literature and Culture*, 27 (1999), 521–30.

Levine, N. "Elizabeth Barrett Browning's Historiographical Poetics," *Modern Language Quarterly*, 77 (2016), 81–104.

Pinch, A. "Rhyme's End," *Victorian Studies*, 53 (2011), 485–94.

Prins, Y. "Victorian Meters," in *Cambridge Companion to Victorian Poetry*, J. Bristow (ed.), Cambridge, Cambridge University Press, 2000.

Rudy, J. "Hemans' Passion," *Studies in Romanticism*, 45 (2006), 543–62.

Stetz, M. "'Ballads in Prose': Genre Crossing in Late-Victorian Women's Writing," *Victorian Literature and Culture*, 34 (2006), 619–29.

Winterer, C. "Victorian Antigone: Classicism and Women's Education in America, 1840–1900," *American Quarterly*, 53 (2001), 70–93.

3 Haunted by Voice

Griffiths, E. *The Printed Voice of Victorian Poetry*, Oxford, Clarendon Press, 1989.

Rowlinson, M. "Lyric," in *A Companion to Victorian Poetry*, eds. Richard Cronin, Alison Chapman, and Antony Harrison, Malden, Blackwell, 2002, 59–79.

Vadillo, A. "Sight and Song: Transparent Translations and a Manifesto for the Observer," *Victorian Poetry*, 38 (2000), 15–34.

4 Floating Worlds: Wood Engraving and Women's Poetry

Cooke, S., and Goldman, P. (eds.) *Readings in Victorian Illustration, 1855–1875: Spoils of the Lumber Room*, Farnham, Ashgate, 2012.

Flint, K. *The Victorians and the Visual Imagination*, Cambridge, Cambridge University Press, 2000.

Golden, C. J. (ed.) *Book Illustrated: Text, Image, and Culture 1779–1930*, New Castle, Oak Knoll, 2000.

Goldman, P. *Victorian Illustrated Books 1850–1870*, London, British Museum Press, 1994.

Goldman, P. *Victorian Illustration: The Pre-Raphaelites, the Idyllic School and the High Victorians*, Aldershot, Scolar Press, 1996.

Kooistra, L. J. "'Illustration,'" in *Journalism and the Periodical Press in Nineteenth-Century Britain*, ed. J. Shattock, Cambridge, Cambridge University Press, 2017, 104–25.

Maidment, B. *Reading Popular Prints 1790–1870*, 2nd ed., Manchester, Manchester University Press, 1996.

Maxwell, R. (ed.) *The Victorian Illustrated Book*, Charlottesville, University of Virginia Press, 2002.

Onslow, B. "Gendered Production: Annuals and Gift Books," in *Journalism and the Periodical Press in Nineteenth-Century Britain*, ed. J. Shattock, Cambridge, Cambridge University Press, 2017, 66–83.

Thomas, J. *Pictorial Victorians: The Inscription of Values in Word and Image*, Athens, Ohio University Press, 2004.

5   Embodiment and Touch

Armstrong, I. "The Gush of the Feminine: How Can We Read Women's Poetry of the Romantic Period?" in *Romantic Women Writers: Voices and Countervoices*, eds. P. Feldman and T. Kelley, Hanover, University Press of New England, 1995, 13–32.

Blair, K. *Victorian Poetry and the Culture of the Heart*, Oxford, Oxford University Press, 2006.

Lootens, T. *The Political Poetess: Victorian Femininity, Race, and the Legacy of Separate Spheres*, Princeton, Princeton University Press, 2017.

Mason, E. *Women Poets of the Nineteenth Century*, Horndon, Northcote, 2006.

McGann, J. *The Poetics of Sensibility: A Revolution in Literary Style*, Oxford, Clarendon, 1996.

Preston, C. J. *Modernism's Mythic Pose: Gender, Genre, Solo Performance*, Oxford, Oxford University Press, 2011.

Rudy, J. R. "Hemans' Passion," *Studies in Romanticism* 45 (2006), 543–62.

6   Publishing and Reception

Chapman, A., and Ehnes, C. "Introduction," *Victorian Poetry* 52 (2014), 1–20.

Erickson, L. *The Economy of Literary Form*, Baltimore, Johns Hopkins University Press, 1996.

Fraser, H., Green, S., and Johnston, J. *Gender and the Victorian Periodical*, Cambridge, Cambridge University Press, 2003.

Hughes, L. K. "What the *Wellesley Index* Left Out: Why Poetry Matters to Periodical Studies," *Victorian Periodicals Review*, 40 (2007), 91–125.

Kooistra, L. J. *Poetry, Pictures, and Popular Publishing: The Illustrated Gift Book and Victorian Visual Culture, 1855–75*, Athens, Ohio University Press, 2011.

Ledbetter, K. *British Victorian Women's Periodicals: Beauty, Civilization, and Poetry*, Basingstoke, Palgrave Macmillan, 2009.

Pulham, P. "'Jewels – delights – perfect loves': Victorian Women Poets and the Annuals," in *Victorian Women Poets*, A. Chapman (ed.), Cambridge, D. S. Brewer, 2003, 9–31.

7 Transatlanticism, Transnationality, and Cosmopolitanism

Boehmer, E. *Indian Arrivals, 1870–1915: Networks of British Empire*, Oxford, Oxford University Press, 2015.

Chapman A. "'I think I was enchanted': Elizabeth Barrett Browning's Haunting of American Women Poets," in *Representations of Death in Nineteenth-Century US Writing and Culture*, L. Frank (ed.), Aldershot, Ashgate, 2007, 109–24.

Chapman, A. and Stabler, J. (eds.), *Unfolding the South: Nineteenth-Century British Women Artists and Writers in Italy*, Manchester, Manchester University Press, 2003.

Finnerty, P. "Women's Transatlantic Poetic Network," in *A History of Nineteenth-Century American Women's Poetry*, J. Putzi and J. Socarides (eds.), Cambridge, Cambridge University Press, 2016, 170–85.

Hughes, L. K. and Robbins, S. (eds.), *Teaching Transatlanticism: Resources for Teaching Nineteenth-Century Anglo-American Print Culture*, Edinburgh, Edinburgh University Press, 2015.

Jackson, V. (ed.), *American Victorian Poetry*, special issue, *Victorian Poetry*, 43 (2005), 157–274.

Keirstead, C. M. *Victorian Poetry, Europe, and the Challenge of Cosmopolitanism*, Athens, Ohio University Press, 2011.

Lootens, T. "Alien Homelands: Rudyard Kipling, Toru Dutt, and the Poetry of Empire," in *The Fin-de-Siècle Poem: English Literary Culture and the 1890s*, J. Bristow (ed.), Athens, Ohio University Press, 2005, pp. 285–310.

McGill, M. *American Literature and the Culture of Reprinting 1834–1853*, Philadelphia, University of Pennsylvania Press, 2003.

Mukherjee, M. "Hearing her Own Voice: Defective Acoustics in Colonial India," in *Women's Poetry, Late Romantic to Late Victorian: Gender and Genre, 1830–1900*, I. Armstrong and V. Blain (eds.), Houndmills, Macmillan, 1999, 207–29.

O'Leary, J. *Settler Songs and Wild Romances: Settler Poetry and the Indigene, 1830–1880*, Amsterdam, Rodopi, 2011.

Simpson, E. "On Corinne, Or Italy," in *BRANCH: Britain, Representation and Nineteenth-Century History*, D. F. Felluga (ed.), www.branchcollective.org/?ps_articles=erik-simpson-on-corinne-or-italy

8 Dialect, Region, Class, Work

Boos, F. S. "'Nurs'd Up Among the Scenes I Have Describ'd': Poetry of Working-Class Victorian Women," in *Functions of Victorian Culture at the Present Time*, C. Krueger (ed.), Athens, Ohio University Press, 2002, 137–56.

Boos, F. S. (ed.) *Working-Class Women Poets in Victorian Britain: An Anthology*, Peterborough, Broadview, 2008.

Goodridge, J. (gen. ed.), *Nineteenth-Century English Labouring-Class Poets*, 3 vols., London, Pickering & Chatto, 2005.

Hodson, J. (ed.), *Dialect and Literature in the Long Nineteenth Century*, London, Routledge, 2017.

Klaus, H. G. *Factory Girl: Ellen Johnston and Working-Class Poetry in Victorian Scotland*, Bern, Peter Lang, 1998.

Maidment, B. (ed.), *The Poorhouse Fugitives: Self-Taught Poets and Poetry in Victorian Britain*, Manchester, Carcanet, 1987.

McCauley, L. "'Eawr Folk': Language, Class and English Identity in Victorian Dialect Poetry," *Victorian Poetry*, 39 (2001), 287–301.

Rosen, J. "Class and Poetic Communities: The Works of Ellen Johnston, 'The Factory Girl,'" *Victorian Poetry*, 39.2 (2001), 207–27.

Sanders, M. *The Poetry of Chartism: Aesthetics, Politics, History*, Cambridge, Cambridge University Press, 2009.

Zlotnick, S. "'A Thousand Times I'd Be a Factory Girl': Dialect, Domesticity and Working-Class Women's Writing in Victorian Britain," *Victorian Studies*, 35 (1991), 7–27.

9 Politics, Protest, Interventions: Beyond a Poetess Tradition

Avery, S. "Telling it Slant: Promethean, Whig, and Dissenting Politics in Elizabeth Barrett's Poetry of the 1830s," *Victorian Poetry*, 44 (2006), 405–24.

Donaldson, S. (ed.), *Critical Essays on Elizabeth Barrett Browning*, New York, G. K. Hall, 1999.

Rigg, P. (ed.), *Augusta Webster*, special issue, *Victorian Poetry*, 55 (2017), 1–124.

Slinn, E. W. *Victorian Poetry as Cultural Critique: The Politics of Performative Language*, Charlottesville, University Press of Virginia, 2003.

Timney, M. "Mary Hutton and the Development of a Working-Class Women's Political Poetics: Chartist Threads," *Victorian Poetry*, 49 (2011), 127–46.

10 Religion and Spirituality

Clarke, M. M. "Emily Brontë's 'No Coward Soul' and the Need for a Religious Literary Criticism," *Victorians Institute Journal*, 37 (2009), 195–223.

Houston, G. T. *Victorian Women Writers, Radical Grandmothers, and the Gendering of God*, Columbus, Ohio State University Press, 2013.

King, J., "Transatlantic Abolitionist Discourse and the Body of Christ in Elizabeth Barrett Browning's 'The Runaway Slave at Pilgrim's Point,'" *Religions*, 8 (2016), 1–24.

Knight, M., and Mason, E. *Nineteenth-Century Religion and Literature: An Introduction*, Oxford, Oxford University Press, 2006.

Lewis, L. M. *Elizabeth Barrett Browning's Spiritual Progress: Face to Face with God*, Columbia, University of Missouri Press, 1998.

Mason, E. *Women Poets of the Nineteenth Century*, Tavistock, Northcote House Publishers, 2006.

Nixon, J. V. "'[S]he shall make all new': *Aurora Leigh* and Elizabeth Barrett Browning's Re-Gendering of the Apocalypse," in *Victorian Religious Discourse*, J. Nixon (ed.), New York, Palgrave Macmillan, 2005, 72–93.

Stone, M., "'A Heretic Believer': Victorian Religious Doubt and New Contexts for Elizabeth Barrett Browning's 'A Drama of Exile,' 'The Virgin Mary' and 'The Runaway Slave at Pilgrim's Point,'" *Studies in Browning and His Circle*, 26 (2005), 7–40.

Williams, W. S. *George Eliot, Poetess*, Burlington, Ashgate, 2014.

11   Children's Poetry

Alexander, C., and McMaster, J. (eds.). *The Child Writer from Austen to Woolf*, Cambridge, Cambridge University Press, 2005.

Alexander, C., and McMaster, J. "Children Writing in Jane Austen's Time," *Persuasions*, 37 (2015), 13–28.

Galway, E. *From Nursery Rhyme to Nationhood: Children's Literature and the Culture of Canadian Identity*, New York, Routledge, 2008.

Garlitz, B. "Christina Rossetti's *Sing-Song* and Nineteenth-Century Children's Poetry," *PMLA*, 70 (1955), 539–43.

Grenby, M. O. "Poetry," *Children's Literature*, Edinburgh, Edinburgh University Press, 2008, 32–60.

Immel, A. and Paul, L. "Poems in the Nursery," *The Oxford Handbook of British Poetry, 1600–1800*, J. Lynch (ed.), Oxford, Oxford University Press, 2016, 88–107.

Kittredge, K. "Early Blossoms of Genius: Child Poets at the End of the Long 18th Century," *Looking Glass: New Perspectives on Children's Literature*, 15 (2011), www.the-looking-glass.net/index.php/tlg/article/view/274/271

Langbauer, L. "Juvenilia and Juvenile Writers," in *The Encyclopedia of Victorian Literature*, 4 vols., D. Felluga (ed.), Oxford, Wiley Blackwell, 2015, 2.861–70.

Meyers, M. "Of Mimicry and (Wo)Man: Infants or Forked Tongue?" *Children's Literature*, 23 (1995), 66–70.

Owen, D. and Peterson, L. (eds.) *Home and Away: The Place of the Child Writer*, Newcastle-on-Tyne, Cambridge Scholars, 2016.

Sickbert, V. "Christina Rossetti and Victorian Children's Poetry: A Maternal Challenge to the Patriarchal Family," *Victorian Poetry*, 31 (1993), 385–410.

Smulders, S. "Sound, Sense, and Structure in Christina Rossetti's *Sing-Song*," *Children's Literature*, 22 (1994), 3–26.

Sorby, A. "Women Poets, Child Readers," in *A History of Nineteenth-Century American Women's Poetry*, J. Putzi and A. Socarides (eds.), Cambridge, Cambridge University Press, 2017, 374–89.

Styles, M., Joy, L., and Whitley, D. (eds.), *Poetry and Childhood*, Stoke-on-Trent, Trentham, 2010.

Taylor, B. "Childhood Writings of Elizabeth Barrett Browning: 'At Four I First Mounted Pegasus,'" in Alexander and McMaster (eds.), *The Child Writer*, pp. 138–53.

Taylor, B. "Elizabeth Barrett Browning and the Politics of Childhood," *Victorian Poetry*, 46 (2008), 405–27.

Tucker, H. "An Ebbigrammar of Motives; or, Ba for Short," *Victorian Poetry*, 44 (2006), 445–65.

Vallone, L. "History Girls: Eighteenth- and Nineteenth-Century Historiography and the Case of Mary, Queen of Scots," *Children's Literature*, 36 (2008), 1–23.

Wakely-Mulroney, K. and Joy, L. (eds.). *The Aesthetics of Children's Poetry: A Study of Children's Verse in English*, New York, Routledge, 2016.

12 Marriage, Motherhood, and Domesticity

Boos, F. S. (ed.), *Working-Class Women Poets in Victorian Britain: An Anthology*, Peterborough, ON, Broadview, 2008.

Harrington, E. *Second Person Singular: Late Victorian Women Poets and the Bonds of Verse*, Charlottesville, University of Virginia Press, 2014.

Hughes, L. K. "Daughters of Danaeus and Daphne: Women Poets and the Marriage Question," *Victorian Literature and Culture*, 34 (2006), 481–93.

Leighton, A. *Victorian Women Poets: Writing Against the Heart*, Charlottesville, University of Virginia Press, 1992.

Peterson, L. H. "Domestic and Idyllic," in *A Companion to Victorian Poetry*, Richard Cronin, Alison Chapman, and Antony H. Harrison (eds.), Oxford, Blackwell, 2002, 42–58.

Rigg, P. *Augusta Webster: Victorian Aestheticism and the Woman Writer*, Madison, NJ, Fairleigh Dickinson University Press, 2009.

13 Sexuality

Bennett, P. "Critical Clitoridectomy: Female Sexual Imagery and Feminist Psychoanalytic Theory," *Signs* 18.2 (1993), 235–59.

Blair, K. *Victorian Poetry and the Culture of the Heart*, Oxford, Clarendon, 2006.

Diedrick, J. *Mathilde Blind: Late-Victorian Culture and the Woman of Letters*, Charlottesville, University of Virginia Press, 2017.

Djikstra, B. *Idols of Perversity: Fantasies of Feminine Evil in Fin-de-Siècle Culture*, New York, Oxford University Press, 1988.

Ehnenn, J. "'Our Brains Struck Fire Each from Each': Disidentification, Difference, and Desire in the Collaborative Aesthetics of Michael Field," in *Economies of Desire at the Victorian Fin de Siècle: Libidinal Lives*, J. Ford, K. E. Keates, and P. Pulham, (eds.), New York, Routledge, 2015, 180–203.

Faderman, L. *Surpassing the Love of Men: Romantic Friendship and Love Between Women from the Renaissance to the Present*, New York, William Morrow & Co., 1981.

Koven, S. *Slumming: Sexual and Social Politics in Victorian London*, Princeton, Princeton University Press, 2006.

Logan, D. *Fallenness in Victorian Women's Writing: Worry, Stitch, Die, or Do Worse*, Columbia, University of Missouri Press, 1998.

Marcus, S. *Between Women: Friendship, Desire, and Marriage in Victorian England*, Princeton, Princeton University Press, 2009.

Meyerowitz, J. "Thinking Sex with an Androgyne," *GLQ*, 17 (2011), 97–105.

Parker, S. *The Lesbian Muse and Poetic Identity, 1889–1930*, London, Pickering & Chatto, 2013.

Prins, Y. *Victorian Sappho*, Princeton, Princeton University Press, 1999.

Vicinus, M. *Intimate Friends: Women Who Loved Women, 1778–1928*, Chicago, University of Chicago Press, 2004.

14 Poets of Style: Poetries of Asceticism and Excess

Bristow, J. (ed.), *The Fin-de-Siècle Poem: English Literary Culture and the 1890s*, Athens, Ohio University Press, 2005.

Condé, A. (ed.), *Decadence and the Senses*, Cambridge, Legenda, 2017.

Harrington, E. *Second Person Singular: Late Victorian Women Poets and the Bonds of Verse*, Charlottesville, University of Virginia Press, 2014.

Hurst, I. *Victorian Women Writers and the Classics: The Feminine of Homer*, Oxford, Oxford University Press, 2006.

Lysack, K. "Aesthetic Consumption and the Cultural Production of Michael Field's *Sight and Song*," *SEL: Studies in English Literature 1500–1900*, 45 (2005), 935–60.

Prins, Y. *Ladies' Greek*, Princeton, Princeton University Press, 2017.

Stetz, M. and Wilson, C. (eds.), *Michael Field and Their World*, High Wycombe, Rivendale Press, 2007.

15 Distant Reading and Victorian Women's Poetry

Fleming, P. "Tragedy, for Example: Distant Reading and Exemplary Reading," *New Literary History*, 48 (2017), 437–55.

Jin, J. "Problems of Scale in 'Close' and 'Distant' Reading," *Philological Quarterly*, 96 (2017), 105–29.

Piper, A. "There Will be Numbers," *Journal of Cultural Analytics*, 2016, DOI: 10.22148/16.006.http://culturalanalytics.org/2016/05/there-will-be-numbers/.

Ramsay, S. *Reading Machines: Towards an Algorithmic Criticism*, Urbana, University of Illinois Press, 2011.

Smith, B. H. "What Was 'Close Reading'? A Century of Method in Literary Studies," *Minnesota Review*, 87 (2016), 57–75.

APPENDIX: POETS' BIOGRAPHIES

Contributors are identified by their initials.

Maria Abdy (1797–1867), known for comic and religious verse and poems on governesses and needlewomen, began writing poetry at a young age. She married John Channing Abdy in 1821. In addition to periodical poems, her first volume, *Poems*, was privately printed in 1834, followed by seven others (1838–62). – AE

Sarah Flower Adams (1805–48), an associate of Robert Browning and Harriet Martineau, is today best known as the author of the hymn "Nearer, My God, to Thee," which was set to music by her sister Eliza, a composer. She also wrote verse drama, critical essays, and poems on political topics. – NH

Grace Aguilar (1816–47), poet, historian, and Jewish theologian, enjoyed a large transatlantic readership. The Aguilar branch of the New York Public Library is named after her. She remains best known for her three-volume *The Women of Israel* (1844), an innovative work of what we might call first-wave feminist religious history. – CL

Margaret Armour (1860–1943) was a Scottish poet and translator. In addition to her three poetry collections – *Songs of Love and Death* (1896), *Thames Sonnets and Semblances* (1897), and *The Shadow of Love and Other Poems* (1898) – she published poetry and art criticism in periodicals. – LK

Elizabeth Barrett Browning (EBB) (1806–61) established her international reputation at mid-career in 1844 under her maiden name "Elizabeth Barrett Barrett" in the two-volume collection *Poems* (in America, *A Drama of Exile, with Other Poems*). Four earlier volumes evince her exceptional learning, originality, and affinities in youth with Romantic currents of thought. Her most influential works (mostly written after marriage to Robert Browning in 1846) include *Sonnets from the Portuguese* (1850); interventions in the

285

transatlantic antislavery movement; and polemical poetical engagements with Italian nation building in *Casa Guidi Windows* (1851),
Poems before Congress (1860), and *Last Poems* (1862). Above all,
Aurora Leigh (1856) – as the first extended portrait of the woman
writer in English poetry and a generically hybrid, epic verse-novel
vitally engaged with the most controversial debates of its time – left
its mark on generations of writers and activists in England, North
America, and Europe, among them many poets represented in this
Cambridge Companion. – MS and BT

Marion Bernstein (1846–1906), located in Glasgow for her writing career,
was a music teacher who suffered from illness and consequent poverty
for most of her life. She is a major political poet, especially engaged with
women's issues, and had a strong relationship with the Glasgow
press. – KB

Mathilde Blind (1841–96), German-born poet, is best known for the
feminist, Darwinian *The Ascent of Man* (1889). Her cosmopolitan
poetics include *Dramas in Miniature* (1891) and *Birds of Passage*
(1895). She additionally wrote the first biography of George Eliot
(1883). Her circle included Amy Levy, W. M. Rossetti, and
A. C. Swinburne. – AV

Charlotte Brontë (1816–55), one of the great novelists of her era,
also published poetry, usually religious in orientation. *Poems
By Currer, Ellis, and Acton Bell* (1846) also features work by her
sisters, Emily (*alias* Ellis) and Anne (*alias* Acton) Brontë. – CL

Frances Brown (1816–79), born into the working class in Stranorlar,
Ireland, lost her sight due to smallpox at eighteen months. Her first
poem appeared in 1840; after many poems in Irish and British periodicals, she published her volume *The Star of Attéghéi* (1844). Soon thereafter, she turned to writing prose. – AE

Elizabeth Duncan Campbell (1804–78), a self-taught Scottish plough-
man's daughter, worked as a herder, weaver, cook, servant, and
laborer. Her four leaflets of poems (1862–7) address the Crimean
War, American slavery, and working-class suffering. *Songs of
My Pilgrimage* (1875), introduced by George Gilfillan, includes
her memoir, "Life of My Childhood." – MS

Elizabeth Carter (1717–1806) was a poet, scholar, and translator, and the
most seriously learned among the Bluestockings. Her English version of
Epictetus was still current into the twentieth century. Samuel
Richardson published her poem "Ode to Wisdom" in the first install-
ment of his novel *Clarissa* in 1747. – MMar

Mary Elizabeth Coleridge (1861–1907) was well known by contemporaries as a novelist and essayist. Today she is better known for her sometimes disturbing, usually short poems, some of which give distinctive turns, in compressed and enigmatic verses, to Gothic themes from the work of her great-great uncle, Samuel Taylor Coleridge. – EHel

Sara Coleridge (1802–52) was the third child and only daughter of the poet Samuel Taylor Coleridge. She published translations from Latin and French, a volume of poetry for children, and a fantasy novel. After her husband's death, she served as editor for her father's literary remains. – NH

Eliza Cook (1812–89), born in Southwark, London, was largely self-taught. *Lays of a Wild Harp* (1835) appeared when she was twenty-three, and her later volumes attracted a wide transatlantic audience. She became a literary celebrity from poems in the radical *Weekly Dispatch*, then founded the immensely popular *Eliza Cook's Journal* (1849–54). After 1854, Cook lived in retirement. – AE

Dinah Mulock Craik (1826–87) was author of the popular *John Halifax, Gentleman* (1856) and other novels. She also published periodical poetry, collected in *Thirty Years: Poems Old and New* (1881). – LK

Sarah Parker Douglas (1824–80), who published as "The Irish Girl," was born in Newry (Ulster) but lived primarily in Ayrshire. Largely self-educated, she published newspaper poems and several collections. After her schoolteacher husband became disabled, Parker attempted to support both of them through writing: she died in poverty in Glasgow. – KB

Eliza Hamilton Dunlop (1796–1880) was an Irish-born Australian émigré. Having published newspaper poems in Ireland, she contributed works to periodicals in New South Wales after her arrival in 1838, including poems about Indigenous Australians and translations of Indigenous song and poetry. – JR

Toru Dutt (1856–77) was born into a prominent Bengali family who converted to Christianity when she was six. Speaking and writing fluently in French and English – she was the first Indian woman poet to publish in English – she visited France (1869), then London and Cambridge, attending Higher Lectures for Women. Dutt navigated between Indian and European literary traditions in her poetry, which is cosmopolitan, lyrical, and highly intertextual. – AC

George Eliot (1819–80) (Marian Evans) began her poetical career after attaining widespread fame as a novelist, at least partly in response to that fame. *The Spanish Gypsy* (1868) is a closet drama in blank verse. *The Legend of Jubal* (1874, expanded 1878) explores a variety of other poetic genres. – CL

"Violet Fane" (Mary Montgomerie Lamb, later Singleton, later Currie, 1843–1905), novelist and poet, was born into a privileged family but lacked family support for her literary aspirations. Her pen name was inspired by Benjamin Disraeli's 1826 novel, *Vivian Grey*. Fane moved in aestheticist circles, and her works often address women's roles and social issues. – JE

Michael Field is the joint pseudonym of Katharine Harris Bradley (1846–1914) and Edith Emma Cooper (1862–1913). Aunt and niece, they lived and wrote together for thirty years and kept a collaborative diary, publishing twenty-seven historical dramas and nine poetry volumes. Early on, Michael Field "swore / Against the world, to be / Poets and lovers evermore" and produced texts characterized by pagan celebration, nature, and same-sex love. After converting to Catholicism, they produced religious verse with the same fervor and sensuality of their earlier texts. Their life and work reflect their Aesthetes' sensibilities, queer-feminist perspectives, and interest in intellectual and formal innovation. – JE

Fanny Forrester (1852–89) was a Manchester-based factory worker (in a dye-house), well known as a contributor to *Ben Brierley's Journal* and many other periodicals in the 1870s. Her Irish mother and two of her siblings were also poets. Forrester's poems have never been collected in volume form. – KB

Tina Galbraith (1837–1923) is reported by James Knox in *Airdrie Bards* (1930) to be a domestic servant in Lanarkshire, and publishing in the local press. No collection is known and no poems have as yet been located outside the selection in Knox's anthology. – KB

Alice E. Gillington (1863–1934) coauthored a book of poems with her sister, May Byron, and placed others in periodicals. She published several collections of Romani folktales and wrote essays for the Gypsy Lore Society based on her observations from living in a caravan among the Roma after 1911. – NH

Dora Greenwell (1821–92), a poet and Christian prose writer, was also a vocal activist who favored female suffrage and opposed vivisection. In addition to periodical poems, she published several volumes including *Poems* (1848), *Stories that Might be True with Other Poems* (1850), *Songs of Salvation* (1873), and *Camera Obscura* (1876). – LK

Janet Hamilton (née Thomson, 1795–1873) worked as a Scottish tambourer from age nine, married at thirteen, bore ten children, and at fifty, having read widely since childhood, taught herself to write. She published dialect and Standard English poetry in *Poems and Essays* (1863), *Poems of Purpose and Sketches in Prose of Scottish Peasant Life* (1865), and *Poems and Ballads* (1868). – LH

Felicia Hemans (1793–1835) was perhaps the most popular English poet from the middle 1820s–1830s. *Records of Woman* (1828), a powerful feminist project, experimented with forms like the dramatic monologue. She was best known as a Christian poet and associated with ideals of motherhood and feminine virtue. "Casabianca" (1826) was a standard recitation piece in English schoolrooms through the nineteenth century. – JR

Emily Hickey (1845–1924) published *A Sculptor and Other Poems* (1881); *Verse-Tales, Lyrics, and Translations* (1889); *Michael Villiers, Idealist, and Other Poems* (1891); and *Poems* (1896). *Michael Villiers*, influenced by EBB's *Aurora Leigh* in its form and focus on gender and class debates, vigorously addresses Irish poverty and Home Rule. – MS

Mary Howitt (née Botham, 1799–1888) married fellow Quaker William Howitt (1792–1879) in 1821; five of their children survived infancy. The couple cowrote *The Forest Minstrel* (1823) and later coedited *Howitt's Journal* (1847–8). But Howitt's poems and ballads, including "The Spider and the Fly," acquired independent standing. – LH

Jean Ingelow (1820–97) first published poems anonymously, but *Collected Poems* (1863), a signed volume, established her reputation, going into twenty-three editions. *The Story of Doom and Other Poems* (1867) was also popular on both sides of the Atlantic. She published in addition four novels and five collections of children's stories. – LK, NH

Maria James (1793–1868), a domestic servant, was born in Wales but emigrated to New York state at age seven. The volume publication of her poems (1839) was sponsored by professor and clergyman Alonso Potter, who also introduced the collection. – KB

Anna Brownell Jameson (1794–1860), a prolific professional writer, is best known for her travel writing, treatises on art, and provocative studies of fictional and famous women. She supported the young founders of the *English Women's Journal* and is noted for her feminist criticism. – MMar

E. Pauline Johnson (1861–1913), also known by her Mohawk name, Tekahionwake, was the Canadian-born daughter of a Mohawk father and English mother. She rose to fame in the late nineteenth century for her dramatic recitations of poems on First Nations topics, most of them published in *The White Wampum* (1895). – JR

Ellen Johnston (c. 1835–73) or "The Factory Girl," a Scottish factory worker, is one of the most important Victorian working-class women poets. Her *Autobiography, Poems and Songs* (1867, 1869) gives a partial account of her life. Though a popular writer for the Dundee and Glasgow press, she died in sickness and poverty. – KB

Frances Anne (Fanny) Kemble (1809–93) was widely known as an actress, poet, and novelist. She married American plantation owner Pierce Butler, whom she later divorced, and published a book against slavery in 1863. Her 1844 *Poems*, which contained many sonnets, was updated in several later editions through 1883. – NH

May Kendall (1861–1943) was born in Yorkshire. Between 1885 and 1898, she published a modern fairy story, two volumes of poetry, three novels, and a short story collection. After 1898, she focused on social work for laborers' rights and equality for women. – MMor

Harriet Hamilton King (1840–1920) expressed her passion for Italian unification in *The Execution of Felice Orsini* (1869), *Aspromonte and Other Poems* (1869), *The Disciples* (1873), and *Letters and Recollections of Mazzini* (1912). Other collections include *A Book of Dreams* (1883), *Ballads of the North and Other Poems* (1889), and *The Prophecy of Westminster* (1895). –MS

Margaret Rebecca Lahee (1831–95), born in Ireland, moved to Rochdale and joined a group of popular Lancashire dialect writers, including Edwin Waugh. Primarily writing fiction and prose, she also published some dialect poems. Lahee apparently lived in a close relationship with a woman, Susannah Wild, for thirty years. – KB

Letitia Elizabeth Landon (L.E.L., 1802–38) was a popular and prolific poet, annual editor, and reviewer. Her earliest poetry was published by William Jerdan, editor of the *Literary Gazette*, with whom she had three illegitimate children. Although highly successful, she faced malicious gossip about sexual impropriety, fueled by her many poems on romantic love. In 1838, she married William

Maclean, moving with him to the Cape Coast, tragically dying of an overdose soon after. – AC

Amy Levy (1861–89), the first Jewish woman to attend Newnham College, Cambridge, wrote feminist dramatic monologues and lyrics that convey late Victorian urban modernity and unrequited lesbian desire. Her brief relationship with Vernon Lee (Violet Paget) inspired several idyllic Italian poems. Levy suffered from major depression and committed suicide at age twenty-seven by inhaling charcoal fumes. – JE

Elizabeth Mary Little (1864–1909) published under the names Lizzie Little and L. M. Little, including three volumes of poetry. Born in Ireland, she was one of three daughters of an improvident father. Her sister Grace, who married the writer Ernest Rhys, also wrote poetry and books for children. – NH

Frederika Richardson Macdonald (1845–1923) was a poet, novelist, and biographer who published under both her maiden and married names. She translated the Ramayana, published several books about Rousseau, and wrote four novels. She was also the first biographer to publish extracts of Charlotte Brontë's letters to Constantin Heger. – NH

Mary MacDonald MacPherson/Màiri Nighean Iain Bhàin, also known as Màiri Mhòr nan Oran ("Big Mary of the Songs") (1821–98), is one of the most important nineteenth-century Scottish Gaelic poets. She apparently trained as a midwife. MacPherson's poems, including significant political verse, were composed and performed orally and transcribed and preserved by her patron Lachlan Macdonald. – KB

Charlotte Mew (1869–1928) published poems and stories in periodicals, including *The Yellow Book*, and one volume of poems, *The Farmer's Bride* (1916). Three of her siblings died in early childhood, while two others were confined to mental asylums. Mew lived with her remaining sister Anne and her mother. – EHar

Alice Meynell (née Thompson, 1847–1922), journalist, essayist, suffragist, and mother of seven surviving children, spent her early life in Switzerland, France, and Italy. She converted to Catholicism in her teens and married Wilfred Meynell in 1877; together they embarked on a strenuous life of journalism. *Preludes* (1875), her earliest poems, garnered praise from Tennyson and Ruskin; her later verse expressed complex attitudes toward motherhood, fallen women, suffrage, and pacifism. She considered her essays (collected in several volumes, beginning with *The Rhythm of Life*, 1893) more important than her rarer poems, though she was twice suggested for the poet laureateship. Recently the subtleties of her poetry, with its fine economies of syntax and form, have returned her to deserved critical attention. – JE, EHel

Jessie Morton (born in Dalkeith c. 1824) published widely in the local Scottish press from a young age and produced one fairly successful collection in 1866 (second edition 1867). Married to James Morton, she kept a stationery shop in Fife. – KB

Constance Naden (1858–89), born near Birmingham, entered the Mason College of Science in 1881. Naden published science and philosophy essays and two volumes of poetry while remaining active in charitable and political causes, including women's suffrage. Naden died of ovarian cysts in 1889. – MMor

Edith Nesbit (1858–1924), known for her children's novels, was cofounder of the Fabian Society and an important socialist poet. Her poetry volumes include *Lays and Legends* (1886), *Songs of Love and Empire* (1898), and *Ballads and Lyrics of Socialism* (1908). Along with her husband Hubert Bland, she disregarded traditional bourgeois ideas of marriage. – AV

Caroline Sheridan Norton (1808–77), poet, novelist, and activist, left her abusive husband in 1835 but then lost custody of her children. She published six collections of poetry, four novels, and numerous pamphlets advocating against child labor and in favor of women's rights to divorce, property, and child custody. – EHar

Eliza Ogilvy (1822–1912), a Scot, wrote a "Natal Address" (1844) for her daughter Rose, who died in 1845. *A Book of Highland Minstrelsy* (1846) established Ogilvy's reputation. She also authored *Poems of Ten Years* (1856) and an 1893 memoir of Elizabeth Barrett Browning, her friend and neighbor in Florence, 1848–52. – EHar

Adelaide O'Keeffe, (1776–1855), Irish daughter of playwright John O'Keeffe, contributed thirty-four poems (a third) to the highly successful *Original Poems for Infant Minds* by Ann and Jane Taylor (1804–5). She also wrote fiction and edited her father's works. – LL

Mabel Peacock (1856–1920), a pioneer folk collector specializing in Lincolnshire dialect, published collections of Lincolnshire tales and rhymes and works on Lincolnshire folklore, some in collaboration with her brother Max or friend Eliza Gutch. – KB

May Probyn, (Juliana Mary Louisa, 1856–1909), aestheticist poet and novelist, converted to Catholicism in 1883. She authored *Poems* (1881), *A Ballad of the Road and Other Poems* (1883), and *Pansies*

(1895), and coauthored *Christmas Verses* (1895) with her friend
Katharine Tynan. Her fiction includes *Robert Tresilian: A Story*
(1880). – AV

Adelaide Procter (1825–64) published many poems in Charles
Dickens's *Household Words* and *All the Year Round*; these were
collected into *Legends and Lyrics* (1858). Procter was a vocal
supporter of women's issues and became the most prominent poet
of the *English Woman's Journal*, in which "A Lost Chord"
appeared. In 1861, she edited *Victoria Regia* for the Victoria
Press. – EHar, LK

Dollie Radford (born Caroline Maitland, 1858–1920) was praised by
contemporaries for her light, romantic lyrics. Yet many of her
poems display her socialist and feminist politics. A friend of
Eleanor Marx, she married the poet Ernest Radford. She also
wrote books for children, a novel, and a play. –NH

Emma Roberts (1791–1840), the Anglo-Indian poet, travel writer,
periodical contributor, and newspaper editor, moved to India from
London in 1828. She temporarily moved back to London in 1832
and became active in metropolitan literary circles, afterward returning to India in 1839. –AC

Agnes Mary F. Robinson (1858–1944), aestheticist poet, critic, and translator, wrote for an English and a French audience. She was the romantic
partner of Vernon Lee until her marriage to the French orientalist James
Darmesteter in 1888. In 1901, seven years after Darmesteter's death, she
married the French biologist Emile Duclaux. – AC

Christina Georgina Rossetti (1860–94) is one of the finest Victorian
poets. She established her reputation with the narrative poems and
lyrics of *Goblin Market and Other Poems* (1862), *The Prince's
Progress and Other Poems* (1866), and *Sing-Song: A Nursery
Rhyme Book* (1872), which were illustrated with wood engravings
after artists' designs. *A Pageant and Other Poems* (1881) show-
cased Rossetti's mastery of the sonnet form, deriving from her
bilingual proficiency in English and Italian traditions. Her collection of devotional poems, *Verses: Reprinted from "Called to be
Saints," "Time Flies," and "The Face of the Deep"* (1893), was her
most popular book of poetry. – LK

Agnes Strickland (1796–1874) is best known for *Lives of the Queens
of England* (coauthored with sister Elizabeth, 1840–8). She coedited *Fisher's Juvenile Scrap-book* (1836–9). Her children's poetry
included *Juvenile Forget-Me-Not* (1827, with sister Catharine Parr
Traill) and *Floral Sketches, Fables, and Other Poems* (1836). – LL

Ann Taylor (later Gilbert, 1782–1866) and Jane Taylor (1783–1824) produced more than twenty poetry books for children. The teenaged Ann won prizes from Darton and Harvey publishers, who commissioned the trend-setting *Original Poems for Infant Minds* (1804–5). "The Star" ("Twinkle, twinkle, little star," *Rhymes for the Nursery*, 1806) by Jane is best known. – LL

Rachel Annand Taylor (1876–1960), prominent in the Celtic Revival, was an Aberdeen University graduate, teacher, and scholar of Renaissance Italy and Scotland. She published three poetry collections between 1904 and 1910, all marked by the influence of the Pre-Raphaelites and decadent movement. – KB

Henrietta Tindall (1818–79), a friend of Mary Russell Mitford, published in annuals before her poems, often on child mortality or working-class suffering, appeared in *Lines and Leaves* (1850) and *Rhymes and Legends* (1879). Queen Victoria personally requested to see Tindall's poem "On the Hartley Colliery Accident . . . 1862." – MS

Graham R. Tomson (née Rosamond Ball, 1860–1911) died as Rosamund Marriott Watson after two divorces and four children with successive partners. Her most successful volumes were *The Bird-Bride: A Volume of Ballads and Sonnets* (1889) and *A Summer Night* (1891); she also edited *Sylvia's Journal* from December 1892 to April 1894. – LH

Charlotte Elizabeth Tonna (1790–1846), alias Charlotte Elizabeth, was a prolific popular religious author from the mid-1820s until her death. She edited both *The Christian Lady's Magazine* and *The Protestant Magazine*. Her ardently Protestant poetry ranges from hymn to blank verse epic. – CL

Elizabeth Tweddell (Mrs. G. M. Tweddell or Florence Cleveland, 1824–99) was married to radical printer, Chartist, poet and well-known local author and activist George Markham Tweddell. Initially known as a North Yorkshire dialect poet under her pseudonym Florence Cleveland, she published *Rhymes and Sketches* in two editions (1875, 1892). – KB

Katharine Tynan (later Hinkson, 1859–1931), friend to Alice Meynell and W. B. Yeats, figured in the Irish Literary Renaissance with *Ballads and Lyrics* (1891), *Cuckoo Songs* (1894), and *The Wind in the Trees* (1898). When her classically trained husband Henry failed to support the family, she turned to potboiling fiction. –LH

Anna Letitia Waring (1823–1910) began writing hymns at an early age and continued to do so throughout her life. Her *Hymns and Meditations* (1850) was popular on both sides of the Atlantic into the twentieth century. She published regularly in religious periodicals such as *Good Words* and the *Sunday Magazine*. – LK

Augusta Webster (née Julia Augusta Davies, 1837–94) was born in Poole, Dorset, to a naval officer with whom Webster often traveled as a young child. In 1851, the family moved to Cambridge, and Augusta attended the Cambridge School of Art. In 1863, she married Thomas Webster, a solicitor; they had one daughter. Webster published seven volumes of poetry, four plays, one novel, and two translations of Greek tragedies. She served on the London School Board and published essays advocating women's suffrage and women's education. Her sonnet sequence, *Mother and Daughter*, was posthumously published in 1895. – MMor

Ethelwyn Wetherald (1857–1940), a Canadian poet and journalist, published three well-received collections of poems. She also wrote essays, stories, and poems for a variety of periodicals, in addition to working as a member of the editorial staffs of several magazines. – NH

Jane Francesca Wilde (1821–96), mother of Oscar Wilde, assumed the name "Speranza" in 1847 to publish works fired with Irish nationalism and expressing her keen sense of the woman artist's role as a prophet to the age. As Lady Wilde, she established a salon in Dublin, and subsequently in London. – MS

Sarah Williams ("Sadie") (1841–68), poet and novelist, lived in London but was half-Welsh and considered a Welsh poet. She published in 1860s periodicals like *Good Words* and produced the posthumous volume *Twilight Hours*. She was chiefly remembered for her most popular poem, "The Old Astronomer to His Pupil." – KB

Florence Wilson (1874–1946), from Ulster, was the well-educated daughter of a mill manager. She wrote poems, stories, and prose on local history and folklore and is particularly known for her use of local dialect. Many of her poems espoused the romantic Irish nationalism of the early twentieth century. – KB

Margaret Louisa Woods (1855–1945) published six volumes of poetry, including her *Collected Poems* (1914) and six novels. Born into a literary household (several siblings were also writers), she married Henry George Woods, who became president of Trinity College, Oxford. – NH

Little biographical information is available on these poets: Jane Euphemia Browne, Georgina Courtenay, Catherine Ann Dorset, Maria Belson Elliot, Isa Forrester, Frances Ridley Havergal, Dorothy Kilner, Mary Ann Kilner, Elsie J. Campbell MacLachlan, Mary MacLeod, Ella Fuller Maitland, Sarah Catherine Martin, Maria Montolieu, Blanche Oram, Arabella Rowden, Menella Bute Smedley, Louisa Stewart, Elizabeth Turner, and Mary E. Wilkins.

"Napoleon III in Italy," 152, 153
Poems, 121, 150, 285
Poems before Congress, 122, 152, 286
"The Romaunt of the Page," 2, 22
"The Runaway Slave at Pilgrim's Point," 4,
    16, 82–4, 122, 147, 169, 207–8,
    210, 257
"A Song for the Ragged Schools of
    London," 148, 155
Sonnets from the Portuguese, 13, 204, 220,
    256, 257, 258, 262, 285
"Tomes of solid Witchcraft," 184
"Void in Law," 156
Baudelaire, Charles
    Fleurs du Mal, 124
    "Harmonie du Soir," 124
Beauties of Poetry and Gems of Art, 74
Ben Brierley's Journal, 132, 135, 288
Benjamin, Walter, 65
Bernstein, Marion, 132, 286
Bethune, George Washington
    The British Female Poets, 29, 32
Bevington, Louisa
    Liberty Lyrics, 155
Bible, 164, 169, 172, 173
Bissell, Mary, 89
Blackwood's Magazine, 38, 80
Blake, William, 45
    Songs of Innocence and Experience, 150
Blind, Mathilde, 7, 45, 147, 152, 155, 157,
    226–7, 255, 286
    The Ascent of Man, 5, 24, 87, 210, 211, 286
    Birds of Passage, 286
    "Chaunts of Life," 226
    Dramas in Miniature, 286
    The Heather on Fire, 158, 234
    "The Leading of Sorrow," 219
    "The Message," 218–19
    "The Mystic's Vision," 8, 222–3
    "The Orange Peel in the Gutter," 226
    "The Russian Student's Tale," 156
    "The Song of the Willi," 221
    "The Street-Children's Dance," 149
Boston Female Anti-Slavery Society, 122
*Boston Miscellany of Literature and
    Fashion*, 164
Botta, Anne C. Lynch, 122
Bourget, Paul, 236
Boyd, Alice, 188
Braddon, Mary Elizabeth
    Garibaldi, 24
Bradley, Katharine. *See* Field, Michael
Brazil, Angela, 191

Bridges, Robert, 34
Brontë, Anne, 286
Brontë, Charlotte, 100, 162–4, 172, 174, 214,
    250, 286, 291
    Jane Eyre, 25, 162, 163, 164
    "The Missionary," 7, 162–4
    Poems by Currer, Ellis, and Acton Bell,
        162, 286
    Shirley, 174
Brontë, Emily, 2, 250, 286
Brown, Frances, 3, 5, 98, 105–11, 133, 286
    "The First," 108
    Granny's Wonderful Chair, 111
    Lyrics and Miscellaneous Poems, 109
    My Share of the World, 111
    "The Pilgrim at the Well," 106
    "Songs of Our Land," 106–7
    The Star of Attéghéi, 109, 286
    "Weep Not for Him That Dieth," 107
Browne, Hablot K., 65, 68
Browne, Jane Euphemia, 182, 295
Browning, Robert, 14, 16, 46, 207, 215,
    240, 285
    "Johannes Agricola," 163
    Pauline, 191
Bryans, E. L.
    "Characteristics of Women's Poetry," 33
Buchanan, Marion, 192
Buchanan, Robert, 79
Bullen, A. H., 47
Burns Festival, 129, 130
Burns, Robert, 129–31, 136, 141, 143
Burton, F. W.
    The Blind Girl at the Holy Well, 106
Butler, Josephine, 156, 157
Byron, May, 288

*Cambridge History of English Literature,
    The*, 182, 191
Campbell, Elizabeth Duncan, 286
    "The Crimean War," 154
    "The Death of Willie, My Second Son," 155
    "Life of My Childhood," 286
    Songs of My Pilgrimage, 286
Carey, Elizabeth, 103
Carroll, Lewis [Charles L. Dodgson]
    Alice in Wonderland, 188
Carter, Elizabeth, 33, 286
    Epictetus, 286
    "Ode to Wisdom," 33, 286
Chace Act of 1891, 121
Chapman, Maria Weston, 122
Chartism, 129, 130, 131, 148, 294

Cambridge Companions to . . .

AUTHORS

Edward Albee edited by Stephen J. Bottoms

Margaret Atwood edited by Coral Ann Howells

W. H. Auden edited by Stan Smith

Jane Austen edited by Edward Copeland and Juliet McMaster (second edition)

Balzac edited by Owen Heathcote and Andrew Watts

Beckett edited by John Pilling

Bede edited by Scott DeGregorio

Aphra Behn edited by Derek Hughes and Janet Todd

Walter Benjamin edited by David S. Ferris

William Blake edited by Morris Eaves

Boccaccio edited by Guyda Armstrong, Rhiannon Daniels, and Stephen J. Milner

Jorge Luis Borges edited by Edwin Williamson

Brecht edited by Peter Thomson and Glendyr Sacks (second edition)

The Brontës edited by Heather Glen

Bunyan edited by Anne Dunan-Page

Frances Burney edited by Peter Sabor

Byron edited by Drummond Bone

Albert Camus edited by Edward J. Hughes

Willa Cather edited by Marilee Lindemann

Cervantes edited by Anthony J. Cascardi

Chaucer edited by Piero Boitani and Jill Mann (second edition)

Chekhov edited by Vera Gottlieb and Paul Allain

Kate Chopin edited by Janet Beer

Caryl Churchill edited by Elaine Aston and Elin Diamond

Cicero edited by Catherine Steel

Coleridge edited by Lucy Newlyn

Wilkie Collins edited by Jenny Bourne Taylor

Joseph Conrad edited by J. H. Stape

H. D. edited by Nephie J. Christodoulides and Polina Mackay

Dante edited by Rachel Jacoff (second edition)

Daniel Defoe edited by John Richetti

Don DeLillo edited by John N. Duvall

Charles Dickens edited by John O. Jordan

Emily Dickinson edited by Wendy Martin

John Donne edited by Achsah Guibbory

Dostoevskii edited by W. J. Leatherbarrow

Theodore Dreiser edited by Leonard Cassuto and Claire Virginia Eby

John Dryden edited by Steven N. Zwicker

W. E. B. Du Bois edited by Shamoon Zamir

George Eliot edited by George Levine and Nancy Henry (second edition)

T. S. Eliot edited by A. David Moody

Ralph Ellison edited by Ross Posnock

Ralph Waldo Emerson edited by Joel Porte and Saundra Morris

William Faulkner edited by Philip M. Weinstein

Henry Fielding edited by Claude Rawson

F. Scott Fitzgerald edited by Ruth Prigozy

Flaubert edited by Timothy Unwin

E. M. Forster edited by David Bradshaw

Benjamin Franklin edited by Carla Mulford

Brian Friel edited by Anthony Roche

Robert Frost edited by Robert Faggen

Gabriel García Márquez edited by Philip Swanson

Elizabeth Gaskell edited by Jill L. Matus

Edward Gibbon edited by Karen O'Brien and Brian Young

Goethe edited by Lesley Sharpe

Günter Grass edited by Stuart Taberner

Thomas Hardy edited by Dale Kramer

David Hare edited by Richard Boon

Nathaniel Hawthorne edited by Richard Millington

Seamus Heaney edited by Bernard O'Donoghue

Ernest Hemingway edited by Scott Donaldson

Homer edited by Robert Fowler

Horace edited by Stephen Harrison

Ted Hughes edited by Terry Gifford

Ibsen edited by James McFarlane

Henry James edited by Jonathan Freedman

Samuel Johnson edited by Greg Clingham

Ben Jonson edited by Richard Harp and Stanley Stewart